Interdependence in Planning

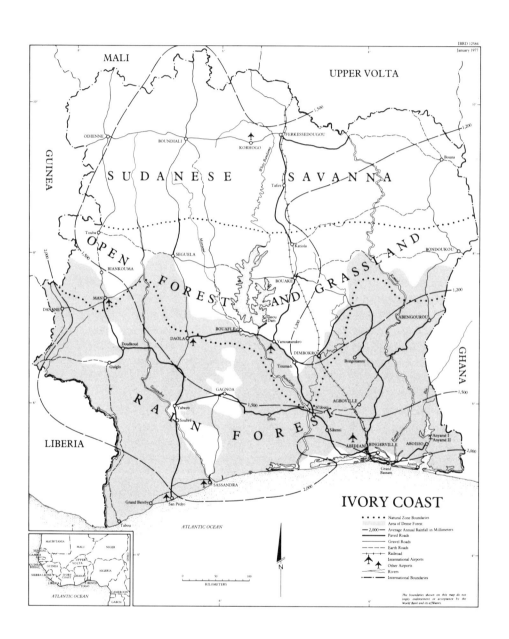

IBRD 12584
January 1977

MALI

UPPER VOLTA

GUINEA

ODIENNE

BOUNDIALI

KORHOGO

FERKESSEDOUGOU

Bouna

S U D A N E S E   S A V A N N A

Tafire

Touba

Katiola

BONDOUKOU

O P E N   F O R E S T   A N D   G R A S S L A N D

SEGUELA

BIANKOUMA

MAN

BOUAKE

ABENGOUROU

DANANE

Doukoue

DAOLA

BOUAFLE

Kossou
Dam

Yamoussoukro

DIMBOKRO

Bongouanou

Guiglo

Toumodi

GHANA

R A I N   F O R E S T

GAGNOA

N'douci

AGBOVILLE

LIBERIA

Yabayo

Soubré

Divo

Sikensi

Anyamé I
Anyamé II

ABIDJAN BINGERVILLE

ABOISSO

Assini

Grand
Bassam

SASSANDRA

Grand Bereby

San Pédro

Tabou

ATLANTIC OCEAN

IVORY COAST

• • • • Natural Zone Boundaries
          Area of Dense Forest
—2,000— Average Annual Rainfall in Millimeters
          Paved Roads
          Gravel Roads
— — —   Earth Roads
          Railroad
          International Airports
          Other Airports
          Rivers
—•—•—   International Boundaries

N

0   50   100
        KILOMETERS

The boundaries shown on this map do not
imply endorsement or acceptance by the
World Bank and its affiliates.

MAURITANIA

MALI

NIGER

SENEGAL
GAMBIA
GUINEA
BISSAU
GUINEA
SIERRA LEONE
LIBERIA
IVORY
COAST
GHANA
TOGO
BENIN
NIGERIA

UPPER
VOLTA

CAMEROON

GABON

ATLANTIC OCEAN

Louis M. Goreux

Interdependence in Planning

Multilevel Programming Studies of the Ivory Coast

with contributions by
Penny Davis and René Vaurs

Published for the World Bank
The Johns Hopkins University Press
Baltimore and London

Library of Congress Cataloging in Publication Data

Goreux, Louis M.   1927–
    Interdependence in planning.
    Bibliography: p. 403.
    Includes index.
    1. Ivory Coast—Economic policy—Mathematical models.
I. Title
HC547.I8G67   330.9'666'805   77-4793
ISBN 0-8018-2001-4
ISBN 0-8018-2006-5 pbk.

Contents

Part Three: Methodology

Tables

Figures

Acknowledgements

THIS STUDY was conducted in the Development Research Center of the World Bank in close cooperation with the administrative services of the Ivory Coast, in particular with the Ministry of Planning. I wish to express my special gratitude to Abdoulaye Koné, minister for economic affairs, finance and planning, and to H. Konan Bédié, former minister of economic affairs and finance, Mohamed T. Diawara, former minister of planning, and Abdoulaye Sawadogo, former minister of agriculture, for their personal advice and cooperation and the contribution made by their staffs.

I thank Emmanuel Dioulo, president of Aménagement de la Région du Sud-Ouest (ARSO), M'Lan Ouattara, director of development studies, and Arthur Achio, chief of the human resource division for their advice and the services rendered by their staffs. I also want to thank Messrs. Doumenc and Kloboukoff, Jean Montenez, Gerard Rebois, and Philippe Villain for their valuable contributions, as well as Paul Baron and Pierre Thénevin, who contributed to the elaboration of a development model for the Southwest.

I am grateful for the cooperation received from the Direction for Developmental Aid in Paris, in particular from Jean Audibert. Special thanks are due to André Guinard from the joint Food and Agriculture Organization—World Bank program, as well as to FAO for having made available the services of I.R. Loerbroks and Henri Quaix.

I owe a debt to several of my former coworkers in the Development Research Center: to Apostolos Condos for his contribution to the study of the urban and educational sectors; to Jacques Loup for his analysis of the livestock sector; and to Durin Kazancigil, Richard Inman, Le'si Vinh, François Nguyen, Ronald Myers, and Narong Thananart, who patiently processed and reprocessed data. I thank also Irma Adelman, Bela Balassa, Charles Blitzer, John H. Duloy, T. Dermot Gately, Roger Norton, Rolland Olivier, and Ardy Stoutjesdijk for their advice. I owe a special debt to Janos Kornai and, in particular, Alan S. Manne for their numerous suggestions.

Finally, I express my thanks to Maria McReynolds, Olga Siwicky, Bakhtaver Divecha, and Michele McKeever, who typed various parts of this manuscript. The final manuscript was edited for publication by David Howell Jones and the index was prepared by Frank Sokolove.

LOUIS M. GOREUX

Part One

Overview

Chapter 1

Objectives and Approach

GOVERNMENT OFFICIALS are obliged to make decisions concerning economywide issues, dealing, for example, with the size of the public budget or the level of the foreign debt. They must also make decisions which affect a particular sector of the economy, such as decisions regarding price-support policy in agriculture. In addition, they often have to make decisions regarding the selection or the mode of implementation of specific investment projects. All these decisions are to some extent related, and all of them should ideally be made in conformity with a common set of objectives which defines the national policy. Since a single person cannot make all these decisions at once, a system of models is needed. This system should make it possible to analyze each component of the economy independently and also to take interdependencies between the components into account whenever necessary. This volume represents an attempt to design such a system and to test its applicability to the economy of the Ivory Coast.

In this system, the components are analyzed independently by solving the models related to a particular project or sector in isolation; interdependencies between components are taken into account by solving the central model, which integrates all the sectoral components in an aggregated form. The central model can be solved for different sets of objectives and constraints, which define alternative policy options. A particular solution of the central model, which defines a set of prices for labor, capital, foreign exchange, and other resources shared among sectors, is associated with each option. When sectoral or project models are solved with that set of prices, due account is taken of resource scarcities associated with the particular policy which has been selected. Decisions made at the level of the project or at the level of the sector can thus be adjusted to changes in national policies. For the system to be workable, the size of the central model must remain

[3]

manageable and the prices derived from it must be reliable. The problem is to satisfy these two requirements simultaneously.

It would clearly be impossible to incorporate the specifications of all possible projects into this system. When a project is small in relation to the rest of the economy, as is usually the case, the specifications of the project need not, however, be incorporated into the system. Decisions regarding such a project do not significantly affect the relative scarcities of national resources and, consequently, their prices. The project may be analyzed on the basis of the interest rate or the foreign exchange rate specified by the central planner. These values are, in this system, the prices obtained in that solution of the central model which corresponds to the policy selected.

A project may, however, be so large that its implementation would affect the relative scarcities of national resources (such as capital and foreign exchange), and hence their prices (interest rate and foreign exchange rate). In such a case, the central planner could not specify the price which should be used by the project analyst, since the amount of this price would depend on whether the project is implemented and, if so, on the manner in which it is implemented. The large project corresponds in this study to the establishment of an iron mine, and this project is treated as a new sector which is incorporated into the central model.

The system makes a distinction between two levels. The models of sectors, or large projects, are at the lower level. The central model, which integrates the models of sectors in an aggregated form, is at the higher level. Small projects are not specified at either of these two levels because they can be appraised on their own merits by using the prices generated through the system. These prices are measures of the relative contributions of different national resources to the satisfaction of the national objectives selected. Their reliability depends greatly on the design of the central optimizing model.

Optimization versus More Traditional Approaches

A dynamic optimizing model may appear unduly complicated for a developing economy. It could, however, be visualized as no more than the synthesis of various planning techniques which have already been applied. When this study was undertaken, three planning techniques were in use in the Ivory Coast: project analysis, the five-year consistency plan, and projections for the year 2000.

These three planning tools are loosely connected to one another.

The first consists in assessing the costs and benefits associated with investment projects and in selecting projects with due regard to rates of return on the invested capital. A private investor is concerned only with the rate of financial return, which is calculated by valuing costs and benefits at actual or expected market prices. A government official allocating public funds among investment projects is interested also in the rate of social return. The latter differs from the former when private costs (or benefits) are not considered to be representative of social costs (or benefits). For example, if many unskilled workers were unemployed, government officials might consider the social cost of employing an additional worker to be substantially less than the wage that a private entrepreneur would have to pay if he were to employ that worker. For this reason, in calculating the rate of social return, project analysts generally value the cost of unskilled labor at a shadow wage which is lower than the prevailing market wage. The differential between market and shadow wages depends on the emphasis that the government places on full employment and the distribution of income. The project analyst is well equipped to assess the technical characteristics of the project, but not to make the price forecasts required to calculate the rate of financial return. He is even less well equipped to forecast the shadow prices of foreign exchange and capital needed to calculate the rate of social return.

The five-year plan based on a Leontief input-output matrix is of little usefulness to the project analyst who is searching for forecasts of market or shadow prices. The plan establishes production targets consistent with the levels of final demand selected as objectives, but it does not provide any price forecasts. On the other hand, alternative projections for the year 2000 may stimulate the conception of far-sighted policies. Without specifying the time path between the present and the year 2000, however, the connection between the projections and the five-year consistency plan remains loose.

In the five-year plan based on a Leontief input-output matrix, consistency is ensured by specifying that, in each sector, net output be equal to net demand: Gross output of a given sector minus intermediate inputs used by other sectors equals investment plus exports minus imports plus private consumption plus public consumption.

In the Leontief model, net demand (which appears in the righthand side of the commodity balance) is taken as given. The gross output required in each sector for satisfying this net demand is computed by inverting the Leontief input-output matrix. In the dynamic optimizing model used here, investments, exports, imports, and private consumption become endogenous variables; they are shifted to the lefthand side of the commodity balance. Public consumption is the only variable which remains exogenous and still appears as a constant in the righthand side of the equation. Such a transformation is reached in four steps.

The first step is to associate a resource matrix with the input-output matrix. Two rows of the resource matrix are already contained in the Ivorian plan. One is a measure of the trade gap, which defines the excess of requirements for foreign exchange over earnings of foreign exchange. The other is a measure of the resource gap, which defines the excess of investment over domestic savings. The resource balances that are being added relate to labor by category of skill, to land by type, and to other physical capital (such as machinery for textile production) by origin and destination. The construction of this resource matrix requires the collection of additional data, such as estimates of the number of workers and the physical capital required to produce a unit of gross output in each sector.

The second step is to introduce supply choices. One choice is between importing certain commodities and producing them. Another choice is between alternative ways of producing some commodities. This is done by incorporating additional columns into the input-output matrices. For example, in the original matrices, the production of all annual crops was represented by a single column. The coefficients in that column were measures of the inputs required for producing a unit of a given mix of crops. This single column has to be replaced by a series of columns representing the various ways in which different crops can be grown. For example, cotton can be grown with or without applying fertilizers, with or without tractors. Each production technology is represented by a column. The coefficients in each column are the technical norms used by the project analyst. These norms can be based on results obtained in experimental stations, on farm survey data, or even on the judgments made by agronomists. With this transformation of the Leontief matrix, the branch "annual crops" has become a sector and the modelbuilder is speaking the same language as the project analyst.

The third step is an extension of the time horizon. In the second five-year plan, the statistical basis was the year 1970, and the input-output matrix was projected for 1975 and 1980. In the optimizing model, the year 1970 still provides the statistical basis; 1975, 1980, 1985, and 1990 are the decision years, and the period 1990–2000 defines the terminal conditions. The matrices representing different points in time are linked through investment activities. Investments are made today because additional capital stocks are required to satisfy tomorrow's demand. Investments become endogenous variables determined through this backward linkage. The projection 2000 is now linked to the statistical basis for 1970 through a series of intermediate stages. The means for progressing from one stage to the next are specified.

The last step is the specification of the objective function. If few choices were available, it would be possible to examine successively all possible outcomes and to choose the best one. Because many choices can be made in each decision year (1975, 1980, 1985, and 1990), the number of feasible outcomes could be enormous. A systematic criterion for selection is needed. The outcome selected is the one which maximizes the value of the objective function, taken here as the discounted utility of per capita consumption by nationals. The whole way from a static Leontief model to a dynamic optimizing model has now been traversed.

The Basic Model

The easiest way to explain a model is probably to specify what is exogenous and what is endogenous. In Table 1.1, this is done for the free-market case, which will be considered for the time being as the basic solution.

Starting with the left side of Table 1.1, the first group of exogenous data defines the resource endowment. At the beginning of the planning period, 1970, the economy inherits fixed stocks of human and physical capital. Physical capital comprises factories, buildings, land, trees, and mines. Minerals and slow-growing trees (100 years and more) are treated as nonrenewable resources. Buildings and factories have stated life expectancies and are identified by their age. The same is true of human capital stocks, including both skilled and unskilled labor. Demographic factors are treated as exogenous; they determine the yearly increments to the potential labor force of unskilled workers. Borrowings of financial capital under special terms—that is, from the World Bank or the European Development Fund (EDF)—are also exogenous; their values are taken as given throughout the planning period.

The second group of exogenous data defines the state of technology. These data measure the technical coefficients of the input-output matrix and of the resource matrix.

The third group defines the conditions under which the Ivory Coast can trade with the rest of the world. The demand for exports of coffee

Table 1.1. Exogenous Data and Endogenous Variables (Free-Market Solution)

Exogenous data	Endogenous variables (1975, 1980, 1985, 1990)
Primary resources	*Investments*
Initial endowment in human and physical capital stocks by vintage.	Level and composition of physical investment by origin and destination.
Life span of capital stocks.	Levels of school enrollments by educational activity subject to constraints for 1975.
Growth rates of the national labor force.	
Projections of soft lending.	
Technology	*Production*
Input-output and capital-output ratios, gestation lags, cost of urbanization, and so forth.	Choice between urban production in the formal and informal sectors.
	Choice between alternative technologies in the rural sector.
	Migrations of unskilled labor between rural and urban areas.
Foreign sector	*Trade*
Price-quantity demand curves for coffee and cocoa.	Exports subject to upper bounds.
Price-quantity supply curve of foreign unskilled workers.	Import substitution for fourteen urban branches and for agricultural products.
Price-quantity supply curve of foreign capital.	Borrowing from abroad at commercial terms except in 1990.
Import prices.	
Export prices and upper limit on volume exported except for coffee and cocoa.	
Demand parameters	*Private consumption by Ivorians*
Population growth rate (ν).	Level and composition of consumption by Ivorians for eight commodity groups.
Income elasticities for eight commodity groups.	
Elasticity of substitution (σ).	
Discount rate (δ).	
Asymptotic growth rate of consumption.	
Demand by public sector	
Civil servants by skill categories.	
Public consumption.	
Nonproductive investments.	

[8]

and cocoa originating from the Ivory Coast is expressed in the form of a quantity-price demand curve. Similarly, supplies of foreign unskilled workers and of foreign capital borrowed on commercial terms are expressed in quantity-price supply curves. In all other cases, the "small-country assumption" is made and the Ivory Coast is treated as a price-taker. An upper limit is set for each type of export other than coffee and cocoa.

The last group of coefficients defines the demand parameters used in the objective function. The rates of population growth through the year 2000 are taken from demographic studies. The effect of urbanization on the pattern of consumption is given from a comparison between the urban and the rural consumption patterns in the base year (see Appendix A, Chapter 9). The income elasticities of demand for eight groups of final consumption goods and services as well as the value of the elasticity of substitution are derived from the econometric analysis of market data. In first approximation, the elasticity of substitution (σ) can be thought of as the common ratio between price and income elasticities. As will be explained in Chapters 8 and 9, the income elasticities and the elasticity of substitution are the parameters of the utility function used to transform consumption into utility. The rate (δ) at which utilities are discounted over time is also a fixed coefficient in any solution of the model. The value of the discount rate (δ), however, is treated as a policy parameter; it implies a choice between increased consumption by the present generation and increased consumption by the future generation. Reducing the discount rate implies lower consumption and higher income taxes today.

Unlike private consumption, the levels and composition of public consumption and public "nonproductive investments" are not treated as variables in the model. Their values are given throughout the planning period. They are assumed to be fixed by government decisions.

The optimized variables appear in the righthand side of Table 1.1. For each decision year (1975, 1980, 1985, and 1990), the levels and composition of the activities defining investment, production, trade, and consumption by Ivorians are treated as endogenous variables.

In the model, there are many choices regarding the composition of the product mix and that of the resource mix. For a given production mix, substitution between resources can occur in two ways: first, by choosing between different ways of producing the same commodity; second, by modifying the composition of the resource endowment through endogenous investment activities—by transforming unskilled labor into skilled labor by means of education, for example. In turn, the production mix can be modified in two ways: first, by choosing the commodity mix of exports and imports; second, by choosing the commodity mix of final consumption.

The primal solution gives the optimal quantities consumed and produced according to the various technologies available, as well as the optimal amounts of resources required to produce them. The dual solution defines what the contributions of an additional unit of resource or product to the value of the objective function would be. These contributions, which are measures of the marginal productivity of resources and the marginal value of products, define the shadow price structure associated with the objectives pursued.

How the Model Works

By means of the model, alternative ways of exploiting domestic primary resources (labor and capital) for the maximization of welfare are investigated. Welfare is defined here as the discounted utility of consumption by nationals.

The primary resources (labor and capital) are transformed into consumption through production and trade activities. These activities use not only labor and capital as inputs, but also intermediate goods. These are themselves produced from labor, capital, and other intermediate goods. Ultimately, the production of any final consumer good can be expressed in terms of its (direct and indirect) requirements of domestic primary resources (labor and capital).

An exported good is a particular type of intermediate product that must be traded for other goods on the world market before it is ultimately transformed into consumer goods for the Ivorian population. Foreign exchange can be thought of as an intermediate resource used for international trading. The marginal unit of foreign exchange is obtained by exporting a given good. The production of this good requires given amounts of labor and capital, which define the domestic resource costs of foreign exchange. Assume that the marginal good is sold at one dollar and that the direct and indirect production requirements for this good amount to only one day of unskilled labor. The free rate of exchange between dollars and *Communauté financière africaine* francs (African financial community, CFA) is the number of CFAF a day that this worker receives. Consumption by foreigners in the Ivory Coast is treated the same way as any other kind of intermediate input. It does not enter into the objective function, which deals only with consumption by nationals.

Investment consists ultimately in trading consumption today for consumption tomorrow. Saving is the consumption forgone today by withdrawing labor and capital from the production of consumer goods today. The labor and capital withdrawn are used to expand the capital (physical and human) which can be used to produce more goods for consumption tomorrow.

Production, trade, and investments are not explicitly considered as objectives in the model. They are only means for producing consumer goods today or tomorrow. The ultimate aim of all these activities is only the satisfaction derived by nationals from consumption throughout the entire planning period. This satisfaction (called the discounted utility of consumption) is the value of the objective function which we maximize.

Intratemporal and intertemporal choices are made simultaneously in the model. For simplicity, these choices will be considered sequentially here. They will be analyzed by combining the quantities from the primal solution with the prices from the dual solution.

Intratemporal choices are concerned with the optimal composition of final demand among consumer goods at a given time and with the most efficient way of supplying these goods. The dual value of a final consumer good measures the contribution of an additional unit of that good to the value of the objective function. At a given time, the dual values of two consumer goods are proportional to their marginal utilities. Assuming the choices of consumers to be rational, marginal utilities are proportional to market prices. Translating dual values into shadow prices, therefore, requires only the choice of a numéraire. The numéraire used here is the dual value of a unit of the Ivorian final consumption basket. Consequently, shadow prices can be interpreted as forecasts of market prices deflated by the cost-of-living index.[1]

Similarly, the dual value of a factor is a measure of the contribution of an additional unit of this factor to the value of the objective function. Using the same numéraire, this contribution can be expressed in terms of consumer goods at base-year prices. The shadow wage of a worker would therefore measure his purchasing power at base-year prices, if that worker was paid according to his marginal productivity, which is the basic assumption here.[2]

Turning now to intertemporal choices, it will be assumed for simplicity below that relative prices remain constant over time, so that a single rate of interest prevails in the economy. This rate, which measures the rate of decline in the dual value of a unit of consumption

1. As shown in the appendix to Chapter 5, the cost-of-living index is computed by weighting the current prices of eight groups of commodities according to their shares in the Ivorian consumption basket.

2. For an illustration, see Table 3.9.

per unit of time, must be equal to the marginal rate of capital productivity. Hence, the dynamic equation of the model may be written in a simplified form as:

(1.1)

$$r_t \quad = \quad \delta \quad + \quad \nu \quad + \quad \gamma_t/\sigma.$$

$$\begin{bmatrix} Marginal \\ rate\ of\ capital \\ productivity \end{bmatrix} = \begin{bmatrix} Rate\ of \\ time \\ discount \end{bmatrix} + \begin{bmatrix} Rate\ of \\ population \\ growth \end{bmatrix} + \begin{bmatrix} Growth\ rate \\ of\ per\ capita \\ consumption \\ divided\ by \\ elasticity\ of \\ substitution \end{bmatrix} , \text{ or}$$

[*Rate of capital productivity*] = [*Rate of decline in the dual value of consumption*].

Because the sum of the discounted utilities of per capita consumption is maximized, the dual value of consumption declines over time on account of three factors which are specified in the righthand side of equation (1.1). The first two[3] are given for any solution of the model. The rate of time discount (δ), which reflects a choice between more utility for the present or the next generation, is treated as a policy parameter, while the rate of population growth (ν) remains constant in all model solutions. The third factor measures the rate of decline in the marginal utility of per capita consumption. It is equal to the growth rate of per capita consumption (γ_t), which is a variable optimized along each point of the time path, divided by the overall elasticity of substitution (σ), which is a behavioral parameter.

For illustration, the values of the first two parameters can be taken as 3 percent a year ($\delta = \nu = 3$) and that of the third as one-half ($\sigma = 0.5$). If, at a given point in time, the marginal rate of capital productivity were equal to 12 percent a year ($r_t = 12$), it would follow from equation (1.1) that the optimal growth rate of per capita consumption would be 3 percent a year ($\gamma_t = 3$). The 12 percent marginal rate of capital productivity would exactly offset the 6 percent endogenous decline in marginal utility (γ_t/σ) and the 6 percent exogenous decline resulting from the values taken for the discount rate and the population growth.[4]

3. If the sum of discounted utilities accruing to each member of the population had been maximized, these two parameters would have been combined in a single one (see Chapter 8).

4. In view of the many choices available in this model, capital productivity is not a constant. Nevertheless, the range of variation is limited by the values selected for the capital-output ratios and the labor-output requirements.

If capital productivity exceeded 12 percent, it would be optimal to invest a little more today; the utility of consumption forgone today would be less than the discounted utility of the additional consumption that could be obtained tomorrow from the additional investment made today. As more is invested today, less is consumed today and the marginal utility of consumption increases today. On the other hand, as the level of consumption increases tomorrow, the marginal utility of consumption declines tomorrow. The increment in the value of the objective function therefore declines with each additional unit of investment made today.[5] The optimal rate of saving is reached when the loss of utility from consumption forgone today is exactly compensated for by the increment in the discounted utility of the additional consumption tomorrow.[6]

The procedure used for optimizing the commodity composition of consumption and the level of savings simultaneously presents conceptual and practical advantages.[7] The system of utility functions required can be specified with a small number of parameters. Those are the income-elasticity coefficients applicable to each commodity group and the overall elasticity of substitution (σ), which can all be estimated from market data.[8] Even if the direct and cross price elasticities implied by that system of utility functions are imperfect, they are better than those implied by the assumptions generally made with dynamic optimizing models. For example, discounted consumption (instead of its utility) is often maximized, whereas the commodity composition of consumption is fixed (Goreux and Manne 1973). It is then implicitly assumed that the elasticity of substitution is zero between commodities (fixed proportions) and infinity between consumption at two different points in time (utility of consumption taken as equal to consumption itself).[9] Moreover, taking the elasticity of substitution over time (σ) as equal to

---

5. This decline is accentuated by the fact that marginal productivity of capital is a decreasing function of capital accumulation.

6. In the last decision year (1990), the stock of capital must be sufficient to sustain a given growth rate of consumption in the postterminal period (1990–2000). This given postterminal growth rate should represent the asymptotic growth rate of the economy.

7. Savings are optimized as in the Ramsey model.

8. The system actually applied is somewhat more complicated, because coefficients of income elasticity are not treated as constant (see Chapter 9).

9. When the consumption of a commodity cannot be replaced in any amount by consumption of another commodity, the elasticity of substitution is equal to zero. On the other hand, when the utility of consumption is equal to consumption itself, marginal utility remains constant and the elasticity of substitution is equal to infinity (see Chapter 8).

infinity creates practical problems. Because the term (γ_t/σ) disappears from the righthand side of equation (1.1), the growth rate of consumption γ_t can no longer be optimized. It would then become optimal to invest or consume everything today depending on whether the marginal productivity of capital (r_t) were higher or lower than the discount rate (δ) plus the rate of population growth (ν), which are both given. Such nonsensical results are avoided in these models by the imposition of constraints on savings or on the growth rate of consumption or investments.[10] There is no need to impose such constraints in the model because the utility of consumption (instead of consumption itself) is maximized. The growth rate of investment remains a truly endogenous variable, yet the time paths of consumption and savings remain credible.

POLICY OBJECTIVES AND SHADOW PRICES

Ideally, when the model is solved with a given set of policy objectives, the primal solution should provide a projection of the quantities produced, traded, and consumed, while the dual solution should provide a projection of prices at which these transactions are conducted. The simplest solution corresponds to the free-market policy. In that case, there is no tariff on imports and there are no subsidies on exports.[11] There is no restriction on the entry of foreign labor nor on the borrowing of capital from abroad. Savings are at their optimal value, which implies the existence of a strong fiscal power able to mobilize the public revenues calculated in the optimal solution by applying the required rate of taxation.[12]

In the free-market solution, the shadow prices of products are interpreted as projections of market prices (deflated by the cost-of-living index). The shadow prices of resources are interpreted as real wages and rent paid by the entrepreneur, private or public, for hiring them. Multiplying the quantities found in the primal solution by the prices found in the dual solution gives the composition and the distribution of the national product at current prices.

The existence of tariffs on imports is one of the factors responsible for the discrepancies between actual market prices and shadow prices

10. These constraints may have a high dual value which obscures the economic interpretation of the dual solution.

11. Because demands for exports of coffee and cocoa originating from the Ivory Coast are assumed to be less than infinitely price-elastic, there are implicit export taxes on cocoa and coffee (see Chapter 13).

12. In some solutions of the model, a constraint is imposed on maximum rates of taxation.

calculated from the free-market solution. The effects of tariffs are simulated in the model by valuing the imported commodities with two different sets of prices. The c.i.f. prices are used to compute the surplus (or deficit) in the balance of foreign trade, whereas the c.i.f. prices plus tariffs are applied to all domestic transactions. Entrepreneurs and consumers in the Ivory Coast make their choices on the basis of prices that include tariffs. Since imports account for approximately 30 percent of the gross domestic products (GDP) in the base year, a substantial change in tariff policy leads to a modification of the entire shadow price structure.

The effects of excise taxes and consumer subsidies can be simulated in a similar manner. Consumers make their choices on the basis of prices that include excise tax (or subsidy), while producers and importers make their production and trade decisions on the basis of prices net of tax (or subsidy). The policy instrument is defined in one case by the level of the ad valorem tariff applied to imports and in the other by the level of the ad valorem excise tax (or subsidy) applied to consumer goods and services.

Although the Ivory Coast has followed an open-door policy since achieving independence in 1960, the implications of changes in that policy were simulated by imposing quotas on the entry of European expatriates, unskilled immigrants from neighboring countries, and foreign capital. The effect of specific government decisions in the public sector was also simulated. These decisions affected, among other things, the level of admissions to public schools, the opening of an iron mine, and the implementation of a large rural employment program in the north (which is the poorest part of the country). Clearly, all the measures listed here could be combined in very many different ways. Among the thirty experiments reported in Chapter 6, the first five simulate the effect of a progressive drive toward autarchy, while the others deal with the implications of specific policy measures taken one by one.

Whether the policy instruments take the form of direct price intervention (that is, tariffs) or the imposition of quotas, their effect on shadow prices can be measured by solving the central model. In either case, decisionmaking can, in principle, be decentralized by the transmission of shadow-price signals from the center to the periphery.

TWO-LEVEL PROGRAMMING

The prices derived from the dual solution of the central model can be reliable only if this model provides a realistic representation of the possibilities of substitution between factors and products. At the same time, the central model should remain relatively small, since it has to be solved many times in order to simulate a wide variety of experiments. Two-level programming is a way of capturing the scope for substitution existing in the various sectors of the economy without unduly increasing the size of the central model.

The starting point is the specification of the unaggregated dynamic economywide model, which is too large to be solved directly. The borderlines between sectors are drawn with a view to maximizing interdependencies within sectors and minimizing them between sectors. In this process, seven sectors are singled out.

Education, which is the key to Ivorization and is the possible subject of some of the most critical decisions of the Ivorian authorities, is treated as a separate sector. Two large projects are also treated as separate sectors. One, the iron mine, could be considered a new sector, since the Ivory Coast would not produce any iron ore if the mine were not to be opened. The other, the Riviera project, has the purpose of developing a center for international tourism in the Ivory Coast. At the time the model was constructed, there was no certainty when or whether these projects would be implemented. All urban activities other than those associated with education or these two large projects are grouped in a single sector called simply "urban." The last three sectors cover the rural activities.

The line of demarcation between the urban and rural sectors depends on the location of the industries processing agricultural goods. Processing industries are included in the rural sectors if the decision to produce the agricultural raw material carries with it the decision to construct the processing factory. Thus, the processing of palm oil is included in the rural models because the decision to grow palm trees for oil necessitates building a factory for processing.

Agriculture in the north and agriculture in the south are treated as separate sectors. The borderline between them is the ecological frontier separating the savanna zone in the north from the forest zone in the south. Most of the commodities produced in these two zones are different. Rice is the most important of the commodities which can be produced in both places. The third rural sector is livestock. In the base period, most livestock products were imported. Domestic production was of limited importance, and the technology applied was traditional. A separate model was constructed for livestock because the Ivorian authorities expressed a special interest in the development of a modern livestock sector.

Once the economy has been decomposed into sectors, the analysis of each sector is conducted by various groups of government officials, each interested in a different type of problem. These differences can be taken into account in the design of the various sectoral models. Strict uniformity is, however, required in the treatment of the commodities produced (and the resources used) by more than one sector. If this uniformity is not enforced from the beginning, it becomes impossible to link the various sectors together later. This lesson was learned the hard way in a multilevel programming study conducted for Mexico. In the concluding chapter of that study, Kornai noted: "Serious problems are encountered when we want to connect models constructed by several individuals. We must say, frankly, that such problems arose in the course of the Mexican work. . . . If researchers are allowed to construct individual models independently, each after his own ideas, the models will be incompatible, and will not fit together within a homogenous system." (Kornai 1973, pp. 546–47)

The problems stressed by Kornai were avoided in the Ivory Coast study. All sectors were formally linked within an unaggregated economywide model which could have been solved at once (by means of simplex algorithm) if a large enough computer had been available. The central model is a compact version of that model, which is arrived at by aggregating the sectoral components. Instead of solving the unaggregated economywide model at once, the central model and the unaggregated sectoral components are solved sequentially.

The sequence between sectoral and central solutions differs from the one described by Dantzig and Wolfe. The latter could be interpreted as a dialogue between the central planner and the sectoral planners, a dialogue which leads ultimately to the formulation of the plan. Each iteration cycle makes it possible for the central planner to gain additional sectoral knowledge by asking the sectoral planner what he would produce and what resources he would need at certain prices. These iterations simulate the exchange of internal memoranda between two levels of the hierarchy. Only the last step of the iterations, the plan, is made public.

The number of iterations between sectors and center is considerably reduced in this system. The initial formulation of the plan and its periodic revisions consist basically of two steps each. The first step takes place essentially at the sectoral level and the second at the central level.

In the first step, each sectoral model is solved independently with alternative sets of instructions received from the center. Each set of instructions can be expressed in terms of prices only, of quantities only, or as a mix between prices and quantities. Applying the alternative sets of instructions to the sectoral models is equivalent to solving these models with parametric variations. At the end of the first step, each sectoral model should operate smoothly and the scope for substitution among central resources should be well known.

The second step is to incorporate aggregated forms of the various sectoral models into the central model. The urban model, which follows a Leontief technology, is incorporated in its reduced form into the central model. As explained in Chapter 12, in the absence of make-or-buy choices, no information would be lost by that transformation although the seventy urban branches would be eliminated from the central model. Because there are make-or-buy choices, the aggregation procedure introduces some inaccuracies. Similarly, a complex educational model is incorporated into the central model in a highly compact form (see Chapter 11). In that case, the only source of error is aggregation over time.

The linkage between the rural and central models could be thought of as an intermediate step in the Dantzig and Wolfe iterative procedure. Instead of proceeding to a series of iterations between sector and center, a group of sectoral solutions is incorporated at once into the central model. Consider the rural sector in the southern part of the Ivory Coast. The sector earns most of the country's foreign exchange by exporting timber, coffee, cocoa, and palm oil. Because labor and capital are the two main central resources required to increase these exports, the central planner may consider the rural sector in the south essentially as a means of transforming labor and capital into foreign exchange. He needs to know how much foreign exchange can be earned in the south by applying different amounts of labor and capital. These data are obtained by solving the rural model of the south for different combinations of the relative prices of foreign exchange, labor, and capital. In one case, a very high premium on foreign exchange may be combined with a low price for labor and a high price for capital. In a second case, the relative prices of labor and capital may be inverted. In two other cases, the premium on foreign exchange may be deleted. If the number of price combinations is large enough and if the price variations are wide enough, the corresponding solutions of the rural model provide a satisfactory representation of the opportunities for earning foreign exchange in the south, depending on the relative scarcities of foreign exchange, labor, and capital. This is the form in which the rural sector of the south is incorporated into the central model. Although this representation is considerably more compact than the nonaggregated sectoral model, it provides the central planner with most of what he needs to know about the south.[13]

Once a compact form of each of the sectoral models has been incorporated into the central model, the types of policy experiments

13. As it turned out, the rural linkage was not very satisfactory. This was largely on account of the fact that work on the rural models could not be pursued until completion of the central model (see Chapter 12).

described earlier can be conducted and dialogue can be engaged in with policymakers. This dialogue could end with the selection of the set of policies that will define the plan. Only then would it be necessary to return to the sectoral models in order to define sectoral targets in detail.

Alternatively, if enough time and resources were available, it would be possible to proceed to a second cycle of iterations before settling upon a final plan. Again, the first step would be conducted at the sectoral level. Each model would be revised in the light of new information and a better knowledge of the value of the central resources. In the second step, the improvements made at the sectoral level would be incorporated into a revised central model.

In this study, the second cycle consisted essentially of enlarging the educational model at the request of the Ivorian authorities. As the results of the Unesco survey became available, the data of the educational model were also revised. It was not possible, however, to revise the rural models during the course of the second cycle; this is the major shortcoming of the study.

What has just been said of the relations between economywide and sectoral analysis applies largely to the relations between sectoral and project analysis. Sectoral models are not constructed by merely consolidating or aggregating project studies. Nevertheless, many of the technical coefficients used in the sectoral models are derived from project studies. Because many projects are small, it is generally assumed that the decision made for a particular project does not affect the shadow prices computed from sectoral or economywide models. Once a large number of project decisions has been made, this assumption is no longer valid, and it becomes necessary to revise the sectoral models.

The system described here provides a logical framework for transmitting information among the central, sectoral, and project levels. The entire system has to be revised periodically to take into account improvements in the data as well as changes in the environment (world prices, for example) or in the policy objectives. When the system is revised, it is fully consistent. Between periodic revisions, research can proceed at each level with a substantial degree of autonomy.

Chapter 2

Organization and Summary

IN A SYSTEM in which everything is interdependent, a full understanding of the effect of a policy measure on one component of the system requires a knowledge of the interactions between that particular component and the rest of the system. Some knowledge of the methodology applied is, therefore, necessary in order to assess the findings. It is useful, however, to have some ideas of the problems and the solutions before getting too deeply involved in methodological issues. On balance, it was considered preferable to start with the findings and to present a summary that may help readers in locating where to find the information that they need in this volume.

Findings (Part II)

The results of the central model are expressed in terms of both quantities and prices for the years 1975, 1980, 1985, and 1990. They are presented in four chapters. The first two are concerned with the free-market policy and the last two with departures from this policy.

FREE-MARKET POLICY (CHAPTERS 3 AND 4)

The free-market solution of the model is conceptually the simplest. The objective is to maximize aggregate growth, and efficiency is the only concern. Moreover, the assumptions made in solving the model in this way do not imply any radical departure from the outward-looking policies followed since independence was achieved in 1960. Tariffs on imports were more moderate than in most developing countries, and few quantitative restrictions were imposed on imports and capital flows. Policies regarding entry of foreign labor were particularly liberal.

The excellent performance recorded from 1960 to 1975 is almost maintained in the free-market solution, and gross national product increases approximately 7 percent a year from 1975 to 1990. With the rapid expansion of exports of tree crops from the forest zone, the share of the rural south in the total population remains about stable. That of the rural north, which declined from 28 percent in 1965 to 18 percent in 1975, falls to 9 percent in the late 1980s. On the other hand, urban population increases steadily, reaching a third of total population in 1990. With the rapid rate of migration, disguised unemployment in urban areas becomes a matter of increasing concern.

The economy remains heavily dependent on foreign capital throughout the planning period, and an increasing part of the return on physical capital invested in the Ivory Coast has to be earmarked for servicing the foreign debt. On the other hand, dependence on foreign technicians declines during the 1980s. By 1990, expatriates have been replaced with nationals in professional positions.

Human investment in postprimary education is treated exactly like any other type of investment. The cultural benefits of being educated are not taken into account in the objective function, and no constraints are imposed on the date by which Ivorization must be completed. Under those conditions, it is optimal to start with the big educational push and to refrain from increasing the number of new enrollments in the late 1970s in order to avoid flooding the market ten years later.

The adjustment problem is particularly severe for three reasons. First, the initial growth of the educational system is considerable; since 1965 new university enrollments have actually increased more than 30 percent a year. Second, the replacement of expatriates represents a one-time shift in demand. Third, in the late 1980s there is practically no demand for replacement after expatriates have left; very few nationals have reached retirement age in 1990, since most of them have graduated since 1960. The paradox of Ivorization is that new enrollments must be curtailed before self-sufficiency is reached, precisely when the demand for expatriates is the greatest.

In the 1980s the wage bill rises 7 percent a year in real terms, whereas the size of the labor force increases at half this rate. The difference is entirely the result of the shifts toward better-paid occupations, since the average of the wages for each skill category does not rise.

POLICY EXPERIMENTS (CHAPTERS 5 AND 6)

One group of policy experiments deals with the freedom of entry to foreign goods, foreign capital, and foreign labor. Another deals with problems of internal distribution (north versus south, rural versus urban, present versus next generation). The effects of events beyond control of the government, such as changes in the terms of trade and in the level of foreign aid, are also simulated.

A progressive drive toward autarchy and nationalism is illustrated by a sequence of steps. The first is the imposition of tariffs on competing imports. As this raises disguised unemployment, the second step is to restrict immigration of unskilled workers and inflow of foreign capital. As the employment situation does not improve, the third step is to launch a large rural employment program in the north. The final step is to restrict the entry of foreign labor. The economy adjusts easily to the first restriction; the objective function declines only 2 percent. When all restrictions are combined, however, the value of the objective function falls 15 percent.

The effects of a given policy measure may depend on the context within which that measure is implemented. Thus, if the rates of taxation cannot be increased, a rural program aiming at increasing employment in the north is not very successful; better distribution of income today leads to reduced aggregate consumption tomorrow. This unfavorable outcome is avoided, however, when the model is solved without a constraint on savings. In that case, which implies the existence of a strong fiscal power, it becomes optimal to save more today in order to compensate for the loss of efficiency in socially oriented investments; here, the level of gross national product (GNP) is hardly affected, whereas its distribution is improved.

Although tariffs on imports are not generally very high, some gains could be made by reducing the protection granted to a number of import-substitution industries. In the experiments made, the removal of tariffs on manufactured imports raised the value of the objective function 3 to 4 percent and resulted in a substantial transfer of income from urban to rural areas. It also contributed to a reduction of the level of disguised unemployment. The reason is that free trade stimulates the production of agricultural export crops and of export industries both of which require more unskilled labor than import-substitution manufacturing industries. When all tariffs are removed, the volume of trade increases about 40 percent and the equilibrium of the balance of payments is reached with a 13 percent devaluation of the currency.

Experiments made to reduce dependence on foreign capital were not encouraging. Achieving Ivorization of capital by 1990 would have a high cost. It would reduce growth without improving the distribution of income.

The growth of the Ivorian economy proved highly sensitive to the assumptions made concerning the terms of trade. A reduction of 10 percent in those terms during the 1970s led to an increase of 5 percent in the shadow price of foreign exchange over the same decade and a loss of 5 percent in private consumption during both the 1970s and the 1980s.

Methodology (Part III)

The results summarized in Part Two illustrate the types of problems that can be analyzed with the system of models described in the eight chapters of Part Three. The first chapter explains how the various parts of the central model fit together, while the other seven chapters deal with the treatment of the various types of economic activities.

CENTRAL MODEL (CHAPTER 7)

The starting point is an unaggregated model of the entire economy, which is expressed in terms of the familiar consumption, production, trade, and investment activities. Because this model is too large to be solved directly, it is aggregated in the form of a central model that describes the way in which primary resources shared between sectors may be transformed into consumer goods and, in turn, into utility, the value of which is maximized. Most intermediate activities do not appear in the central model explicitly. Their levels and their resource requirements are, however, implicit in any solution of the model, and they can be calculated from that solution. Thus, final demand by consumers is optimized among eight commodity groups, one of which is clothing. The model specifies the amounts of primary resources (labor of each skill category, type of capital stocks, and foreign exchange) required to supply a unit of clothing to consumers. Such requirements include the resources needed by the textile industry and by the industries providing the inputs used in producing textiles. The levels of gross output of these industries are not among the variables optimized in the central model, but they can be derived from the optimal solution of that model.

CONSUMPTION AND UTILITY (CHAPTERS 8 AND 9)

Intratemporal and intertemporal consumption choices are made simultaneously by maximizing the value of a nonlinear utility function. Variations in the demand for each commodity group results from the combination of endogenously determined income and price-substitution effects and of an exogenous time trend which reflects the impact of population growth and urbanization. The implicit demand functions can be estimated from market data. The commodity-specific parameters are the time trend and the coefficients of income elasticity. The overall elasticity of substitution (σ) is the common ratio between the coefficients of price elasticity and income elasticity.

Reasonable time paths of consumption and investments are obtained by maximizing the sum of the discounted utilities of consumption without applying any constraint on rates of saving. In truncating the time horizon at the year 1990, it is assumed that, at that time, the economy has already reached its asymptotic growth rate. Investments made in 1990 are constrained to raise capital stocks at a level sufficient for sustaining the asymptotic growth rate during the period 1990–2000. In a two-factor economy with labor augmenting technical progress, the asymptotic growth rate of per capita consumption would be the rate of increase in labor productivity. In this rather complex model, the asymptotic growth rate had to be determined by iterations. Although its value was not modified during the course of the policy experiments, the horizon effects in the year 1990 remained generally minor.

INVESTMENTS (CHAPTERS 10 AND 11)

In the urban sector, physical investment activities generate capital stocks in the form of vehicles, construction, and machinery, which may be specialized in terms of their utilization. For example, machinery installed in a textile factory can be used only for producing textiles. Because investment activities have different gestation lags and capital stocks have different life spans, a problem of time aggregation arises in this dynamic model, which is not specified annually but only at five-year intervals.[1]

The problem of time aggregation is particularly complex in the case of human investments in education. Students enrolling at the same time in a given cycle of studies do not graduate simultaneously, because a number of them have to repeat several grades. The aggregation procedure applied here permits this multiple lag structure to be taken into account and provides a realistic picture of the educational system. The aggregation error is minimal, and only a few rows have to be added to the central model on account of the educational sector. From

---

1. The gestation lag is the interval between the time a capital good is invested and the time the capital stock generated from the investment is available for production.

the optimal solution of that model, disaggregated yearly data can be derived regarding size of the student population by cycle of studies and educational inputs.

Production and Trade (Chapters 12 and 13)

The production and trade activities defining the inputs and the primary resources required to produce a unit of output are specified in the sectoral models, but they do not appear in the central model. In the latter, a rural sector is represented by a group of solutions of the optimizing model of that rural sector. Each sectoral solution defines the amounts of final consumer goods and export goods that can be produced with given quantities of central resources, those which are shared among sectors, such as capital and foreign exchange. The optimal combination of these sectoral solutions is selected by solving the central model. Because the sum of the nonnegative weights applied to each sectoral solution cannot exceed unity, sufficient amounts of sector-specific resources must be available to ensure the feasibility of the combination selected. There is no need to include in the central model constraints on sector-specific resources, such as land and water, which cannot be used outside of the sector concerned.

In the case of the urban sector, where a commodity can be produced according to a single technology, the input-output matrix is square if domestic production is used as the source of supply whenever there is a choice between producing and importing the same good. The resources required directly and indirectly for supplying a unit of a given type of final demand can then be calculated by inverting the input-output matrix. A similar calculation can be made when importing, instead of production, is used as the source of supply whenever there is a choice; the input-output matrix then remains square and can still be inverted. The calculation leads to different resource requirements for supplying the same final demand item. The urban sector is represented in the central model by two matrices defining the central resources required for supplying a unit of the various final demand items in two different ways. With the production matrix, whenever there is a choice between producing and importing, domestic production is used as the source of supply. With the import matrix, importing is used as the source of supply whenever there is a choice. In relation to the current trade literature, the import matrix could be visualized as the basis of reference used by Balassa (1965) and Corden (1966) to calculate rates of effective protection. The production matrix would be the one from which Bruno (1972) calculates domestic resource costs.[2] The model used here rests on less restrictive assumptions than the two preceding, since any combination of the supply activities defined by the import and production matrices can be selected.

The model can be solved with or without tariffs. The simulation of ad valorem tariffs is obtained by solving the model iteratively, but the convergence is very fast.

LABOR (CHAPTER 14)

In the Ivory Coast there are simultaneously a large influx of foreign labor and a serious problem of underemployment among nationals. Foreign labor consists of professionals coming mainly from Europe and of unskilled labor migrating from neighboring countries, in particular from Sahel countries. The three critical areas of underemployment for nationals are seasonal unemployment in agriculture, disguised urban unemployment, and underemployment of school dropouts who wish to occupy clerical positions and do not want blue-collar jobs. These particular features of the labor market in the Ivory Coast are reflected in the design of the model.

Services of European expatriates are treated the same way as any other imported services, and the Ivory Coast is a price-taker. In the case of unskilled workers migrating from neighboring countries, the Ivory Coast is treated as a price-influencer. There is an upward supply curve for unskilled foreign labor, which implies that foreign migrants receive a lower salary than nationals performing the same task and having the same productivity.

In rural areas, seasonal unemployment is estimated by setting a reservation price for labor, which assumes that labor will not work below a minimum level of remuneration. In urban areas, disguised unemployment is defined as the production of services which are imperfect substitutes for the goods and services of the formal sector. The rate of substitution becomes increasingly unfavorable to the informal sector as the output of the latter rises. Surplus labor can therefore be employed at decreasing returns. In the free-market solution, these informal services account for about 5 percent of the value added by the formal sector.

Migrations from rural to urban areas have a real cost in additional urban services. Because this cost is assumed to increase linearly with the

---

2. Domestic production is used by Bruno as the source of supply if some production has been recorded during the year for which the input-output table was constructed.

rate of migrations, the elasticity of migration in relation to the wage differential between urban and rural areas remains constant.

Finally, the model recognizes the possibility of substitution between labor of skill categories requiring relatively close qualifications. This is of particular relevance for the skill categories affected by school ·dropouts.

Multilevel Programming (Part IV)

The starting point in Chapter 7 was an economywide model that was too large to be solved directly. This model was reduced to a manageable size by aggregating its sectoral components. It led to the central model, which was solved many times in order to assess the effects of alternative policies and their sensitivity to external events. Once a given solution of the central model has been selected, the disaggregated sectoral results can be arrived at by returning to the sectoral models and solving them for the quantities and prices obtained in the selected solution of the central model. Solving the sectoral models and the central model sequentially in this fashion leads to a solution of the nonaggregated economywide model (the one too large to solve directly) that is feasible but generally suboptimal. The loss of optimality remains, however, small if the aggregation of the sectoral models does not result in a substantial loss of information regarding ways of replacing one central resource with another within sectors. With appropriate aggregation procedures, the loss of optimality need not be of greater concern than the effects of errors made in estimating statistical parameters or in projecting exogenous variables, such as future levels of commodity prices in world markets.

The nature of the formal linkages and the errors attached to them are analyzed in Chapter 15, while the particular features of the urban and rural models are reviewed in the last two chapters of this volume.

FORMAL LINKAGES (CHAPTER 15)

The iron mine is treated as a new sector, since no iron ore will be produced in the Ivory Coast unless the mine is constructed. There is no choice regarding the size and the nature of the investments required. Choices concern only the date at which investments should be initiated; construction may start in 1975, 1980, or 1985, or it may not occur during the planning period. Because the mine requires capital and earns foreign exchange in substantial quantity, its construction affects the shadow prices of capital and foreign exchange. Consequently, the gain (or loss) resulting from the construction of the mine cannot be calculated on the basis of the prices which would have prevailed without the mine. The gain (or loss) has to be measured by solving the central model with and without the mine. Whether it is optimal to construct the mine depends on the relative shadow prices of capital and foreign exchange; it depends on the options selected regarding trade and financial policies, as well as on variations in the terms of trade.

The columns of the matrix representing the rural sector in the central model correspond to solutions of the nonaggregated rural models that are associated with different patterns of agricultural development in each rural subsector (south, north, and livestock). A combination of these solutions is selected in the central model by optimizing the allocation of central resources among the three rural subsectors and the rest of the economy. The optimal combination depends on the policies adopted (for example, on the level of protection granted to urban industries or on restrictions to the entry of foreign labor), as well as on external events (such as changes in the terms of trade or in the level of foreign aid).

Agriculture in the south may be visualized by the central planner as a means of transforming labor and capital into foreign exchange. The ways of proceeding to such a transformation are, unfortunately, represented in the central model by too few solutions of the sectoral model, and the loss of information is significant. In the case of the urban sector, not all possible ways of saving foreign exchange through import substitution are taken into account. Some information is therefore lost, but the loss on that account is small.

URBAN AND RURAL MODELS (CHAPTERS 16 AND 17)

The nonaggregated urban model consists of three matrices. The input-output matrix and the resource matrix define the state of the technology. There is no technological choice in fifty-eight branches, but there is a choice between domestic production and import in another fourteen branches. The final-demand matrix defines the composition of eighteen types of final-demand items in terms of the products and services of the seventy-two urban branches. From these three basic matrices is derived the aggregate matrix which is incorporated into the central model. This matrix, the reduced form of the urban model, defines the amounts of central resources required (directly and indirectly) to supply one unit of each of the eighteen types of final-demand items. Each item can be supplied in three different ways resulting from three given combinations of the import and production activities in the fourteen branches in which there is a make-or-buy choice.

The level of final demand for urban goods and services can be optimized by solving the central model. Alternatively, the central resources required for a given level of final demand can be calculated by solving the urban model alone. The impact of import substitution can be assessed by comparing the results obtained with the resource matrices associated with the two extreme make-or-buy choices. Given the shadow prices of the central resources, the relative profitability of the various urban branches can also be calculated through simple matrix operations.

In the case of agriculture, two small models not formally linked with the rest of the economy were experimented with before the central model had been constructed. The first was used to assess the profitability of tractors and animal traction in the north of the Ivory Coast. Because of the short rainy season, labor and traction requirements are spread unevenly throughout the year, and they are specified monthly in the model. The analysis suggests that the use of tractors would not generally be profitable because their yearly rate of use would be too low. Animal traction appears more promising, because oxen could be fed on fallow crops, which form part of the rotation of crops required for maintaining fertility. The model was also used to assess the scope for substitution between labor and capital. It showed that a variation in the rate of interest substantially affects not only the ratio between labor and capital but also the level of commodity output and the use of purchased inputs.

A dynamic model of the forest zone in the southwest was used to assist in the formulation of the development program in that region. The problem was to coordinate the exploitation of forest resources with the planting of tree crops, to assess the relative profitability among tree crops and the optimal timing of investments. The most serious constraints to the expansion of all tree crops are the availability of labor, the infrastructure required for receiving additional migrants, and the equipment for clearing land. In the solution selected, the size of the agricultural labor force was increasing fivefold between 1970 and 1990, and average employment per year and per worker was rising by one quarter. The most critical issue was the availability of capital for implementing the investment program.

After the first development plan of the southwest had been made, the plan was revised in the context of the entire forest area of the south, and the static model of the north was transformed into a dynamic model in order to facilitate analysis of linkages between north and south. A third dynamic model was also constructed to assess the prospects for the development of a livestock industry. The three rural models were fully consistent with each other, and they could, in principle, have been solved as a single model of the rural sector. This was not done, however, because the sectoral model would have been too large and its solution too costly. Instead, each of the three rural models was solved separately. Linkages among the three rural models and between the rural sector and the rest of the economy were taken into account simultaneously by solving the central model.

In the system, the sectoral models and the central model are solved sequentially. A cycle of solutions could be associated with the preparation of a draft of the national plan. Several cycles of solutions would, therefore, be required to prepare successive drafts of the plan. After the plan has been completed and before it is revised, work on the sectoral models and the central model can proceed with a great deal of autonomy.

At the time of formulation of the plan, there are formal upward and backward linkages between the sectoral models and the central model. In the case of a small project, there is no need for an upward linkage because such a project does not significantly affect the shadow prices of the central resources, such as foreign exchange and capital. The downward linkage consists in solving the model of the project with the shadow prices found in the optimal solutions of the central and sectoral models. After many small projects have been analyzed, it becomes necessary to revise the sectoral model in the light of the information collected at the project level.

Part Two

Findings

Chapter 3

The Free-Market Solution

THE FREE-MARKET SOLUTION is used here as the point of reference because it is conceptually the simplest.[1] Its objective is maximization of aggregate growth. Efficiency is the only concern. Since some of the implications of this solution may appear as politically undesirable, the ways to correct them will be analyzed in Chapter 6, which deals with policy experiments.

The Overall Picture

The broad economic trends summarized in Table 3.1 provide a rosy picture. The excellent growth performance recorded between 1965 and 1972 is maintained almost throughout the planning period.

The net inflow of capital and the wage bill of expatriates continue to increase until 1980; afterwards, both decline sharply. During the 1980s, net capital inflow is reduced by CFAF71 billion.[2] This loss of resources is more than compensated for by the replacement of expatriates;[3] by 1990, what might be called the Ivorization of professional cadres— *l'ivoirisation des cadres*—has been completed. The Ivorization of capital— *l'ivoirisation des capitaux*—remains a problem, however. In 1990, 11 percent of commodity exports go to the servicing of the debt contracted

---

1. For a distinction between exogenous data and endogenous variables, see Table 1.1.
2. This is the difference between +21 and −50 shown for 1980 and 1990 in row 8 on the left side of Table 3.1. In this book the word "billion" is used according to the American and French systems, in which 1 billion equals 1,000 million.
3. The wage bill of expatriates declines by CFAF113 billion, which is the difference between the values of 118 and 5 shown for 1980 and 1990 in row 11 on the left side of Table 3.1.

[33]

Table 3.1. The Main Economic Aggregate at 1970 Prices (Free-Market Solution)

Economic variable	Absolute levels (billions of CFAF at 1970 prices)					Average yearly growth rates (percent)					
	1970 historical	1975	1980	1985	1990	1965–72[a] historical	1970–75	1975–80	1980–85	1985–90	1970–90
1. GNP[b]	366	510	722	1,033	1,467	7.1	6.9	7.2	7.4	7.3	7.2
2. Private consumption	233	326	439	632	881	n.a.	7.0	6.2	7.6	6.9	6.9
3. Public consumption	44	64	91	127	179	n.a.	9.0	7.3	6.9	7.1	7.3
4. Total investments	95	136	213	269	357	10.1	9.0	7.3	6.9	7.0	7.3
5. Physical investments[c]	78	100	156	196	278	n.a.	5.1	9.4	4.7	7.2	6.6
6. Human investments	17	36	57	73	79	n.a.	17.6	9.6	5.0	1.6	8.0
7. Domestic savings	89	120	192	274	407	8.6	6.2	9.8	7.4	8.7	7.9
8. Net capital inflow	6	16	21	–5	–50	n.a.	22.0	5.6			
9. Commodity exports f.o.b.	125	185	254	329	460	7.6	8.1	6.6	5.3	6.9	6.7
10. Commodity imports c.i.f.	108	159	227	288	396	8.6	8.0	7.4	4.8	6.6	6.7
11. Wage bill of expatriates	68	94	118	88	5	n.a.	6.7	4.8	–5.7	–42.7	–14.0
12. Ivorians of high skills[d]	9	27	73	175	293	n.a.	24.0	22.0	19.0	10.9	14.9
13. Ivorians of medium skills[d]	12	23	45	73	128	n.a.	14.1	14.3	10.0	11.8	12.5

n.a. Not available.
a. Growth rates in real terms given in *Current Economic Situation and Prospects of the Ivory Coast* (Washington, D.C.: World Bank Report no. 296-IVC, April 11, 1974. Circulation restricted—for World Bank internal use only).
b. Row 1 = row 2 + row 3 + row 4 − row 8.
c. Row 5 + row 6 = row 7 + row 8.
d. Number of Ivorians employed (outside education) by skill categories weighted by wages.

[34]

abroad and to the remuneration of the foreign capital invested in the Ivory Coast.[4]

Replacing expatriates with nationals during the 1980s requires a considerable effort in the field of education during the 1970s. At the beginning of the planning period, priority is given to the formation of human capital. Investments in postprimary education increase from 17 percent of total investments in 1970 to 27 percent in 1980 (Table 3.2).

Between the time a person enters high school and the time he graduates from a university, ten to fifteen years elapse. Because of this long lag, the growth of enrollments in high schools must be reduced well before self-sufficiency is reached in the labor market. Between

4. This percentage refers to the net outflow of capital, after deduction of the current inflow. It is lower than the debt-service ratio, which refers to the gross outflow of capital.

Table 3.2. Educational Data (Free-Market Solution)

Item	1970	1975	1980	1985	1990
Students newly enrolled (thousands)					
First year of high school	15.8	27.3	27.4	31.6	42.1
First year of higher education	0.9	2.6	3.1	5.0	5.0
Total students (thousands)					
Secondary education	54.5	95.9	138.0	151.0	155.0
Higher education	2.8	12.1	12.5	13.9	20.8
Expatriates (thousands)	21.7	28.4	36.0	25.1	1.9
Ratios					
Public recurrent expenditures on postprimary education over total recurrent public expenditure	0.18	0.23	0.24	0.21	0.17
Human investment in postprimary education over total investment	0.17	0.27	0.27	0.27	0.22

	1965–72	1970–75	1975–80	1980–85	1985–90
Average yearly growth rate (percent)					
New enrollments in high schools	14.0	11.6	0.1	3.0	5.0
New enrollments in higher education	31.0	21.0	3.8	9.7	0.1
Students in secondary education	18.8	12.0	7.6	1.8	0.5
Students in higher education	22.01	23.0	9.9	2.9	1.9
Public recurrent expenditure on postprimary education	13.5	15.1	8.5	3.8	2.0

1970 and 1975, new enrollments in high schools and in higher education increase 11.6 percent and 21 percent a year, respectively. Between 1975 and 1980, precisely when the number of expatriates is at its peak, these growth rates are severely curtailed to avoid flooding the market ten years later (see Chapter 4)

The rapid growth of the economy, together with the early educational push, leads to a transformation of the occupational and regional distribution of the population in the 1980s. Student population as a percentage of the total labor force reaches a peak in 1980. By 1985, the large flow of students enrolled in the 1970s has entered the labor market, affecting the distribution of income significantly (see Chapter 4).

The urban share of the labor force continues to increase rapidly in the 1970s (Table 3.3). As the problem of disguised urban unemployment becomes more severe in the 1980s, the disparity between urban and rural wages is somewhat reduced. Incentives for migrating from rural to urban areas become weaker, and the growth rate of the urban population declines from about 7 percent a year around 1970 to slightly more than 4 percent a year in the 1980s (Table 3.4). During that decade, the rural population increases about 2 percent a year, while the increase in the population as a whole is approximately 3 percent a year.

The most striking feature is the disparity between the picture in the south and that in the north. In relation to the total labor force, employment in the south (the rich forest zone) remains almost stable, but employment in the north (the savanna zone) dwindles. This situation induces large migrations of labor from the north and reduces the need for foreign migrants. A considerable reduction of the population in the north is an implication of the laissez-faire policy and

Table 3.3. Composition of the Labor Force (Free-Market Solution)
(Percent)

Segment of labor force	1965	1970	1975	1980	1985	1990
Unskilled labor						
North rural	28	24	18	14	9	8
South rural	49	48	49	48	49	46
Urban	18	21	25	29	31	33
Skilled labor	5	7	8	9	11	13
Total	100	100	100	100	100	100

Table 3.4. Composition of the Total Population: Past Trends and Projections (Free-Market Solution)[a]

Segment of population	1965	1970	1975	1980	1985	1990
	Millions of persons					
Rural	3.31	3.67	3.84	4.11	4.63	5.11
Urban	0.99	1.39	1.99	2.69	3.33	4.14
Subtotal	4.30	5.06	5.83	6.80	7.96	9.25
Immigrant labor	...[b]	...[b]	0.13	0.07	0.04	0.40
Total (including immigrant labor)	4.30	5.06	5.96	6.87	8.00	9.35
	Yearly growth (percent)					
	1965–70	1970–75	1975–80	1980–85	1985–90	
Rural (with immigrant labor)	2.1	1.6	1.0	2.2	2.2	
Urban	7.0	7.4	6.2	4.3	4.5	
Total (without immigrant labor)	...	2.9	3.1	3.2	3.1	
Total (with immigrant labor)	3.3	3.3	2.9	3.1	3.2	

a. Estimates made in 1972. On the basis of the first population census, made in April 1975, total population in mid-1975 amounts to 6.7 million, of which approximately 2 million would have been born of foreign parents. From 1970 to 1975, total population would have risen on the average by somewhat more than 5 percent a year, immigration accounting for half the growth.

b. African migrants are included in the population until 1970. From 1970 until 1990, agricultural workers migrating from neighboring countries are treated as foreigners. The size of the Ivorian population (including African migrants in the country by 1970) is an exogenous datum common to all experiments. The numbers of foreign agricultural migrants and of Ivorians migrating from rural to urban areas are endogenous variables in the model; their values vary with the experiment.

may be considered politically undesirable. It will be discussed again in connection with the policy experiments.

The Mechanism of Price Formation

Market prices result from the interactions between the demand for final consumer goods and the supply of those goods. This interaction is illustrated for the year 1980 by Tables 3.5 through 3.8.

For each of the eight groups of final consumer goods, Table 3.5 shows prices (deflated by the cost-of-living index) in row 1 and quantities consumed in rows 2 and 3. All figures are expressed as indexes, taking the 1970 levels as unity. The index of aggregate consumption (row 2) is obtained by multiplying the index of per capita consumption (row 3) by 1.34, which measures the given population growth. The interesting feature of the table is the decomposition of the

Table 3.5. *Private Consumption by Ivorians: Prices, Quantities, and Budget Shares (Free-Market Solution)*

Item	Housing	House- hold goods	Trans- porta- tion	Clothing	Bever- ages and miscel- laneous	Cereals	Meat	Tradi- tional foods	Total consump- tion
				Index:	*1970 = 1.00*				
Variations in prices and quantities									
1. Prices (deflated by cost-of-living index)[a]	1.38	0.98	0.77	0.89	0.76	1.13	1.45	0.73	1.00
2. Aggregate quantities consumed[b]	1.76	2.14	2.47	2.07	2.27	1.49	1.42	1.39	1.89
3. Quantities consumed per capita[c]	1.31	1.59	1.84	1.54	1.69	1.11	1.05	1.33	1.41
Specific impact of									
4. Urbanization	1.36	1.35	1.30	1.24	1.35	1.06	1.14	0.96	1.21
5. Income per capita (deflated by cost-of-living index)[d]	1.20	1.17	1.22	1.19	1.14	1.08	1.19	1.03	1.16
6. Prices (deflated by cost-of-living index)[e]	0.80	1.01	1.17	1.05	1.10	0.97	0.78	1.04	1.00

Elasticity coefficients

					Percentage				
Elasticity in relation to									
7. Income per capita	1.29	1.10	1.37	1.25	0.87	0.55	1.31	0.20	1.00
8. Price[f]	−0.53	−0.52	−0.74	−0.45	−0.43	−0.27	−0.65	−0.10	−0.50
Consumer budget shares									
9. 1970 consumption at 1970 prices	7.6	13.5	13.6	16.5	11.5	6.3	8.3	22.7	1.00
10. 1980 consumption at 1970 prices	7.1	15.3	17.8	18.1	13.8	5.0	6.2	16.7	1.00
11. 1980 consumption at 1980 prices	10.7	16.4	14.9	17.3	11.5	6.1	9.8	13.3	1.00

a. Price variations are computed from the dual solution.

b. Quantity variations are computed from the primal solution.

c. Row 3 = row 4·row 5·row 6.

d. Income effect at constant prices with variable income elasticity, which in 1980 reaches the value given in line 7. Along the Engel path the same level of total utility would be reached with an increase of 15.1 percent in total per capita consumption; this barely exceeds the 16 percent arrived at here using the 1970 prices as weights.

e. Substitution along an eight-dimensional isoutility surface. The percentage variation derived from line 1 multiplied by the price elasticity shown in line 8 gives the percentage price effect that can be derived from line 6. Thus, for housing, the price increase of 38 percent combined with a price elasticity of −0.53 leads to a 20 percent decline in prices [(0.38)(−0.53) = −0.20].

f. Apparent price elasticity, computed ex post and not entering into the model.

Table 3.6. Production Costs in 1980 (Free-Market Solution)

Item	Consumer goods		Capital goods			Tradi-tional com-merce
	Housing	House-hold goods	Vehicles	Ma-chines	Con-struction	
			Index: 1970 = 1.00			
1. Shadow prices of output	1.38	0.98	1.00	0.99	1.07	1.06
Cost component[a]			*Percentage share*			
2. Unskilled labor	1	5	1	1	16	94
3. Medium-skilled labor	1	7	8	8	11	2
4. Highly skilled labor	1	23	17	35	39	3
5. Capital	95	23	12	14	15	0
6. Foreign exchange	2	42	62	42	19	1
Total	100	100	100	100	100	100

a. For each good, production costs are computed by weighting resource requirements with the shadow prices of twenty-two types of resources (eleven for labor, ten for physical capital, and one for foreign exchange). Labor skills are regrouped here into three categories, while capital is aggregated into a single category. Resource requirements and shadow prices are derived from the model solution.

increase in per capita consumption (row 3) into the specific impacts of urbanization, income, and prices. Those are shown in rows 4–6.

Assume that between 1970 and 1980 average income per capita remains unchanged in rural and urban areas and that the relative price of housing also remains the same. The national demand for housing would increase faster than the size of the total population because, during that decade, people move from rural to urban areas. In the savanna zone, housing is not a problem, but in Abidjan it is. The urbanization effect of 36 percent shown in row 4 takes care of this particular problem.

This shift in the composition of the population between urban and rural areas does not affect all types of consumer goods equally. Although it increases the demand for housing, it reduces the demand for traditional foods. On the whole, however, urbanization increases the national demand for consumer goods substantially, as can be seen in the last column of Table 3.5. The 89 percent increase in aggregate consumption (row 2) results from the combination of three elements: a 34 percent increase attributable to population growth alone, a 21 percent increase attributable to urbanization alone, and a 16 percent increase attributable to income growth alone (1.89 = 1.34·1.21·1.16). This increase of 16 percent in per capita consumption is distributed among the eight groups of consumer goods (row 5) on the basis of the income elasticities shown in row 7. Thus, with an elasticity of 1.29, demand for housing increases 20 percent on account of income alone.

Consider the aggregate demand for housing at constant prices: the population effect is 1.34, the urbanization effect is 1.36 (row 4), and the income effect is 1.20 (row 5). These three factors combined lead to an increase of 119 percent in the aggregate demand for housing (2.19 = 1.34·1.36·1.20). The total supply increases only 76 percent. The market is cleared through a price increase of 38 percent (row 1), which reduces the effective demand 20 percent (row 5);[5] the implied price elasticity of -0.53 is shown in row 8.[6]

Satisfaction of demand is one element in the mechanism of price formation; the other is the cost of supplying goods to consumers.

5. $1.76/2.19 = 0.8 = 1 - 0.2$.
6. $(0.8 - 1)/(1.38 - 1) = -0.53$.

Table 3.7. The Structure of the Domestic-Resource Cost of Foreign Exchange Earned through Exports or Saved through Import Substitution in 1980 (Free-Market Solution) (Percent)

Cost component	Exports				Import-substitution activities		
	Agricultural products from the south		Industrial products				Marginal (clothing)
	Average	Marginal[a]	Processed foods	Miscellaneous	All urban products	Household goods	
Unskilled labor	33	14	25	18	2	2	3
Medium-skilled labor	4	7	15	12	14	9	11
Highly skilled labor	10	19	33	34	47	59	47
Urban capital	3	8	27	36	37	30	39
Rural capital	50	52					
Total	100	100	100	100	100	100	100

a. Marginal import-substitution activity is defined as the difference between two activities which are both positive in the optimal solution.

Table 3.8. The Domestic Resource Cost in 1980 (Free-Market Solution)
(Percent)

Cost component	Foreign exchange	House-hold goods	Vehicles	Machinery	Construc-tion
Unskilled labor	14	11	10	7	19
Medium-skilled labor	7	10	12	11	12
Highly skilled labor	19	31	29	43	42
Urban capital	8	26	17	17	17
Rural capital	52	22	32	22	10
Total	100	100	100	100	100

Examine the cost of supplying housing and household goods in Table
3.6. The prices appearing in the first two columns of line 1 are the
same as those in Table 3.5. This time they represent the marginal
supply cost, decomposed in terms of primary resources in rows 2–6.
Consider the group called "household goods." It consists of several
commodities combined in fixed proportions within the group. Some of
those goods can be either produced locally or imported. Labor, capital,
and various intermediate goods are required for the manufacture of
the goods that are produced locally. The costs shown in rows 2–6 are
computed by adding to the direct resource requirements the indirect
requirements represented by intermediate goods. Thus, direct and
indirect foreign exchange requirements account for 42 percent of the
total costs of household goods, but for only 2 percent of the costs of
housing services. In the latter case, 95 percent of the total costs are
rents on buildings.

Foreign exchange can be earned by exporting or saved by replacing
imported goods with domestically produced goods. The domestic
resource cost of foreign exchange is computed by deducting the cost of
production of the exported good, which is the indirect foreign exchange cost, from the foreign exchange earned by exporting it. The
same applies to the replacement of an imported good with one
produced locally. Table 3.7 illustrates the structure of the domestic
resource cost of foreign exchange with seven examples. As shown in
the first line, the import-substitution industries employ much less
unskilled labor than do the export industries. For the former, skilled
labor is the largest item of cost. To increase the profitability of import-
substitution industries, therefore, it is necessary to replace expatriates
with nationals.

Agricultural exports from the south remain the dominant source of
foreign exchange in 1980. The foreign exchange costs, shown in line 6

of Table 3.6, can be replaced by the domestic resource cost of the foreign exchange earned from marginal agricultural exports given in the second column of Table 3.7. This leads to Table 3.8, in which production costs are expressed in terms of labor and capital only. Ultimately, the shadow price of any good is measured by weighing the primary resource requirements by the shadow prices of these resources, which are given in Table 3.9.[7]

The shadow prices of labor and capital are measures of the yearly rental values of these resources. For any given category of labor skill, say clerical skill, the rental value is the annual salary of a clerk. This salary is formally measured in the model by the contribution of the clerk to the value of the objective function. Because shadow prices are deflated by the cost of living of the current year, salaries are expressed in CFAF at 1970 prices. This is a familiar measurement which can be easily compared with market wages, even if clerks do not all receive, in practice, the same salary.

With respect to physical capital, the meaning of the shadow price is less obvious. There are ten types of physical capital used in the urban sector, identified by sector of origin (vehicles, machines, construction) and destination (textile mill, machinery factory). Consider the case of buildings for housing or office use. If the need for buildings had been expressed in terms of two-bedroom apartments or square meters of office space, the shadow price of the capital would have been a familiar

---

7. The quantities of primary resources required for supplying a given good are not known before solving the model. There are alternative ways of supplying a given good; the most efficient way is selected in the optimization process.

Table 3.9. Shadow Wages at 1970 Prices and Rental Values as Percentages of Capital Values

Type of labor or capital invested for urban use	1975	1980	1985
	Millions of CFAF per worker per year		
1. Unskilled rural laborer	0.071	0.071	0.077
2. Unskilled urban laborer	0.117	0.104	0.104
3. Specialized worker	0.270	0.240	0.149
4. Clerk	0.390	0.346	0.363
5. Professional (M.A. level)	3.017	3.400	3.815
	Rental value as percentage of capital value		
6. Vehicles	27	29	29
7. Machinery	23	20	27
8. Buildings	22	25	27

concept; the shadow price of a two-bedroom apartment would have been the annual rent paid for this apartment. The model does not go into this degree of disaggregation, however. All urban buildings except schools fall into a single category. The types, sizes, and number of the buildings required are summarized in a single number, which is a quantity index. It measures the worth of the buildings in billions of CFAF at 1970 prices. The rent paid in 1975 for these buildings is equal to the number of units used multiplied by the rental value per unit— that is to say, per billion CFAF worth of buildings at 1970 prices. This is the shadow rent shown in the first column of row 8 of Table 3.9.

The rental value per unit of a building reflects four elements: the cost of construction of the building, the interest rate, the anticipated life span of the building (the period during which it can be used before needing replacement), and the gestation lag (the interval between the time the investment is made and the time the building is usable). The combination of these four elements is illustrated in Table 3.10. In this

Table 3.10. Capital Value, Rent, and the Capital-Recovery Factor

Item	Number of units
1. Volume of capital stocks[a]	1.00
2. Current value of capital[b]	1.10
3. Current value of annual rent[c]	0.22
Components of capital-recovery factor:[d]	
4. Interest charges on expenditures before occupancy[e]	0.044
5. Interest charges on capital value after occupancy[f]	0.150
6. Amortization[g]	0.006
7. Total[h]	0.200

a. Five hundred two-bedroom apartments, each worth CFAF2 million at 1970 prices, are the physical capital utilized: 500·0.002 = 1.

b. Volume of capital multiplied by shadow price of construction activity rounded to 1.1 (first column of row 1, Table 3.6).

c. Shadow price for renting one unit of capital stock (first column of row 8, Table 3.9).

d. Ratio between annual recurrent charges for occupying the apartment and current capital value of the apartment.

e. A lag of two and one-half years between initial expenditures and availability for occupancy.

f. Fifteen percent a year interest on buildings.

g. Life span equal to twenty-five years.

h. Sum of rows 4, 5, and 6 and ratio of row 3 to row 2.

simplified example, the cost of construction and the interest rate are assumed to be constant throughout the planning period. The ratio between annual rent paid (row 3 and capital value (row 2) is equal, by definition, to the capital-recovery factor (row 7). The difference between the latter (0.20) and the rate of interest (0.15) accounts for the amortization of the building and for interest charges between the time construction starts and the time the building is ready for occupancy.

What occurs in the model is more complicated, however, because the cost of construction (fifth column of Table 3.6) and the interest rate do not remain constant over time. As in the real world, a particular type of physical capital may be in short supply at a given time and there may be a surplus of it at another time. These changes are reflected by variations in the rental value per building unit. This is why the ratios between rents paid on different types of physical capital do not remain constant over time (see Table 3.9 and equation 10.10).

The Overall Picture Reviewed at Current Prices

The picture given in Table 3.1, at the beginning of this chapter, was expressed in terms of quantity indexes at 1970 prices. Multiplying these quantity indexes (derived from the primal solution) by price indexes (derived from the dual solution) leads to the projection in current prices presented in Table 3.11.[8] The upper part of this table is similar to Table 3.1. The numbers are not quite the same, because the current price structure differs from the 1970 price structure. For broad economic aggregates, such as the GNP, however, the differences do not exceed a few percentage points. The interesting part of the table is the lower one, which shows imputed returns on labor and capital.

THE EQUALITY BETWEEN MARGINAL COSTS
AND MARGINAL RETURNS

As will be recalled from Chapter 1, the model transforms the primary domestic resources (labor and capital) into utility of private consumption by Ivorians. This utility is equal to the value of private consumption measured at current prices (after appropriate deflation).[9]

8. Table 3.11 gives the year-by-year composition of the minimand (see Table 7.4).
9. The shadow prices are indexes with base unity for 1970. They are obtained by dividing the dual values found in the model by an index of the cost of living (1970 = 1.00). This index is computed by weighting the dual values of the eight groups of final consumer goods by their current shares. The shadow prices are therefore expressed in 1970 prices.

Table 3.11. Composition and Distribution of the GNP *at Current Prices Deflated in 1970* CFAF *(Free-Market Solution)*

	Billions of CFAF deflated at 1970 prices			Percentage shares		
Component of the GNP	1975	1980	1985	1975	1980	1985
1. Consumption (private and public)	394	534	758	76	73	72
2. Physical investments	103	159	184	20	21	18
3. Public exogenous investments	21	27	36	4	3	4
4. Urban investments	63	94	113	12	12	11
5. Iron mine	0	20	0	0	3	0
6. Riviera project	0	0	13	0	0	1
7. Rural investments	19	18	22	4	3	2
8. Human investments	43	74	97	8	10	9
9. Buildings and other expenses	9	14	16	2	2	1
10. Teachers	18	33	38	3	4	4
11. Students	16	27	43	3	4	4
12. Financial investment abroad[a]	−23	−29	+7	−4	−4	1
13. GNP[b]	517	738	1,046	100	100	100
14. Returns on labor	283	383	538	55	52	51
15. Unskilled rural labor	86	92	111	17	12	11
16. Unskilled urban labor	54	65	80	10	9	8
17. Skilled labor	127	199	304	25	27	28
18. Students	16	27	43	3	4	4
19. Returns on capital	227	338	487	44	46	47
20. Urban	118	187	313	23	25	30
21. Iron mine	0	0	13	0	0	1
22. Riviera project	0	0	4	0	0	1
23. Rural (mostly to the south)	109	151	157	21	20	15
24. Other rents (mainly on exports)	7	17	21	1	2	2

a. Minus sign indicates net inflow of capital.
b. Row 1 + row 2 + row 8 + row 12 = row 13 = row 14 + row 19 + row 24.

In addition to the utility of private consumption, which is maximized, public consumption requirements have to be satisfied. These are specified exogenously in terms of quantities of various goods and services.[10] Multiplying these quantities by the shadow prices of the

10. Quantities of these good and services are in turn expressed in terms of man-years of civil servants belonging to specified skill categories.

corresponding goods and services gives the current cost of public consumption. This cost is added to the value (or utility) of private consumption. The sum, which appears in row 1 of Table 3.11, is a measure of the current value of total consumption, public and private. This value is decomposed into the relative contributions of the various primary resources in the lower part of the table. Contributions are measured here with the assumption of a perfectly competitive market, where each resource is rewarded on the basis of its marginal productivity.

In the imputation procedure, all production and trade activities are treated as intermediate transactions for which marginal costs and returns cancel each other. For example, the domestric resource cost of "household goods" (second column in Table 3.8) appears in the lower part of table 3.11 under "returns on labor and capital." The marginal value of these goods (which is equal to the marginal cost in the optimal solution) appears in the upper part under row 1, "value of consumption."

Consider another example. The marginal cost of an investment activity in 1975 must be equal to the discounted sum of the marginal returns on the capital stocks generated by that activity. When the entire planning period (including the postterminal period) is taken as a whole, costs and returns must cancel each other, but within a single year they do not. The cost of the investment made in 1975 appears in the lower part of the table as returns on labor and capital for that year. Because investments made in 1975 do not contribute to consumption before 1980, the returns on those investments do not appear in row 1 for 1975. To balance the accounts within each decision year, investments must be valued at current costs in rows 2–11 in the upper part of the table.

Returns on labor are shown in the table according to the GNP concept. Since foreigners are treated as intermediate inputs, they do not appear in the table, either as consumers in the upper part, or as wage earners in the lower part.[11] Since labor is treated as human capital, moreover, the full cost of postprimary education appears in row 8 as investment. Usually only school buildings are treated as investments. Here, even the salaries forgone by students while attending university are counted as investment costs (row 11); therefore, they appear as returns on labor in row 18.

Exogenous public investments, row 3, correspond to the category

11. The procedure followed here is the one applied to "nonresidents" in national accounting. The UN methodology recommends treating foreign tourists and technical assistance experts as nonresidents; the procedure used here is therefore orthodox, even if it differs from the one applied in the Ivory Coast.

called "nonproductive investments" in the Ivorian accounts. Since they do not generate any direct return, they have no counterpart in the lower part of the table. They are treated, in the model, in much the same way as public consumption. Urban investments in row 4 are investments in the form of vehicles, machinery, and construction for urban uses, which were discussed in the preceding section. The iron mine and the Riviera project are two large investments that have been isolated from other urban investments. In the free-market solution, it is optimal to start the iron ore project in 1980 and the Riviera project in 1985. Iron ore is exported in 1985 and a positive rent occurs for the mine during that year (row 21). The Riviera provides housing services for nationals and hotel facilities for foreigners; some returns on the capital already invested occurs in 1985 (row 22).

In rows 14–18, returns on labor refer only to nationals. In rows 19–23, returns on capital relate to all forms of physical capital (renewable or not) that are located within national boundaries. No distinction is made with respect to ownership, whether private, public, or foreign. Returns on foreign investments appear as a positive component in the balance of financial transactions with the rest of the world shown in row 12. In brief, it could be said that the GNP concept is applied in the case of returns on labor, while the GDP concept is used in the case of returns on physical investments.

The last row, 23, is a residual. In this particular case, the major part of it accounts for rents on manufactured exports.[12] This residual is sufficiently small not to obscure the interpretation of the imputed returns.[13]

RETURNS ON LABOR AND CAPITAL

The distribution of the imputed returns between labor and capital are shown as shares of the GNP in the bottom righthand corner of

12. For each of the five groups of manufactured exports there is an upper limit to the volume exported. When this limit is binding, the marginal return on the exported good exceeds its marginal cost of production, and the difference between the two is a measure of the rent on manufactured exports. The limitation imposed on the volume of manufactured exports is more likely to reflect implicit supply constraints, however—management, export promotion, and the like—than the inelasticity of world demand. Consequently, the rent on manufactured exports should be interpreted as returns on factors not explicitly introduced in the model, rather than as the rent resulting from a partially monopolistic position.

13. When the residual item is large, the analysis of imputed returns becomes meaningless. This can be the price of "improving the credibility" of the primal picture by adding constraints that are somewhat "artificial." A constraint is artificial when its cost has no clear economic meaning.

Table 3.11. Between 1975 and 1985, the share of labor declines from 55 percent to 51 percent, while that of capital increases from 44 percent to 47 percent. This somewhat disconcerting feature reflects two factors—the increasing importance of replacement and the heavy borrowings from abroad.

Since investments are counted on a gross basis in the upper part of the table, the cost of replacement is counted as gross returns on capital in the lower part of the same table. Replacement was only 24 percent of gross urban investments in 1975. It becomes 28 percent of it in 1980 and 37 percent in 1985. This development is characteristic of a dynamic economy starting with young capital stock. Can it be responsible for the increasing capital shares? This question is explored in Table 3.12. The cost of replacement (row 3) is excluded from the adjusted GNP (row 4) and from the returns on capital (rows 6 and 7). At the same time, a correction is made for the returns on education; those were measured on the basis of the salaries forgone by students attending university (row 11 of Table 3.11). Scholarships and other indirect benefits may account for only a quarter of the salaries forgone. The difference between the two is also deducted from the adjusted GNP (row 4) and from returns on labor (row 5). These two corrections combined improve the picture only slightly: labor shares decline from

Table 3.12. Distribution of the GNP Less Replacement, Corrected for Student Returns (Free-Market Solution)

Component of the GNP	Billions of CFAF at 1970 prices			Percentage shares		
	1975	*1980*	*1985*	*1975*	*1980*	*1985*
1. GNP from Table 3.11	517	741	1,048	...	...	...
2. Salaries forgone by students less scholarships and indirect benefits[a]	11	20	32	...	...	...
3. Replacement of urban capital and of installations in iron mine	15	26	44	...	...	...
4. Adjusted GNP[b]	491	695	972	100	100	100
5. Returns on labor	272	363	506	55.4	52.3	52.0
6. Returns on total capital (less replacement)	212	315	443	43.2	45.3	45.7
7. Returns on urban capital[c]	103	161	271	21.0	23.2	26.6
8. Other rents	7	17	21	1.4	2.4	2.3

a. Amounts in row 2 are equal to three quarters of those in row 18, Table 3.11.
b. Adjusted GNP = row 1 − row 2 − row 3 = row 5 + row 6 + row 8.
c. Amounts in row 7 are included in those in row 6.

55.4 percent to 52.0 percent and capital shares increase from 43.2 percent to 45.7 percent.

The increase in inflows of foreign capital provides the basic answer. As noted before, returns on labor relate only to nationals; returns on capital relate to all physical capital located in the country. The problem of the ownership of capital may be illustrated by the iron-mining sector. In 1985, the sector reaches the stage of full exploitation, and the decomposition of the resource cost is shown in Table 3.13. In row 4, the net return (inclusive of any pure Ricardian rent) is calculated by subtracting from export earnings (row 6) all current operating costs (rows 1, 2, 3, and 5). This rent of CFAF12.5 billion is the figure appearing as returns on capital in row 21 of Table 3.11. If the mine were owned by a foreign firm, this rent would be the return to the foreign firm before tax. Assume now that the mine is owned by the state, which borrows the financial capital required for the installation. In 1980, this capital appears in the upper part of Table 3.11 as a + under physical investments (row 5) and as a − under financial investments (row 21). In 1985, the entire CFAF13 billion (row 21) is not a net profit to the state. The servicing of the foreign debt contracted in 1980 has to be deducted first. Whatever ownership arrangements are made, borrowing during the 1970s is equivalent to preempting a significant fraction of returns on capital for the servicing of the foreign debt during the 1980s.

The effect of heavy borrowing from abroad is illustrated in Table 3.14, which refers to endogenous borrowing at commercial terms. Interest payments on this debt increase from 1.2 percent of GNP in 1975 to 5.1 percent in 1985 (row 5). When this amount is deducted from the returns on all capital located in the Ivory Coast (row 6), the share of

Table 3.13. *Resource Cost of the Iron Mine in 1985*
(Free-Market Solution)

Cost component	Billions of CEAF at 1970 prices	Shares of domestic resource cost
1. Unskilled labor	.27	1
2. Skilled labor	4.04	17
3. Urban capital	7.40	30
4. Iron mine	12.50[a]	52
5. Imports	3.11	. . .
6. Exports[b]	27.32	100

a. Net of depreciation calculated in current costs.
b. Row 1 + row 2 + row 3 + row 4 + row 5 = row 6.

Table 3.14. Borrowing from Abroad[a] *and Preemption of Returns on Capital Located in the Country (Free-Market Solution)*

Item	1975	1980	1985
	Quantities in billions of CFAF *at 1970 prices*		
1. Foreign capital borrowed (endogenous)	20.0	26.8	19.6
2. Interest payments on above (endogenous)	4.8	20.9	40.3
	Values in billions of CFAF		
3. Interest payments valued at shadow prices	6.6	28.1	53.9
4. GNP[b]	517	738	1,046
	Percentage share		
5. Return on foreign capital[c]	1.2	3.8	5.1
6. Return to all capital[d]	43.9	45.8	46.6
7. Return on Ivorian capital and on capital acquired by foreigners before 1972[e]	42.7	42.0	41.5

a. Endogenous borrowing is made at commercial terms with increasing interest rates. This excludes exogenous borrowing either contracted before 1972 or contracted during the planning period at concessional terms (from the World Bank, French cooperation, and the like). Yearly borrowings are shown in row 1 and cumulated interest charges in row 2.
b. Row 13 of Table 3.11.
c. Row 5 = 100 times row 3 over row 4.
d. Row 6 = 100 times row 19 of Table 3.11 over row 4.
e. Row 7 = row 6 minus row 5.

the returns on Ivorian-owned capital actually declines from 42.7 percent in 1975 to 41.5 percent in 1985.[14] Through its effect on relative prices, borrowing from abroad improves the share accruing to Ivorian labor relative to that accruing to Ivorian capital. It leads, however, to an increasing share of the domestic capital owned (directly or indirectly) by foreigners and this may be considered as politically undesirable. As stressed at the beginning of this chapter, the Ivorization of professionals is completed by the end of the planning period, but the Ivorization of capital is not.

THE PRIVATE SECTOR VERSUS THE PUBLIC SECTOR

A fraction of the returns on capital is pre-empted for the repayment of the foreign debt. Of the remainder, the major part goes to the public sector. In the urban sector, most large enterprises are joint ventures

14. Ivorian-owned capital is defined as capital owned by nationals (in both the private and public sectors) and capital acquired by foreigners before 1972 and still in their possession.

between the state and foreign firms. In rural areas, land is owned privately or collectively. The state, however, recovers part of the land rent in the form of export taxes.[15] In the case of wood exports, taxes may be considered as the "pure rent" accruing to the owner of nonrenewable resources. For economic purposes, trees taking a century to grow are similar to mineral resources.

15. In the free-market solution, there is an implicit export tax on coffee and cocoa, because the demand for Ivorian exports is taken as less than infinitely price elastic (see Chapter 13).

Table 3.15. Comparative Contributions of the Private and Public Sectors in Investment Financing (Free-Market Solution)

Item	Billions of CFAF at 1970 prices			Percentage shares		
	1975	1980	1985	1975	1980	1985
1. Consumption	394	534	758	100	100	100
2. Private sector	310	415	758	79	78	79
3. Public sector	84	133	161	21	22	21
4. Gross investments	146	233	281	100	100	100
5. Private sector	46	71	113	31	31	40
6. Public sector	77	133	175	53	57	62
7. Net capital inflow	23	29	−7	16	12	−2
8. GNP[a]	517	738	1,046			
9. Return to private sector[b]	356	486	710	69[d]	66[d]	68[d]
10. Returns from labor income	276	371	514	97[e]	97[e]	96[e]
11. Returns from capital and others	80	115	196	34[f]	32[f]	38[f]
12. Private investments[c]	46	71	113			
13. Human investments	13	24	40	30[g]	32[g]	41[g]
14. Salaries forgone by students (less scholarships received)	11	20	32	75[h]	75[h]	75[h]
15. Monetary contribution	2	4	8			
16. Physical investments	33	47	73	32[i]	30[i]	40[i]

a. Row 8 = row 1 + row 4 − row 7.
b. Row 9 = row 2 + row 5 = row 10 + row 11.
c. Row 5 = row 12 = row 13 + row 16.
d. Percentage share of the private sector in GDP.
e. Percentage share of the income of labor going to the private sector.
f. Percentage share of the returns from capital going to the private sector.
g. Percentage of human investments financed by the private sector.
h. Scholarships are taken as a quarter of salaries forgone by students.
i. Percentage of physical investments financed by the private sector.

In the free-market case, there is no constraint on savings. Whether savings originate in the public or the private sector does not affect the solution. Nevertheless, the distinction is made in Table 3.15 in order to give some feeling of the relative importance of the two sectors.[16] As shown in row 5, the private sector is responsible for approximately a third of gross savings. This proportion applies to physical investment (row 16) as well as to human investment (row 13). The main private contribution to investments in postprimary education takes a nonmonetary form. It is the value of salaries forgone by students less scholarships received (row 14). For physical investments in the urban sector, the private contribution was, in the early 1970s, primarily in the field of housing, shops, and small enterprises. In the rural sector, investments often take the form of a joint venture between the state and the landowner. The latter usually receives public aid for improving his land and for planting his trees. The state recovers its investment through export taxes.

With this system, only about a third of the returns on physical capital ends in the hands of the private sector (row 11 at right). Three-quarters of private income originates from the returns on labor. The important social problem is the distribution of the wage bill, which is the subject of the next chapter.

16. The distinction becomes operative when there is a binding constraint on savings (see Chapters 5 and 10).

Chapter 4

Returns on Labor

THE DISCUSSION OF IMPUTED RETURNS to this point has been centered on the distinction between labor and physical capital. In this chapter the focus is on the distribution of the wage bill among skill categories. All workers belonging to the same skill category are assumed to have the same productivity and, consequently, to command the same "efficiency wage." Skills can be acquired through education, here treated as an endogenous investment activity.

In the model, the association between skill and efficiency wage is not a rigid one. First, a distinction is made between unskilled rural and unskilled urban workers. The wage differential between them reflects the cost-of-living differential between urban and rural areas. Second, a distinction is made between expatriates and nationals belonging to the same skill category. The ratio between their efficiency wages declines progressively from 1.75 in 1970 to unity in 1990. This reduction reflects an assumed gain in the productivity of the nationals, a gain which follows a learning curve. Third, promotion to the highest skill category is gained through experience, not formal training. Fourth, substitution possibilities exist among close skill categories.

The size and distribution of the wage bill are computed from the numbers of Ivorians employed in each skill category and their efficiency wages; both factors are endogenous variables in the model, and their values vary from one solution to another. To facilitate comparison with the results presented in the preceding chapter, the free-market case will be retained.

The first section illustrates the functioning of the labor market; the second deals with the problem of Ivorization; and the third, with the distribution of the wage bill.

The Labor Market

Eleven types of labor are differentiated in the model. Each type has its own wage. There is one market for unskilled agricultural workers, there is a second for unskilled urban workers, and there are nine others, one for each type of skilled labor. The nine skill categories are listed in rows 1–9 of Table 4.3. The interrelations among these different markets are illustrated by Figure 4.1. To simplify the diagram, the nine types of skilled labor have been grouped together.

To start with the right side of the diagram: Most of the demand for labor is determined endogenously; labor requirements are linked to a great variety of economic activities. For example, the production of CFAF1 billion worth of electrical machinery (at 1970 prices) requires specified numbers of engineers, qualified workers, and unskilled urban workers. These labor norms do not remain constant throughout the planning period; they incorporate gains in the productivity of labor that vary from one skill category to another. In the case of agriculture, labor norms are differentiated according to the technology applied. For example, one hectare of rice can be cultivated using the traditional method and only unskilled agricultural workers. But it can also be cultivated by applying a modern method, in which case fewer agricultural workers will be needed, but some skilled labor will be required for supervision and for the repair of tractors. In addition to that endogenous labor demand, a small exogenous demand for civil servants affects some categories of skilled labor.

The total demand for each type of labor must be met either by nationals or by foreigners. Imported labor is important at the extremes of the wage spectrum: migrant workers from neighboring countries form a large part of the labor employed in the southern plantations, while expatriates, most of them from France, occupy many of the professional positions.

The national labor force consists of stocks of labor in various skill categories with specified life expectancies and students who are in the education pipeline. The inherited stock of unskilled labor is enlarged each year by those newly entering the labor force. Unskilled workers can move between rural and urban areas, the rate of migration being a function of the wage differential between these two areas. Not all unskilled urban workers find employment in the formal sector. Those left over are employed in the informal urban sector, producing traditional services. This may be considered as a disguised form of unemployment. Postprimary education links the market for unskilled urban workers and the market for skilled labor. It is treated in the

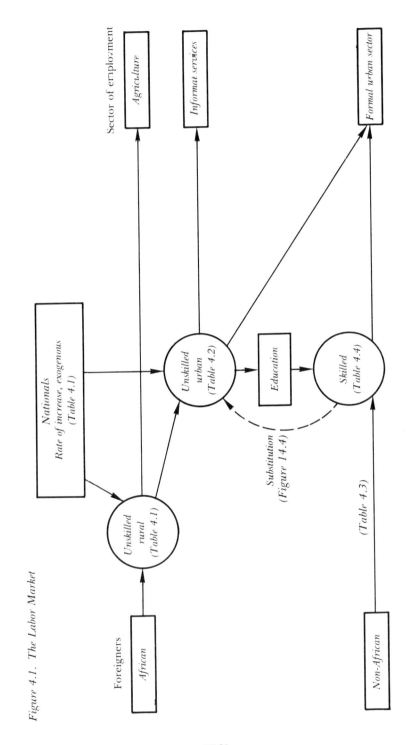

Figure 4.1. The Labor Market

Sector of employment

Agriculture

Informal services

Formal urban sector

Nationals
Rate of increase, exogenous
(Table 4.1)

Unskilled
urban
(Table 4.2)

Education

Skilled
(Table 4.4)

Substitution
(Figure 14.4)

Unskilled
rural
(Table 4.1)

Foreigners

African

Non-African

(Table 4.3)

model as an investment activity requiring children with primary education, teachers, school buildings, and the like as inputs.[1]

Start with the balance between the urban and rural labor forces. The exogenous data (those which remain constant in all solutions of the model) are summarized in the upper part of Table 4.1. The size of the labor supply, which is expressed in adult male equivalents (row 1), is subject to significant errors. On the one hand, the labor supply was derived from the number of the total population which had been underestimated before the results of the 1975 census became available. On the other hand, the rate of female participation in the active labor force is bound to be defined in a somewhat arbitrary manner. An error in the size of the labor supply has, however, limited consequences on the findings of the model, provided that that error is offset by another of the same magnitude in the estimation of labor requirements. During the base year, these two errors were offsetting each other approximately, since the excess of the labor supply over the calculated labor

1. Primary education is treated as an exogenous activity; under no circumstances could primary school graduates be in short supply.

Table 4.1. The National Labor Force: Labor Balance for Unskilled Agricultural Workers (Case F1)[a]

Segment of labor force	Thousands of persons			Yearly growth rate (percent)		
	1970	1980	1990	1970–80	1980–90	1970–90
Assumptions						
1. National labor force	1,582	2,177	3,141	3.3	3.7	3.5
2. Urban labor force before migrations	459	627	890	3.2	3.5	3.3
3. Rural labor force before migrations[b]	1,123	1,550	2,251	3.3	3.8	3.5
Variables						
4. Migrations from rural to urban areas	0	269	577	. . .	. . .	. . .
5. Rural labor force after internal migrations[b]	1,123	1,281	1,674	1.4	2.7	2.0
6. Migrations from abroad	0	79	109	. . .	. . .	. . .
7. Rural employment (unskilled)[b]	1,123	1,360	1,783	1.9	2.8	2.3

a. Figures shown in rows 1–3 are taken as exogenous data. Figures shown in rows 4–7 are optimal values obtained by solving the model; these values differ from case to case.
b. Only unskilled agricultural workers are included in the rural labor force.

requirements during that year led to a reasonable estimation of labor unemployment.

The assumptions made in the upper part of Table 4.1 are common to all experiments. In the lower part of the table, the numbers of migrants from rural areas to urban (row 4) and from neighboring countries to rural areas (row 6) vary from one experiment to another. The values shown here for migrants and for rural employment (row 7) are those found in the free-market solution.

The urban labor force is defined in Table 4.1 as the difference between the national labor force (row 1) and the part of it employed in rural areas (row 5). Table 4.2 shows how the urban labor force (row 3) can be decomposed into skilled labor and students withdrawn from the labor market (row 4) and unskilled urban workers (row 5). The last, together with some of the skilled workers who could not find employment fitted to their qualifications (row 7), share the tasks that do not require qualifications in the formal (row 8) and informal sectors (row 9).

In turn, skilled labor can be decomposed into categories.[2] For each category, the excess of total demand over the supply of nationals is the number of expatriates required. Their numbers are shown for the free-market solution in Table 4.3. Consider the balance for labor with qualifications acquired through university training. Demand exceeds the supply of nationals in 1980; hence, expatriates have to be employed. Because marginal productivity must always equal marginal cost

2. Labor balances for the three categories of skilled labor are given in Table 11.6.

Table 4.2. *The National Labor Force: Balance for Unskilled Urban Labor (Case F1)*[a] (Thousands of persons)

Segment of labor force	1970	1975	1980	1985	1990
1. Active urban labor force[b]	459	533	726	744	890
2. Migrations from rural areas	0	107	269	403	577
3. Total urban labor force	459	640	896	1,147	1,467
4. Skilled labor requirements plus students withdrawn from the labor force	138	198	288	379	505
5. Unskilled[c]	321	442	608	768	962
6. Skilled laborers performing unskilled tasks	17	19	18	. . .	84
7. Employment in unskilled category	338	461	626	768	1,046
8. Formal sector	303	404	500	601	726
9. Informal sector (disguised unemployment)	35	57	126	167	320

a. Figures in row 1 are exogenous; the others are endogenous.
b. Row 1 + row 2 = row 3 = row 4 + row 5.
c. Row 5 + row 6 = row 7 = row 8 + row 9.

Table 4.3. The Wage Bill of Expatriates: Distribution of Imported Skilled Labor among Skill Categories (Free-Market Solution)

	Skill category	Thousands of workers					Wages received by expatriates[a] (millions of CFAF)
		1975	1980	1985	1990	2000	
1. λ = 2	Specialized workers						0.368
2. λ = 3	Qualified workers	4.9	1.8				1.175
3. λ = 4	Clerks						0.680
4. λ = 5	High school graduates (humanities)	7.0	9.9	6.4			2.100
5. λ = 6	High school graduates (sciences)	7.0	11.9	7.7			2.625
6. λ = 7B	University graduates (short cycle)	0.3	0.4	2.8			4.000
7. λ = 9	High school teachers	2.2	3.1	1.3			4.000
8. λ = 7	Professionals (long university cycle)	5.3	8.6	7.6	0.9		5.250
9. λ = 8	Senior professionals	1.7	0.3				8.750
10. λ = 2–9	Total number of expatriates	28.4	36.0	25.1	0.9		

		Billions of CFAF				
11. λ = 2–8	Wage bill of expatriates	94	118	88	5	

		Percentage premium over consumption				
12.	Premium of wages paid to expatriates	10	7	6		
13.	Coefficient of equivalence between expatriates and nationals[b]	1.46	1.26	1.11	1.00	1.00

a. Wages received by expatriates are exogenous data; they remain constant throughout the planning period (except in the case of the first two skill categories, λ = 2 and λ = 3, for which wages rise 2 percent a year). Expatriates pay an income tax rising from 9 percent of their salaries in 1975 to 12 percent in 1990. The 10 percent premium in 1975 is computed from the dual solution of the model. It expresses the fact that CFAF1 million (before tax) paid to an expatriate is worth CFAF1.1 million of consumption by the average Ivorian. This premium is largely the result of the foreign exchange component of wages received by expatriates.

b. The coefficient of equivalence is the ratio between the efficiency wages received by expatriates and those received by nationals belonging to the same skill category. This coefficient is specified exogenously; it reflects "learning by doing."

in the model, the efficiency wage of a national is the marginal cost of hiring an expatriate to perform the identical task. The purchasing power of an expatriate with a university degree is equal to CFAF4 million at 1970 prices (row 6 of Table 4.3).[3] On the one hand, the marginal cost of providing a unit of consumption happens to be 7 percent higher for an expatriate than for a national in that particular solution (row 13 of Table 4.3).[4] On the other hand, the marginal productivity of an expatriate is assumed to be 26 percent higher than that of a national belonging to the same skill category. As a result, the efficiency wage of a national is CFAF3.4 (= 4 × 1.07/1.26) million.

In the case of clerks (or specialized workers), it is never optimal to employ expatriates (rows 1 and 3 of Table 4.3). The difference between the shadow price of a specialized worker (or a clerk) and that of an unskilled worker (rows 2, 3, and 4 of Table 3.9) gives a measure of the training cost (see Chapter 11).

In the Ivory Coast, at the time this study was made, the marginal cost of employing expatriates clearly affected the levels of wages paid to nationals, especially in private and semipublic sectors. Nevertheless, the link was less rigid than it is in the present model. The link may progressively fade away, moreover, as the relative number of expatriates declines in the 1980s. This progressive fading away does not occur in the model.

The Problem of Ivorization

In the free-market solution, full Ivorization is reached by 1990 without the setting of a date by which the process should be completed. Postprimary education, which is treated like any other import-substitution activity, proves to be socially profitable. This is no wonder, inasmuch as the shadow wage of the average expatriate in 1980 is thirty-four times that of the unskilled urban worker.[5]

The private rate of return on education is higher than the social rate of return for two reasons: First, most of the direct costs are covered by the state; earnings forgone by students are partly compensated for by

3. This is the equivalent of US$16,000 at 1970 prices.
4. This cost is determined endogenously in the model, as explained in Chapter 14.
5. As can be seen in Table 4.3, in 1980 the shadow price of the average expatriate is (118/36)(1.07) = CFAF3.507 million. The shadow price of an urban unskilled worker during the same year is CFAF0.104 million, as shown in Table 3.9.

scholarships.[6] Second, salaries are more closely correlated with educational levels in the Ivory Coast than in the industrial countries.

Apart from these economic considerations, there are obvious psychological and political reasons for replacing expatriates with nationals in responsible positions commanding high salaries. All the incentives point in the same direction, and the pressure for expanding educational facilities is enormous.

Between 1965 and 1972, new university enrollments increased 31 percent a year, on an average (see Table 3.2). If increases of this magnitude were to be maintained for too long, the deficit in skilled labor would eventually turn into a huge surplus. Because of built-in foresight, this does not occur in the model. The marginal costs of training a student in the 1970s must be compensated for by marginal returns in later decades.

Human and physical investment are competing activities. Both compete for the use of public funds and skilled labor, two resources which are scarce during the 1970s. Postprimary education is a major user of public funds (almost a quarter of current public expenditures) and highly skilled labor (teachers and students withdrawn from the labor market). While human and physical investment compete for resources in the 1970s, in the 1980s they produce trained labor and physical capital, which are complementary resources. The size of the demand for engineers depends on the number of factories which have been built. If too much is devoted to human investments and not enough to physical investment in 1980, not all the students graduating in 1985 can find jobs in the country.

How great the adjustment problem is depends on the length of time that the training requires. The problem is relatively easy to solve in the case of technical education; it takes only a year or two to train a specialized worker. The adjustment problem becomes critical in the case of higher education; at least ten years elapse between the time a person enters high school and the time he graduates from a university. Figures 4.2 through 4.4 and Table 4.4 illustrate the magnitude of this problem, using the results of the free-market case.

Comparison of Figures 4.2 and 4.4 shows that the growth rates of enrollments in high schools and universities must be severely curtailed ten years before the country reaches self-sufficiency. This is precisely when the number of expatriates is the largest and the pressure for training more nationals to replace the expatriates is likely to be the strongest. Figure 4.2 shows that the reduction in the growth rate of

---

6. See rows 18 of Table 3.11 and 2 of Table 3.12.

Figure 4.2. Growth Rates of New Enrollments
(Free-Market Solution)

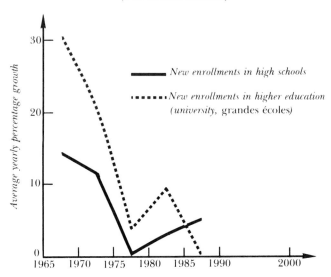

Figure 4.3. Growth Rates of Supply and Demand for High Skills
(Free-Market Solution)

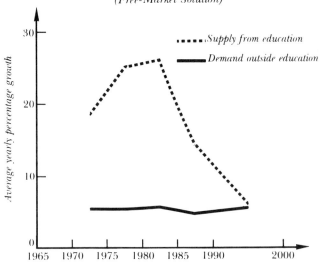

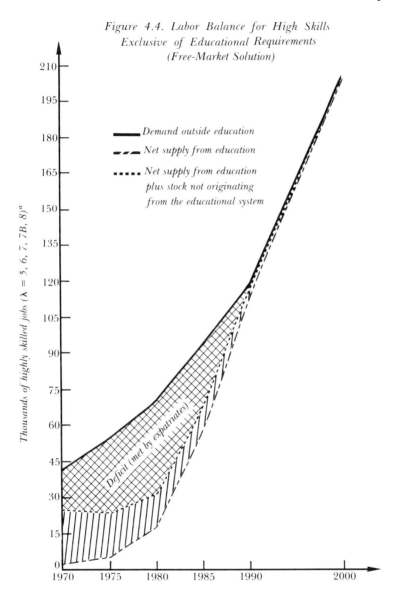

Figure 4.4. *Labor Balance for High Skills Exclusive of Educational Requirements (Free-Market Solution)*

a. See Table 4.3.

Table 4.4. Demand for and Supply of High Skills (λ = 5 through λ = 8), Excluding Teachers and Students

Element of demand or supply	1970	1975	1980	1985	1990	2000
Absolute values (thousands of persons)						
1. Demand outside the educational sector	42	55	71	93	118	205
2. Stock not originating from the educational sector	22	18	13	9	4	0
3. Supply from the educational sector (excluding teachers and students)	3	6	18	58	113	205

	1970– 75	1975– 80	1980– 85	1985– 90	1990– 2000
Growth rates (average yearly percentage)					
1. Demand outside the educational sector	5.4	5.2	5.7	4.9	5.7
2. Supply from the educational sector (excluding teachers and students)	18.7	25.0	26.0	14.3	6.1
3. New enrollments in high schools	11.6	.1	3.0	5.0	. . .
4. New enrollments in university and higher education	21.0	3.8	9.7	.1	. . .

enrollments is not caused by a fall in the final demand for skilled labor; this demand increases at a fairly constant rate (no less than 5 percent a year nor more than 6 percent a year). Figures 4.3 through 4.5 illustrate the three factors responsible for the curtailment of enrollments. The first is the replacement of expatriates, which is a one-time shift in demand. Assume that half the stock of skilled labor must be replaced within a few years by an increase in the annual flow of graduates. Clearly, a smaller annual flow will be needed after the replacement of expatriates has been completed.

The second factor is the replacement of less well-trained nationals with those who are better trained. At the beginning of the planning period, a number of professional positions are held by persons who did not go through the educational system. These persons are progressively replaced, largely through attrition. Demand for this type of replacement will have disappeared by 1990, while the students graduated after 1960 will not retire before 2000. As a result, between 1990 and 2000 no professional will need to be replaced.

The third factor is a particular feature of Ivorization: the need of the educational system to train its own teachers and professors for both high schools and the university. When postprimary education in the Ivory Coast began, almost all the faculty had to be imported. Today there is a huge demand for Ivorian professors. During the decade after

Figure 4.5. Balance for High School Teachers (Free-Market Solution)

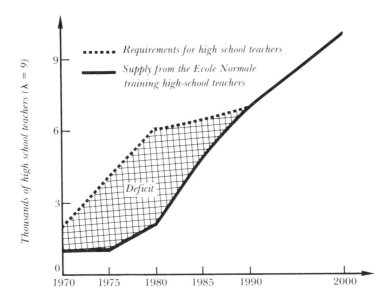

Figure 4.6. New Enrollments in the Ecole Normale (Free-Market Solution)

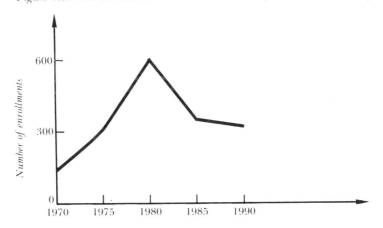

all the foreign professors have been replaced, there will be a dramatic fall in the demand for new professors. This is illustrated in the case of high school teachers by Figures 4.5 and 4.6.

Full Ivorization of high school teachers by 1990 does not appear, at first glance, to be a difficult target, but to reach it without creating a surplus after 1990 is not easy. As shown in Figure 4.6, the number of students admitted to the Ecole Normale (which trains high school teachers) must rise from 300 in 1975 to 600 in 1980, but it must then be reduced to 356 in 1985 and 327 in 1990. Suppose that Ivorization is to be reached in 1985 instead of 1990: 1,000 students instead of 600 will have to be enrolled in 1980, yet no more than 350 students should be enrolled in 1985 and 1990. The major obstacle to earlier Ivorization, therefore, is not the initial absorptive capacity of the educational system; professors can be imported, and students can be sent abroad. The major obstacle is a political one: it is the difficulty of reducing enrollments after the initial push.

The problem is illustrated by Figure 4.7, in which one of the first experiments conducted with the model is summarized. In case 1, an upper bound to the size of enrollments was imposed in 1975. In case 1A, this constraint is dropped. Without the constraint, new enrollments in high schools jump by a third in 1975 then fall by a third in 1980. Because the increase one year is corrected by a decrease the next, the labor market remains in equilibrium during the 1980s. With the early push, the wage bill of expatriates increases 4 percent in 1975, when more teachers are required; it declines 74 percent in 1985, when the students graduate. Because expatriates have been replaced with nationals, the shadow wage of high school graduates falls in 1985; it recovers in 1990.

Little economic gain is achieved by allowing the absolute number of new enrollments to decline in 1980: the value of the objective function increases only 0.5 percent in case 1A. Such a small gain hardly justifies the social problems it creates. Consequently, apart from case 1A, a monotonicity constraint was imposed.[7] That is, the absolute level of new enrollments in high schools and in universities was never allowed to fall from one year to the next in any of the experiments reported in this volume. The growth rate of new enrollments can decline, but it can never become negative.

It may be asked whether the reduction in the growth rate of enrollments is exaggerated in the optimal solution. As a result of an underestimate of the scope for substitution between skilled and un-

---

7. Because an upper limit on enrollments was imposed in 1975, the monotonicity constraint was seldom binding.

Figure 4.7. The Effect of Releasing the Constraint on New Enrollments in High School during 1975 (Cases 1A and 1)

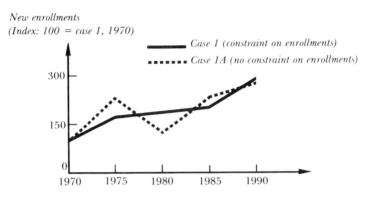

New enrollments
(Index: 100 = case 1, 1970)

——— Case 1 (constraint on enrollments)
••••••• Case 1A (no constraint on enrollments)

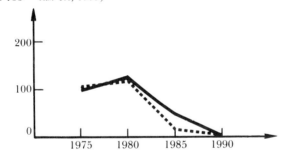

Wage bill of expatriates
(index: 100 = case 1A, 1975)

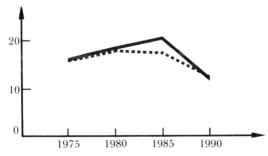

Ratio of efficiency wage of high school graduates
to that of unskilled urban workers

skilled labor,[8] as well as between labor and capital,[9] the model could be underestimating the demand for skilled labor after the expatriates have been replaced with nationals. Gains in the productivity of labor could have been overestimated, moreover. In the free-market solution, demand for skilled labor increases 6 percent a year after 1990. The practical issue is whether this growth rate is substantially underestimated.[10]

Skilled labor is defined here as labor having formal postprimary educational training. The intercountry comparison conducted by Psacharopoulos (1973) shows that the ratio between the skilled and the total labor force is correlated with the level of GDP per capita. For data relating to the mid-1960s, the share of the labor force that is skilled is 1.5 percent for Nigeria, 1.8 percent for Ghana, 2.6 percent for Uganda, and 3.0 percent for Kenya,[11] whereas it is 41 percent for northwestern Europe and 65 percent for the United States. When could the Ivory Coast reach the present stage of the developed countries?

An answer is provided in Table 4.5. Footnote 6 to this table gives the growth rates applicable to the postterminal period (1990–2000) of the Ivory Coast model. The first three rows of the table show when and at what income level the Ivory Coast would reach the point at which 41 percent and 65 percent of the labor force would be skilled if the postterminal growth rates were extrapolated. The last two rows give the statistics applicable to northwestern Europe and the United States in the mid-1960s. By the year 2030, the Ivory Coast would reach the level of northwestern Europe in the mid-1960s, and the GNP per capita in

8. The assumptions made with respect to skill substitution are described in Chapter 14. The general hypothesis is that a substantial scope for substitution exists between neighboring skill categories, but not between extremes of the spectrum of skills.

9. Substitution is specified in the model in three ways. The first is the choice of the product mix for final consumption. The second is the choice between importing and producing. The third is the choice of the technology to be applied to the production of a given good in the rural sector. Technological choices are not, however, available in the urban sector, except for the choice between producing in the formal sector or the informal sector.

10. The sensitivity of the growth of enrollments to the assumptions made with respect to the demand for skilled labor can be analyzed more conveniently with the simplifed sectoral model described in Chapter 11 than with the central model.

11. These are the four African countries for which data are to be found in Psacharopoulos's study. Among developing countries in other regions, there is a striking difference between Brazil (3.2 percent of the labor force is skilled) and South Korea (15.8 percent skilled). Western Europe is represented here by Great Britain, Norway, and the Netherlands—the only three European countries (apart from Greece) for which data are given by Psacharopoulos. These percentages are to be obtained by adding those shown under columns L_s and L_h of Table F1 in Psacharopoulos (1973, p. 183).

Table 4.5. Skilled Labor as a Percentage of the Total Labor Force: Intercountry comparisons[a]

Country or region	Year	GNP *per capita*[b] *(U.S. dollars at 1971 prices)*	Skilled labor as percentage of total labor force[c]
Ivory Coast	1990	676	13
	2030	2,207	41
	2046	3,542	65
Northwestern Europe	1965	2,366	41
United States	1965	4,607	65

a. Skilled labor is defined here as labor with formal training through postprimary education. In the Ivory Coast model, this requires enrollment *en sixième*, which is the first grade of high school.

b. GNP per capita at 1971 prices and growth rates 1965–71 are from the *World Bank Atlas/1973*. Data given here are extrapolated from the following assumptions of yearly growth rates in the postterminal period:

Income per capita	3.0 percent a year
Size of the total labor force	3.0 percent a year
Demand for skilled labor	6.0 percent a year

c. George Psacharopoulos, *Returns to Education: An International Comparison* (Amsterdam, London, and New York: Elsevier Scientific Publishing Company, 1973), Appendix F, "The Distribution of the Labor Force by Educational Level," Table F1, p. 183.

the Ivory Coast would be only 7 percent lower. By the year 2046, the Ivory Coast would have the share of skilled labor of the United States in the mid-1960s, with a GNP per capita 23 percent lower. In an international context, the Ivory Coast figures are not unreasonable.

Assume now that the supply of skilled labor increases at a rate somewhat greater than 6 percent. The wage differential between skilled and unskilled labor would decline faster than is indicated by the model. This would not be a catastrophe. The additional cost of training would not necessarily be justified on grounds of efficiency and equity, however. Additional investments in informal education might do better according to both criteria. This assumption was tested by incorporating a program of practical agricultural training into the free-market solution. The program contributed to an increase in aggregate output. In addition, it raised the income of rural labor 4 percent in 1985 and 11 percent in 1990; unfortunately, it had no significant effect in the 1970s.

Distribution of the Wage Bill

The results on the distribution of the wage bill among Ivorians are summarized in Table 4.6. The share of skilled labor in the total labor

Table 1.6. Employment of Nationals, Excluding Students (Free-Market Solution)

Segment of labor force	1975	1980	1985	1975	1980	1985	1975–80	1980–85
	Thousands of workers			*Percentage of total labor force*			*Annual growth rates (percent)*	
Size of labor force								
1. Unskilled labor, rural	1,206	1,282	1,454	67	61	58	1.2	2.6
2. Unskilled labor, urban	451	626	768	25	30	31	6.8	4.2
3. Skilled labor[a]	144	205	278	8	9	11	7.3	6.3
4. Total labor force	1,801	2,113	2,500	100	100	100	3.1	3.4
	Billions of CFAF							
Returns imputed to labor								
5. Unskilled labor, rural	85	91	108	32	26	22	1.2	3.5
6. Unskilled labor, urban	53	65	80	20	18	16	4.2	4.2
7. Skilled labor	127	199	304	48	56	62	9.4	8.9
8. Total returns to labor force	265	355	492	100	100	100	6.0	6.7
	Millions of CFAF *per worker*			*Index: 1975 = 100*				
Imputed average return								
9. Unskilled labor, rural (row 5 over row 1)	0.071	0.071	0.074	100	100	108	0.0	0.9
10. Unskilled labor, urban (row 6 over row 2)	0.117	0.104	0.104	100	89	89	–2.3	0.0
11. Skilled labor (row 7 over row 3)	0.881	0.971	1.093	100	110	124	2.0	2.4
12. Overall average ($\bar{w}_t$) (row 8 over row 4)	0.147	0.168	0.197	100	110	135	2.7	3.2

a. There are eleven skill categories identified by subscript λ. The number of workers in a category is designated by L_λ and the efficiency wage by w_λ. Skilled labor is an aggregate covering nine skill categories. The number of workers shown in row 3 is obtained by taking the sum of L_λ for all nine categories. The imputed returns shown in rows 7 and 8 are obtained by taking the sum of the products $w_\lambda L_\lambda$ for nine and eleven skill categories, respectively. The average returns shown in rows 11 and 12 are derived from wages for each skill category $w_{\lambda t}$ by weighting them according to the share of each skill category $L_{\lambda t}/\sum_\lambda L_{\lambda t}$.

force rises over time (row 3). There is an even more rapid increase in the share of skilled labor in the imputed returns on all types of labor (row 7). As a result, the imputed return per worker rises more rapidly for skilled labor (row 11) than for unskilled (rows 9 and 10).

Taking the Ivorian labor force as a whole, the real wage bill (deflated by the cost of living) rises 6.7 percent a year between 1980 and 1985. Since the size of the labor force increases 3.4 percent a year during that period, the average income per worker rises 3.2 percent a year. This sizable increase in income per worker occurs despite a decline of 1 percent a year in the weighted average of the salaries applicable to each skill category.[12] This paradox reflects the modification in the composition of the labor force. There is an overall shift toward better-paid occupations. This shift in distribution induces an annual increase of 4.3 percent in the average return per worker between 1980 and 1985.

The shift in distribution may be visualized as the modification of the wage pyramid shown in Figure 4.8.[13] The composition of the labor force is expressed along the horizontal axis in the form of cumulated shares. The proportion of skilled workers in the total labor force increases from 7 percent in 1970 to 13 percent in 1990 (first two columns of row 1 of Table 4.7), while that of unskilled agricultural workers in the total labor force declines from 71 percent in 1970 to 54 percent in 1990. The 1975 efficiency wages (third column of Table 4.7) are shown along the vertical axis; they are the weights used to measure the effect of a change in the composition of the labor force.

The 1970 wage pyramid is the shaded area. Its surface measures the average return per worker at 1975 wages: CFAF138,000 a year. In 1990, two blocks have been added to the 1970 pyramid. The surface of these two blocks (black rectangles) is equal to 39 percent of the surface of the original 1970 pyramid. At the 1975 wage levels, the average return per worker would have become CFAF192,000 (138 × 1.39) a year in 1990.

12. The average wage is computed by weighting salaries $w_{\lambda t}$ with time-invariant weights (the shares of each skill category in 1975—$L_{\lambda 75}/L_{75}$). For the average return, the weights vary with time ($L_{\lambda t}/L_t$).

13. Columns have length $\alpha_{\lambda t}/L_t$ and height $\bar{w}_{\lambda 75}$; the total surface $\Sigma_\lambda \alpha_{\lambda t} \bar{w}_{\lambda 75}$ is thus a measure of the average income per worker at 1975 wages.

Table 4.7. Distribution of the Labor Force among Three Segments

	Share of the labor force (percent)		Efficiency wages, 1975 (thousands of CFAF at 1970 prices)
Segment of the labor force	*1970*	*1990*	
Skilled labor	7	13	884
Unskilled urban labor	22	33	117
Unskilled agricultural labor	71	54	71
Total labor force	100	100	
1970			138
1990			192

*Figure 1.8. The Effect of the Change in the Composition of the Labor Force
on Average Return, with Efficiency Wages of 1975 Used as Weights*

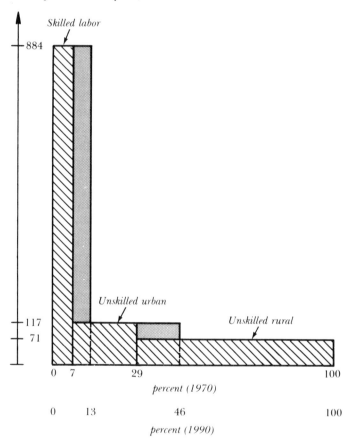

Cumulated percentage from rich to poor

Promotions from agricultural to unskilled urban work (small black
rectangle) account for one-seventh of the gain. Promotions from
unskilled to skilled labor (large black rectangle) account for the rest.

Skilled labor does not represent a homogenous group. In the model,
it consists of nine skill categories ranging from specialized workers to

senior professionals. The decomposition procedure applied in Figure 4.8 can be repeated by decomposing the group referred to as skilled labor into nine subgroups. This would ultimately lead to an eleven-step pyramid. Promotion between 1970 and 1990 would then be represented by the addition of ten blocks. Together, these ten blocks account for 64 percent of the surface of the original 1970 pyramid. Between 1970 and 1990, average income per worker increases, on an average, 2.5 percent a year on account of promotions alone.

When labor is treated as a single homogenous resource, there is a rather mysterious increase in the productivity of labor. When labor is disaggregated into skill categories, most of the mystery disappears. Three-quarters of the gain in labor productivity between 1970 and 1990 is explained by a modification in the composition of the labor force, which reflects an upgrading of the human capital stock.

These results should be interpreted cautiously. First, the efficiency wages derived from the dual solution of the model can differ from market wages. Second, the distribution of income can be modified by a progressive income tax. Nevertheless, it may be noted that this description of the free-market solution is fairly similar to the one given by Langoni for Brazil. Analyzing historical data on the distribution of income in that country, Langoni writes:

i) In the case of Brazil, the increase in inequality is closely linked to the behavior of the labor market;

ii) the increase in inequality is a consequence (and not the cause) of the classical changes brought about by the process of economic development in the long run; in particular, it is associated with the reallocation of labor between sectors (from the primary to the urban sector), and regions (from the less developed to the more developed ones), as well as with the qualitative improvement of the labor force, especially in terms of educational standards and age composition. It is worthy noticing that the degree of inequality is higher in the urban sector than in the primary sector, in the dynamic regions than in those that exhibit a low growth rate, and among individuals with higher education than among illiterate people;

... This unbalanced growth, which is inherent to the process of economic development, induces a disproportionate increase in the demand for skilled labor, thus causing the salaries of this category of workers to grow faster than those of unskilled labor ...

[F]rom a statistical point of view, the contribution of the differences in educational level for explaining the inequality in the distribution of income increased by 33 percent between 1960 and 1970. On the other hand, among all variables taken into account, education was by far the most important one for explaining individual differences in income: in 1970, its contribution to overall inequality stood at approximately 13 percent, as against 2.1 percent for the variable occupational situation (employer, employee, self-employed) which may be regarded as a measure of access to ownership. (Langoni 1973)

The differential among efficiency wages is large because the cost of importing an engineer from Paris is approximately fifty times as high as that of importing an agricultural worker from neighboring Sahel countries.[14] Table 4.7 shows that the efficiency wage ratios are high, but not ridiculously so, in relation to the ratios of market wages reported by Psacharopoulos (1973) for Ghana, Uganda, and Nigeria. All these ratios, however, are considerably higher than those found in the industrial countries.

In the Ivory Coast, as in a number of fast-growing developing countries.[14] Table 4.8 shows that the efficiency wage ratios are high, but is the attribution of this rent. In an economy where capital is not privately owned, the rent returns to the state, which pays for all educational investments. In an economy where all capital is privately owned, the rent returns to the individual, who pays for being educated. Receiving free education and keeping the rent is having the best of two worlds.

Clearly, education cannot be the privilege of the rich. One solution is for individuals to pay for their education but to receive loans (covering monetary costs and earnings forgone) to be repaid after graduation. Another solution adopted by several industrial countries is the provision of free education and a highly progressive income tax. The second solution is similar to the one applied in the Ivory Coast for the financing of agricultural investments. The state contributes to the cost of setting up a coffee plantation. When the trees bear fruit, the state recovers its initial investment in the form of an export tax on coffee.

Changes in the income tax system are difficult to bring about, and free education may be a political necessity. Because anticipations are based mainly on present wage differentials, the anticipated rate of return on education for individuals is extremely high. This may lead to an enormous pressure to increase enrollments and, hence, to a greater number of students and lower professional wages than in the optimal solution of the model. Nevertheless, the growth rate of enrollments will

14. The Sahel is a region of West Africa that forms a belt between the tropical area and the Sahara; the principal countries referred to here are Mali, Upper Volta, and Niger.

*Table 4.8. Market Wage and Shadow Wage Ratios by Educational Level:
Intercountry Comparison*

Country or group of countries	University over secondary	University over no education
	Market wages in the 1960s[a]	
High-income countries	1.7	2.4[b]
Medium-income country (Mexico)	2.3	10.5
African countries		
Ghana	4.9	20.8
Kenya	2.4	8.9
Uganda	3.7	30.0
Nigeria	4.4	22.6
	Shadow wages in 1975	
Ivory Coast model[c]	2.2	29.8

a. George Psacharopoulos, *Returns to Education: An International Comparison* (Amsterdam, London, and New York: Elsevier Scientific Publishing Company, 1973), Table 8.4, p. 132.

b. Higher education over primary; no data are available for wage earners without primary education.

c. Free-market solution; higher education is taken as the average between long and short university cycles ($\lambda = 7$ and $7B$); secondary education is taken as *bachelier lettres* ($\lambda = 5$); no education is taken as unskilled urban ($\lambda = 1$).

have to be severely curtailed at some point around 1980. Whether it is done five years earlier or later will make a great difference.

In conclusion, the replacement of expatriates with nationals has many favorable consequences. It reduces the cost of skilled labor, thus removing a serious handicap to the industrialization of the country. It also reduces disparity between the wages of skilled and unskilled labor, which is now very high. This, however, occurs only in the 1980s. Before that time a serious problem of income distribution may arise.

Chapter 5

Market Imperfections

A PERFECTLY COMPETITIVE MARKET was postulated in the two preceding chapters, and all taxes were assumed to be neutral. This chapter is concerned with two types of imperfections of the market—tariffs on imports and constraints on savings.

Foreign Exchange

The earning of foreign exchange is treated as the production of any intermediate good that is ultimately transformed into goods consumed by nationals. The shadow price of foreign exchange is determined endogenously in the model, as is the shadow price of any other intermediate good. Its value depends on whether or not tariffs are imposed on imports.

FREE TRADE

Following Bruno (1972), the direct and indirect domestic resource cost (DRC)[1] of earning (or saving) one unit of foreign exchange through an export (or an import-substitution) activity is calculated as follows:[2]

---

1. See Table 3.7, which shows the structure of the DRC of export and import-substitution activities.

2. The computation is more easily stated in algebraic terms:

$$(5.1) \qquad f = r_x + \sum_j p_j q_{xj},$$

where j = subscript characterizing primary domestic resources, x = subscript characterizing export activity, p_j = shadow price of a domestic primary resource, f = shadow price of foreign exchange, q_{xj} = quantity of primary domestic resource j

The domestic resource requirements, expressed in quantities of domestic resources per unit of foreign exchange earned, are multiplied by the shadow prices of the corresponding domestic resources. The costs thus obtained are then added up for each of the primary domestic resources used. The shadow price of a unit of foreign exchange is equal to the DRC of the marginal export (or import-substitution) activity. All export and import-substitution activities for which the DRC is higher (or lower) than the shadow price of foreign exchange are unprofitable (or profitable) and excluded from (or included in) the optimal solution. If the DRC of an export activity is lower than the shadow price of foreign exchange, it would be profitable to expand exports. The expansion of exports may be limited by the market outlet. In this case, there accrues to this export activity a rent that is equal to the difference between the shadow price of foreign exchange (marginal return) and the DRC (marginal cost).[3]

The mechanism of formation of the shadow price of foreign exchange can be illustrated diagrammatically by making several simplifying assumptions. In the model, a distinction is made among more than twenty different primary domestic resources, and the shadow price of each resource is a variable. In Figure 5.1, the relative prices of these resources are assumed to remain constant. This permits the expression of all domestic resource requirements in terms of a single resource, taken here as man-years of workers belonging to a given skill category.[4] The profitability of each export (or import-substitution) activity can, in this case, be unequivocally characterized by the number of man-years required to earn (or save) one unit of foreign exchange. This ratio is shown along the vertical axis on the right. Ranking the export activities in increasing order of the DRC ratio and representing along the horizontal axis, from left to right, the amount of foreign exchange earned leads to the export-supply curve *TF* of Figure 5.1. Ranking the import-substitution activities in increasing order of the DRC

---

required (directly or indirectly) to earn one unit of foreign exchange (net of indirect imports) through export activity x, $r_x > 0$ export activity profitable and fully used, $r_x = 0$ export activity marginal and partly used, and $r_x < 0$ export activity unprofitable and unused.

In Figure 5.1, labor is the single primary domestic resource, which commands the shadow wage (w). The labor requirement for the marginal trading activity (at the point of equilibrium, F) is called L_{mg}. Formula (5.1) can be rewritten thus:

(5.2) $$f = (w)(L_{mg}), \text{ with } r_{mg} = 0.$$

3. This is the rent referred to in Chapter 3, note 12.

4. These requirements could be interpreted as a quantity index of the DRC at constant factor prices.

Table 5.1. The Effects of the Removal of Tariffs on Imports in 1980

Economic variable	Figure 5.1		Model solution		Variation $\left(100 \dfrac{T1 - F1}{F1}\right)$
	Free trade solution	Tariffs solution	Free trade (F1)	Tariffs (T1)	
	Quantities[a]		Billions of CFAF at 1970 prices		Percent
	Horizontal axis[b]				
1. Deficit on noncommodity trade	O'N	O'N	48	49	+2
2. Noncompeting imports	NM'	NM'	116	118	+2
3. Competing imports	MI^F	MI^T	111	35	−68
4. Net capital inflow	OX	OX	21	23	+0
5. Exports	XE^F	XE^T	254	179	−30
	Shadow Price of Foreign Exchange[c]				
Numéraire	Vertical axis				
6. Consumption	f^F	f^T	1.35	1.19	−12
Wages					
7. Unskilled agricultural workers	...	...	19.80	18.90	−5
8. Unskilled urban workers	...	...	13.00	12.00	−8
9. Professionals	...	...	0.40	0.36	−10
Rental value					
10. Machinery equipment	...	...	6.50	5.27	−19
11. Urban buildings	...	...	5.22	4.53	−13

a. Composition of the foreign exchange balance at c.i.f. and f.o.b. prices with 1970 official exchange rate.
b. Row 1 + row 2 + row 3 = row 4 + row 5.
c. CFAF1 billion of traded goods, valuing imported goods at c.i.f. in the free-trade solution and at c.i.f. plus tariffs in the tariff solution.

Figure 5.1. *Tariffs and the Shadow Price of Foreign Exchange*

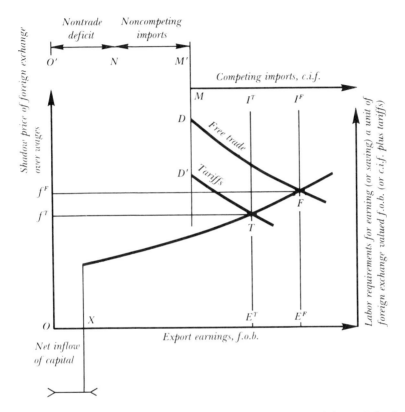

ratio and representing along the horizontal axis, from right to left, the amount of foreign exchange saved leads to the import-demand curve *DF* for the goods which can either be produced locally or imported. For the sake of simplicity, these curves are shown in Figure 5.1 as representing smooth functions instead of step functions.

The horizontal origins (*X* and *M*) of the export-supply curve and of the demand curve for competing imports do not coincide. Exports and competing imports are only two of the five components of the balance of payments listed in rows 1–5 of Table 5.1. The origin of the import-demand curve is defined by the sum (0'*M*') of the deficit on noncommodity trade (0'*N*) and of noncompeting imports (*NM*'). The origin of the export-supply curve is defined by the net inflow of capital (0*X*). The simplifying assumption made in the diagram is that these two quantities

(0X) and (0'M') are not affected by changes in the value of foreign exchange. As will be seen from Table 5.1, these assumptions are approximately satisfied in the model.

The optimal solution is reached at point F, where the import-demand curve (DF) and the export-supply curve (TF) intersect. For the marginal export (or import-substitution) activity corresponding to point F, the DRC of earning (or saving) one unit of foreign exchange is equal to the shadow price of foreign exchange. This cost is measured in thousands of man-years along the vertical axis on the right. Assume that it takes ten units of labor (each unit representing 1,000 man-years) to earn one unit of foreign exchange (defined here as CFAF1 billion at the rate of CFAF250 per SDR which prevailed during the base year).[5] The ratio between the shadow price of foreign exchange and labor is equal to 10; it is the ordinate of f^F, shown along the vertical axis on the left side.[6]

TARIFFS ON IMPORTS

Assume now that exports remain untaxed and unsubsidized but that tariffs are imposed on competing imports. Assume also that all production, trade, investment, and consumption decisions are made on the basis of prices, inclusive of tariffs. Foreign exchange earned (or saved) is still measured on the basis of c.i.f. and f.o.b. prices along the horizontal axis, but their profitability is now measured on the basis of the prices inclusive of tariffs along the vertical axis (see Chapter 13). The export-supply curve TF is not affected, but the import-demand curve is shifted downward. Because imported goods cost more now in CFAF, fewer man-years are required to produce CFAF1 billion worth of imported goods. Because the ordinates are expressed in terms of direct and indirect costs and earnings, the amplitude of the downward shift is related, not to the nominal tariff, but to the level of effective protection (see Chapter 13). Since this protection is not the same for all goods, the shape of the import demand curve and the ranking of the import-substitution activities are modified by the imposition of tariffs. The new equilibrium is at point T, at which the export-supply curve TF intersects the new import-demand curve D'T. The quantities exported and imported fall; the shadow price of foreign exchange declines in relation to the shadow price of domestic resources from f^F to f^T.

5. The value of SDR is based on the value of a basket of currencies used by the IMF as numéraire. For long-term projections, it is preferable to define the exchange rate in relation to such a weighted average than in relation to the U.S. dollar.
6. For unskilled urban workers, this ratio in 1980 is equal to 13 with free trade and 12 with tariffs, as shown in row 8 of Table 5.1.

Compare this simplified diagrammatic presentation with what actually occurs in the model. The upper part of Table 5.1 gives the components of the balance of payments, which were shown along the horizontal axis of Figure 5.1. Deficit on noncommodity trade (row 1) plus noncompeting imports (row 2) plus competing imports (row 3) must be equal to net capital inflow (row 4) plus exports (row 5). In Figure 5.1, it was assumed that tariffs affect only competing imports and exports. Table 5.1 shows that it is not quite true, but almost. When tariffs are imposed, the volume of competing imports (row 3) and the volume of exports (row 5) decline sharply, while none of the other three components (rows 1, 2, and 4) is affected by as much as 10 percent.

The lower part of the table deals with the shadow price ratios between foreign exchange and selected domestic resources. In Figure 5.1, the ratio fell from f^F to f^T with the imposition of tariffs. It was possible to use a single ratio because the relative prices of all domestic primary resources were assumed to remain constant. The purpose of this simplification was to keep the chart two-dimensional. In the model, the size of the fall in the value of foreign exchange depends on which domestic resource is used as the numéraire. The decline is only 5 percent in relation to agricultural wages, whereas it is 19 percent in relation to machinery (see last column of Table 5.1). The effect of imposing tariffs on manufactured goods is to raise the rental value of machinery in relation to agricultural wages, because tariffs stimulate domestic production of manufactures at the expense of agricultural production for export. The former requires, directly and indirectly, more machinery and less unskilled labor than the latter (see the left- and right-hand columns of Table 3.7).

If relative prices of primary domestic resources had not been affected by a change in protection policies, the impact of such a change on particular industries could have been calculated from the rate of effective protection. For example, it would have been possible to draw precisely the export-supply curve (TF) and the import-demand curves with tariffs ($D'T$) and without tariffs (DF). Each export industry or import-substitution industry could have been related to a particular segment along these curves. Knowing the equilibrium points with tariffs (T) and without tariffs (F), the import-substitution industries to be closed and the export-industries to be promoted could have been identified.[7] This would, however, have given an incorrect picture of the "resource pull" if the relative prices of the primary resources were

---

7. Import-substitution industries penalized by a negative rate of effective protection might also fall into this category.

substantially affected by the imposition of tariffs.[8] This is a limitation of the effective-protection approach based on a partial-equilibrium analysis, which is pointed out by Srinivasan (1975). This limitation is eliminated here by treating the prices of primary resources as endogenous variables.

Savings

Foreign exchange earnings were treated only as a means of increasing the utility of goods consumed by Ivorians. The level of exports was optimized by equalizing the domestic resource cost of earning an additional dollar through exports to that of saving an additional dollar through import substitution. Levels of investment and savings are treated in much the same way, but the tradeoff is now intertemporal instead of intratemporal.

As explained earlier, the choice between consumption and savings depends on the value of two key parameters of the objective function. The first is the elasticity of substitution between consumption today and consumption tomorrow. It is treated as a given behavioral parameter measurable from econometric analysis of market data. The second is the rate at which utilities are discounted over time. It is treated as a policy parameter characterizing a choice between more consumption by present or by future generations.

The choice between consumption and savings can be modified by changing the value of the discount rate. A less straightforward procedure (which corresponds to a second-best solution and assumes the absence of strong powers) is to introduce an institutional constraint on savings without changing the value of the discount rate.[9] These two different procedures were compared by conducting two sets of controlled experiments. The results of the first set of experiments are summarized in the first three columns of Table 5.2. The discount rate, equal to 4 percent a year in the reference case, is raised progressively to 7 percent, then 11 percent. In the last three columns of the table, there

8. In formula (5.1), the sign of r_x depends not only on q_{xj} but also on prices p_j. Clearly, if the price of a resource vital to a given production activity goes up 10 percent while that of the resource vital to another activity goes down 10 percent, the relative profitability of the two production activities will be affected. The values of q_{xj} may also be affected by a modification in the technologies selected.

9. This procedure is inconvenient in that it mixes constant and variable price relationships. On the one hand, the constraint on savings is expressed on the basis of relations at constant prices (see Chapter 10). On the other hand, choices in the model are made on the basis of variable prices.

Table 5.2. The Open and Closed Savings Loops

Period, item, or year	Open loop: Percentage rate of time discount			Closed loop: Strength of savings constraint		
				None (case T1)	Light (case T3)	High (case T4)
	4	7	11			
Growth rate of private consumption	*(average yearly percentage)*					
1. 1970–90	6.4	6.0	5.6	6.7	6.5	6.2
2. 1970–75	4.7	6.0	7.2	5.9	6.5	7.2
3. 1985–90	8.0	5.9	5.0	6.7	6.1	5.6
Rental values of capital stocks in 1980	*(percentage increase over reference case)*					
4. Vehicles	0	16	26	0	18	46
5. Machinery	0	17	33	0	15	35
6. Construction	0	16	26	0	13	28
Relative prices of consumer goods in 1980						
7. Housing over clothing	0	13	25	0	13	27
Shadow price of savings	*(percentage premium on savings)*					
9. 1975	0	0	0	0	20	73
10. 1980	0	0	0	0	24	59
11. 1985	0	0	0	0	22	64

is no constraint on savings in the reference case T1; the tightness of the constraint is increased progressively in cases T3 and T4.

Whichever way savings are reduced, the growth rate of consumption throughout the twenty-year period declines (row 1). Consumption increases at the beginning of the period (row 2) and falls at the end (row 3).

Figure 5.2 illustrates the effect of an increase in the discount rate. The solid line shows the percentage change in consumption when the discount rate is raised from 4 to 7 percent; the dotted line shows the corresponding percentage change when the discount rate is raised from 4 to 11 percent. In Figure 5.3, the heavy line measures the percentage variation in consumption resulting from the introduction of a light constraint on savings; the dotted line corresponds to the tight constraint. The two procedures lead to very similar results.

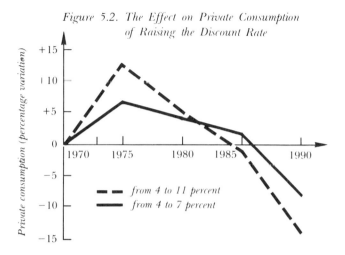

Figure 5.2. The Effect on Private Consumption of Raising the Discount Rate

- - - - from 4 to 11 percent
——— from 4 to 7 percent

Figure 5.3. The Effect on Private Consumption and Domestic Saving of Introducing a Constraint on Savings

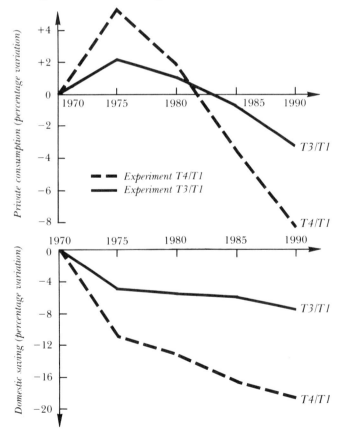

- - - - Experiment T4/T1
——— Experiment T3/T1

As regards the prices in the lower part of Table 5.2, rows 4, 5, and 6 show the increase in rental values of the three types of urban capital stocks. Row 7 shows the increase in the relative price of housing services (essentially rents on buildings) and clothing (which requires much less capital). Here again, the increase in the price of housing in relation to that of clothing is quite similar in the two sets of experiments. The difference is in the shadow price of savings (three bottom rows of Table 5.2).

In the first set of experiments, there is no shadow price on savings, and the cost of using capital is raised by increasing the interest rate. As will be recalled from Table 3.10, the rental value of one unit of capital stock corresponds to the capital-recovery factor, and this factor increases with the rate of interest. More simply, the annual rent increases with the interest charge.

In the second set of experiments, the rental value of capital stocks rises because a penalty is imposed on the use of capital (see formula 10.6). This penalty is equal to the shadow price of savings shown in rows 9–11 in Table 5.2. This shadow price can be interpreted as the scarcity premium commanded by savings when the level of savings is below its optimal value. The shadow price of savings is equal to zero when the constraint is removed.

Because public funds are a source of savings, public funds also command a scarcity premium (see Table 10.1). This premium is approximately 10 percent less than the premium on savings (rows 1 and 2 of Table 5.3). When public funds increase, less than the full

Table 5.3. *Shadow Prices of Foreign Capital and Constraints on Savings in 1980*

Item	Shadow price		
	Case T1 (no constraint)	Case T3 (light constraint)	Case T4 (heavy constraint)
Savings	0	0.24	0.59
Public revenues[a]	0	0.21	0.53
Foreign exchange	1.19	1.17	1.17
Foreign capital[b]	1.19	1.42	1.74

a. The shadow price of public revenues is approximately equal to nine-tenths of the shadow price of savings.

b. Because 40 percent of foreign capital is assumed to be borrowed by the public administration, there is a loss of $0.4 \times 0.1 = 0.04$ in the form of public consumption. The shadow price of foreign capital is therefore equal to the shadow price of foreign exchange plus 96 percent of the shadow price of savings (see Chapter 10).

increment is saved. Part of the increment induces an increase in the current expenditures of the public administration. This part can be considered as lost; it does not contribute (through additional investments) to an increase in private consumption, which is the variable entering in the objective function.

Constraining savings and public revenues below their optimal level reduces the value of the objective function by 0.2 percent in case T3 and 1.7 percent in case T4. Cutting the tax rate from its optimal value of 0.129 to 0.11 reduces the maximand only 0.2 percent. Cutting it further from 0.11 to 0.09 reduces the maximand an additional 1.5 percent. Losses are far from being proportional to the reduction in the taxation rate. The maximand is almost flat near the top but it declines steeply as one goes away from the top.

The open savings loop, introduced by Ramsey (1928), is frequently used in the growth theory literature. Most numerical models, however, have been based on a closed savings loop (Taylor 1975). For example, the method of estimating shadow prices for the project evaluation presented in the UNIDO manual (Das Gupta, Sen, and Marglin 1972) is based on a closed savings loop. The shadow price of savings and investments is one of the principal shadow prices in the literature on

Table 5.4. Endogenous Borrowing and Shadow Prices of Foreign Capital, 1975–90

	Constraint on savings		
	None	*Light*	*Heavy*
Year or period	*T1*	*T3*	*T4*
Endogenous borrowing	(*billions of* CFAF)		
1. 1975	17.0	13.4	8.7
2. 1980	26.8	26.8	15.6
3. 1985	35.8	19.7	8.2
Shadow price of foreign capital	(*1970 = 100*)		
4. 1975	1.03	1.27	1.92
5. 1980	1.20	1.40	1.74
6. 1985	1.19	1.41	1.83
7. 1990	1.39	1.46	1.55
	(*average yearly percentage*)		
8. 1975–80	3.1	2.0	−2.0
9. 1980–85	−0.2	0.2	1.0
10. 1985–90	3.3	0.7	−3.3
11. 1975–90	2.1	0.9	−1.4

project appraisal. The fact that this shadow price disappears with the open savings loop can lead to confusion. The confusion disappears when reference is made to the shadow prices of primary resources. Ultimately, what matters is the rental value of a unit of capital stock. The experiments reported in Table 5.2 show that rental values can be increased in two ways. With the open loop, the shadow price of savings remains equal to zero but the pure time-discount rate is raised. With the closed loop, the discount rate remains unchanged, but a penalty is imposed on the use of savings, and its level is raised by tightening the constraint on savings. Similar results may be obtained by adjusting the time-discount rate in the first case and the tax rate in the second. Nevertheless, a basic difference between the two methods remains. With the first, the savings rate and, consequently, the tax rate are optimized, and a strong fiscal authority is thus postulated. With the second, the tax rate is given and the fiscal authorities do not have the power to raise it. As will be shown in the experiments to be described in Chapter 6, whether fiscal authorities are able to adjust the tax rate in response to new policy objectives or new events can make a great deal of difference.

Foreign Capital

Net inflow of capital from abroad makes a positive contribution to the balance of payments as well as to the balance between savings and investments. Since an additional unit of foreign capital contributes to a simultaneous easing of these two balances, the shadow price of foreign capital is equal to the sum of the shadow prices of foreign exchange and savings. Table 5.3 shows that the shadow price of foreign capital increases from 1.19 in case T1 to 1.74 in case T4. The closed-loop model leads to a higher premium on foreign capital than does the open-loop model, because in the former the level of savings is assumed to be below optimum. This is in the tradition of the two-gap models of Chenery and others.

The fact that foreign capital commands a higher premium with than without a constraint on savings does not mean that it is optimal to borrow more with than without the savings constraint present. The capital borrowed today has to be repaid tomorrow; what matters is the effect of the constraint on the variation of the shadow price of foreign capital over time.

Table 5.4 shows that the optimal level of borrowing is reduced by the constraint on savings—the amounts borrowed decline in rows 1–3 when going from the T1 column to the T4. Foreign capital is cheaper in 1975 than in 1990 without a constraint on savings; the reverse is true with a heavy constraint on savings (first and third columns of rows 4 and 7). Without any constraint on savings, the shadow price of capital increases on an average 2.1 percent a year; with a heavy constraint on savings, it declines 1.4 percent a year (row 11). By reducing the ratio between the price of foreign capital in 1990 and the price in 1975, the constraint on savings reduces the profitability of borrowing.

Appendix. Shadow Prices and Own Rates of Interest

The symbol Π refers to the variables entering into the dual equations. The symbol p_j refers to shadow prices, which are measured by the ratios between the dual value of variable Π_j and the dual value of the numéraire Π. The latter is defined as a weighted average of the dual values of the eight final consumer goods.

$$\Pi_t = \sum_i \alpha_{it}\Pi_{it} \text{ with } \sum_i \alpha_{it} = 1.0, \text{ for } i = 1, \ldots, 8,$$

the shadow price of variable j is given by:

$$p_{j,t} = \Pi_{j,t}/\Pi_t \text{ with } p_{j,0} = 1.0, \text{ for all } j.$$

The own rate of interest on a given variable defines the average rate of depreciation of the dual value between two points in time:

$$\Pi_{t+\tau}/\Pi_t = (1 + r)^{-\tau},$$

where r = own interest rate on consumption over the period $t, t + \tau$, and

$$\Pi_{j,t+\tau}/\Pi_{j,t} = (1 + r_j)^{-\tau},$$

where $\Pi_{j,0} = 1.0$ and r_j = own interest rate or variable j over the period $t, t + \tau$. The average rate of variation of the shadow price of variable j between two points in time is a function of the own rates of interest on the numéraire and on variable j:

$$\frac{p_{j,t+\tau}}{p_{j,t}} = \left(\frac{1 + r}{1 + r_j}\right)^{\tau} = \left(1 + \frac{r - r_j}{1 + r_j}\right)^{\tau},$$

where $\dfrac{r - r_j}{1 + r_j}$ = rate of growth of shadow price p_j between t and $t + \tau$.

The own rate of interest on variable j can be derived from the shadow price of variable j and the own rate of interest on the

*Table 5.5. Own Rates of Interest on Consumption and
Foreign Capital, 1975–85*
(Percent a year)

Period	Case T1	Case T3	Case T4
Consumption			
1. 1975–80	15.9	15.6	12.0
2. 1980–85	17.8	16.3	15.4
Foreign capital			
3. 1975–80	12.5	13.4	14.3
4. 1980–85	18.1	16.2	14.3

numéraire. Thus, from the rates of variation of the shadow prices of
foreign capital shown in rows 8 and 9 of Table 5.4 and the own rates of
interest on consumption shown in rows 1 and 2 of Table 5.5, the own
rates of interest on foreign capital shown in rows 3 and 4 of Table 5.5
can be derived.

In Chapter 6, the impact of a given factor is measured by applying
controlled experiments. Results are often presented as percentage
variations by comparing the solution with the factor (denoted below
with ′) to the solution without that factor (denoted below without ′).
The percentage variation of the shadow prices of variables i and j are
measured by:

$$x_i = 100 \left(\frac{p_i'}{p_i} - 1\right) = 100 \left(\frac{\Pi_i'/\Pi'}{\Pi_i/\Pi} - 1\right) \text{ and}$$

$$x_j = 100 \left(\frac{p_j'}{p_j} - 1\right) = 100 \left(\frac{\Pi_j'/\Pi'}{\Pi_j/\Pi} - 1\right).$$

The percentage variation of the price ratio between variables j and i is
measured by:

$$x_i{}^j = 100 \left(\frac{\Pi_j'/\Pi_i'}{\Pi_j/\Pi_i} - 1\right).$$

It follows that:

$$x_j - x_i = (1 + .01x_i)x_i{}^j.$$

Chapter 6

Policy Experiments

TWO TYPES OF POLICIES are simulated. One has to do with the relation between the Ivory Coast and the rest of the world; it characterizes the freedom of access to foreign goods, foreign labor, and foreign capital. The other has to do with the distribution of the national product; it characterizes the distribution of gains between present and future generations, among regions, and between an educated elite and the rest of the population. These two types of policies and the instruments for implementing them are specified in the upper part of Table 6.1. The lower part of that table is taken up with factors beyond government control, such as variations in the level of foreign aid or in the terms of trade. The policies and factors listed in Table 6.1 could be combined in many different ways. Out of all possible combinations, thirty-three have been selected in the manner described in the appendix (Tables 6.16 and 6.17). A particular solution of the model is associated with each of the thirty-three selected combinations, and the comparison among these various solutions is presented in two different ways.[1]

First, a sequence of five solutions simulates a progressive drive towards autarchy and nationalism. Each solution differs from the next by the imposition of additional restrictive measures. At one extreme, the first solution is associated with an outward-looking policy very close to free trade. At the other extreme, the fifth solution reflects a resolutely inward-looking policy.

Second, the effects of given policies (or events) are analyzed with a series of binary comparisons. Between the two terms of the comparison the only difference is the existence (or absence) of a given measure. The sensitivity to the environment is tested by replicating the experi-

1. From any given solution of the central model, the corresponding solutions of the disaggregated sectoral models can be derived in the manner described in Chapters 12 and 15.

Table 6.1. Types of Experiments

Subject of policy measure	Instrument of control
Freedom of foreign access	
Commodity imports	Tariff
Foreign labor	Quota
Foreign capital	Quota
Enclave project (iron ore)	Approval
Internal distribution	
Public savings versus private consumption	Taxation rate
Agricultural employment in the North	Program
Relative prices to consumers	Excise taxes and subsidies
Education	Levels of enrollments
Factors not under government control	
Grants from abroad	
Terms of trade	
Scope for import-substitution	

ment under different conditions, as outlined in Table 6.2. For example, the first policy objective listed in that table is to raise agricultural employment in the north (the poorest part of the country) by implementing a labor intensive agricultural program in that region. In order to assess the consequences of such a policy, the model is solved with and without that program, under two different situations. In one case, there is no constraint on savings and the rate of taxation is optimized, which postulates the existence of a strong fiscal power. In the other case, there is a constraint on savings, and the rate of taxation cannot be raised because the fiscal power is assumed to be weak. As will be seen, the effect of the employment program greatly depends on which of the two assumptions is made.

The Progressive Drive toward Autarchy

The progressive drive toward autarchy is presented in the form of five projections. In the first, the situation is fairly similar to the one that prevailed in the early 1970s. The constraint on savings is not severe. Tariffs on noncompeting imports are maintained at their existing levels, but tariffs on competing imports are suppressed. In the second projection, tariffs on competing imports are reinstated. In the following projections, additional restrictions are imposed one after the other.

The policy changes are summarized in the top part of Table 6.3 and their economic implications in the lower part. The first column gives

Table 6.2. Policies and Factors beyond Government Control

Policy or factor under investigation		Environment					
		Fiscal power		Tariffs on competing imports		Scope for import substitution	
Objective	Instrument	Strong[a]	Weak	Yes	No	Large	Small
Promoting employment in the north	Implementing an agricultural program	x					
Ivorization of capital	Equilibrium of capital flows in 1990		x				
Protecting manufacturing industries	Tariffs on imports	x		x		x	
		x					x
			x				x
Altering patterns of consumption	Excise tax and consumers' subsidies	x		x		x	
		x		x			
			x				
Modification in the scope for import substitution		x		x	x		
Variations in the level of foreign aid		x		x			
		x			x		x
			x		x		
Changes in the terms of trade		x		x			

a. When a strong fiscal power is postulated, there is no constraint on savings.

the absolute values of selected economic aggregates in projection 1. The following columns show, for each of the other four projections, the percentage changes from projection 1, which is used as the common basis of reference.[2]

The comparison between the first two projections is summarized by the percentage changes given in column 2. The imposition of tariffs on competing imports promotes import substitution. By the end of the planning period, the volume of imports has declined more than 20 percent. Because import-substitution industries are more capital intensive than export industries, the level of physical investment increases in 1975. Because these industries are less efficient than the export industries, the level of consumption declines during all years, and the discounted utility of consumption for the entire planning period declines 2.1 percent. The most alarming feature is the increase in disguised urban unemployment. By the end of the period, it is 35.5 percent higher than in projection 1.

To reduce unemployment, immigration of unskilled workers from neighboring countries is prohibited in projection 3. In addition, the capital balance has to be in equilibrium by the end of the planning period. Because nationalization of foreign firms is not allowed, capital borrowing has to be curtailed before 1990. What are the effects of these two measures? The exclusion of unskilled foreign migrants would substantially reduce disguised unemployment, but the restriction of the inflow of capital would tend to increase it. With the two measures combined, disguised urban unemployment is reduced in 1975 and 1990 but remains unaffected in 1980 and 1985. In 1975, the restriction of the inflow of capital hardly affects consumption, but it reduces physical and human investments substantially. The value of the objective function declines a further 2.4 percent. Restricting capital inflows slows the replacement of expatriates with nationals. In 1985, the wage bill of expatriates is 2.5 times as large as in the previous case.

A step toward reducing urban unemployment was made in projection 3. Is it possible to improve the situation further by launching a large-scale agricultural employment program in the north? This attempt, made in projection 4, is rather disappointing. Disguised urban unemployment is reduced 13 percent in 1990 from that seen in projection 3, but aggregate consumption declines more than 8 percent.

2. The five projections correspond to five of the fifteen experiments listed in Table 6.16. Solution 1 has been excluded from the comparison because the scope for import substitution and export promotion was greater than in the other solutions. The five solutions selected (2, 3, 4, 5, and 6) in Table 6.16 were conducted under identical technological conditions; they differ only in the policy followed.

Table 6.3. *The Effects of Progressively More Nationalistic Policies*

Policy		Projection[a]				
		1	2	3	4	5
Imposing tariffs on competing imports			X	X	X	X
Prohibiting the immigration of unskilled workers				X	X	X
Restricting capital imports by prohibiting a net capital outflow in any year				X	X	X
Implementing a rural employment program in the North					X	X
Restricting entry to foreign skilled labor[b]						X

Implication	*Year*	CFAF (Billions)	\<=== *Percentage variation in relation to projection 1* ===\>			
		1	2	3	4	5
Discounted utility of private per capita consumption by nationals (maximand)		100	−2.1	−4.5	−10.0	−15.4
Private consumption by nationals	1975	327	−1.0	−1.5	−2.1	−3.6
	1980	443	−1.7	−5.3	−6.7	−11.3
	1985	587	−0.9	−4.1	−6.2	−10.2
	1990	764	−2.0	−2.5	−10.8	−12.8
Physical investments (endogenous component)	1975	69	8.2	−14.7	−24.4	−42.4
	1980	80	2.2	15.4	+6.4	−27.4
	1985	150	−16.0	−18.9	−25.1	−22.5
	1990	175	−5.2	−6.5	−14.3	−18.3

Human investments in postprimary education	1975	29	−0.7	−8.3	−8.0	5.2
	1980	51	−3.0	−20.2	−25.1	−19.2
	1985	49	−3.6	1.8	−7.5	−13.4
	1990	62	−1.4	5.1	−1.0	−7.7
Imports (valued at c.i.f.)	1975	140	0.0	−7.7	−11.3	−19.2
	1980	195	−13.8	−13.5	−19.1	−27.8
	1985	267	−18.7	−21.4	−29.6	−39.0
	1990	342	−21.3	−16.4	−29.8	−33.9
Wage bill of foreign skilled labor[b]	1975	64	0.0	−6.1	−7.7	−6.1
	1980	72	−0.4	−3.6	−5.6	−58.3
	1985	15	−23.3	91.8	91.8	..
Employment of Ivorians in high skills[c]	1975	47	0.0	0.9	0.9	0.9
	1980	93	−3.0	−6.9	−6.9	−0.4
	1985	187	−3.9	−11.1	−12.2	−6.9
	1990	288	−3.7	−8.0	−12.5	−11.5
(Thousands)						
Unskilled urban labor employed in the informal sector[d]	1975	106	1.0	−29.3	−22.6	−17.2
	1980	201	14.9	13.4	31.3	88.1
	1985	321	18.1	19.5	17.6	21.7
	1990	372	35.5	12.9	−1.1	2.4

a. Projections 1–5 correspond to solutions 2, 3, 4, 5, and 6 listed in Table 6.16. In all cases there is a constraint on savings.
b. In all projections, no imports in 1990; in projection 5, no imports in 1985 or 1990.
c. Numbers of those who have graduated, weighted by wages.
d. Disguised urban unemployment.

The objective function falls another 5 percent—a high price to pay for a small gain in employment. There are two causes for this disconcerting finding. First, the level of public savings is reduced by the requirement of additional public expenditures to finance the agricultural program. Investments and, in turn, aggregate growth are thereby curtailed. Second, there is a shortage of agricultural workers in the south. Agricultural migrations from north to south are reduced as more employment is now available in the north. Migrant workers from neighboring countries are not allowed in the country. The wage differential between rural and urban workers declines, but the reduction is not large enough to attract a sufficient number of workers from the informal urban sector into plantations of the forest zone.

In projection 5 (the righthand column), an additional restriction is imposed: entry of skilled foreign labor is severely limited in 1980 and prohibited altogether thereafter. While consumption hardly declines in 1975, physical investments fall drastically, and serious problems of underutilization of capacity arise. The objective function declines another 5 percent and ends up 15.4 percent below the point at which it began in projection 1. When import restrictions were imposed on labor or on capital, adjustment was relatively rapid; when import restrictions are imposed on both at once, adjustment takes a decade.

The Rural Employment Program in the North

In the series of experiments just described, the unfavorable effects of the rural employment program were unexpectedly large. The value of the objective function declined 5 percent between projections 3 and 4. To gain a better understanding of the program, its effect can first be considered in the north by solving the sectoral model in isolation—that is to say, by ignoring interactions between the north and the rest of the economy. These interactions will be taken into account in a second stage by solving again the economywide model with and without program, but in an economic environment more favorable than in projections 3 and 4.

The partial-equilibrium analysis at the level of the sector is illustrated in Table 6.4. In the upper part of the table, the benefits accruing to the north are measured by comparing the levels of employment, investments, and subsidies corresponding to the solutions of the sectoral model of the north with and without program. Table 6.4 shows that the gain in employment resulting from the program becomes progressively larger. By the end of the planning period, employment is almost 150

Table 6.4. Costs and Benefits of the Agricultural Development Program in the North (Partial-Equilibrium Analysis)
(Percent)

Item	1975	1980	1985	1990
Benefits to the rural north	(percentage of increase)			
Employment of unskilled labor	15	27	84	147
Investments	412	616	598	320
Public subsidies	400	457	500	366
Costs to the economy	(share of national aggregate)[a]			
Investment of the program as percentage of total endogenous physical investment	3.4	6.0	6.8	5.9
Subsidy of the program as percentage of public saving	3.3	3.2	2.8	2.3
Subsidy of the program as percentage of GDP	0.4	0.8	0.8	0.7

a. In comparison with solution F1.

percent higher with than without the program. This spectacular result is reached by means of a fivefold increase in investment and public subsidy. For the rural north, such increments appear enormous. In terms of national aggregates, they remain modest. This is shown in the lower part of Table 6.4 by comparison with the free-market solution of the economywide model.[3] Investments associated with the program account for only 6 percent of total endogenous physical investments; the public subsidies involved account for about 3 percent of public savings and less than 1 percent of GDP.

In the general-equilibrium analysis, the decline in production between projections 3 and 4 was partly the result of a labor shortage in the south. Such a shortage occurred because agricultural workers from neighboring Sahelian countries were not allowed to enter. In the two new experiments, this problem is avoided by allowing free entry of foreign labor. The decline of the objective function is reduced from 5 to 2.2 percent when the constraint on savings is maintained (experiment 1B/1). It is reduced to 0.9 percent when the constraint on savings is also eliminated (experiment F2/F1).

The effect of relieving the constraint on savings is illustrated in Figure 6.1. With a strong fiscal power (experiment F2/F1), it becomes optimal to compensate for the loss of efficiency associated with the program by saving and investing more (upper part of Figure 6.1). As a result, consumption declines only at the beginning of the planning

3. The free-market solution without program (F1) was reviewed in Chapters 3 and 4.

Figure 6.1. The Effects of an Agricultural Employment Program in the North on Consumption and Investment (Table 6.6)

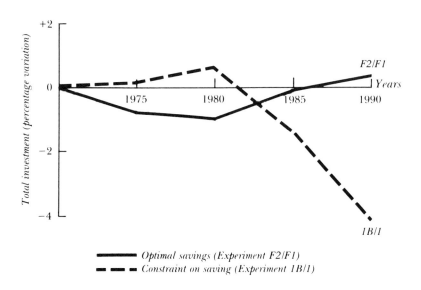

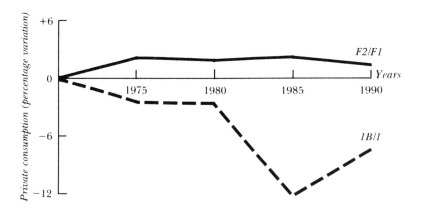

Table 6.5. *The Agricultural Development Program in the North: The Impact of the Employment Program on the Maximand and Own Rate of Interest on Consumption*

	Comparison	
Item	F2/F1	1B/1
Environment		
Entry of foreign workers allowed	Yes	Yes
Existence of tariff on competing imports	No	No
Constraint on savings	No	Yes
Existence of tariff on noncompeting imports	No	Yes
Results Impact of employment program on maximand (discounted utility—percentage variation)	−0.9	−2.2
Own rate of interest on consumption (yearly percentage 1975–85)		
Without program	16.0	14.8
With program	16.7	14.1

period (lower part of Figure 6.1). With a weak fiscal power, the opposite occurs; because of the constraint on savings less is invested, and consumption falls sharply in 1990.

A detailed comparison of the two experiments is presented in Table 6.6. The impact of the program is expressed in the upper part in terms of percentage changes in the primal and dual variables. It is expressed in the lower part by the absolute difference between the values of the primal variables with and without program. In the case of experiment 1B/1, in which there is a constraint on savings, the two bottom rows show the premium which savings command over consumption in the solutions with and without program.

With a strong fiscal power (experiment F2/F1, reported at the left), it becomes optimal to increase taxes when the program is implemented. Throughout the entire planning period, the increase in tax proceeds amounts on an average to 1.2 percent of GDP (first row of Table 6.6). Because of the increase in public savings (row 6), higher physical investments made in the north (row 1) hardly affect the level of physical investments made in the rest of the economy (row 2); human investments even increase slightly (row 3).

With a weak fiscal power, the constraint on savings precludes any increase in the rate of taxation (right part of Table 6.6). Public savings decline (row 6); additional investments required by the program result in a sharp decline in physical investments in the rest of the economy, especially in the eighties (row 2). The premium on savings more than

Table 6.6. The Impact of the Agricultural Development Program (General-Equilibrium Analysis)

	Policy							
Economic variable	Optimal savings and free trade (Experiment F2/F1)				Constraints on savings and tariffs on noncompeting imports (Experiment 1B'1)			
	1975	1980	1985	1990	1975	1980	1985	1990
Primal solution								
Increment of tax proceeds as percentage of GDP	0.9	1.6	1.4	0.9	...[a]	...[a]	...[a]	...[a]
	Percentage variation associated with program							
Gross domestic product	0.1	0.1	0.7	+0.6	-1.0	0.0	-4.0	-5.0
Private consumption	-0.8	-1.0	-0.1	0.3	0.1	0.6	-1.4	-4.1
Total investments	2.0	1.8	2.2	+1.4	-2.4	-2.5	-12.4	-7.5
Private savings	-0.8	-1.0	-0.1	+0.3	0.1	0.6	-1.4	-4.1
Public savings	4.4	4.0	4.4	+2.7	-2.0	-0.8	-16.3	-17.0
Ivorians employed in highly skilled occupations	0.0	0.3	0.7	+1.7	0.0	-0.2	-2.7	-6.8
Ivorians employed in medium-skilled occupations	0.0	4.4	4.2	+7.1	0.5	0.5	-1.5	-3.2
Disguised urban unemployment	15.9	-8.3	0.0	-6.3	0.2	-4.2	0.0	20.3

Dual solution

	F2−F1				1B−1			
Premium on savings[b]	...	...	...	...	116.0	176.0	148.0	169.0
Revaluation (−) or devaluation (+)	−1.0	−3.4	6.0	−5.4	6.3	11.0	10.0	1.0
Value of foreign capital	−1.0	−3.4	6.0	−5.4	24.0	30.0	29.0	22.0
Efficiency wage of agricultural workers	5.6	5.3	8.7	1.6	5.6	11.5	8.1	11.9
Wage differential (λ = 5 over λ = 0)	−5.9	−6.4	−6.2	1.5	−2.3	−2.2	−0.9	3.1

Differences in the uses and origins of the investment funds[c]

Absolute impact in billions of CFAF

	F2−F1				1B−1			
1. Physical investment in the north	2.4	3.2	4.0	4.4	2.4	3.2	4.0	4.4
2. Physical investment in rest of economy	−0.3	−0.3	0.0	−1.4	−5.8	−4.7	−28.4	−23.2
3. Human investments	0.6	0.9	1.3	2.1	−0.1	−3.6	−5.4	−4.6
4. Total investment	2.7	3.8	5.8	5.1	−3.1	−5.1	−29.8	−23.4
5. Private savings	−4.3	−1.7	0.0	0.5	0.4	0.3	−1.8	−8.2
6. Public savings	7.0	5.5	5.8	4.6	−1.1	−7.8	−20.0	−27.2
7. Net capital inflow	2.7	0.0	0.0	0.0	−2.4	2.4	−8.0	12.0

Percentage premium

	F2−F1				1B−1			
8. Premium of savings over consumption without program	...	...	...	...	25.0	17.0	21.0	19.0
9. Premium of savings over consumption with program	...	...	...	...	54.0	47.0	52.0	52.0

a. A tax increase is precluded.
b. With optimal savings the shadow price of savings is always equal to zero. With a constraint on savings the percentage increase with program is obtained by dividing the figures shown in row 8 by those in row 9.
c. Row 1 + row 2 + row 3 = row 4 = row 5 + row 6 + row 7.

doubles (from 21 to 51 percent, on an average, throughout the planning period). The premium on foreign capital almost doubles (from 45 to 84 on an average). In comparison, the increase in agricultural wages (10 percent on an average) appears modest.

Several lessons may be drawn. First, the partial-equilibrium analysis may be misleading in that it ignores the effect of the additional sectoral investments on the rest of the economy; this effect may be modest in the short term but substantial in the long term. Second, when the project is assessed within a general-equilibrium framework the results may be highly sensitive to the policy and the economic environment. In this case, the assumptions made on the strength of the fiscal powers are critical.

If a government places more emphasis on the distribution of income without altering its rate of time preference, the rate of taxation must increase substantially (experiment F2/F1). If the tax rate remains constant, the government is in effect raising its preference for the present generation and penalizing future generations (experiment 1B/1). Giving more to the poor today without taking it from the rich reduces aggregate consumption tomorrow. The community is then trading better distribution of income today for less aggregate consumption tomorrow.

If the emphasis placed on the distribution of income coincides with an increase in the saving effort of a country receiving foreign aid, the premium on foreign capital is hardly affected (experiment F1/F2). If it does not (experiment 1B/1), the premium on foreign capital in the receiving country rises; in this example, it rises from 45 percent to 84 percent. This increase in the shadow price of foreign capital is unavoidable with a constant level of foreign aid.

Restrictions on Capital Flows

In the free-market solution described in Chapters 3 and 4, all expatriates are replaced with nationals before the end of the planning period. A substantial share of the physical capital is owned by foreigners, however, and an increasing proportion of export earnings goes into servicing foreign debt. This may be considered an undesirable dependence from abroad. The object of experiment F5/F4 (Table 6.7) is to assess the cost of achieving the Ivorization of capital by 1990. During that year, in case F5, the capital balance must be in equilibrium without

Table 6.7. Restrictions on Capital Flows (Experiment F5/F4) [a]
(Percent)

Economic variable	1975	1980	1985
Primal solution			
Decline in borrowing as percentage of average export earnings	−1.6	−2.5	−16.5
	Percentage change from case F4 to case F5		
Private consumption	−2.7	−2.5	−5.8
Total investments	3.3	−5.5	−0.3
Export of commodities (f.o.b.)	−0.6	−3.5	−6.7
Imports of commodities (c.i.f.)	−0.6	−11.1	−11.2
Import bill for foreign unskilled labor	−23.2	−77.0	−100.0
Disguised urban unemployment	25.0	0.0	26.5
Dual solution			
Foreign exchange in relation to the cost of living	2.0	5.9	9.1
Foreign exchange in relation to capacity in machinery	4.1	10.6	13.1
Wage differential between *bachelier lettres* and unskilled urban worker	8.7	3.2	8.1

a. Optimal savings and free trade in both case F5 and case F4. In Case F5, the inflow of capital is reduced in 1975, in 1980, and, especially, in 1985, because net capital flow is constrained to be zero in 1990. The relative loss in the maximand is 3.2 percent.

any borrowing from abroad in commercial markets.[4] By setting a ceiling on debt servicing in 1990, the Ivorization constraint reduces the amounts that it is optimal to borrow in earlier years. The reduction in borrowings is shown as a percentage of export earnings in the first row of Table 6.7.[5]

Because of reduced inflows of capital, private consumption declines, and the value of the objective function falls 3.2 percent. Imports are reduced more severely than exports. Although the number of migrants from neighboring countries is severely curtailed, disguised urban unemployment increases, and the wage differential between skilled and unskilled labor widens. It is optimal to reduce borrowing as late as possible—that is, in the decision year 1985. During that year, the shadow price of foreign exchange increases 9 percent. On the whole, the price of reaching this goal of self-reliance is high.

4. Borrowings at special terms (from the World Bank or the International Monetary Fund) is still allowed, but the level of such borrowings is taken as exogenous.
5. Borrowings in case F5 minus borrowings in case F4 divided by average export earnings for F4 and F5.

Table 6.8 The Effects on Economic Aggregates and Shadow Prices of the Removal of Tariffs on Imports

				Comparison		
Item	*F1/T1*	*F12 T4* / *T5 T1*		*2A/3A*	*2/3*
		F12 T4			

Item	*F1/T1*	*F12 T4* *T5 T1*	*2A/3A*	*2/3*
Environment				
Reduction of estimated scope for import substitution	no	yes	yes	yes
Constraint on savings	no	no	no	yes
Experiment				
Suppression of tariffs on all imports	X	X		
30 percent excise tax on beverages, 30 percent subsidy on housing		X		
Suppression of tariffs on competing imports only			X	X
Effect of reducing tariffs on imports		*Percentage variation*		
Discounted utility of private consumption	4.4	3.2	2.4	1.6
Rent on plantations and forests as share of the maximand	40.0	38.0	10.0	8.0
Year 1980				
Private consumption (quantity index at 1970 prices)	2	3	1	2
Disguised urban unemployment	−14	−15	−5	−13
Exports f.o.b.	42	39	18	12
Imports c.i.f.	49	33	17	16
Foreign exchange deflated by cost-of-living index	13	10	9	5
Year 1985				
Private consumption (quantity index at 1970 prices)	3	1	3	1
Disguised urban unemployment	−25	−12	−10	−15
Exports f.o.b.	53	49	23	16
Imports c.i.f.	59	45	26	23
Foreign exchange deflated by cost-of-living index	13	15	9	+9
Foreign exchange deflated by resource-cost index	12	17	9	+8
Foreign exchange over efficiency wage of professionals ($\lambda = 5$)	8	14	13	+1
Foreign exchange over rental value of machinery equipment	21	24	1	22
Foreign exchange over rental value of buildings	10	13	11	4

Table 6.8. *(continued)*

		Comparison		
Item	*F1/T1*	*F12 T4* / *T5 T1*	*2A/3A*	*2/3*
Implied elasticities of exports and imports in relation to the devaluation (foreign exchange deflated by cost of living)[a]	3.9 (0.6)	3.4 (0.4)	2.5 (0.5)	2.5 (0.6)

a. Average for 1980 and 1985, with standard deviation in parenthesis.

Protecting Manufacturing Industries

The effect of imposing tariffs on manufactured imports has already been illustrated (Figure 5.1 and Table 5.1). The results over time of the removal of tariffs on imports can now be compared with four different experiments, which are described in the upper part of Table 6.8. In the first two experiments, tariffs are removed on all nonagricultural imports. In the last two, they are removed only for those manufactured goods which compete directly with domestic production—that is, for which there is a make-or-buy choice.

The purpose of tariffs is to protect industrial production against competition from imports. The average rate of effective protection is close to 60 percent (see Chapter 13). It is much higher than the average nominal rate of ad valorem tariffs, because the share of value added by many import-substitution industries is low and because there is no subsidy on exports. When tariffs are removed, prices of imported goods decline in relation to those of domestically produced goods. This was represented on Figure 5.1 by an upward shift of the demand curve for imports. The new equilibrium point (*F* instead of *T*) corresponds to a higher volume of imports and exports and to a higher value of the shadow price of foreign exchange—that is, to a devaluation.[6]

The lower part of Table 6.8 shows that, depending on the year and the experiment, the increments in the volume of imports range from 16 percent to 59 percent and those of the price of foreign exchange from 5 percent to 15 percent. Elasticities of the volume of trade in relation to the price of foreign exchange have been computed by least squares. The elasticity is equal to 2.5 in the last two experiments; it reaches 3.9

6. CFAF1 billion of foreign exchange can buy more imported goods when those goods are valued at c.i.f. than when they are valued at c.i.f. plus tariffs.

Figure 6.2. The Effects of Grants on Private Consumption and Domestic Saving (Table 6.14)

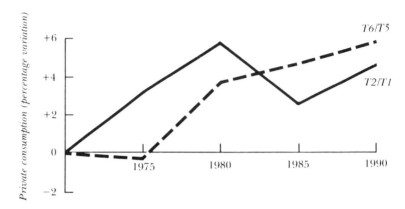

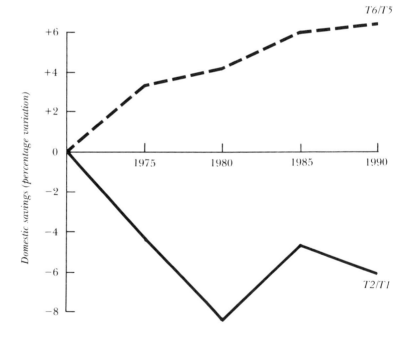

━ ━ ━ *Grant in 1975, with a constraint on savings (Experiment T6/T5)*
────── *Continuous grant, without a constraint on savings (Experiment T2/T1)*

in the first, where the scope for import substitution is greater. The increase in trade is always associated with a gain in social welfare. Whereas the increase in the volume of imports ranges from 16 percent to 59 percent, however, the increase in the value of the maximand ranges from 1.6 percent to 4.4 percent. A 10 percent increase in the volume of trade is therefore associated with a 1 percent increase in welfare.[7]

Because a removal of tariffs does not affect the shadow prices of all primary resources equally (second to sixth rows from the bottom of Table 6.8), it is not possible to forecast the effects of tariffs accurately by simply computing "effective rates of protection." It is necessary to compare the solutions of the model with and without tariffs. The effect of tariffs on the trade pattern is shown in Table 6.9. As these data derived from sectoral solutions are much more disaggregated, the comparison is limited to the removal of tariffs on competing imports only and to a single year (1980).[8] Half the increase in exports originates with the urban sector (Table 6.9a); the gain in urban exports comes entirely from processed foods and textile products (Table 6.9b). On the other hand, the increment in total imports is accounted for entirely by larger imports of urban goods (Table 6.9a). Since the volume of noncompeting imports (those items which cannot be produced locally) remains almost unchanged, the increase occurs in the fourteen products for which there is a make-or-buy choice (Table 6.9c). With tariffs, local production accounted for 65 percent of the total supply of the fourteen products listed; imports accounted for the remaining 35 percent. Without tariffs, the share of domestic production falls to 45 percent and that of imports rises to 55 percent. As shown from the breakdown by branches, extreme specialization, which is a frequent implication of linear programming models, does not occur here (see Chapter 12).

It has been noted before that free trade stimulates employment. Table 6.10 shows the effect of removing tariffs on industrial imports. The upper part of the table deals with the demand for labor in the rural and urban sectors. In all years, employment increases. In 1975, 35 percent of the additional jobs are created in the urban sector and 65 percent in the rural. In 1985, the proportions are reversed: 60 percent of the additional employment occurs in the urban sector. The lower part of the table shows that half the additional jobs are taken by

7. Discounted utility of consumption and GDP are fairly sluggish indicators.
8. The solution of the disaggregated urban model is derived from the solution of the central model, as explained in Chapter 12.

migrants from the neighboring countries. The other half contributes to a reduction of disguised urban unemployment

The removal of tariffs stimulates employment for two reasons. First, the better allocation of resources induces a higher level of activity. Second, export industries are more labor intensive than import-substitution industries. As was noted in Chapter 3 (Table 3.7), gaining one dollar through exports instead of saving it through import substitution requires more unskilled workers and fewer highly skilled workers. In 1980, expatriates remain the marginal source of supply for the latter, and each of their man-years costs approximately forty times that of an unskilled worker—hence the increase in the total number of

Table 6.9. *The Effects on the Structure of Trade of the Removal of Tariffs on Competing Nonfood Imports in 1980 (Cases 2A and 3A)*

6.9a.   *Exports and Imports by Sector*

	Absolute increase (case 2A minus case 3A) (billions of CFAF)	
Sector of origin	Exports f.o.b.	Imports c.i.f.
Rural sector (south)	+10.6	+0.1
Urban sector	+17.5[a]	+30.0
Iron mine[b]	+7.4	−2.9
Total	+35.5	+28.0

6.9b.   *Exports of the Urban Sector by Category*

	Absolute values (billions of CFAF at market prices)		Relative increase between case 3A and case 2A (percent)
Type of urban export	Case 2A	Case 3A	
Processed food	14.7	9.0	63
Textile products	28.5	10.0	185
Petroleum products	12.5	12.5	0
Transfer industries	15.0	15.0	0
Miscellaneous	0.0	0.0	0
Total	70.0	46.5	52
Total (at f.o.b. prices)	(50.9)	(33.4)	(53)

a. 17.5 = 50.9 − 33.4 (last row of Table 6.9b).
b. The mine is implemented earlier. By 1980 it exports more and requires less of imported capital goods.

Table 6.9.   *(continued)*

6.9c.   *Imports of the Urban Sector by Category*

Type of urban import	Absolute values (billions of CFAF at market prices)		Share of supply (percent)	
	Case 2A	Case 3A	Case 2A	Case 3A
First transformation of metals	0.9	0.0	4.9	0.0
Construction materials	1.9	0.0	12.1	0.0
Chemicals and pharmaceuticals	11.2	9.8	53.7	46.7
Furniture	3.0	0.0	70.3	0.0
Assembly of vehicles	16.5	13.8	64.5	56.7
Electrical and mechanical equipment	38.2	32.7	55.4	48.8
Agricultural machinery	0.0	0.0	0.0	0.0
Basic fabrics	34.3	19.9	72.9	53.9
Industrial textiles	7.1	0.0	84.9	0.0
Clothing	11.7	0.0	77.2	0.0
Vegetable oil products	5.2	0.0	50.3	0.0
Rubber products	1.0	0.0	13.4	0.0
Paper products	8.0	5.7	62.1	41.5
Glass products and ceramics	0.9	0.7	51.2	38.9
Total competing imports	38.9	82.7	55.3	35.5
Noncompeting imports	93.6	92.9	100.0	100.0
Total urban imports	232.5	175.6	. . .	. . .

Table 6.10. *The Effects of the Removal of Tariffs on the Labor Market (Cases F1 and T1)* (Thousands of jobs)

Item	Difference between case F1 (free trade) and case T1 (tariffs)		
	1975	1980	1985
Additional labor demand			
Rural sector	29.4	28.5	39.6
Formal urban sector	11.2	27.9	58.4
Total	40.6	56.4	98.0
Sources of supply			
Informal urban sector	14.4	21.0	55.7
Foreign unskilled labor	29.4	37.8	41.4
Foreign skilled labor	−3.2	−2.4	0.9

jobs created and the reduction in the number of expatriates, as shown in Table 6.10.

The reduction of industrial protection also modifies the internal price structure. In the first experiment (removal of all tariffs on nonagricultural imports), prices of agricultural consumer goods increase 25 percent in relation to those of nonagricultural consumer goods in 1980; rents accruing to the plantations in the south rise 40 percent (Table 6.8). The improvement in the agricultural terms of trade reduces the wage differential between urban and rural unskilled workers and, consequently, the incentive to migrate from rural to urban areas. This also contributes to the reduction of disguised urban unemployment.

Only four experiments are reported in Table 6.8. Six other experiments (not reported in this book) have been conducted at various stages of the work. These have led to forty observations (four decision years in each experiment). The removal of tariffs led to a lower level of disguised urban unemployment in thirty-two out of forty observations. In the remaining eight observations (some of the decision years in some of the experiments), the level of employment was not materially affected.

Excise Tax and Consumption Subsidies

Not all price changes associated with a reduction of tariffs may be welcome. Consider the group of consumer goods called beverages, which consists mainly of wines, liquors, and tobacco. The supplies are largely imported. If tariffs on these goods are removed, consumption will increase, which is precisely what the Ministry of Health wants to avoid. In the model, excise taxes take care of this problem. The proceeds of the excise tax on alcoholic beverages may be used to subsidize consumer prices of other products considered more valuable socially. Granting a subsidy of 30 percent on housing and levying an excise tax of 30 percent on beverages represent the strategies analyzed in Table 6.11.

Start with the first experiment summarized on the left side of Table 6.11. In 1975, the price paid by consumers for housing does not decline 30 percent as was intended. It declines only 18 percent because the price before subsidy rises 18 percent.[9] The housing subsidy generates a

9. The 30 percent subsidy is given by the following calculation: $(1 - 0.176)/(1 + 0.177) = 1 - 0.3$.

Table 6.11. The Effects on Quantities Consumed and on Prices of Granting a 30 Percent Subsidy on Housing and Levying a 30 Percent Tax on Beverages in 1975, 1980, and 1985
(Percentage change)

Economic variable	Experimental F3/F1 [a]			Experiment F12/F1 [b]		
	1975	1980	1985	1975	1980	1985
Quantities						
Consumption of housing	13	21	19	22	27	22
Consumption of beverages	−14	−10	−12	−14	−11	−14
Activity of the construction sector	12	−1	9	1	−3	6
Investment in construction	18	−2	17	3	−2	8
Total investment	2	0	3	−2	−4	−3
Exports f.o.b.	−9	0	0	0	0	−1
Imports c.i.f.	−8	−1	1	2	3	1
Disguised urban unemployment	18	0	3	32	17	21
Prices [b]						
Housing (price paid by consumers)	−18	−25	−30	−29	−36	−33
Housing (price before subsidies)	18	7	2	1	−6	−3
Beverages (price paid by consumers)	31	35	33	31	30	39
Beverages (price before tax)	+1	4	2	1	0	7
Rental value of buildings	19	8	2	1	−7	−3
Foreign exchange	−1	3	1	1	1	8

a. The experiments are defined as follows:

	Cases			Experiments	
	F1	F3	F12	F3/F1	F12/F1
Free trade and optimal savings	X	X	X		
Subsidy on housing and tax on beverages		X	X	X	X
Reduced scope for import substitution			X		X
Maximand (index and percentage variation)	100.0	98.9	98.0	−1.1	−2.0

b. Deflated by cost-of-living index.

boom in the construction sector. In 1975, investment in construction rises 18 percent and the activity of the construction sector 12 percent. Despite that, the rental value of buildings (which is the major component of the cost of housing services) rises 19 percent. The rental value of buildings does not return to its original level before 1985. Only then do consumers benefit fully from the 30 percent subsidy on housing.

In the first experiment, the aims of the scheme are fully reached after one decade. Because the scheme was launched when capital was fully utilized, its initial effect was partly inflationary. In the second experiment (right side of Table 6.11), the scheme is launched in the middle of a recession.[10] In 1975, the boost in housing is just what is needed to avoid a drop in the activity of the construction industry and in the rental value of buildings before subsidies (both actually rise 1 percent in 1975). Prices paid by consumers for housing decline 29 percent. The aim of the scheme is reached from the beginning.

The Scope for Import Substitution

A recession in 1975 has been simulated in the last experiment by introducing, together with the tax-with-subsidy scheme, a constraint on the scope for import substitution. The specific effect of this constraint is the object of the two experiments reported in Table 6.12.

The distinction between competing and noncompeting imports cannot be altogether satisfactory. Suppose that the items which could be produced locally were defined too optimistically; this error in estimation is now corrected. What are the implications of the correction? Table 6.12 shows that they are not quite the same with a constraint on savings and tariffs (right side) as with savings unconstrained and free trade (left side).

Start with the common features. In both cases, a number of items formerly produced locally must now be imported. The volume of imports and the premium on foreign exchange therefore rise. At the same time, the demand for capital and its rental values declines (the recession simulated in the previous experiment). Because export activities require less highly skilled labor than do import-substitution activities, the demand for highly skilled labor declines and the import bill of expatriates falls. In 1980 and 1985, the extent of the decline ranges from 21 percent to 27 percent. The import of engineers is replaced by the import of manufactured goods.

Turn to the differences. The increase in imports is higher with than without tariffs, a situation which could have been expected. With tariffs, a larger share of the supply originates from import-substitution activities. Since the tariff solution is more severely affected by the constraint imposed in this experiment (less scope for import-substitution), it might have been expected that the loss in the maximand would be larger. The opposite occurs. Because tariffs were encouraging import substitution unduly, reducing its scope does not result in a large welfare loss.[11]

10. The recession is simulated by reducing the scope for import substitution, as in experiment F12/F4, reported below in the left side of Table 6.12. In 1975 the effect of this measure alone is to reduce both the volume of physical investments and the rental value of buildings 10 percent. Here this is called a recession.

11. The decline in the shadow price of savings should be noted.

Table 6.12. *The Effects on Quantities Consumed and on Prices of a Reduction in the Estimated Scope for Import Substitution* [a]
(Percentage variation)

Economic variable	Experiment F12/F4 (no tariffs, no constraint on savings)				Experiment T5/T4 (tariffs and constraint on savings)			
	1975	1980	1985	1990	1975	1980	1985	1990
Quantities								
Private consumption	1	0	−3	−5	−1	−2	−1	0
Total investments	−5	−5	−4	−4	−9	1	2	0
Physical investments (endogenous)	−10	−3	−3	−5	−19	1	7	1
Human investments	7	−9	−9	−4	12	1	7	1
Exports (f.o.b.)	8	0	0	0	14	2	2	2
Imports (c.i.f.)	10	4	1	0	18	15	11	2
Import bill of expatriates	−7	−21	−24	0	−21	−27	−27	0
Imported unskilled workers	−20	−30	...	−11	−22	...	...	−2
Nationals employed in highly skilled jobs	0	4	−3	−5	0	5	3	0
Nationals employed in medium-skilled jobs	−1	−4	−4	−12	−2	−9	−3	1
Disguised unemployment	25	17	21	9	26	17	3	0
Prices								
Foreign exchange	5	3	6	3	10	4	−2	2
Capacity in buildings	−10	−2	−8	−1	−49	−24	−11	−5
Savings	...	...	...	...	−44	−19	−20	−8

a. The value of the maximand is reduced 2.1 percent in experiment F12/F4 and 0.8 percent in experiment T5/T4.

Foreign Aid

Variations in the level of foreign aid are largely beyond the control of the receiving country. Nevertheless, the impact of an additional grant may be affected by the policies followed in the receiving country. This is illustrated by the three experiments summarized in Tables 6.13 and 6.14. In the first experiment, the grant is assumed to be permanent; it amounts, on the average, to 7 percent of what export earnings would have been without the grant. In the second and third, the grant is temporary; it amounts to 9.4 to 10 percent of export earnings, but it is given only during the first five years of the planning period.[12] In the

12. In 1975 the grant is equal to CFAF16 billion, which is approximately equivalent to US$70 million.

Table 6.13. A Permanent Grant in Foreign Exchange versus a Temporary Grant, with Optimized and Constrained Savings (Experiments T2/T1, F6/F4, and T6/T5)

Time profile of the grant and variables affected	T2/T1 (Tariff, no constraint on savings)	F6/F4 (No tariff, no constraint on savings)	T6/T5 (Tariff and constraint on savings)
Grant as percentage of export earnings without grant		*Percentage variation*	
1975	4.3	9.4	10.0
1980	7.8	0.0	0.0
1985	8.8	0.0	0.0
1990	8.0	0.0	0.0
Implications over the entire time period			
Discounted utility of maximand	5.35	2.86	4.64
Rent of forestries and plantations as a fraction of the maximand	−8.2	−3.5	−11.5
Indexes[a]		*Index: T6/T5 = 1*	
Levels of grants (present value)	1.97	1.00	1.00
Efficiency			
Increment in maximand over present value of grant	0.57	0.59	1.00
Present value of increments in GDP over present value of grant	0.35	0.58	1.00
		Multiplier	
Present value of increments in GDP over present value of grant	1.44	2.39	4.16

a. All flows are discounted at 10 percent a year.

Table 6.14. Average Effect of the Grant throughout the Planning Period (Experiments T2/T1, F6/F4, and T6/T5) [a]

Economic variable	T2/T1	F6/F4	T6/T5
		Percentage variation	
Private consumption	4.0	2.5	3.5
Domestic savings	−5.9	−0.7	5.0
Investments	1.1	0.1	8.8
Exports	−3.5	−0.5	−0.8
Imports	5.0	2.2	5.3
		Percentage premium	
Average premium on savings without grant	0.0	0.0	57
Average premium on savings with grant	0.0	0.0	33

a. Private consumption declines slightly at the beginning of the planning period but increases substantially at the end. More detailed data, analyzed by five-year periods, are given in Table 6.20.

first two experiments there is no constraint on savings, but in the third, one is introduced.

The third case is the success story. Domestic savings increase an average of 5 percent. A grant of $1 at the beginning of the period induces a gain of $4 in GDP.[13] The multiplier effect is large. In the second case, domestic savings are hardly affected; a grant of $1 is worth US$2.4 in GDP. In the first case, domestic savings decline 5.9 percent on an average; a grant of $1 is worth only US$1.4 of increased GDP.

When the grant is permanent (T2/T1), most of it goes into consumption. Investments increase only marginally; greater imports are secured with smaller exports. This behavior is rational if the rate of preference for the present remains unchanged and if it is believed that the grant is permanent. When permanent income rises, it would indeed be unreasonable to reduce consumption.

With a temporary grant and a constraint on savings, the story is quite different. The windfall income may be what was required to launch a program which had to be postponed because of a lack of cash. This is precisely what occurs in the third experiment (T6/T5). The full amount of the grant received in 1975 goes into additional investments, as shown in Tables 6.14 and 6.20. Without the grant, investment and savings were below their unconstrained optimal level. During 1975, the premium of savings over consumption was 41 percent. With the grant, the premium falls to 11 percent; the constraint on savings is no longer significant.

If the principal aim of international aid is efficiency, there is a strong case for temporary aid (comparisons F6/F4 and T6/T5). Planning for inflows of long-term aid may be counterproductive.

If the major aim is equity, international aid should contribute to an increase in consumption as well as investments in the poor countries. The first experiment (T2/T1) satisfies this income-redistribution objective.

The Terms of Trade

In several respects, a decline in the terms of trade is comparable to a reduction in the volume of grants received. The similarities and

---

13. The coefficient of four is a measure of the ratio between the present value of the increments to the GDP throughout the planning period and the present value of the grants received. Present values are measures of the sum of the annual increments (to GDP or to grants) discounted at the rate of 10 percent a year.

differences can be noted by comparing the experiment F10/F11 in Table 6.15 with the experiment F6/F4 in the middle of Table 6.13

In the years 1975 and 1980, the f.o.b. prices for exports are 10 percent lower in case F10 than in case F11. Exports valued f.o.b. decline by more than 10 percent; the volume of exports declines 5 percent on an average and the shadow price of foreign exchange rises 5 percent. The decline of the terms of trade does not affect the shadow prices of all primary domestic resources equally. The price ratio between foreign exchange and domestic resources increases 7 to 13 percent in the case of physical capacities and only 2 percent in the case of professional labor.

In the years 1985 and 1990, the f.o.b. prices for agricultural exports are the same in cases F6 and F5. After the price recovery, the value of exports and the shadow price of foreign exchange return almost to their original level (the difference between cases F10 and F11 becoming negligible).

During the first decade, private consumption declines 4 percent. This

Table 6.15. The Decline in the Terms of Trade (Experiment F10/F11, Optimal Savings and Free-Market Solutions) [a]

Economic variable	1975	1980	1985	1990
Postulated percentage decline in terms of trade	−10.0	−10.0	0.0	0.0
Primal solution				
Increase (+) or decline (−) in borrowing as percentage of average export earnings	−1.4	5.2	1.4	0.0
	Percentage variation between Cases F10 and F11			
Private consumption	−3.9	−4.5	−4.3	−6.8
Total investments	−11.9	−2.0	−4.6	−4.3
Exports of commodities (f.o.b.)	−11.5	−19.5	−3.2	−1.2
Imports of commodities (c.i.f.)	−17.2	−11.5	−5.2	−0.8
Import bill for foreign unskilled labor	−8.9	−51.8	−75.9	−45.9
Disguised urban unemployment	58.9	0.0	9.3	0.0
Dual solution				
Foreign exchange in relation to the cost of living	4.6	5.6	1.8	2.5
Foreign exchange in relation to high-school graduates ($\lambda = 5$)	2.3	2.6	2.1	10.2
Foreign exchange in relation to capacity in machinery	10.0	7.4	−1.9	1.9
Wage differential ($\lambda = 5$ over $\lambda = 1$)	10.2	4.9	4.4	−1.5

a. The decline in the maximand is 6.4 percent.

is a steep fall, but Ivory Coast exports account for 35 percent of the GDP. Domestic savings fall more steeply than private consumption (-12 percent), which affects investments adversely. During the second decade, consumption does not return to its original level. The export earnings forgone in the first decade have reduced capital accumulation and, thereby, the growth potential of the second decade.

The effect of lower export prices in the 1970s has been somewhat mitigated by the possibility of borrowing more from abroad on commercial terms. Since the model is optimized simultaneously through the entire planning period, it is assumed that the variations in the terms of trade across the entire horizon are perfectly predictable. Because it is known in 1975 that "things will grow worse before they become better," a little less is borrowed in 1975 in order that much more can be borrowed in 1980 when the fall in prices hurts the most.

A 10 percent decline in the terms of trade in the course of ten years results in a 6 percent loss in the value of the maximand (Table 6.15). A grant equal to 10 percent of export earnings during five years led to a 3 percent gain in the value of the maximand (experiment F6/F4 in Table 6.13). It was noted, in the preceding section, that temporary grants are more efficient than permanent grants. In case of shortfalls in export earnings, therefore, compensatory lending appears to be an efficient form of international aid.

The series of experiments just reviewed show that the impact of a particular policy measure is not always easily predictable. Without a model, one may easily neglect some interactions that have an important bearing on the ultimate results. The general equilibrium model, which takes these interactions systematically into account, may help in avoiding such errors and in finding the combination of measures likely to achieve the desired objective. The results of the model could not, however, influence policy decisions if the persons making them could not be convinced of the soundness of the results. The causal relations and the economic rationale leading to the results need to be explained in relatively simple terms. It has been attempted to provide such an explanation in this chapter which concludes with a summary of the findings.

Policy Options

The free-market solution led to a rosy picture with respect to aggregate growth. It nevertheless raised a number of problems: depopulation of the north, disguised urban unemployment, high housing costs, growing foreign claims on returns from domestic investments, and increasing disparities in income.

In the free-market solution, agricultural employment in the savanna zone falls from 24 percent of the total labor force in 1970 to 8 percent in 1990 (see Table 3.3). This trend may be reversed by an investment program financed out of public funds. The effect of the program is to increase in 1990 the share of agricultural employment in the north from 8 percent to 20 percent. The cost of the program can be assessed with partial- or general-equilibrium analysis. The partial-equilibrium analysis conducted at the sectoral level is misleading because it ignores the effect on the rest of the economy of the additional investments required by the program. The general-equilibrium analysis has the advantage of taking intersectoral linkages into account. It leads to different results depending on the assumptions made of the strength of the fiscal authorities. If the government cannot raise tax rates, the growth of the GDP is appreciably curtailed. If the government has enough power to adjust tax rates, it becomes optimal to compensate for the loss of efficiency resulting from socially oriented investments by increasing public savings. In the latter case, the GDP does not decline, and the loss of aggregate consumption is only temporary.

Given the specifications of the model, no satisfactory way was found for reducing disguised urban unemployment below the levels reached in the free-market solution. One reason for this failure is that free trade stimulates agricultural exports and urban processing industries, both of which are more labor intensive than the urban import-substitution industries. The essential requirements of the latter are capital and skilled labor. Prohibiting immigration from neighboring countries was not a satisfactory solution. It induced an increase in agricultural wages and, therefore, a reduction of migrations from rural to urban areas. With the migration behavior simulated in the model, however, the effect on migration flows was not large enough. Disguised unemployment did not disappear in the cities, and the output of the southern plantations was adversely affected by labor shortages.[14] In addition, closing the borders to migrant labor penalized neighboring Sahelian countries, which are not as well endowed as the Ivory Coast.

In the free-market solution, all expatriates are replaced by nationals in the 1980s without the necessity of a date being set by which Ivorization must be completed. This requires a considerable training effort. Recurrent expenditures in postprimary education increase in relation to total recurrent public expenditures from 18 percent in 1970

---

14. A limitation on migrations from abroad could be combined with constraints on internal migrations, but the effect of such constraints was not simulated in the model.

to 24 percent in 1980. Because ten years elapse between the time a person enters high school and the time he graduates from a university, and because the replacement of expatriates is a one-time demand, it is optimal to curtail the growth rate of enrollments in high schools severely in the late 1970s, long before Ivorization is completed. It may be extremely difficult, however, for the authorities to curtail the growth of enrollments at the time that the number of expatriates is at its peak. The shortage of graduates in the 1970s could therefore turn into a large surplus in the 1980s. This risk does not exist in the model because demand and supply are optimized simultaneously throughout the planning period, but the risk exists in the real world.

By the end of the planning period, expatriates are no longer needed but the use of foreign capital remains optimal. The cost of achieving Ivorization of capital by 1990 would be high. This would imply a significant reduction of inflows of capital in earlier years and would result in lower investments and slower growth. In addition, it would penalize low-income groups more heavily than high-income groups. If the use of foreign capital could be optimized according to national objectives, the limitation on inflows of capital should probably be the amounts which foreigners are prepared to lend.

Although tariffs on imports are moderate in comparison with those imposed by most developing countries, some gains could be made by reducing protection for a number of import-substitution industries. In the experiments conducted, the removal of tariffs on manufactured imports raised the social welfare index (discounted utility) by 3 to 4 percent and resulted in a substantial transfer of income from the urban to the rural sector, most of the gain going to the south. To maintain the balance of payments in equilibrium after removal of the tariffs, the currency would need to be devalued by approximately 13 percent in real terms. Uniform tariffs on imports, together with export subsidies could lead to a situation close to the free-trade solution.[15]

The composition of the pattern of consumption resulting from free trade may not be considered socially optimal. Society may attach different values to particular consumer goods (such as housing and alcoholic beverages or tobacco) from those attached by individual consumers. Excise taxes and consumer subsidies have been used here as the policy instrument for adjusting the free-trade pattern of consumption to social preferences. This instrument is more efficient than tariffs

---

15. The world demand for imports of coffee and cocoa from the Ivory Coast is less than infinitely elastic. Consequently, it would be optimal to impose an export tax in the absence of any tariff on imports.

on imports. Since it penalizes both domestic production and imports, it does not stimulate the production of inefficient domestic industries.

In one experiment, a subsidy scheme for housing was launched during a period of full employment, and the initial effect was inflationary. In another experiment, such a scheme was launched in a recession year; the result was stimulation of the activity of the construction industry without concomitant inflation. The housing scheme did not, however, relieve the unemployment problem. The reason may be that no technological choice is available to the construction industry in the model, and the introduction of such choices would be an obvious improvement.

Policy changes may be required to reflect a modification in the relative emphasis placed on different objectives. They may also be needed as responses to events beyond control of the government. This was the reason for simulating technical changes in the scope for import substitution, modifications in the level of foreign aid, and variations in the terms of trade. The experiments reported here are purely illustrative. In practice, the experiments must be designed especially for the particular problem under investigation.

Appendix

The experiments reported in this chapter were based on comparisons between the thirty-three solutions specified in Tables 6.16 and 6.17. Policy instruments (or factors beyond government control) are identified horizontally and solutions vertically. When changes are cumulated from one solution to the next, the bloc is triangular; this applies to solutions 2, 3, 4, 5, and 6 of Table 6.16, which correspond to the five projections of the progressive drive toward autarchy. After the review of the first set of experiments by the Ivorian authorities, the educational submodel was revised, and the economywide model was solved again according to the specifications given in Table 6.17. Most of the binary comparisons reported subsequently are based on the second set of solutions.

In view of the interdependence between policies and events, the effect of a given measure must be assessed by solving the model with and without that measure within a specified environment. Nevertheless, the sign of the effect (if not its magnitude) may often be foreseen. From the various experiments conducted, an attempt has been made in Table 6.18 to indicate the likely sign of the effects of various policies and measures on major economic variables. The sign may not remain

Policy Experiments **[121]**

Table 6.16. Cumulated Changes

Policy instrument	Solution														
	1A	1	1B	2A	2	3A	3	4	5	5A	5B	5C	5D	5E	6
Imposition of tariffs on noncompeting imports	X	X	X	X	X	X	X	X	X	X	X	X	X	X	X
Imposition of a ceiling on new high-school enrollments in 1975		X	X	X	X	X	X	X	X	X	X	X	X	X	X
Imposition of a constraint on savings	X	X	X		X		X	X	X	X	X	X	X	X	X
Downward revision of the scope for import substitution and for promotion of industrial exports[a]				X	X	X	X	X	X	X	X	X	X	X	X
Imposition of tariffs on competing imports						X	X	X	X	X	X	X	X	X	X
Reduction of capital imports in 1975, 1980, and 1985[b]								L	L	L	L	H	H	H	H
Prohibition of entry to foreign agricultural workers								X	X	X	X	X	X	X	X
Implementation of a rural employment program in the north		X							X	X	X	X	X	X	X
Elimination of the iron-ore project										X	X	X	X	X	X
Elimination of the Riviera project												X			
Restriction of entry to foreign skilled labor[c]													L	H	H

a. This reflects an error in estimation rather than a policy decision.

b. L = light constraint (net capital outflow cannot exceed CFAF15 billion in any year); H = heavy constraint (net capital outflow prohibited in every year).

c. L = light constraint (ceiling on entry of foreigners in 1980 and 1985); H = heavy constraint (low ceiling on entry of foreigners in 1980; entry of foreigners prohibited in 1985).

constant throughout the planning period. Thus, when the constraint on savings is tightened (first column of Table 6.18), more is consumed today and less tomorrow. In the second row of the first column, the plus sign at the left indicates that consumption increases at the beginning (1975 and 1980), while the minus sign at the right indicates that it declines at the end (1985 and 1990). (The effect from year to year can be seen in Table 6.19.) In the case of the employment programs, the sign of the effect depends on whether there is a

Table 6.17. Controlled Experiments[a]

Assumption	F1	F2	F3	F4	F5	F6	F7	F8	F9	F10	F11	F12	T1	T2	T3	4	T5	T6
Policies																		
Free trade[b]	X	X	X	X	X	X	X	X	X	X	X	X						
Imposition of tariffs[c]													X	X	X	X	X	X
Imposition of constraints on savings[d]															L	H	H	H
Implementation of a rural employment program in the north				X														
30 percent excise tax on beverages; 30 percent subsidy on housing			X	X	X	X	X	X				X						
Reduction of capital imports in 1975, 1980, and 1985[e]					X													
Data																		
Grants received[f]						0						C			0			
10 percent increase in agricultural export prices in 1985 and 1990							X											
10 percent decline in agricultural export prices in 1975 and 1980								X	X	X								
10 percent increase in the estimation of agricultural resources									X									
10 percent increase in industrial export prices											X							
Reduction of the estimated scope for import substitution												X					X	X
Elimination of the intermediate import-substitution strategy	X	X	X															

a. This set of solutions differs from the one presented in Table 6.16 in two principal respects: First, the educational data were revised and the decomposition of skill categories increased. Second, agricultural export prices were revised upward for 1975 and 1980.
b. All tariffs on imports are eliminated.
c. 1973 import duties imposed on all imports.
d. L = light constraint; H = heavy constraint. Without constraint, the rate of taxation (in relation to the GDP) is a variable optimized. With constraint the rate of taxation is given.
e. Borrowing is reduced by prohibiting a net capital outflow in the terminal year, 1990.
f. C = continuous grants; 0 = grant received once, in 1975.

Table 6.18. Summary of Policy Measures

Economic variable	Reduction of the rate of overall taxation		Increase in agricultural employment in the north		Grants received		Constraint on savings		Temporary loss in terms of trade	Reduction in borrowing from abroad	Reduction in tariffs on imports	Reduction in scope for import substitution
	Yes	*No*	*Yes*	*No*	*Permanent*	*Temporary*	*Yes*	*No*	*No*	*No*	*Yes and No*	*Yes and No*
Quantities (primal solution)[a]												
Gross domestic product	−				+	+	+		−	−	+	−
Average consumption	+	−		+	+	+	+		−	−	+	−
Domestic savings	−	+		+	−	+	−		−	+	− +	−
Borrowing from abroad[b]	−			+	+	−	+		+	−	+	
Investments	−	+		+	−	+	+		−	−	+	+
Exports	−				−	−	+	−	−	+	− +	+
Imports	−			−	+	+	+		−	+	+	+
Employment of highly skilled nationals							+		−	−		
Disguised urban unemployment	+	+		−	+	+	−		+	+	−	+
Prices (dual solution)												
Premium on savings	+		+			−	−		+	−	−	
Rental values of capital stocks	+		+			−	−		+	+		
Premium on foreign exchange			+		−	−	+		+	+	+	+
Premium on foreign capital	+		+		−	−	+		+	+		
Wage differential[c]	+		−		−	−	+		+	+	+	+
Rent of plantations	+		+		−	−	−		−	−	+	+

a. When the impact at the beginning of the planning period is different from that at the end of the period, the sign (+ or −) is shown at the left of the column for the beginning of the period and at the right for the end of the period. No sign is shown where its value is uncertain.

b. Borrowing is limited by repayment capacities.

c. Skilled labor over unskilled.

Table 6.19. A Comparison of the Effects of Light (Case T3) and Heavy (Case T4) Constraints on Savings (Percentage variation)

Economic variable	1975 Experiment		1980 Experiment		1985 Experiment		1990 Experiment	
	T3/T1 a	T4/T1 b	T3/T1 a	T4/T1 b	T3/T1 a	T4/T1 b	T3/T1 a	T4/T1 b
	Primal solution							
Private consumption	2.1	5.4	1.1	2.0	−0.7	−3.5	−3.3	−8.3
Total investments	−6.3	−14.3	−4.0	−12.9	−8.5	−17.7	−5.5	−12.7
Physical investments (endogenous only)	−2.7	−9.9	−5.7	−16.2	−12.9	−28.3	−7.1	−18.1
Human investments	−17.2	−31.8	−3.8	−14.0	−11.2	−8.3	−6.6	−10.3
Difference (−decline, +increase) in the percentage of total investments financed from net foreign capital inflow	−2.0	−4.8	1.3	−1.3	−2.8	−0.9	3.4	9.1
Wage bill of expatriates	−3.8	−8.4	5.7	4.9	−1.0	2.3		
Wage bill of Ivorians employed in highly skilled occupations	0.0	−2.8	−4.5	−7.1	−2.4	−7.9	−6.2	−14.8
Wage bill of Ivorians employed in medium-skilled occupations	0.0	−0.1	−6.6	−12.1	−4.4	−12.3	−5.5	−13.0
Disguised urban unemployment	−2.2	0.6	0.0	1.5	10.7	52.5	0.0	40.0

Dual solution

Cost of living (used as deflator)	1.5	0.0	+2.8	18.5	9.7	31.4
Price of housing services	1.9	2.3	16.9	25.1	6.0	18.5
Devaluation (+) or re-evaluation (−) of domestic currency	1.9	18.3	−2.1	−2.0	1.4	2.0
Value of foreign capital	23.2	86.7	16.9	45.4	18.7	54.1
Rental value of machinery equipment per unit of capacity	1.7	1.0	15.3	35.4	11.9	39.6
Rental value of buildings per unit of capacity	2.4	4.4	12.5	28.0	6.7	20.5
Efficiency wage of urban unskilled workers ($\lambda = 1$)	−0.9	−4.6	−7.0	−10.0	−10.3	−29.9
Efficiency wage of high school graduates ($\lambda = 5$)	−0.3	−0.6	−3.3	−6.3	−1.4	−4.9
Wage differential ($\lambda = 5$ over $\lambda = 1$)	0.7	+4.3	4.3	3.9	9.9	34.8
Foreign exchange over unskilled labor ($\lambda = 1$)	5.5	24.1	4.4	8.7	13.0	42.2
Foreign exchange over rental of buildings	2.0	14.2	−13.1	−23.4	−5.6	−15.0

Entire planning period

Discounted utility of consumption			−0.2	−1.7
Relative returns to stocks of forestries and plantations			11.8	36.1

a. Light constraint on savings.
b. Heavy constraint on savings.

Table 6.20. A Permanent versus a Temporary Grant in Foreign Exchange with Free and Constrained Savings, Selected Years
(Percentage variation)

	1975		
Economic variable	*Experiment T2/T1* [a]	*Experiment F6/F4* [b]	*Experiment T6/T5* [c]
Grant as percentage of domestic savings without grant	4.7	13.5	14.8
Grant as percentage of export earnings without grant	4.3	9.4	10.0
Primal solution			
Private consumption	3.2	2.3	−0.3
Domestic savings	−4.4	−4.0	3.3
Total investments	1.8	0.7	17.2
Exports of commodities	−0.6	−4.0	−3.8
Imports of commodities	6.7	7.5	4.9
Imports of foreign skilled labor	−1.0	3.7	12.9
Ivorians employed in medium skills	0.0	0.6	0.0
Ivorians employed in high skills	0.4	0.0	2.2
Disguised urban unemployment	15.9	20.3	0.0
Dual solution			
Dual value of foreign exchange undeflated	−10.8	−9.8	−13.3
Cost of living used as deflator	−5.1	−8.0	−6.6
Re-evaluation (−) of the domestic currency	−5.9	−2.0	−7.2
Reduction in the saving premium[d]			−73.3
Rental value of machinery equipment per unit of capacity	5.8	6.0	20.7
Efficiency wage of urban unskilled workers ($\lambda = 1$)	1.9	−10.6	−5.2
Efficiency wage of high-school graduates ($\lambda = 5$)	−7.8	−8.6	−6.4
Wage differential ($\lambda = 5$ over $\lambda = 1$)	−9.5	2.2	−1.3
Foreign exchange over unskilled labor ($\lambda = 1$)	−12.5	0.9	−8.6
Foreign exchange over high school graduates ($\lambda = 5$)	−3.2	−1.3	−7.4
Foreign exchange over rental of building capacity	−10.4	−8.4	−16.1
Foreign exchange over rental of machinery capacity	−11.1	−7.5	−23.3

a. Tariff but no savings constraint.
b. No tariff or savings constraint.
c. Tariffs and savings constraints.
d. In case T5, the premium on saving over consumption is equal, respectively, to 41, 48, 51 and 88 percent in each of the time periods.

Table 6.20. *(continued)*

	1980		
Economic variable	*Experiment T2/T1*[a]	*Experiment F6/F4*[b]	*Experiment T6/T5*[c]
Grant as percentage of domestic savings without grant	8.7	0.0	0.0
Grant as percentage of export earnings without grant	7.8	0.0	0.0
Primal solution			
Private consumption	5.8	3.7	3.7
Domestic savings	−8.5	0.7	4.2
Total investments	−0.8	−1.0	3.4
Exports of commodities	−2.1	2.6	−6.7
Imports of commodities	5.5	1.5	5.3
Imports of foreign skilled labor	5.4	−2.1	5.1
Ivorians employed in medium skills	−1.5	1.9	7.0
Ivorians employed in high skills	0.9	5.5	7.5
Disguised urban unemployment	0.0	0.0	−4.0
Dual solution			
Dual value of foreign exchange undeflated	−13.5	−6.2	−9.7
Cost of living used as deflator	−8.2	−6.7	−9.4
Re-evaluation (−) of the domestic currency	−5.6	0.5	−0.2
Reduction in the saving premium[d]			−51.9
Rental value of machinery equipment per unit of capacity	3.8	−2.9	−20.9
Efficiency wage of urban unskilled workers ($\lambda = 1$)	−10.3	−6.5	−3.2
Efficiency wage of high-school graduates ($\lambda = 5$)	−10.3	−6.9	−6.8
Wage differential ($\lambda = 5$ over $\lambda = 1$)	0.0	−0.4	−5.5
Foreign exchange over unskilled labor ($\lambda = 1$)	−3.5	0.4	−6.6
Foreign exchange over high school graduates ($\lambda = 5$)	−3.5	0.8	−1.1
Foreign exchange over rental of building capacity	−12.9	3.5	19.9
Foreign exchange over rental of machinery capacity	−9.3	3.7	26.2

Table 6.20. *(continued)*

	1985		
Economic variable	Experiment T2/T1 [a]	Experiment F6/F4 [b]	Experiment T6/T5 [c]
Grant as percentage of domestic savings without grant	8.8	0.0	0.0
Grant as percentage of export earnings without grant	8.8	0.0	0.0
Primal solution			
Private consumption	2.6	2.9	4.6
Domestic savings	−4.7	−0.6	6.0
Total investments	2.2	−0.6	8.5
Exports of commodities	−5.2	−0.3	4.2
Imports of commodities	3.3	−0.5	8.8
Imports of foreign skilled labor	4.9	−1.3	−13.1
Ivorians employed in medium skills	−0.2	3.3	6.3
Ivorians employed in high skills	0.7	2.1	7.5
Disguised urban unemployment	0.0	0.0	−4.0
Dual solution			
Dual value of foreign exchange undeflated	−9.0	−5.6	−14.6
Cost of living used as deflator	−9.0	−4.4	−15.7
Re-evaluation (−) of the domestic currency	0.0	−1.3	1.4
Reduction in the saving premium [d]			−30.7
Rental value of machinery equipment per unit of capacity	−3.1	−3.4	−8.2
Efficiency wage of urban unskilled workers ($\lambda = 1$)	−10.0	−3.4	−5.8
Efficiency wage of high-school graduates ($\lambda = 5$)	−9.0	−5.5	−14.5
Wage differential ($\lambda = 5$ over $\lambda = 1$)	1.0	−2.1	−9.2
Foreign exchange over unskilled labor ($\lambda = 1$)	1.1	−2.2	−9.3
Foreign exchange over high school graduates ($\lambda = 5$)	0.0	0.0	−0.2
Foreign exchange over rental of building capacity	0.4	3.5	14.5
Foreign exchange over rental of machinery capacity	2.8	2.3	10.4

a. Tariff but no savings constraint.
b. No tariff or savings constraint.
c. Tariffs and savings constraints.
d. In the experiment, the premium on saving over consumption is equal, respectively, to 41, 48, 51 and 88 percent in each of the time periods.

Table 6.20.   *(continued)*

Economic variable	1990		
	Experiment T2/T1 [a]	*Experiment F6/F4* [b]	*Experiment T6/T5* [c]
Grant as percentage of domestic savings without grant	7.0		
Grant as percentage of export earnings without grant	8.0	0.0	0.0
Primal solution			
Private consumption	4.4	0.9	5.9
Domestic savings	−6.0	1.1	6.5
Total investments	1.1	1.1	6.2
Exports of commodities	−5.9	−0.1	3.0
Imports of commodities	4.3	0.1	2.3
Imports of foreign skilled labor	0.0	0.0	0.0
Ivorians employed in medium skills	3.6	1.9	7.5
Ivorians employed in high skills	0.1	1.1	5.7
Disguised urban unemployment	0.0	−10.2	−10.6

a. Tariff but no savings constraint.
b. No tariff or savings constraint.
c. Tariffs and savings constraints.
d. In the experiment, the premium on saving over consumption is equal, respectively, to 41, 48, 51 and 88 percent in each of the time periods.

constraint on savings; thus, a distinction between these two eventualities is made in Table 6.18. Similarly, in the case of grants from abroad, a distinction is made between a permanent grant without a constraint on savings (experiment T2/T1) and a temporary one with a constraint on savings (experiment T6/T5). When the sign of the effect varies with factors not specified in Table 6.18, no plus or minus sign is shown.

The last two tables supplement the summary data presented earlier in discussing two types of experiments. Table 6.19 shows how the effect of tightening the savings constraint varies over time; it relates to the analysis presented early in the chapter. Similarly, Table 6.20 shows how the effects of different types of grants vary over time, which supplements the information given in the section on foreign aid.

The solutions of the disaggregated sectoral models can always be derived from the optimal solution of the central model. For economy of space, however, few of the disaggregated sectoral solutions have been reported in this chapter.

Part Three

Methodology

Chapter 7

The Model

THE CONSTRUCTION OF THE CENTRAL MODEL was influenced by two major considerations. The first was to generate reasonable shadow prices which could be used for decentralized decisionmaking. The second was to keep the size of the model manageable so that a sufficiently large number of experiments could be conducted.

With dynamic optimizing models, it is not too difficult to obtain a reasonable primal solution. It is, however, more difficult to obtain a reasonable dual solution at the same time. By "reasonable" is meant shadow prices which have a straightforward economic interpretation and which vary in much the same way as market prices do. This is achieved here by introducing enough scope for substitution and enough nonlinear relationships while avoiding the use of artificial "smoothing devices."[1]

The problem with general-equilibrium models is that they are either too aggregated to be useful for practical purposes or too large to be manageable. In this two-level planning exercise, the attempt to overcome this difficulty has been made by decomposing the economywide model into a linked series of sectoral models.

This introductory chapter to the methodological part of the volume explains this search for a manageable optimizing model able to generate reasonable shadow prices. The chapter is divided into seven sections. The first highlights the importance of the nonlinear objective function. The following two sections deal with the nonaggregated model. The model is described first in terms of the familiar consumption, investments, production, and trade activities. A distinction is then made between national and sectoral activities in the

1. The introduction of nonlinear relationships, although not common, can be done quite easily in the case of decreasing returns or increasing costs. See Chapter 9, Appendix B; Duloy and Norton (1973); Takayama and Judge (1971).

[133]

manner used by Dantzig and Wolfe (1961) and by Kornai and Liptak (1965). The next three sections deal with the aggregated form of the economywide model. This is the "central model" from which the results described in the previous part of this volume were derived. In the concluding section, the way in which market imperfections and government interventions are simulated in the model is described.

The Nonlinear Maximand

It is most important to reflect decreasing returns in the objective function. Here, this is done by maximizing the discounted value of the utility of consumption—not the discounted value of consumption itself. The utility maximand performs two sets of choices. The first is at the level of aggregate intertemporal choice—the allocation of resources between consumption and savings. Following Ramsey, the level of savings is derived from the optimization process and not from a fixed coefficient measuring the propensity to save. The second set of choices is at the micro-economic level—the allocation of consumption among eight groups of consumer goods. Following both Ramsey and Frisch, utilities derived from consumption are assumed to be additive.

Consider first the intertemporal substitution between consumption and savings. Assume that there is a single commodity in the economy and that this commodity can be transformed into usable capital stocks overnight. By investing one more unit yesterday and one fewer today, the stock of capital is increased by one unit today but remains unchanged thereafter.[2] The dual value of a unit of capital stock today ($\Pi_{k,t}$) must therefore be equal to the difference between the dual value of a commodity unit yesterday (Π_{t-1}) and today (Π_t):[3]

$$(7.1) \qquad \Pi_{k,t} = \Pi_{t-1} - \Pi_t$$

2. This statement assumes that it is optimal to invest some positive amount both yesterday and today. It is also assumed that output is net of replacement requirements and that capacity, therefore, has an infinite service life.

3. The dual equation of investment activities made at times $t - 1$ and t can be written:

$$\pi_{t-1} = \pi_{k,t} + \pi_{k,t+1} + \pi_{k,t+2} + \dots,$$

$$\pi_t = \pi_{k,t+1} + \pi_{k,t+2} + \dots,$$

which gives by subtraction:

$$\pi_{t-1} - \pi_t = \pi_{k,t}.$$

In a one-commodity economy, the dual value of that commodity may be taken as the numéraire—that is to say, the value in relation to which all other values are measured. The righthand side (RHS) of equation (7.1) then measures the depreciation of the numéraire per unit of time—that is to say, the difference it makes to the value of the maximand whether the same unit is consumed yesterday or today. The utility of consumption is defined as

$$(7.2) \qquad U = -c^{(1-1/\sigma)} \qquad \text{with } 0 \le \sigma < 1,$$

where c measures the level of per capita consumption and σ is a constant. The rate of change in the numéraire (the unit of time being here the day) can be written:[4]

$$(7.3) \qquad \frac{\Pi_{t-1} - \Pi_t}{\Pi_t} = \delta + \nu + \frac{g_t}{\sigma},$$

where δ = rate at which utilities are discounted over time, ν = rate of population growth, g_t = rate of growth in per capita consumption, and σ = elasticity of substitution between per capita consumption at various points in time.

In an economy with a single commodity and a single factor of production, the system can be closed by specifying the marginal productivity of capital (r_t).[5] The dual equation of the production activity defines the shadow price of capacity as the ratio between the dual value of the capacity constraint and that of the single good (used here as the numéraire):

$$(7.4) \qquad \frac{\Pi_{k,t}}{\Pi_t} = r_t.$$

Equations (7.1), (7.3), and (7.4) characterize the investment, consumption, and production activities, respectively. Their combination gives the basic dynamic equation:

$$(1.1) \qquad r_t = \delta + \nu + \frac{g_t}{\sigma}.[6]$$

When the elasticity of substitution (σ) between two units of consump-

---

4. See Chapter 8.

5. In a constant-returns economy with a single factor, the marginal productivity of capital would be the economywide output-capital ratio. With two factors (labor and capital) receiving equal shares, the marginal productivity of capital would equal half the output-capital ratio.

6. This equation holds only if the optimal levels of the consumption, production, and investment activities always remain positive.

tion (one corresponding to a lower level of consumption today and the other to a higher level tomorrow) is infinite, utility of consumption becomes identical to consumption itself (equation 7.2) and the marginal utility of consumption remains always equal to unity.[7] In that particular case, the link between the marginal productivity of capital (r_t) and the growth rate (g_t) of per capita consumption disappears from dynamic equation (1.1). This is precisely the source of the problems encountered with a linear maximand measuring the discounted value of consumption (instead of its utility).

For finite values of the elasticity of substitution ($0 < \sigma < \infty$), marginal utility ($u > 0$) is a decreasing function of the level of per capita consumption. Consumers are no more indifferent between an additional unit of consumption today and an additional unit tomorrow, if their level of consumption is lower today than it will be tomorrow. The isoutility curve (see Figure 8.1) between consumption at two different points in time becomes nonlinear, and the degree of nonlinearity is measured by $1/\sigma$. This can be seen from the first and second derivatives of the utility function (7.2):

$$(7.2')\qquad u = \frac{dU}{dc} = -\left(1 - \frac{1}{\sigma}\right)c^{-1/\sigma} \qquad \text{with } 0 < \sigma < 1,$$

$$(7.2'')\qquad \frac{du}{dc} = -\frac{1}{\sigma}\frac{u}{c}.$$

The relative variation in marginal utility $\Delta u/u$ associated with a given relative variation in per capita consumption $\Delta c/c$ can be derived from (7.2') as:

$$(7.5)\qquad \frac{\Delta u}{u} = \left(1 + \frac{\Delta c}{c}\right)^{-1/\sigma} - 1.$$

With the value of the elasticity of substitution, $\sigma = 0.5$, used here:

$$\frac{\Delta c}{c} = +0.1 \Rightarrow \frac{\Delta u}{u} = (1.1)^{-2} - 1 = -0.17,$$

$$\frac{\Delta c}{c} = -0.1 \Rightarrow \frac{\Delta u}{u} = (1.1)^{2} - 1 = +0.21.$$

Hence, the marginal utility of consumption declines 17 percent

---

7. For $\sigma > 1$, the measure of utility is a positive number and the negative sign disappears from the RHS of equation (7.2). Hence, $U = c$ for $\sigma = +\infty$.

when per capita consumption rises 10 percent; it increases 21 percent when per capita consumption declines 10 percent. If devoting an additional 10 percent of consumption to savings today would permit consumption to rise more than 10 percent tomorrow, this would mean a deterioration in the terms of trade between consumption today and consumption tomorrow of more than 32 percent.[8] Clearly, even if the marginal productivity of capital happens to be very high (or low) today, it would not pay to save (or to consume) everything today. The progressive deterioration (or improvement) in the terms of trade would lead to an intermediate point between these two extremes.

Intertemporal choices should ideally be made within an infinite time horizon. With a truncated horizon and without postterminal constraint, it would always be optimal not to invest in the terminal year, since investments made in that year would only affect capacities available for production after that year. A satisfactory approximation of the model with an infinite time horizon can, however, be obtained if it can be assumed that the growth rate in the terminal year is sufficiently close to its asymptotic value. The method applied here for truncating the time horizon is based on this property (see Chapter 8). On the one hand, the sum of the discounted utilities of consumption after the terminal year (1990) is a finite number which can be expressed as a function of the discounted utility of consumption in the terminal year and of the asymptotic growth rate ($\bar{\gamma}$). It is therefore possible to define the objective function as the sum of the discounted utilities of consumption over an infinite time horizon, although the latest decision year refers to 1990. On the other hand, investments in the terminal year (1990) must be sufficient to enable the economy to grow at the asymptotic rate $\bar{\gamma}$ during a postterminal period, taken here as the decade 1990–2000; this defines the postterminal constraints through which investments in the terminal year are valued. In a simple model the asymptotic growth rate $\bar{\gamma}$ could be calculated algebraically; here it is arrived at by solving the model iteratively, but the convergence is rapid.

In the various policy experiments reported in Chapter 6, the optimal values of consumption and investments in the terminal year did not remain constant.[9] It could still be assumed, however, that the economy had reached its asymptotic path in the terminal year, and it

8. $(1 - 0.17)/(1 + 0.21) = 1 - 0.32$.
9. It would therefore have been improper to keep a constant value for terminal capital stocks or for the shadow price at which these stocks should be valued, as would have been necessary with simpler truncation procedures.

did not prove necessary to modify the value of the asymptotic growth rate $\bar{\gamma}$ from one experiment to the other. The truncation procedure just described combined with the nonlinearity of the objective function has made it possible to optimize the time paths of consumption and investments without introducing any smoothing device. Most other dynamic models contain some kind of smoothing device, which can take the form of constraints on savings, on investments, or on consumption.[10] Those devices obscure the dual solution and reduce the scope for intertemporal tradeoffs, which are the raison d'être of dynamic optimization.

Having outlined the method used for analyzing intertemporal tradeoffs, it is possible to look at intratemporal consumption tradeoffs. For a zero consumption level, the marginal utility of the consumption of any commodity would approach infinity. Consumption must therefore be positive for all commodities. By definition, the dual value (Π) of the commodity balance is a measure of the marginal contribution of a unit of that commodity to the value of the objective function. Hence, at any given point in time:

$$(7.6) \qquad \frac{\Pi_A}{\Pi_B} = \frac{u_A}{u_B},$$

for any two commodities A and B. Assuming optimum allocation among consumer goods, marginal utilities (u) and market prices (p) must be proportional; thus:

$$(7.7) \qquad \frac{u_A}{u_B} = \frac{p_A}{p_B}.$$

It follows that dual values must also be proportional to market prices:

$$(7.8) \qquad \frac{\Pi_A}{\Pi_B} = \frac{p_A}{p_B}.$$

Equation (7.7) is the familiar demand equation which is established by maximizing the utility of consumption subject to a budgetary constraint. The common ratio (u_i/p_i) is the cost of the budgetary constraint, which is often called the "Lagrange multiplier." Here, it is desirable to go one step further in the general-equilibrium approach. Income is treated as an endogenous variable by replacing the budgetary constraint by constraints expressed in terms of pri-

10. Alan S. Manne (1973, p. 110) uses a "gradualistic consumption path" in the Mexico model.

mary resources. In the model, commodity balances are linked to these resource constraints through supply activities (either producing the commodity locally or importing it). The dual equation of any such supply activity operated at a positive level in the optimal solution states that the dual value of the commodity balance (marginal utility) is equal to the marginal cost of supply. The price system of the dual solution is therefore Pareto optimal:

$$(7.9) \qquad \frac{p_A}{p_B} = \frac{\Pi_A}{\Pi_B} = \frac{u_A}{u_B} = \frac{marginal\ cost\ of\ supplying\ A}{marginal\ cost\ of\ supplying\ B} \ .$$

Activities of the Unaggregated Model

The model can be visualized as an extension of the multiperiod model outlined above in equations (7.1), (7.3), and (7.4). Instead of a single commodity, there are eight consumer goods and a variety of intermediate goods. Instead of a single aggregate called capital, there are many stocks of physical capital (such as coffee plantations or machinery for producing textiles); there are ten stocks of human capital (nationals trained in given skill categories) and there are stocks of financial capital. In addition, there is a resource called foreign exchange which provides the link between the economy of the Ivory Coast and the rest of the world. During each time period, instead of a single production and a single investment activity, there are many different production, trade, and investment activities. Through these activities, national resources are transformed into consumer goods, which in turn are transformed into utility. The three main types of activities will be reviewed in turn.

CONSUMPTION

There are three consumer groups in the model: the public administration, foreigners, and nationals. Since their demands are the largest, it is assumed for the sake of simplicity, that only nationals adjust the composition of their consumption to variations in relative prices.

For public administration, the level of consumption is considered to be a matter of government policy and is treated as an exogenous variable. For European expatriates, salaries are given (they increase 1 percent a year, in real terms), but the total wage bill is an endogenous variable, depending on the number of expatriates required. The model selects the number of expatriates required in each skill category, in much the same way that it selects the volume of imports for each type of physical commodity. For Africans migrating from neighboring countries, the basic real wage increases 2 percent a year; in addition, the supply curve is upward sloping.[11] The wage bill is computed separately for European expatriates and for African migrants. To each group a different set of propensities to consume and to remit savings abroad is applied. Consumption and remittances are computed by multiplying the variable wage bill by the given coefficients of propensity. They are valued in terms of consumption forgone by nationals and of foreign exchange withdrawn.

The treatment of consumption by nationals is quite different.[12] The model optimizes simultaneously both the time path of total per capita consumption and the composition of consumption among eight commodity groups within each representative year. The intertemporal tradeoffs were illustrated earlier by using a simplified one-commodity model. This led to the simple relation (1.1) linking the optimal growth rate of aggregate consumption to the marginal productivity of capital. This relation still provides a useful representation of intertemporal consumption tradeoffs, but it is a simplified one. The single commodity balance is now replaced by eight commodity balances to which are associated eight dual values Π_{it}, one for each group of final consumer goods and services. The dual value Π_t of aggregate consumption is no longer independent of the product mix. It is now an index number, and can only be computed, ex post, by weighting the eight values Π_{it}, one for each individual consumption good.

It is assumed that for each commodity group there is a national market with a single price. The national demand on this market is the sum of the rural and urban demands, which are based on different sets of coefficients of income elasticity and patterns of consumption (see Chapter 9, Appendix A). The growth rates of these two populations are taken as given, and it is assumed that per capita income increases at the same rate in the two groups. This rough projection model leads to two sets of estimates. The first is the effect that urbanization would have on national demand in the absence of any change in the average per capita income of the urban and rural populations. The second is the effect that the same percentage increase of per capita income in rural and urban areas would have on national demand; the second relation defines, for each projection year, the aggregate income elasticity. The utility function of the average Ivorian is computed from these

11. Africans having settled in the Ivory Coast before 1970 are treated as nationals.
12. In the terminology of Tendulkar (1971), the consumption loop is "closed" for foreigners and "open" for nationals.

two sets of estimates (see Chapter 9). As the migration level computed in the optimal solution does not generally differ greatly from the level assumed in the rough projection model, this procedure leads to an acceptable approximation of the effect of urbanization on the composition of demand. It also leads to an acceptable approximation of the average income elasticities.

INVESTMENTS

There are two main types of intertemporal linkages in the central model. The first occurs through the maximand; it is the choice between consumption today and consumption tomorrow. The second occurs through the investment activities. The usual practice is to assume for capital stocks either a constant service life or else a constant rate of depreciation. Instead, a vintage model has been used. This requires a precise formulation of the initial conditions, since the demand for replacement during the planning period is largely determined by the levels of investments in the years preceding the planning period. In the case of a young and dynamic economy such as that of the Ivory Coast, it leads to a more realistic estimate of the demand for replacement. This demand can vary considerably. At one extreme is the case of vehicles (the type of capital goods with the shortest life span). For these, the replacement demand (expressed as a share of gross investment) rises from 35 percent in 1970 to 65 percent in 1980. At the other extreme are the Ivorian secondary school teachers. The replacement demand for these remains practically nil until 1990.

The representation of investment activities is the simplest in the case of vehicles, machinery, and construction. At the time of investment ($\bar{t}$), the capital good characterized by subscript k is withdrawn from the commodity balance for that good. The capital stock thus generated can be utilized from time $\bar{t} + p_k$ to time $\bar{t} + p_k + lf_k$, where p_k and lf_k characterize, respectively, the time lag in the creation of the capacity and the life span of this capacity.

For tree crops and for the iron mine, investment activities are treated as projects. They are represented by columns recording year by year the necessary resources as minuses and the outputs as pluses.

In the case of human investments, the level of an educational activity initiated in year $\bar{t}$ is defined by the number of students entering a given study cycle in that year. The costs of this activity in year $t \geq \bar{t}$ are expressed in terms of students (labor force forgone), of teachers, of school buildings, and so on. They are incurred for the students of vintage $\bar{t}$ still in the educational cycle in year t. Students who successfully complete the cycle of study are promoted to a higher skill level.

They can enter the labor market or start with a cycle of higher studies. The benefits of education occur after the student has entered the labor market. They are measured, throughout his productive life, by the productivity differential associated with the upgrading of his skills.

The unit of time used to describe investment activities is the year (years of schooling, years of productive life, and so forth). The representation of these activities in the central model would be quite straightforward if this model were annual and if the time horizon were not truncated. Because there is a five-year interval between two consecutive decision years, a problem arises of aggregation over time. The aggregation procedure followed is described in Chapter 10 for physical investments and Chapter 11 for human investments. Initial conditions are discussed in Chapter 11, while terminal conditions are analyzed in relation to the asymptotic properties of the model in Chapter 8.

PRODUCTION AND TRADE

In the rural sector, the same commodity can be produced with different activities. Rice can be grown by applying a traditional, an improved, or a modern technology. Each technology is associated with a specific set of coefficients measuring unitary output and unitary requirements in the form of intermediate inputs (fertilizers, seeds, and so forth) and of factors (land, labor, and so forth). These coefficients are based on agronomical norms. In some cases, they are derived from systematic experiments or from farm-management surveys. In others, they reflect the judgment of well-informed individuals. Much the same sources of data are employed in project evaluation.

In the urban sector, the coefficients of the production activities are derived from national accounts, occasionally supplemented by engineering data. They are expressed in the form of an input-output matrix and of a resource matrix. The latter defines what each urban activity requires in labor by skill category and capacities by type of capital good. No reliable engineering estimates of alternative technologies were found (see Chapter 16).

Import activities are very much like production activities. They increase supplies in the commodity balance of the imported item by withdrawing resources from the foreign exchange balance. Since commodity balances are measured at retail market level, import activities also withdraw supplies from the balance of commercial services. In the free-trade solution, the cost of these services measures the difference between prices paid by consumers and prices c.i.f.

In the urban sector, the problem of choice between import and production activities is simplified by drawing a distinction among three types of commodities. Thirty-seven nontradables must always be produced locally; twenty-one noncompeting imports must always be imported; fourteen competing imports can be either produced locally or imported. The urban input-output matrix is therefore composed of $72(= 37 + 21 + 14)$ rows and $86(= 72 + 14)$ columns. The existence of make-or-buy choices for competing imports in the urban sector raises the same type of problems as the existence of alternative production technologies in the rural sector. It transforms the square Leontief matrix into a rectangular matrix that cannot be inverted.

Two-Level Decomposition

Having reviewed activities according to their nature, it is possible to consider how they can be decomposed by sectors. In Table 7.1 a distinction is drawn among five main groups. The first three deal with activities specific to the rural, urban, and educational sectors, respectively. The fourth deals with two large projects (the iron mine and Riviera), which are treated as independent sectors rather than as branches of the urban sector. They correspond to new types of possible investment activities. The date of implementation is the choice variable, but the size of the project is given. The last group deals with national activities that affect all sectors. This group covers consumption, borrowing from abroad, importing commodities, and labor services, as well as labor migration from rural urban areas.

Figure 7.1 shows how the economywide model can be decomposed. All national constraints (those affecting at least two sectors) are grouped at the top, and all constraints that affect only one sector are shown at the bottom.[13] For the sake of simplicity, the two special projects and the livestock sector have been omitted, while education has been treated as a national activity. The three sectors singled out in Figure 7.1 are the urban, the south rural, and the north rural sectors.

The commodity balances (that is, rice, textiles, cotton, and machines) are treated as national rows. Foreign exchange is treated as a national resource, because every sector has either a surplus or a deficit of foreign exchange. The same applies to skilled labor (locally trained or imported), since this resource is shared among all sectors. Unskilled

13. A sectoral constraint must have nonzero entries for only the activity columns belonging to that sector.

Figure 7.1 Illustrative Model before Aggregation (Year *t*)

	Rural north					Rural south					Urban			
	Invest in		Produce			Invest in			Produce		Invest in		Produce	
Type of row (maximand, commodity, and resource balances)	Tractor pool	Land clearing	Cotton	Rice	Hire from labor pool	Tractor pool	Land clearing	Coffee planting	Rice	Hire from labor pool	Machinery	Textiles	Textiles	Machinery
	No	Yes				No	Yes				No			
Maximand														
National														
Commodity balances														
Final consumer goods—rice				+1					+1 −					
Final consumer goods—textiles													+1 −	
Final consumer and capital goods—machines	−1					−1					−1	−1 −	+1	
Intermediate goods only—cotton		+1											−	
Resource balances														
Pool of rural migratory labor					−1					−1				
Urban unskilled labor												− −		
Skilled labor		− − −				−	− −				− −		
Foreign exchange								+			−	− − −		
School buildings														
Sectoral														
Urban														
Capacity for producing textiles												+	−	
Capacity for producing machinery											+	+		−
Rural south														
Unskilled labor (by type and quarter)						−	−		−	− +1				
Tractor pool (by quarter)						+	+		−	−				
Lands (by type and nature of planting)							+	+	−	− −				
Rural north														
Unskilled labor (by type, quarter and district)		−	−	−	+1									
Tractor pool (by district and quarter)	+	+	−	−	−									
Lands (by type and district)		+	+	−	−									

choice of technologies

	National																Constant of the righthand side (− requirements + inherited capacities)
	Invest in					Import				Export		Consume					
Hire from labor pool	Stu-dents	Schools	Rice	Ma-chinery	Cot-ton	Labor		Capital	Cot-ton	Tex-tiles	Rice	Tex-tiles	Ma-chinery				
						Skilled	Un-skilled										
	Yes			No				Yes		No		Yes					
t	$t-\tau$	t	$t-\tau$	t	t	t	t	t	$t-\tau$	t	t	t	t	t			t
								+			+	+					
			+1			−	−				−1				$\geq$	+ Public consumption	
−						−	−			−1		−1			$\geq$	+ Public consumption	
−			−1	+1		−						−1			$\geq$	+ Public consumption	
				+1				−1							$\geq$	0	
−1						+1									$\geq$	− Labor stock	
+1	−	−1													$\geq$	− Labor stock	
	+	−				+									$\geq$	− Labor stock	
					−	−	−	−	−	−	+1	+	+		$\geq$	− Net inflow of capital	
	−	+													$\geq$	− Capital stock surviving	
															$\geq$	− Capital stock surviving	
															$\geq$	− Capital stock surviving	
															$\geq$	− Labor stock	
															$\gtreqless$	Capital stock surviving	
															$\geq$	− Capital stock surviving	
															$\geq$	− Labor stock	
															$\geq$	− Capital stock surviving	
															$\geq$	− Capital stock surviving	

urban labor, which can be employed as such in the urban sector or upgraded through education, has also to be treated as a national resource. For unskilled agricultural labor, the situation is more complex. Each rural sector has its own labor endowments in the form of children, adult females, and adult males attached to particular areas. Migrations between sectors and from abroad occur through a fictitious labor pool, which is represented by a national row. Each sector can hire labor from the pool at a price corresponding to the marginal cost of import. When a worker is hired in the north, there is no additional cost; when he is hired in the south, there is an additional cost; and when he is hired in urban areas, there is a higher additional cost, which increases with the number of migrants.

If postprimary education had been treated as a separate sector, school buildings would have been the only type of resource specific to that sector, since skilled labor and unskilled urban labor are national resources.[14] This was the reason for treating education as a national activity and, consequently, the stock of school buildings as a national resource.

Only two urban rows are shown in Figure 7.1. In actuality, there are nine types of urban resources: two capital stocks in the form of vehicles and buildings and seven capital stocks in the form of machinery differentiated according to use. In addition, there are five constraints defining upper bounds to the five groups of urban exports. In total, however, there are many more national rows than urban rows that have nonzero entries in the urban-activity columns. For that reason, it is not convenient to solve the urban model independent of the economywide model. When the urban model is solved alone, the shadow prices of all the national rows (with nonzero entries in the urban-activity columns) have to be taken as given. These prices are the signals sent by the center to the sector with the decomposition procedure of Dantzig and Wolfe.

The case of the rural sectors is different. In the north, a distinction is made among three districts and five types of land within each district. Consequently, there are fifteen sectoral rows characterizing land resources. Capital stocks in the form of tractors are represented by twelve rows in each district corresponding to the four seasons. Labor resources specific to the sector are represented by thirty-six rows corresponding to the three types of labor in three districts during four seasons. In total, there are sixty-three different sectoral resources for each of the representative years in the rural model for the north. This number far

---

14. Assuming that teachers can be employed outside the educational system.

exceeds that of the national resources and national commodities used or produced by that sector, and the same applies to the rural model for the south. When one of the rural models is solved alone, the number of shadow prices which have to be taken as exogenous (national rows) is small in relation to the number of the shadow prices computed in the sectoral model (sectoral rows).

The ratio between the number of sectoral and national rows is indicative of the degree of autonomy of the sector. The previous review suggests that, in a two-level decomposition of the economywide model, educational and urban activities should be treated as national, while rural activities could be treated as sectoral. With the iteration procedure of Dantzig and Wolfe, the rural models can be solved with the shadow prices of the national resources obtained by solving the central model in the previous iteration. This procedure has the advantage of recognizing the relative autonomy of the sectors. It does not, however, reduce the size of the overall model, and the practical problem is the sheer size of the unaggregated model outlined in Table 7.1. Each of the three rural models contains approximately 1,000 rows. The urban model is almost as large, when each of the seventy-two branches is represented by a separate row for each of the representative years. Finally, the educational model would have been of a huge size if all relations reflecting the complex lag structure prevailing in the sector had been made explicit year by year. Altogether, this would have led to a 5,000-row model. With the two-stage procedure outlined in Table 7.2, this 5,000-row model is condensed into one of 500 rows, which is called the central model.

Aggregation

Most of the activities described in Table 7.1 do not enter directly into the central model. Instead, they enter into the sectoral models outlined in the upper part of Table 7.2. Those models are used to generate the sectoral matrices that are incorporated into the central model (lower part of Table 7.2). Consider the case of the rural sector in the south. Exports represent four-fifths of the value of net sectoral output. National resources account for slightly less than half the total resource cost and labor for almost two-thirds of the national resource cost.[15] In first approximation, the sector may be considered by the central

---

15. The average ratio throughout the entire planning period may be derived from Table 15.3.

Table 7.1. Sectoral Decomposition and Activity Choices

Rural sector	Urban sector
Sectoral coverage and description	
Supplying agricultural, forestry, and livestock products in raw and processed forms for final consumption ($i = 6, 7, 8$), for consumption by foreigners, for intermediate use by other sectors (cotton, for example), and for export.	Supplying urban goods and services for final consumption ($i = 1, \ldots, 5$), for consumption by foreigners and the public administration, for intermediate use by other sectors (fertilizer, for example), for investment (vehicles, machinery, and construction), and for export.
Hiring unskilled labor from district resources and from the central pool; hiring skilled labor for central pools only.	Hiring labor, skilled and unskilled, from central pools.
Purchasing intermediate inputs from the urban sector (fertilizers) and from abroad (noncompeting imports).	Purchasing intermediate inputs from the rural sector (cotton, for example) and from abroad (noncompeting imports).
Subdivisions	
North (savanna zone), subdivided into three districts. South (forestry zone). Livestock (mainly in the north).	Formal sector consisting of seventy-two input-output branches with time-variant coefficients. Informal sector supplying competing urban services ($i = 2, 3$) at decreasing returns.
Investment	
Investing in tractors, in draft animals, in cattle breeding, in land improvements (four types), and in plantations by type (outgrowers and industrial estates) and commodities (nine).	Investing three capital goods into nine capital stocks (some differentiated by destination). Time lags and life spans of capital stocks differentiated by capital goods; no technological choices.
Supply	
Producing eighteen commodities, with a choice between four technologies for each commodity.	In fifty-eight branches, no choice of supply technologies. In fourteen branches, choice between producing and importing.
Exports	
Exporting twelve commodities with net exportable surplus at prices f.o.b.; fixed export prices with upper bounds on quantities for ten commodities; variable export prices for coffee and cocoa.	Exporting five groups of products at fixed prices with upper bounds on quantities. Fixed composition of each group among products of the seventy-two branches; time-variant coefficients.

Table 7.1. (continued)

Education	Special projects

Sectoral coverage and description

Transforming unskilled labor with primary education into labor of seven skill categories (= 2, . . . , 8). Enrolling students into various educational cycles.

Hiring teachers.

Purchasing current material inputs (electricity, for example) and capital goods (construction) from the urban sector.

Two large projects:
Iron mine, producing only foreign exchange.
Riviera, producing foreign exchange (through tourism) and housing ($i = 1$).

Investment

Technological choices in human investments (educational cycles). No choice in physical investments (school buildings).

Single technology.

Choice of optimal date for implementation

Table 7.1. (continued)

	National	
Borrowing from abroad	*Trade and migration*	*Consumption*
	Sectoral coverage and description	
Exogenous activities for borrowing at concessional rates and at commercial rates before 1973	Importing unskilled agricultural workers at increasing costs and skilled labor at fixed costs. Moving unskilled workers from rural to urban areas at increasing cost	Public consumption exogenous. Private consumption by foreigners (African and non-African) computed with fixed wages and propensities but variable numbers of workers (closed loop).
Endogenous activities for borrowing at commercial rates in 1975, 1980, and 1985.	Importing food (i = 6, 7, 8) at fixed costs.	Private consumption by the average Ivorian endogenous; absolute level, composition among eight groups (i = 1, . . . , 8) and time path simultaneously optimized (open loop).
	Subdivisions	
		Fixed composition of each consumption group (public, foreign, and i = 1, . . . , 5) among products of the seventy-two urban branches; time-variant coefficients.

Figure 7.2. Production-Efficiency Frontier of the Rural Sector

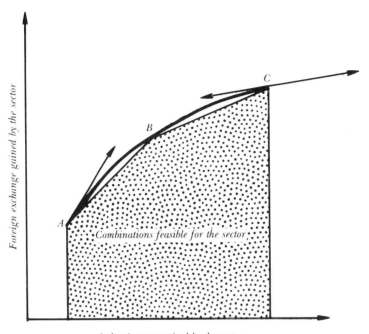

Labor input required by the sector

planner as a means of transforming labor into foreign exchange. With this simplification, the only information required for solving the central model is the sectoral efficiency frontier *ABC* of Figure 7.2. The three points (*A*, *B*, and *C*) along this frontier can be obtained by solving the rural model for three different values of the ratios of the shadow price of labor to that of foreign exchange. The tangents to the efficiency frontier in *A* and *C* are taken as the extreme values of the range within which the ratio of the shadow price of labor to that of foreign exchange can vary in the central model. Any point on or below the efficiency frontier *ABC* satisfies the sectoral constraints (that is, land constraints); any point above it does not.

The curvilinear frontier *ABC* is approximated by the two linear segments *AB* and *BC*. This is done by incorporating into the central model a matrix of three rows and three columns. The variable activity levels are the nonnegative weights applied to the three rural solutions. In the rural matrix incorporated in the central model, the coefficients

Table 7.2. Sectoral Models and Their Aggregated Form in the Central Model

Rural sector (North, south, livestock)	Special projects
Sectoral models	
Type	
Dynamic optimization; three sectoral models of 600 rows and 900 columns each; maximization of returns on rural resources.	Project evaluation.
Central variables taken as exogenous	
Dual values of central resources and commodities produced or used in 1975, 1980, 1985, 1990, and 2000; intermediate urban inputs expressed in terms of central resources.	Dual values of central resources and products in 1975, 1980, 1985, 1990, and 2000; intermediate urban inputs expressed in terms of central resources.
Sectoral solution	
Optimal production of final consumer goods ($i = 6, 7, 8$) and exports; requirements for central resources and products in 1975, 1980, 1985, 1990, and 2000.	Social profitability of the project.
Central model	
Sectoral matrix	
H: 15 columns (3 for each of the three rural sectors and each of the two projects) and 90 rows through the planning period.	
Three vectors defining optimal solutions for each sector, with a $+1$ entry in the sectoral convexity constraint.	Three vectors defining costs and benefits of each project initiated alternatively in 1975, 1980, and 1985 with a $+1$ entry in the project convexity constraint.
Central activities	
Weights applied to each sectoral solution (optimal mix among the three sectoral combinations).	Weights applied to each project initiated at alternative dates; total size given.
Aggregation loss	
Only three sectoral combinations allowed out of an infinite number possible.	

Table 7.2. (continued)

Urban sector	Education[a]
Sectoral models	
Type	
Consistency for 1970; simulation for 1975, 1980, 1985, 1990, and 2000 (increment from 1990 until 2000).	Recursive, yearly from 1950 until 2000. Consistency for enrollments from 1950 until 1972. Simulation of enrollments after 1972.
Central variables taken as exogenous	
Final demand vector, y_t, and choice of import-substitution activity; m = import all fourteen competing items; p = produce all fourteen items; i = import specified items and produce the rest.	For each educational cycle, annual growth rate of enrollments defined for successive five-year periods (1972–77, 1977–82, and so forth).
Sectoral solution	
Gross output per branch and requirements for central resources every five years.	Effect of educational activities on availability of resources in 1975, 1980, 1985, 1990, and 2000 (increment from 1990 to 2000).
Central model	
Sectoral matrix	
D: 54(= 3 × 18) columns and 20 rows for 1975, 1980, 1985, 1990, and 2000.	**E**: 56 (= 14 × 4) columns and 90 rows throughout the planning period.
Reduced-form matrices $\mathbf{D}_{mt} + \mathbf{D}_{it} + \mathbf{D}_{pt}$, with $\mathbf{D}_m = \mathbf{R}_m(\mathbf{I} - \mathbf{A}_{mt})^{-1}\mathbf{F}_t$ for t = 1975, 1980, 1985, 1990, and 2000.	Sectoral solution taking unitary levels of investment for 1975, 1980, 1985, and 2000 and given rates of increase within each five-year period (1972–77, 1977–82, and so forth).
Central activities	
Vectors of final demand, $\mathbf{Y}_t$, measuring demand, $\mathbf{Y}_{mt}$, and the mix of import-substitution activities ($\mathbf{Y}_{it} - \mathbf{Y}_{mt}$ and $\mathbf{Y}_{pt} - \mathbf{Y}_{mt}$).	Activity level of each type of investment during each division year 1975, 1980, 1985, and 1990.
Aggregation loss	
Only 2 × 18 = 36 different combinations allowed for replacing competing imports with production out of a total of 213 possible combinations.	Aggregation over time: difference between five-year interpolation growth rates selected and implied in the optimal solution.

a. The sectoral models for physical and financial investments are similar to the educational model for human investments. A recursive yearly model was used for financial transactions abroad. The coefficients for physical and financial investments enter the central model in the form of the K matrix.

Table 7.2. (continued)

Utility of consumption

Sectoral models

Type

Projection model: Rural (and urban) demand projected on the basis of rural (and urban) demand function; average demand function derived from total demand projected with the same growth in per capita income in both groups.

Central variables taken as exogenous

Numbers of urban and rural populations in 1975, 1980, 1985, 1990, and 2000. Income-elasticity functions for rural and urban populations.

Sectoral solution

Specific urbanization effect with zero per capita growth, c_{i0t}/c_{i00}. Aggregate income-elasticity function, $c_{ist} = c(i, s, t)$, satisfying additivity $c_{st} = \Sigma_i c_{ist}$.

Central model

Sectoral matrix

U: $144 (= 18 \times 8)$ columns and 17 rows for 1975, 1980, 1985, and 1990.

Values of consumption $\bar{C}_{ist}$ and utilities $\bar{U}_{ist}$ for different rates of income growth, s, for each commodity i and in each year $t = 1975, 1980, 1985,$ and 1990, with a $+1$ entry in the interpolation constraint.

Central activities

Interpolation weight W_{ist} defining the level of consumption for each commodity.

Aggregation loss

Difference between urbanization rates selected and projected plus linear approximation errors.

of the labor and foreign exchange rows measure the coordinates of points A, B, and C—that is, the labor input required and the foreign exchange gained in each of the three optimal rural solutions. All the resource constraints specific to the rural sector (that is, land, water, and so forth) are replaced in the central model by a single constraint expressing the requirement that the sum of the weights applied to the different rural solutions cannot exceed unity. This implies that the optimal solution of the central model cannot correspond to a point of Figure 7.2 above the linear approximation ABC of the efficiency frontier, so that all sectoral constraints (omitted from the central model) are thereby satisfied (see Chapter 9, Appendix B).

If it were true that the sector employed a single national resource (labor) and produced a single national resource (foreign exchange) during a single year, the aggregation error would be negligible. It would result from the piecewise linear approximation of the efficiency frontier ABC shown in Figure 7.2. Because the sector uses and produces more than two national resources (or commodities) during more than one year, tradeoffs become multidimensional, and the error of aggregation is substantial. This is discussed algebraically in Chapter 12 and geometrically in Chapter 15.

The aggregation procedure used for the urban and educational sectors differs from the one just described. All resources used by these sectors are treated as national rows and are incorporated into the central model. However, a large number of the equations shown in the upper part of Table 7.2 do not need to appear in the central model. All intermediate variables, together with the equations determining their values, are eliminated from the "reduced-form" matrices shown in the lower part of Table 7.2. Consider the case of the urban sector, in which there is no technological choice. Suppose that there is no make-or-buy choice either: the direct and indirect resource requirements for each type of final demand could be calculated exactly by inverting the input-output matrix, which is square (see Bruno 1967). Levels of gross output in the seventy-two urban branches and the corresponding commodity balances would not appear explicitly in the central model. No information would be lost, however. Once the central model had been solved, gross output by branch could be derived unequivocally from the final demand vector found in the optimal solution (see Chapter 12).

In actuality, there are make-or-buy choices in the urban sector. For this reason, three reduced-form matrices (instead of one) are incorporated into the central model. With the first, goods are produced domestically whenever there is a choice between producing and importing; with the second, goods are imported whenever there is a choice; with the third, domestic production is selected as the source of supply for only some of the commodities for which a make-or-buy choice exists. Because not all possible combinations of make-or-buy choices in the urban sector are taken into account in the central model, this procedure introduces some errors; they are analyzed in Chapter 12.

The most successful aggregation procedure is that applied to the educational sector. Full justice is done to the multiple-lag structure. Choices among alternative educational investments are preserved. The only error results from time aggregation, and this error is small, as explained in Chapter 11.

The Central Model

The aggregated sectoral matrices described in the lower part of Table 7.2 are the building blocks of the central model. A sketch of these blocks is presented in Figure 7.3. It shows that intertemporal linkages occur through three matrices. The first, **H**, deals with the three rural sectors and the two special projects. The second, **E**, deals with human investments and the third, **K**, with physical and financial investments. The three other matrices are restricted to intratemporal linkages. One, **D**, is the reduced form of the urban model. The second, **U**, is the utility matrix transforming consumption of eight types of goods into utility. The last, **C**, deals with all remaining central activities. These six matrices together with the maximand and the RHS define the central model.[16]

Figure 7.3 gives a feel for what the intertemporal linkages are. Figure 7.4, the enlargement of one diagonal block of Figure 7.3, helps in the understanding of how the model works. In order to illustrate the linkages between a diagonal block and the rest of the model, Figure 7.4 shows a few rows and columns which do not belong to the diagonal block. The additional rows, at the top, are the maximand and the constraints on rural resources (for the three rural sectors) and on project size (for the two special projects). The additional columns, at the left, summarize the activities of the rural sectors and of the special projects in terms of central commodities and central resources.

16. The six matrices were constructed separately. The work of programming was performed by Narong Thananart for matrices **K** and **C**, by Vinh Le-Si for matrices **D** and **H**, and by François Nguyen for matrices **E** and **U**. The six matrices were called on disc memory, and the model was solved mainly by François Nguyen. It was possible to handle minor modifications in the coefficients directly through the APEX linear programming routine, major ones by recomputing the sectoral matrices.

Figure 7.3. The Central Model: The Overall Picture[a]

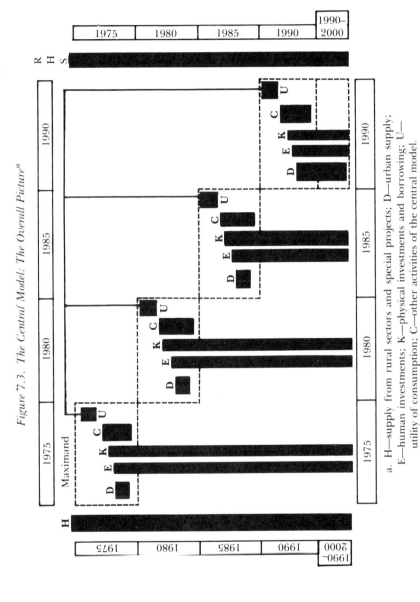

a. H—supply from rural sectors and special projects; D—urban supply; E—human investments; K—physical investments and borrowing; U—utility of consumption; C—other activities of the central model.

		Activities of rural sectors and special projects	Urban activities supplying through production and import						Investing (or deinvesting) in			
			Consumer goods for				Capital goods for investment	Goods for export	Human capital	Physical urban capital stocks	Financial liabilities abroad	
			Ivorians	Non-Africans	Africans	Public administration						
									Technological choices			
					Yes					No		
Type of row	Number	(3+2)3 =15[b]	5×3 =15	3	3	3×3 =9	3×3 =9[b]	5×3 =15	14	2+7 =9	4	

Maximand

Type of row	Number	
Constraints on rural resources or project size	5[b]	+1..
	(9)	
Accounting row for total utility in year t	1	
Nonfood consumption (i = 1, . . . , 5)	5	
Consumption of food (i = 6, 7, 8)	3	
Linear interpolation	(16)	
Utility function for nonfood (i = 1, . . . , 5)	5	
Utility function for food (i = 6, 7, 8)	3	
Migrating from rural to urban areas	1	
Substituting skills	4	
Importing unskilled agricultural workers	1	
Supplying informal traditional urban services	1	
Borrowing from abroad	1	
Commodity balances	(21)	
Food (i = 6, 7, 8; cereals, meat, others)	3	+..
Nonfood (i = 1, . . . , 5; housing, household goods, . . .)		+
For consumption by Ivorians	5	
For consumption by non-Africans	1	
For consumption by non-Ivorian Africans	1	
Goods and services for public consumption and intermediate	3[c]	−..
Capital goods: vehicles, machinery, construction	3	−..
Export goods (x = 1, . . . , 5)	5	
Resource balances	(21)	
Used for the production of urban goods and services		
Cotton	1	+..
Labor, urban unskilled (λ = 1)	1	−..
Labor, skilled, by categories (λ = 2, . . .)		−..
Labor, skilled, by categories (λ = 8)[e]	7	−..
Stocks of capital goods, by origin and destination	9	−..
Foreign exchange	1	+..
Not used for the production of urban goods		
Rural unskilled labor (λ = 0)	1	−..
Capital stocks: school buildings	1	

Letters on the matrix: H, E, K, D

+1.. (financial liabilities abroad, borrowing row)
+1+1 entries in commodity balance rows
−.. / −1.. / +.. entries in E and K blocks
+ + in foreign exchange row

Supplying tra- ditional urban services infor- mally or nonlinearities	Importing				Substi- tuting a higher skill category for a lower	Migrat- ing from rural to urban areas	Utility from		Accounting activities			
	Unskilled agri- cultural labor	Skilled labor by category	Food prod- ucts	Cot- ton			Food items	Nonfood items	Food con- sump- tion	Non- food con- sump- tion	Util- ity
Yes			No			Yes			Not applicable			
10	8	7	3	1	4×8=32	8	$\begin{array}{c}3\times18\\=54\end{array}$	5×18=90	3	5	1

											+	
												≤ 1
						+..	+..				−1	= 0
							+..	−1				= 0
						+..	**U**		−1			= 0
							+1..					≥ 1
						+1..						≥ 1
					+1..							≤ 1
				+1..								≤ 1
	+1..											≤ 1
+1..												≤ 1
												≤ 1
		−..	−..	+1+1						−1		≥ 0
+..						−..				−1		≥ 0
		−..										= 0
		−..										= 0
			− −									≥ + $\overline{GC}$
			C									≥ 0
												≤ EX$_x$
			+1									= 0
−..						+..						≥ − $\check{L}_{lt}$
		+			+..							≥ −L_{At}
		+			−..							≥ −L_{At}
												≥ −$\check{K}_{kt}$
	−..	−..	−									≥ −$\check{F}_t$
+..		− −			−..							≥ − $\check{L}_{0t}$
												≥ −$\check{K}_{ct}$

[notes to figure appear at foot of page 160]

Within a diagonal block, the rows are divided into four groups. The first group is composed of accounting rows, which are not needed in the solution process but which are included in the model to keep track of certain aggregate values such as GDP (see Table 7.5). Those could be eliminated with minor rearrangements. The second group deals with the piecewise linear approximations to nonlinear relationships; these are programming devices for introducing nonlinearities into a model solved with linear programming techniques. The last two groups of constraints are the commodity and resource balances.

The columns are classified into eight groups. Going from right to left, the first group deals with accounting activities; those are the homologues of the accounting rows (if the latter were eliminated, the former would disappear). The second group deals with the utility of final consumption. This is measured in the model through the utility matrix, **U**, which is linked upward to the maximand and downward to the eight commodity balances of final consumer goods for Ivorians. The next four groups deal respectively with internal migrations between rural and urban areas, with substitution between skill categories, with import of commodities and labor services from abroad and with the production of traditional urban services in the "informal sector."

The seventh group deals with investment activities outside the rural sectors and the special projects. A distinction is made between human, physical, and financial investments. Lending abroad reduces resources available for consumption today and increases them tomorrow in much the same way that investing at home does. Borrowing from abroad (which can be considered as a negative investment) and investing at home in physical assets are the activities included in the **K** matrix. Investing in human capital through postprimary education defines the activities of the **E** matrix. In the tops of the **E** and **K** matrices (the only parts appearing in Figure 7.4), the cost of a human or a physical investment is shown as a minus, while the money just borrowed is shown as a plus. In the remainder of these matrices (which appear in Figure 7.3), the signs are inverted; costs are replaced by returns and borrowings by repayments.

The last group of columns in the diagonal block defines urban

[Notes to Figure 7.4]

a. In year 1990 there is no borrowing activity from abroad. In the postterminal period (1990 to 2000), there are activities for importing skilled labor and resource constraints for physical capacities, skilled labor, labor substitution and foreign exchange.
b. Time-invariant rows and columns.
c. Include two rows of goods and services for the public administration and commercial services used by other sectors.
d. In the first set of experiments these constraints did not exist; labor was downgraded directly from a higher to a lower skill category.
e. In order to illustrate substitution between skills, two lines are used instead of one for skilled. In the last set of experiments, four additional skill categoried are included.

supply activities. The urban sector can supply eighteen different groups of goods and services in three different ways. Each way is associated with a particular mix of the make-or-buy choice for fourteen competing commodities (those are used as intermediate inputs by the urban sector but do not appear in the central model). A commodity balance corresponds to each type of goods supplied by the urban sector. On the one hand, the contributions of the urban supply activities are accounted for by +1 coefficients in the commodity balance rows. On the other hand, the requirements of these activities are accounted for by minus coefficients in the resource balance rows.[17] Since the minus coefficients account for both direct and indirect resource requirements, the matrix **D** (reduced form of the urban model) is very dense (see Table 16.6).

Outside the diagonal block, the activities of the rural sectors and the special projects are summarized by a set of columns running throughout the planning period. Several columns are associated with a given sector; each defines a particular sectoral program. The ultimate effect of that program on national resources and products is measured by the coefficients of the column associated with that program. Each rural column corresponds to a particular program and the coefficients of that column are obtained in solving the rural model according to that program. The positive row entries account for supplies of food products, cotton, and foreign exchange. In the columns corresponding to the iron-mining project, there is a positive entry in the foreign exchange row. In the case of the Riviera project, positive row entries account for supplies of housing services for residents and of foreign exchange earned from foreign tourists.

Having reviewed the main rows and columns of Figure 7.4, linkages can be illustrated by analyzing the closed consumption loop for foreigners. Consider the case of a French engineer who belongs to the skill category $\lambda = 8$. Assume that because of his experience he has a marginal productivity 30 percent higher than that of his Ivorian counterpart. Assume further that he receives a salary of CFAF4 million after tax, that he spends in the Ivory Coast 15 percent of his salary on food (5 percent on each of the items $i = 6, 7$, and 8), and 45 percent on nonfood items and that he repatriates the remaining 40 percent. With these assumptions, the coefficients of the last column under the heading "importing skilled labor by categories" would read thus from top to bottom: $-0.2(= 4 \times 0.05)$ for each of the three commodity balances $i = 6, 7$, and 8 shown in Figure 7.4 under a single line, $-1.8 =$

---

17. The entries for export supply activities in the foreign-exchange row are shown by pluses, since the foreign exchange gained by exporting an urban good exceeds the foreign exchange lost by producing it.

(4 × 0.45) in the commodity balance for nonfood consumption by non-Africans, +1.3 in the labor balance relating to his skill category, and −1.6 = (4 × 0.4) in the foreign exchange balance. Assume that it is optimal for the country to hire 1,000 such engineers and no other non-Africans. Requirements amount to 1,800 in the commodity balance "nonfood consumption by non-Africans." These have to be met by the cheapest combination of three activities shown under the heading "urban activities supplying consumer goods for non-Africans through production and imports."[18]

When it is optimal to import foreigners in a given skill category, the efficiency wage of nationals belonging to this category reflects the cost of hiring foreigners, subject to the assumed productivity differential. When it is not optimal to import foreigners, the efficiency wage has to be calculated from the training cost of nationals. This could not be done, however, by considering only the diagonal block of Figure 7.4. It would be necessary to take into account intertemporal linkages by returning to the overall picture of Figure 7.3.

Combining all periods of time, the columns and rows corresponding to Figures 7.3 and 7.4 are listed in Tables 7.3 and 7.4. These two tables correspond to the free-market solution, which is the simplest. The rows, which fulfill only an accounting function in the free-market case, are shown separately in Table 7.5.[19] A number of these rows (those preceded by the letter *P*) become binding constraints in policy experiments.

One striking feature of the model is the high ratio between the number of activities and the number of constraints. Two-thirds of the columns listed in Table 7.3 are interpolation weights used for piecewise linear approximations. Even if those were eliminated by replacing nonlinear relations by linear, the ratio between columns and rows would remain greater than 2. This is shown in Table 7.6.

---

18. The +1 coefficients appearing in these columns express only the fact that demand cannot exceed supply in the commodity balance. They should not be confused with the +1 coefficients appearing in the rural columns. On the one hand, the costs of urban supply activities are fully taken into account by the minus coefficients in the central resource balances; no resources used by urban activities have been left out. On the other hand, all resource constraints specific to the rural sectors (plantations, land, and the like) are replaced by a single constraint expressing the fact that the sum of the weights applied to the sectoral solutions cannot exceed unity.

19. An accounting row is here defined as a row which can be eliminated without affecting the optimal solution. Such rows may have nonzero dual values; for example, in order to compute gross imports and gross exports in addition to net trade, two rows with nonzero dual values must be added.

The Dual Solution

Only the free-market solution, which leads to the most straightforward interpretation of the dual, will be considered. In Table 7.4, the first column lists the constraints. The second and third columns explain the functions performed by each type of constraints and the economic interpretation of the dual values. The fourth and fifth columns give the constant term in the righthand side (RHS) of the constraint and the composition of the minimand; the latter shows how the value of consumption is imputed among factors.

Start with the commodity balance for final consumption good i. The dual value of this constraint measures the contribution of a unit of commodity i to the value of the objective function. It can be written:

$$(8.26') \qquad \Pi_{it} = N_t^{-1}(1 + \delta)^{-t} u_{it},$$

where $N_t = N_0(1 + v)^t$ = the size of the population at time t; δ = the rate at which utilities are discounted over time; and u_{it} = the marginal utility of per capita consumption of commodity i.

Using as numéraire the dual value Π_t of the Ivorian consumption basket, dual values can be expressed in terms of shadow prices as:

$$p_{it} = \Pi_{it}/\Pi_t,$$

where

$$\Pi_t = \sum_i \alpha_{it}\Pi_{it}, \text{ with } \sum_i \alpha_{it} = 1 \text{ and } \Pi_{i0} = \Pi_0 = 1.$$

The shadow price p_{it} is interpreted as a projection of the real price of commodity i. This projection is subject to the assumptions made in the free-market solution. Because of the equality between marginal returns and marginal costs (equation 7.9), the dual value of any commodity balance is a measure of the marginal cost of producing a unit of that commodity, and the dual value of a resource balance is a measure of the marginal productivity of a unit of that resource. Using the same numéraire (Π_t), all prices and returns are expressed in real terms.

For each of the five groups of manufactured exports, there is an upper bound to the volume exported. When this constraint is binding, the marginal return of the export activity exceeds its marginal costs, and the dual value of the constraint is a measure of the difference between the two. If the upper bound constraint reflected only the inelasticity of demand, the dual value could be interpreted as the rent accruing to the exporter; as in the case of cocoa and coffee, this rent could in principle be captured by the

Table 7.3. List of Activities (Free-Market Model)

Chap-ter	Ma-trix	Nature of activities	Sector or product	Activities
		Sectoral or project activities summarizing		
12	H	Rural sectors	North, south, livestock	3
12	H	Special projects	Iron mine, Riviera	2
		Nonlinear relations		
9	U	Transforming consumption into utility	Type of consumer goods (i)	8
14	C	Migrating from rural to urban areas		1
14	C	Substituting labor skills[b]	Skill used as substitute	4
14	C	Importing unskilled agricultural labor		1
14	C	Supplying urban services through the informal sector		1
10	K	Borrowing from abroad		1
		Urban supply activities delivering		
9	D	Final consumption for Ivorians	Group $i = 1, \ldots, 5.$	5
14	D	Final consumption for foreigners	Africans and non-Africans	2
10	D	Capital goods	Vehicles, machinery, construction	3
12	D	Export goods	Five groups ($x = 1, \ldots, 5$)	5
		Investment activities		
11	K	Students newly enrolled in a cycle of study	Skill after graduation	7
10	K	Physical investment	Origin	
10	K	By origin only	Vehicles	1
10	K	By origin and destination	Construction	1
10	K	By origin and destination	Machinery	1
		Trade activities		
14	C	Imports of skilled workers	Skilled labor	7
13	C	Imports of food	Goods for final consumption ($i = 6, 7, 8$)	3
12	C	Importing cotton instead of reducing exports		1
		Accounting columns		
9	U	Total utility		1
9	U	Consumption for Ivorians	Groups ($i = 1, \ldots, 8$)	8
		Total		

a. When no number appears, the choice is made for the entire planning period. When the number is 3, the decision years are 1975, 1980, and 1985. When the number is 4, the decision years are 1975, 1980, 1985, and 1990. When the number is 5, the decision years are 1975, 1980, 1985, 1990, and 2000.

Table 7.3. (continued)

differentiated by				
	Choice regarding		*Year*[a]	*Total number of activities*
				(15)
Weights applied to sectoral activities			3	9
Time of implementation			3	6
				(932)
Interpolation weights for approximating a curve by linear segments			21	672	4
"	"	"	8	4	32
"	"	"	8	4 or 5	144
"	"	"	8	4	32
"	"	"	10	4	40
"	"	"	4	3	12
				(216)
Mix between importation and production of fourteen items			3	4	60
"	"	"	3	4	24
"	"	"	3	4	36
"	"	"	3	4	60
				(103)
Education technology			2 or 1	4	63
Destination				
All urban branches			1	4	4
Schools, all urban branches			2	4	8
Six specified urban branches, all other urban branches			7	4	28
				(51)
			1	5	35
			1	4	12
			1	4	4
				(36)
				4	4
				4	32
				1,353

b. In the first set of experiments, substitution at decreasing returns was replaced by straight downgrading.

Table 7.4. List of Constraints (Free-Market Model)[a]

Number of rows a year	Number of years[b]	Total	Name	Function
				Primal constraints
		1	Maximand	Maxizing discounted utility of consumption
		(6)	*Constraints on weight applied to*	
		3	Rural sectoral solutions	Satisfying rural constraints
		2	Iron mine and Riviera projects	Specifying project size
		(65)	*Linear interpolation of*	
8	4	32	Utility function	Enforcing decreasing returns
8	4 (or 3 or 5)	33	Other nonlinear functions	Enforcing decreasing returns or increasing costs
		(93)	*Commodity balances*	
8	4	32	Final consumer goods for Ivorians	Limiting demand to availabilities
2	4 (or 5)	9	Final consumer goods for foreigners	Limiting demand to availabilities
2	4	8	Public consumption	Satisfying given public needs
4	4	16	Capital and intermediate goods	Limiting demand to availability
5	4 (or 3)	19	Export goods	Limiting export specialization
1	5	5	Foreign exchange	Limiting demand to availability
1	4	4	Supply adjustment for cotton	Increasing supply cost when urban demand exceeds rural supply
		(93)	*Primary domestic resource balances*	
9	5 (or 4)	43	Labor by skill category	Limiting demand to availability or supply
10	5	50	Physical capacities	Limiting demand to availability or supply
9	4	36	*Accounting rows*	
67		293	Total	

a. Additional accounting and policy rows are shown in Table 7.5.
b. When the number of decision years is 4, those refer to 1975, 1980, 1985 and 1990. When the number is 5, the additional year refers to increments between 1990 and 2000.

Table 7.4. (continued)

Dual value	Right-hand side	Minimand (cost minus return) $\Sigma_t \, \Sigma \, (\text{RHS})_t \, (dual \, value)_t$
Discounted values of		
Return on rural resources	+1	+Returns to rural resources
Profit (or loss) from project	+1	+Profit (or + loss) from project
Utility loss[c]	+1	−Maximand − value of private consumption
Rents	+1	+Rents
Market price	0	
Marginal cost	0	
Marginal cost of public consumption	+	−Value of public consumption
Marginal cost		
−Marginal costs + marginal return	+	+Rents on urban exports
Efficiency value of foreign exchange	−	+Return on foreign capital
Differences between prices c.i.f. and f.o.b.		
Efficiency wage	−	+Return on labor
Efficiency rental value of capacities	−	+Return on domestic capital (excluding rural)
		−Maximand (return minus cost)

c. Utility loss is defined as the consumption increment required to reach bliss, priced at current marginal utility minus the utility gained in reaching bliss. No loss would occur if marginal utility were constant; see Figure 7.5.

Table 7.5. *Additional Rows for Accounting and Policy Experiments*[a]

Variable to be measured or additional constraint	Number of rows per year	Number of years	Total
Economic aggregates			(60)
GDP		4	
Total consumption		4	
Total physical investment		4	
Total human investment		4	
P Private savings		4	
P Public expenditures on postprimary education		4	
Public expenditures (including education)		4	
Public revenues		4	
P Public savings (resource balance)		4	
P Net inflow of capital from abroad		5	
Debt repayment abroad		4	
Total imports		5	
Total exports		5	
Agricultural exports forgone by urban purchases		5	
Labor and educational data			(81)
P Wage bill paid to non-Africans		5	
P Wage bill paid to non-Ivorian Africans		4	
Weighted index of Ivorians employed in medium skills		4	
Weighted index of Ivorians employed in high skills		4	
Ivorians employed, by skill category ($\lambda = 1, \ldots, 8$)	8	(4 or 5)	
P New enrollment in first grade of high school		4	
P New enrollment in university		4	
Student population in technical schools		4	
P Student population in secondary education		4	
P Student population in higher education		4	
Cumulated number of dropouts		5	
Tariff experiments (existing and reduced tariffs)			(28)
P Public revenues including tariffs	2	4	
P Total imports at prices c.i.f. plus tariffs	2	5	
P Trade balance with tariffs	2	5	
Additional constraints			(65)
Four additional skill categories	4	4 (or 5)	
Employment of Ivorians in these four categories	4	4 (or 5)	
Linear interpolation for skill substitution in two categories	2	5	

a. Rows preceded by *P* become binding constraints in policy experiments.

Table 7.5. (continued)

Variable to be measured or additional constraint	Number of rows per year	Number of years	Total
P Monotonicity constraints on new enrollments	2	4	
P Monotonocity constraints on size of school populations	2	4	
Allocation of urban investment in 1970		1	
Total listed above[b]			234
Rows listed in Table 7.4			293
Grand total[b]			527

b. Numbers refer to last set of experiments.

state through an export tax. Upper bounds to manufactured exports are, however, more likely to reflect implicit supply constraints dealing, for example, with management or export promotion. The dual value would then account for returns on factors not explicitly identified in the model.

Consider now the sectoral constraints at the top of Table 7.4. By limiting to unity the sum of the weights applied to the sectoral solutions, the constraint effectively enforces all the constraints which are specific to the sector. The dual value of the weight constraint therefore is a measure of the sum of the discounted returns imputed to all sectoral resources.[20] In the case of the iron mine, the size of the mine is given; the only variable is the date at which the mine should be opened. The dual value of the weight constraint is a measure of the discounted net benefit (or loss) attached to the mining project. For each of the sectors (or projects), the weight constraint covers the entire time horizon. The dual value of the constraint, therefore, is a measure of the return imputed to the resources that are specific to the sector (project) throughout the planning period. Imputed returns can nevertheless be computed year by year; national resource costs need only be subtracted from the value of the national resources and commodities produced during each representative year.

The dual values of the interpolation constraints enforcing nonlinear relationships can be interpreted as rents. Consider, for example, the interpolation constraint relating to the upward-sloping supply curve of unskilled labor migrating from neighboring countries. The dual value

20. It also includes the costs of the rural constraints other than those expressed in the form of resource balances. Thus, it includes the rent on exports of coffee and cocoa, which is equal to the quantity exported multiplied by the difference between marginal return and marginal cost.

Table 7.6. Ratio between Activities and Constraints

Type of model	Activities	Constraints	Ratio
Tables 7.3 and 7.4 as they are	1,353	293	4.6
Tables 7.3 and 7.4 after replacing all nonlinear functions by linear ones and removing the 36 accounting rows and columns	450	192	2.3
All rows and columns appearing on the last set of experiments	1,642	527	3.1

of the constraint is equal to the difference between marginal and average import costs multiplied by the number of migrants (see Figure 14.1). Similarly, the interpolation constraint enforcing decreasing marginal utilities is a measure of the consumer's surplus.

As regards the composition of the minimand in the last column of Table 7.4, in the top two rows, the contribution to the minimand and the dual values of the constraints are the same. In the next two rows, the constants of the interpolation constraints on the righthand side (RHS) are still equal to unity but the constraints are time-specific. The dual values, therefore, need to be added up over time to calculate the contribution to the minimand. In the case of the interpolation constraints used to transform consumption into utilities, the sum of the dual values of these constraints is negative. In absolute terms, this sum is a measure of the excess of consumption priced at its dual value over the maximand.

In the commodity balance rows, the contribution to the minimand is obtained by multiplying the RHS by the dual value of the constraint and summing up the products over time. The exogenously given requirements for public consumption are valued in the same way as private consumption and are measured negatively, while the contributions of the net inflow of foreign capital and the rent on manufactured exports are counted positively. Finally, in the two bottom rows, the contributions of the primary domestic resources are counted positively. The minimand, therefore, imputes the value of consumption (public and private) net of rents to national labor and domestic capital.[21] When the imputed returns to factors were shown for the years 1975, 1980, and 1985 in Table 3.11, the value of investments had been added to that of consumption. We do not

21. Since the value of final demand is ultimately imputed to primary resources, the model can be simplified by expressing final demand in terms of direct and indirect resource requirements whenever possible. This is precisely what was done in incorporating reduced-form matrices into the central model.

need to do so in Table 7.4. By measuring the sum of the discounted utility of consumption over an infinite time horizon, the contribution of investment is accounted for in terms of future consumption (see Chapter 8).

Government Intervention

The model described in the preceding pages has been modified to simulate various types of government intervention. This can easily be done if the policy measures take the form of quantitative restrictions, which is accomplished by modifying the coefficients (that is, the discount rate, the level of public consumption, the weights applied to a project or a rural solution, and so forth). Alternatively, additional constraints can be introduced into the model (quotas for the entry of foreign labor, for the inflow of foreign capital, for university enrollments, and for savings, for example). Government interventions dealing with price policies, such as excise taxes or tariffs on imports, are more difficult to simulate. Because they affect the dual solution, an iterative procedure is required.

In a model in which consumption does not react to variations in prices, excise taxes can be ignored. Here, because they affect the pattern of consumption, they cannot be ignored. Consider the case of alcoholic beverages. One of the main purposes of the tax is to reduce the consumption of alcohol, a commodity to which society attaches a lesser value than do individual consumers. The impact of the tax can be simulated by introducing into the model a double price structure. Prices inclusive of tax are used to optimize the patterns of private consumption. Prices net of tax are used to optimize resource allocation.

The problem of tariffs on imports (or export subsidies) is very similar. In this instance, however, the tariff structure does not affect only consumer choices; it also affects the make-or-buy choice. Prices inclusive of tariffs (or subsidies) are used to optimize production, trading, and consumption choices. Prices net of tariffs (or subsidies) are used to ensure equilibrium in the balance of payments.

This dual price structure is somewhat cumbersome because it requires iterative solutions. With free trade, there is a single foreign exchange balance in which imports are valued at c.i.f. prices and exports at f.o.b. prices. With tariffs there are two such balances. The true balance of payments becomes an accounting row measuring by its slack the foreign-exchange surplus or deficit. The distorted balance of payments, in which imports are valued at c.i.f. prices plus tariffs and exports at f.o.b. prices plus subsidies, becomes the binding constraint. This is the constraint which determines the dual values on the basis of which choices are made. This constraint must include in its RHS an iterative constant, $\bar{T}$, where $\bar{T}$ is an estimation of the proceeds of tariffs net of subsidies. When the true balance of payments is in equilibrium, the constant $\bar{T}$ is identical to the proceeds of tariffs net of subsidies. With the iterative procedure described in Chapter 13, convergence is very fast.

The model can be solved with alternative sets of tariffs. A set of shadow prices corresponds to each set of tariffs, but, in any given solution of the model, decisions are made on the basis of a common set of shadow prices in the private and public sectors.

When shadow prices are used to select public investments on the basis of social cost-benefit analysis, the procedure is different. Allocation of resources is made in the private sector on the basis of prices inclusive of tariffs and in the public sector on the basis of shadow prices, which exclude the price distortions resulting from the imposition of tariffs. This raises a logical problem. On the one hand, tariffs are set by government representatives. On the other, tariffs are excluded for allocating government funds among projects. The rationale for this position is that the government cannot be treated as a single decision-making body. This position is stated clearly by W. M. Corden:

> Tariffs [may] have been imposed to achieve certain purposes concerned with the production pattern with which the appraisers of investment projects are not in sympathy, such as to shift income distribution towards the protected industries or to foster certain types of production for the sake of externalities believed to be generated. The project appraisers cannot get the tariffs reduced explicitly, but they can modify or even eliminate their effects by providing what is, essentially, offsetting protection for the project industries.
>
> We may have a situation where one part of the government—one department or minister, or one set of advisers—has different objectives from another part, and each has control of part of the decision-making machinery. Instead of a single government policy being pursued, one department of government then maximises its "objective function"—conceived of here as depending on efficiency of resource allocation (Pareto criterion), qualified perhaps for income distribution considerations—subject to the constraint of policies imposed by other departments and their backers. This sounds a little cynical, but does so only because it is put so bluntly. (Corden 1974)

Chapter 8

The Choice between Consumption and Savings

THE MODEL COMBINES Ramsey's principle for optimizing savings (Ramsey 1928) with Frisch's generalized demand system (Frisch 1959). As a result, the allocation of resources between consumption and savings is optimized simultaneously with the composition of final demand among consumer goods. Although intertemporal and intratemporal choices are made simultaneously in the model, they are analyzed in two separate chapters. This chapter deals with the optimization of the consumption path over time; there is no constraint on savings; consumption is treated as a single good. The next chapter deals with the optimal composition of consumption, which is disaggregated into eight commodity groups; the endogenous price and income effects will then be analyzed, taking the choice between consumption and savings as given.

The first section of this chapter gives the specifications of the additive utility function. This function is expressed as a generalized constant elasticity of substitution (CES) function (Arrow, Chenery, Minhas, and Solow 1961). In accordance with estimates derived from generalized demand systems (in countries other than the Ivory Coast), the overall elasticity of substitution, σ, is taken as less than unity (generally 0.5). For this reason, the utility maximand always converges. In the second section the relationships between the optimal growth rate of per capita consumption and the marginal productivity of capital are analyzed algebraically. Numerical examples show that credible savings rates can be reached by combining values of the elasticity of substitution and of the pure time-discount rate which are also credible. In the third section, a simplified algebraic version of the Ivory Coast model is reviewed in the context of the golden-rule literature (Phelps 1966). In the last two sections, the simplified algebraic model is translated into programming terms. The notations used throughout this chapter in the one-product, two factor model are here summarized for convenience:

Endogenous variables

$Y_t = I_t + C_t$		
$\quad = Y(K_t, L_t, t)$	Net national product	> 0
K_t	Stock of renewable capital	> 0
$I_t = \dot{K}_t$	Net investments (= savings)	
C_t	Consumption	> 0
$U_t = U(c_t)$	Utility of per capita consumption	< 0
$c_t = C_t/N_t$	Per capita consumption	> 0
$r_t = \partial Y_t/\partial K_t$	Marginal productivity of capital	> 0
$w_t = \partial Y_t/\partial L_t$	Marginal productivity of labor	> 0
$k_t = K_t/Y_t$	Capital-output ratio	> 0
$s_t = I_t/Y_t$	Savings ratio	$0 < s < 1$
$x_t = e^{-\zeta t}K_t/L_t$	Capital/labor augmented ratio	> 0
$z_t = e^{-\zeta t}C_t/L_t$	Consumption/labor augmented ratio	> 0
γ_t	Growth rate of per capita consumption	
$g_t = \nu + \gamma_t$	Growth rate of total consumption	

Exogenous variables

$N_t = e^{\nu t}\bar{N}_0$	Size of population	> 0
$L_t = e^{\nu t}\bar{L}_0$	Size of the labor force	> 0
K_0	Initial capital stock	> 0

Exogenous time-in variant parameters

ν	Growth rate of population	> 0
ζ	Growth rate of labor productivity	≥ 0
$\bar{\gamma}$	Postterminal growth rate of per capita consumption	> 0
σ	Elasticity of substitution of per capita consumption at various points in time	$0 < \sigma < 1$
$\bar{\sigma}$	Elasticity of substitution between labor and capital	$0 < \sigma < 1$

Superscript and subscripts

$\hat{}$	Superscript identifying asymptotic values	
t and τ	Time subscripts	> 0
T	Terminal point for optimization	> 0

The Objective Function

Utility $U(c)$ is an isoelastic Bernouilli function. It is most easily defined by starting from the marginal utility of consumption and its derivative:

$$(8.1) \qquad u = \frac{dU}{dc} = Ac^{-1/\sigma},$$

$$(8.2) \qquad \frac{du}{dc} = -A\frac{1}{\sigma}c^{-1/\sigma-1} = -\frac{1}{\sigma}\frac{u}{c},$$

where A is an arbitrary positive constant and c (the level of per capita consumption) is nonnegative.

The marginal utility of consumption must be positive and must be declining when consumption rises. Equation (8.2) shows that these two conditions require the value of σ to be nonnegative. Equation (8.2) can be rearranged as (8.2'), which shows that $-\sigma$ is a measure of the elasticity of consumption in relation to the marginal utility of consumption:

$$(8.2') \qquad \frac{dc}{c} = -\sigma\frac{du}{u},$$

where $\sigma \geq 0$.

Integrating (8.1) gives the utility function:

$$(8.3) \qquad \begin{aligned} U &= \bar{U} + A\frac{\sigma}{\sigma - 1}c^{1-1/\sigma} \quad \text{for} \quad \sigma \neq 1 \quad \text{and} \\ U &= A\log\frac{c}{\bar{c}} \qquad\qquad \text{for} \quad \sigma = 1, \end{aligned}$$

where A is an arbitrary positive constant and $\bar{U}$ an integration constant. By appropriate selection of these constants, the utility function can be rewritten:

$$(8.4a) \qquad U = -c^{-(1/\sigma-1)} \quad \text{for} \quad 0 \leq \sigma < 1,$$

$$(8.4b) \qquad U = \ln c \qquad\qquad \text{for} \quad \sigma = 1,$$

$$(8.4c) \qquad U = +c^{1-1/\sigma} \qquad \text{for} \quad \sigma > 1.$$

The value of the objective function is defined as the sum of the discounted utilities of consumption over an infinite time horizon:

$$(8.5) \qquad V = \sum_{t=0}^{t=\infty} (1 + \delta)^{-t}U(c_t),$$

where c and t are nonnegative. It will be noted that equation (8.5) implies the "noncomplementarity between periods" postulate of Debreu (1960) and the "stationary" postulate of Koopmans (1960).

From (8.2′), $-\sigma$ was interpreted as a price elasticity of demand. From the combination of (8.4) and (8.5), σ can be reinterpreted as the elasticity of substitution between consumption at different points in time. This can be shown in a simple way by considering the levels of consumption c_0 and c_t at times zero and t and writing the value of the objective function as:

$$(8.6) \qquad \mu V = c_0^{1-1/\sigma} + (1 + \delta)^{-t} c_t^{1-1/\sigma}, \quad \text{for} \quad \sigma \neq 1,$$

where μ is a dummy variable defined as $\mu = +1$ for $\sigma > 1$ and $\mu = -1$ for $0 < \sigma < 1$.[1]

Elevating the left- and righthand sides to power $1/\sigma - 1$, equation (8.6) can be rewritten as:

$$(8.6′) \qquad (\mu V)^{-1/\rho} = a[hc_0^{-\rho} + (1 - h)c_t^{-\rho}]^{-1/\rho},$$

where $\rho = 1/\sigma - 1$, $h = [1 + (1 + \delta)^{-t}]^{-1}$, and $a = [1 + (1 + \delta)^{-t}]^{-1/\rho}$.

Function (8.6′) is very similar to the constant elasticity of substitution (CES) function of Arrow, Chenery, Minhas, and Solow (1961):

$$(8.6″) \qquad\qquad Q = a[hK^{-\rho} + (1 - h)L^{-\rho}]^{-1/\rho}.$$

For Q given, equation (8.6″) defines an isoproduct curve in the K, L space and σ measures the elasticity of substitution between capital (K) and labor (L) along this isoquant. For V, the sum of discounted utilities given, (8.6′) defines an isoutility curve in the c_0, c_t space shown in Figure 8.1; σ is a measure of the elasticity of substitution between consumption at time zero (c_0) and at time t (c_t) along this isoquant. The CES distribution parameter $(1 - h)/h$ is equal to unity when utilities are not discounted; it is less than unity when the pure time-discount rate (δ) is positive. Calling w and r the marginal product of labor and capital, the relative returns to factors are measured, respectively, by

$$\frac{wL}{rK} = \frac{1 - h}{h} \left(\frac{L}{K}\right)^{1-1/\sigma}$$

1. With $n + 1$ points in time $t(= 0, \ldots, n)$, the righthand side (RHS) of equation (8.6′) would be rewritten as:

$$\left[\sum_{t=0}^{t=n} e^{-\delta t} c_t - \rho\right]^{-1/\rho},$$

which is the generalized CES function introduced by Bergson (1936).

Figure 8.1. The Isoutility Curve for δ = 0

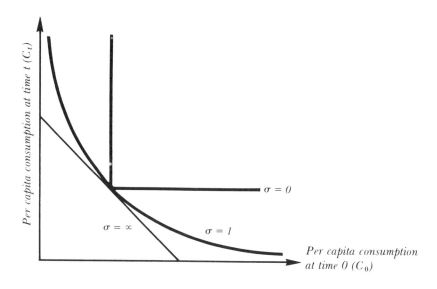

Figure 8.2. Marginal Utility (+) and Utility (−) for 0 < σ < 1

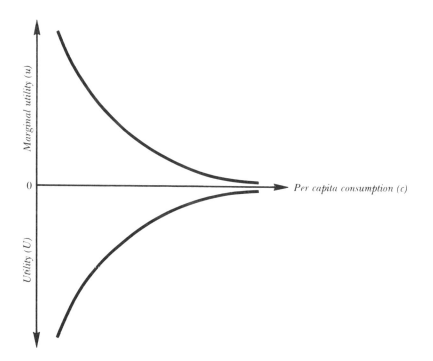

Table 8.1. Constant-Elasticity-of-Substitution Production and Utility Functions

$\rho = \dfrac{1}{\sigma} - 1$	Production function	Utility function		$\sigma = \dfrac{1}{1+\rho}$
$\rho = +\infty$	Harrod and Domar $Y = kK$	$U = 0$ and	$c_t \equiv \bar{c}$	$\sigma = 0$
$0 < \rho < \infty$	$Y = a[hK^{-\rho} + (1-h)L^{-\rho}]^{-1/\rho}$	$U = \bar{U} - Ac^{-(1/\sigma - 1)}$	Bliss $= \bar{U}$	$0 < \sigma < 1$
$\rho = 0$	Cobb and Douglas $Y = aK^h L^{1-h}$	$U = A \ln (c/\bar{c})$		$\sigma = 1$
$-1 < \rho < 0$	$Y = a[hK^{-\rho} + (1-h)L^{-\rho}]^{-1/\rho}$	$U = Ac^{1-1/\sigma} - \bar{U}$	Unbounded	$1 < \sigma < \infty$
$\rho = -1$	Linear $Y = ahK + a(1-h)L$	$U = c$		$\sigma = +\infty$

and

$$\frac{(1 + \delta)^{-t} u_t \, c_t}{u_0 \quad c_0} = (1 + \delta)^{-t} \left(\frac{c_t}{c_0}\right)^{1-1/\sigma}.$$

The difference between the lefthand-side members of (8.6') and (8.6") reflects the difference between the assumptions made on returns to scale. In (8.6"), constant return to scale is assumed; this requires the production function to be homogenous of degree one in K and L. The constant return-to-scale assumption can be tested empirically, because the three variables are measured in cardinal units. In (8.6'), V is not defined cardinally but ordinally. Its value is used only to order the preferences of consumers along different utility-indifference curves. Any monotonic transformation of V, such as $V^{-1/\rho}$, does not affect this ordering.

The impact of σ on the shape of the isoutility curve is illustrated in Figure 8.1. The indifference curve is linear for $\sigma = \infty$, logarithmic for $\sigma = 1$ and right-angle for $\sigma = 0$. For $\sigma > 1$, the indifference curves cut the axes, and U is measured by a positive number. For $0 < \sigma \le 1$, the indifference curves do not cut the axes, and U is measured by a negative number. The corresponding formulas of the production and undiscounted utility functions are shown in Table 8.1.

The analysis presented in Chapter 9 can now be anticipated briefly by disaggregating consumption into n commodity group $i = 1, \ldots, n$. The objective function (8.5) becomes:

$$V = \sum_t (1 - \delta)^{-t} \sum_i U_{it}(c_{it}),$$

which can be rewritten:

(8.5a) $\qquad V^{-1/\rho} = [\sum_t (1 - \delta)^{-t} \sum_i A_i c_i^{-\rho_i}]^{-1/\rho},$

where

$$\rho_i = \frac{1}{\eta_i \sigma} - 1, \, \rho = \frac{1}{\sigma} - 1, \quad \text{and} \quad \sigma = \sum_i \eta_{it} \frac{c_{it}}{c_t}.$$

Equation (8.5a) is a generalized CES function. As will be seen in Chapter 9, parameters η_i (income elasticity) and σ (overall elasticity of substitution) can be estimated econometrically from the quantities and prices recorded in the market. The concept of the generalized demand system was introduced by Frisch (1959). Since then, a number of empirical studies have been conducted. The results reported by Sato (1972) and Lluch (Lluch and Williams 1973) indicate that σ is significantly lower than unity, especially in low-income countries.[2] This implies that the utility function is always bounded for nonnegative discount rates (δ). The fact that the elasticity of substitution, σ, could be econometrically estimated from generalized demand systems does not seem to have been recognized in the growth theory literature of the 1960s.[3]

In this study, experiments were conducted only for values of σ lower than unity; therefore, the objective function always converges. As shown in Figure 8.2, when per capita consumption tends toward infinity, utility tends toward zero from below; marginal utility tends also toward zero, but from above.

The Simplified Algebraic Model

In the actual programming model, time is a discrete variable. In this simplified algebraic presentation, time is treated as a continuous variable and the objective function (8.5) is rewritten as:

$$(8.5') \qquad V = \int_{t=0}^{t=\infty} e^{-\delta t} U(c_t)\, dt,$$

where utility (U) is still defined by (8.4a).

In a one-product closed-economy model, there is a single commodity balance:

$$(8.6a) \qquad Y_t \quad = \quad I_t \quad + \quad C_t.$$

$$[\text{Production}] = [\text{investment}] + [\text{consumption}].$$

In this balance, C_t refers to total consumption; instead, in the objective function, c_t refers to per capita consumption. Taking the initial population N_0 as unity, C_t is related to c_t through the population growth rate ν taken as a time-invariant parameter:

$$(8.6b) \qquad C_t = e^{\nu t} c_t,$$

where $\bar{N}_0 = 1$.

Physical capital is assumed here to be the only renewable resource and not to depreciate through time; investment is therefore equal to

2. The empirical estimation of CES production functions also suggests that when factors are defined broadly (such as labor and capital), the elasticity of substitution, σ, is less than unity.

3. As noted by Sato (1972), the coefficient $\omega = -\sigma^{-1}$ was not interpreted by Frisch (1959) as the overall elasticity of substitution. See also Kendrick and Taylor (1969).

net physical capital formation:

(8.6c) $$I_t = \dot{K}_t.$$

Production is a constant return to scale function of capital, K_t, and labor, L_t. Labor is an exogenous variable increasing at the same rate, ν, as population. The production function, twice continuously differentiable in K and strictly concave, is of the form:

(8.6d) $$Y_t = Y(K_t, t) \quad \text{with} \quad K(0) = \bar{K}_0.$$

Combining equations (8.6a) through (8.6d), per capita consumption can be written:

(8.6) $$c_t = e^{-\nu t}[Y(K_t, t) - \dot{K}],$$

where $c_t > 0$, $Y_t > 0$ and $K_t > 0$.

Replacing, in (8.5'), c_t by its value from (8.6), the objective function is of the form:

(8.5″) $$V = \int_{t=0}^{t=\infty} F(K_t, \dot{K}_t, t)dt.$$

With F strictly concave in K_t and $\dot{K}_t$, the necessary and sufficient condition for V to be a maximum is the Euler equality:

(8.7) $$\frac{\partial F}{\partial K} = \frac{d}{dt}\left(\frac{\partial K}{\partial \dot{K}}\right) \quad \text{for all } t.$$

It can be rewritten, in this case, as:

(8.7') $$r_t = \delta + \nu - \frac{\dot{u}_t}{u_t},$$

where $r_t = \partial Y/\partial K$ is the marginal productivity of capital.

With a CES utility function, the last term is:

$$\frac{\dot{u}_t}{u_t} = -\frac{1}{\sigma}\frac{\dot{c}_t}{c_t}.[4]$$

Defining the growth rate of per capita consumption by the variable parameter:

$$\gamma_t = \frac{\dot{c}_t}{c_t},$$

4. $\dot{u}_t = \dfrac{du(c_t)}{dc_t}\dfrac{dc_t}{dt}$, where the derivative of marginal utility is given from equation

(8.2) by $\dfrac{du(c_t)}{dc_t} = -\dfrac{1}{\sigma}\dfrac{u_t}{c_t}$.

equation (8.7') becomes:

$$r_t = \delta + \nu + \frac{\gamma_t}{\sigma}.$$

The Euler equality, therefore, defines the optimum growth rate of per capita consumption, γ_t, in relation to the marginal productivity of capital, r_t (which is an endogenous variable), and to the three time-invariant parameters σ, δ, and ν:

(8.8) γ_t = σ (r_t − δ − ν).

$$\begin{bmatrix} Optimal\ growth \\ of\ per\ capita \\ consumption \end{bmatrix} = \begin{bmatrix} elasticity \\ of\ substi- \\ tution \end{bmatrix} \begin{bmatrix} marginal \\ productivity \\ of\ capital \end{bmatrix} - \begin{matrix} pure\ rate \\ of\ time \\ discount \end{matrix} - \begin{matrix} rate\ of \\ population \\ growth \end{matrix} .$$

This is the key equation defining the dynamics of the model. It may, therefore, be useful to derive it in a more intuitive way (without using the Euler theorem). Consider, first, the case of a stationary population ($\nu = 0$) where time is not discounted ($\delta = 0$). Assume that one additional unit is invested today (at time t) and one less tomorrow (at time $t + \Delta t$). Capital stock increases by one unit tomorrow (at time $t + \Delta t$), but remains unchanged thereafter. Optimal saving implies that the satisfaction derived from the additional consumption tomorrow exactly compensates for the satisfaction forgone today. The latter is equal to $u(c_t)$, which defines the marginal utility of a unit of consumption today. The former is the amount $(1 + r_t \Delta t)$ valued at $u(c_{t+\Delta t})$, which defines the marginal utility of a unit of consumption tomorrow. In addition to the unit saved today the increment $r_t \Delta t$ is received tomorrow; this increment may be visualized as the return on a unit of capital lent for the period Δt at the prevailing interest rate, r_t (this is the marginal productivity of capital treated as constant during the small interval Δt). The optimality condition can therefore be written as:

(8.9) $$u(c_t) = (1 + r_t \Delta t) \cdot u(c_{t+\Delta t}), \quad \text{or}$$

(8.9') $$r_t \cdot u(c_{t+\Delta t}) = -\frac{u(c_{t+\Delta t}) - u(c_t)}{\Delta t}.$$

When the interval of time Δt tends toward zero, the righthand side (RHS) of (8.9') tends toward the derivative of the marginal utility of consumption in relation to time, that is to say, $-\dot{u}_t$. Simultaneously, the second term of the lefthand side (LHS) tends toward $u(c_t)$. Equation (8.9') can therefore be rewritten as:

(8.7") $$r_t = -\frac{\dot{u}_t}{u_t},$$

which is identical to equation (8.7′) for $\delta = \nu = 0$. Equation (8.7″) says that, with optimal savings, the marginal productivity of capital must be just equal to the rate of decline over time in the marginal utility of consumption. With a CES utility function, the latter is equal to γ_t (the rate of increase over time of per capita consumption), divided by σ (the elasticity of substitution between consumption at two different points in time). Hence: $\gamma_t = \sigma r_t$.

Assume now that population rises at the rate ν. By investing one additional unit today and one less tomorrow, $1 + r_t \Delta t$ additional units of consumption are still disposed of tomorrow. But those have to be shared among a number of consumers multiplied by $1 + \nu \Delta t$. Consequently, the increase in per capita consumption becomes $(1 + r_t \Delta t)/(1 + \nu \Delta t) \to 1 + (r_t - \nu)\Delta t$, for $\Delta t \to 0$. In the lefthand side (LHS) of equation (8.7″), r_t must now be replaced by $r_t - \nu$.

Assume, finally, that utility of consumption is discounted over time at rate δ. In the RHS of (8.9), the utility of consumption tomorrow $u(c_{t+\Delta t})$ must be divided by the discount factor $1 + \delta \Delta t$. The first term of the RHS of (8.9) becomes:

$$\frac{1 + r_t \Delta t}{(1 + \nu \Delta t)(1 + \delta \Delta t)} \to 1 + (r_t - \nu - \delta)\Delta t, \text{ for } \Delta t \to 0.$$

Replacing r_t by $r_t - \nu - \delta$ in (8.7″) leads to (8.7′), hence to (8.8).

The numerical values implied by equation (8.8) are illustrated in Table 8.2. One single value, $\nu = 0.03$, is used for population growth. Two alternative values are used for the elasticity of substitution, $\sigma = 0.2$ and 0.5; they correspond to the lower and upper ranges of the econometric estimations conducted for developing countries (Lluch and Williams 1973). Three alternative values are retained for the pure discount rate, δ, and for the marginal productivity of capital, $r_t = \partial Y_t / \partial K_t$.

Consider a row of Table 8.2, with which a given value of the marginal productivity of capital (r_t) is associated. Plausible values of

Table 8.2. *The Optimal Growth Rate of Per Capita Consumption* γ_t
(8.8) $\gamma_t = \sigma(r_t - \delta - \nu)$ for $\nu = 0.03$

Marginal productivity of capital	$\delta = 0$		$\delta = 0.05$		$\delta = 0.10$	
	$\sigma = 0.5$	$\sigma = 0.2$	$\sigma = 0.5$	$\sigma = 0.2$	$\sigma = 0.5$	$\sigma = 0.2$
$r_t = 0.10$	0.035	0.014	0.010	0.004	−0.015	−0.006
$r_t = 0.15$	0.060	0.024	0.035	0.014	0.010	0.004
$r_t = 0.20$	0.085	0.034	0.060	0.024	0.035	0.014

the growth rate of per capita consumption (γ_t) can be found for appropriate combinations of the values of σ and δ. For example, given $r_t = 0.15$, $\gamma_t = 0.035$ for $\sigma = 0.5$ and $\delta = 0.05$.

In equation (8.8), time is treated as a continuous variable. In numerical applications, time is often treated, instead, as a discrete variable identifying the year. As shown below, equation (8.8) is replaced by:

$$(8.32) \qquad (1 + \gamma_t)^{1/\sigma} = (1 + r_t)(1 + \delta)^{-1}(1 + \nu)^{-1}.$$

For $\sigma = 0.5$, $\delta = 0.05$ and $r_t = 0.15$ the value of γ_t becomes 0.0295 instead of 0.035 (Table 8.2). The coefficient δ corresponds then to a 5 percent a year discount rate and the coefficient γ_t to a 2.95 percent annual growth in per capita consumption. The difference between 3.5 and 2.95 is significant and should not be overlooked in numerical models.

Treating time as a continuous variable, equation (8.8) shows that the same value of γ_t can be obtained for different combinations of the values of σ and δ. A modification $\Delta\sigma$ in the value of the elasticity of substitution can be compensated for by a variation $\Delta\delta$ in the rate of discount. Compensated variations are defined by:

$$(8.8') \qquad \Delta\delta = \frac{\gamma_t}{\sigma}\frac{\Delta\sigma}{\sigma + \Delta\sigma}.$$

Thus, for $r_t = 0.15$ and $\nu = 0.03$, the same growth rate $\gamma_t = 0.03$ can be obtained either with the combination of $\sigma = 0.25$ and $\delta = 0$ or with the combination of $\sigma = 0.5$ and $\delta = 0.06$. The impact of variations compensated for in σ and δ has been tested with a small version of the Ivory Coast model.[5] Table 8.3 shows that the optimal rate of saving is hardly affected by reducing σ from 0.5 to 0.3 provided the value of δ is simultaneously reduced according to (8.8').

The value of the elasticity of substitution, σ, can be estimated empirically from market data (see Chapter 9). Given observable values of the growth rate of per capita consumption (γ_t) and of the marginal productivity of capital (r_t), a value of the pure time-discount rate can be derived from equation (8.8).

The alternative method is to solve the model for different values of δ and to select the appropriate value of δ on the basis of its implications. The selection is then made on the basis of projected

---

5. The experimental version of the model consists of 130 equations, whereas there are 500 equations in the final version.

Table 8.3. *The Effect of Variations of σ and δ Compensated for on the Optimal Rates of Saving*

Year	σ = 0.5 δ = 0.053	σ = 0.3 δ = 0.016
1975	0.247	0.246
1980	0.288	0.284
1985	0.315	0.307
1990	0.296	0.295

a. Variations compensated for are calculated from equation (8.8′) for the asymptotic values $\hat{y} = 0.028$ and $\hat{r} = 0.14$, given $\nu = 0.031$.

intertemporal consumption tradeoffs and feasible savings efforts. Figure 8.3 shows three alternative time paths of consumption and savings associated with three different values of the pure time preference (δ). The choice between these three alternatives is a political option. A higher level of consumption in 1990 requires a greater savings effort in the 1970s, and this effort must be politically feasible.

The numerical value of the discount rate is affected by the formulation of the objective function. In this study, the objective function V, given in equation (8.5′), is the discounted utility of per capita consumption. Some authors define, instead, an objective function V' which is the sum of the discounted utilities accruing to each member of society. Since their number is N_t, the objective function becomes:

$$V' = \int_0^\infty N_t e^{-\delta' t} U(c_t) dt.$$

With objective function V', the population growth rate (ν) disappears from equation (8.8): $\delta + \nu$ is replaced by δ'.[6] When parameters δ and ν are time invariant, as is the case here, the two formulations lead to the same result provided $\delta' - \delta = \nu$. The difference $\delta' - \delta$ shows that the discount rate has to be interpreted differently with objective functions V' and V.

The Optimal Path

Equation (8.8) defines the optimal growth of per capita consumption (γ_t) in relation to the marginal productivity of capital (r_t). It does

6. In the RHS of equation (8.9), the individual gains are divided by $1 + \nu\Delta t$, but the gain of society is multiplied by $1 + \nu\Delta t$; thus, ν disappears.

Figure 8.3. *The Impact of Alternative Values of the Time-Discount Rate (δ) on the Time Path of Consumption and Savings*

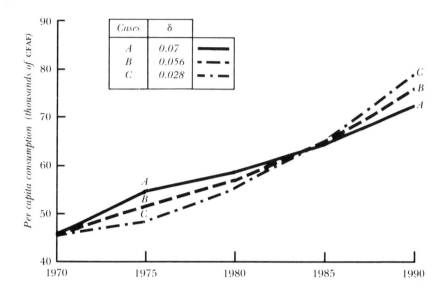

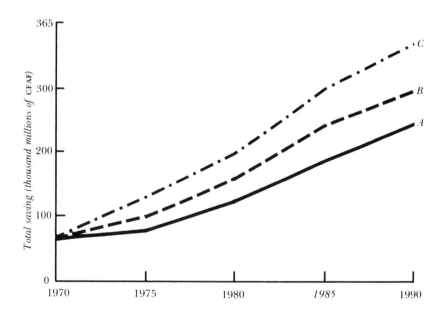

not, however, specify the growth path, except when the marginal productivity of capital remains constant.

This case, which corresponds to a labor-surplus economy with a fixed capital-output ratio (k), should first be disposed of. The marginal productivity of capital remains constant $(r = k^{-1})$. Consumption, investment, capital stocks, and production all grow at the same rate $(\gamma + \nu)$ throughout the optimization horizon $(t = 0, \ldots, \infty)$. At time zero, consumption $C_0 = (k^{-1} - \gamma - \nu)\bar{K}_0$ can be lower than, equal to, or higher than the historical level depending on the initial capital stock $(\bar{K}_0)$.

If capital per worker grew at the constant rate γ, the labor surplus would normally be expected to be absorbed at some stage. The interesting problem is the elimination of the labor surplus. Chakravarty (1969) and Manne (1974) analyze this problem by drawing a distinction between a modern sector and a traditional one. A one-sector model will be adhered to here, but the case will be considered in which labor and capital both have nonzero marginal productivities and are substitutable, the one for the other. The Ramsey model will provide a start (see Ramsey 1928), before considering a more complex one that provides a reasonable approximation of the actual programming model.

THE RAMSEY MODEL

Population and technology are stationary $(\nu = \zeta = 0)$; time is not discounted $(\delta = 0)$; the time variable t thus disappears from the objective function in equation (8.5′). For the sake of simplicity, Ramsey's disutility of labor will be omitted and the utility at the bliss level will be taken as zero. The objective function can then be written in the simple form:

$$V = \int_{t=0}^{t=\infty} U[Y(K) - \dot{K}]dt.$$

Because U is a function of K and $\dot{K}$ only, the Euler equality takes the simplified form:

$$U + \dot{K}U_{\dot{K}} = 0.$$

Treating it as an end-point problem in the (t, K) plane leads to:

$$(8.10) \qquad\qquad \dot{K} = \frac{-U}{u}.$$

The Ramsey rule states that, at every point in time, investment valued at marginal utility of consumption ($\dot{K}_t u_t$) must be equal to the distance from bliss (U_t). This rule is illustrated in Figure 8.4, where utility is measured as a negative number along the vertical axis and consumption as a positive number along the horizontal axis. Since there is a single good in the economy, investment and consumption can both be measured along the horizontal axis. At a given time the supply of goods is equal to OB; how should this supply be allocated between consumption and savings? This is done by drawing from B the tangent to the utility curve and projecting the point of tangency, C, vertically in A. It is optimal to consume $\overline{OA}$ and to save $\overline{AB}$. The distance from bliss (U) is $\overline{AC}$; the marginal utility (u) is measured by $\tan \alpha$; equation (8.10) is satisfied since:

$$\dot{K}u = (\overline{AB}) \tan \alpha = -\overline{AC} = -U.$$

Figure 8.4. The Ramsey Saving Rule

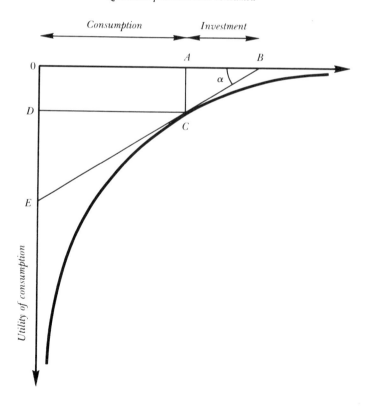

Quantities produced and consumed

Along the vertical axis, investment and consumption valued at marginal utility ($u = \tan \alpha$) are measured by OD and DE, while the consumers' surplus is measured by the part below E. At each point in time the sum of the three is equal to bliss (zero). With the CES utility function:

(8.4a) $$U = -c^{1-1/\sigma},$$

(8.4b) $$u = \frac{1 - \sigma}{\sigma} c^{-1/\sigma}, \quad \text{for} \quad 0 \le \sigma < 1.$$

Bliss is taken as zero and U is the negative number measuring the distance from bliss. With a stationary population, c and C can be made identical by taking the initial population as unity. The combination of (8.10), (8.4a) and (8.4b) gives:

(8.11) $$\frac{\dot{K}}{C} = \frac{-U}{cu} = \frac{\sigma}{1 - \sigma}, \quad \text{hence} \quad s = \frac{\dot{K}}{\dot{K} + C} = \sigma.$$

The optimal saving plan is to keep the saving ratio (s) constant and equal to the elasticity of substitution (σ) of consumption at various points in time. The application of equation (8.8) shows that the growth rate of consumption (γ_t) is equal to the saving ratio ($s = \sigma$) multiplied by the marginal productivity of capital:

$$\gamma_t = s r_t.$$

The marginal productivity of capital (r_t) does not affect the optimal saving ratio.[7] It affects only the growth rate of consumption and, therefore, the length of time required to reach bliss. This length depends a great deal on the assumptions made on the production function. At the limit, bliss will never be reached (see Weizsäcker 1965) with the decreasing return to scale production function:

$$y = K^b \quad \text{if} \quad b \le \sigma < 1.$$

THE MODEL WITH LABOR AUGMENTING TECHNOLOGICAL PROGRESS

The size of the population and the labor force are increasing at the constant rate ν. Utilities are discounted at the constant rate δ. Production is represented by a CES function with constant return to scale. The elasticities of substitution of consumption and production are both less than unity. Technological progress is Harrod-neutral and has for effect to increase the number of "efficiency units" of

---

7. As noted by Ramsey (1928), this does not remain true when utilities are discounted.

labor at the constant rate ζ. This could be called a Phelps-Mirrlees model since both authors have analyzed models with similar characteristics (see Phelps 1966 and Mirrlees 1967).

We know from the golden rule (Phelps 1966, Samuelson 1965) that, if the system converges, the economy will grow asymptotically at the rate $\nu + \zeta$, which is the growth rate of the number of efficiency units of labor. It is therefore convenient to express all variables in terms of efficiency units of labor:

Augmented ratio of capital to labor $\qquad x_t = L_0^{-1} e^{-(\zeta+\nu)t} K_t,$

Augmented ratio of output to labor $\qquad y_t = L_0^{-1} e^{-(\zeta+\nu)t} Y_t,$

Augmented ratio of consumption to labor $z_t = L_0^{-1} e^{-(\zeta+\nu)t} C_t,$

Ratio of capital to output $\qquad\qquad k_t = \dfrac{x_t}{y_t} = \dfrac{K_t}{Y_t},$

Savings ratio $\qquad\qquad\qquad s_t = 1 - \dfrac{z_t}{Y_t} = 1 - \dfrac{C_t}{Y_t} = \dfrac{I_t}{Y_t}.$

The derivatives of x_t and z_t in relation to time are:

$$\dot{x}_t = e^{-(\zeta+\nu)t} \dot{K}_t - (\zeta + \nu)x_t, \quad \text{and}$$

(8.12)
$$\frac{\dot{z}_t}{z_t} = \frac{\dot{c}_t}{c_t} - \zeta.$$

The commodity balance $(C_t + \dot{K}_t - Y_t = 0)$ and the Euler equality become, respectively:

(8.13)
$$z_t + \dot{x}_t + (\zeta + \nu)x_t - y(x_t) = 0,$$

$$r_t - \nu - \delta = -\frac{\dot{u}_t}{u_t} = +\frac{1}{\sigma}\frac{\dot{c}_t}{c_t} = +\frac{1}{\sigma}\left(\frac{\dot{z}_t}{z_t} + \zeta\right), \quad \text{or}$$

(8.14)
$$\frac{\dot{z}_t}{z_t} = -\zeta + \sigma(r_t - \nu - \delta),$$

where the initial capital constraint is given by:

(8.15)
$$x_0 = L_0^{-1} \bar{K}_0.$$

Production $y(x_t)$ is defined as the CES function:

(8.16)
$$y(x_t) = a[hx_t^{-\rho} + 1 - h]^{-1/\rho},$$

where a and h are positive constants and $\bar{\sigma} = (1 + \rho)^{-1}$ is the elasticity of substitution between labor and capital (the bar on top distinguishes it from σ used for the elasticity of substitution of consumption). The marginal productivity of capital derived from (8.16) is:

$$\frac{dy}{dx} = (ha^{-\rho})\left(\frac{x}{y}\right)^{-(1+\rho)},$$

where $ha^{-\rho}$ is a constant term. Since:

$$\frac{dy_t}{dx_t} = \frac{\partial Y_t}{\partial K_t} = r_t \quad \text{and} \quad \frac{x_t}{y_t} = k_t,$$

the marginal productivity of capital (r_t) is related to the capital-output ratio (k_t) by:

(8.17) $\quad \dfrac{r_t}{r_0} = \left(\dfrac{k_t}{k_0}\right)^{-1/\bar{\sigma}} \quad$ or $\quad \log(k_t/k_0) = -\bar{\sigma}\log(r_t/r_0).$

The elasticity of the capital-output ratio in relation to the marginal productivity of capital is therefore equal to $-\bar{\sigma}$. The three parameters of the production function will be expressed below in terms of the initial value of the variables (x_0, y_0) which define the initial capital-output ratio $(k_0 = x_0/y_0)$; of the initial value of the marginal productivity of capital (r_0) and; of the elasticity of substitution $(\bar{\sigma})$.

Having defined the production function (8.16) and the initial conditions (8.15), the growth path is fully specified by the two differential equations (8.13) and (8.14). Although these equations cannot be directly integrated (except for particular values of the parameters), the main properties of the optimal growth path can be analyzed.

In Figure 8.5, capital per efficiency unit of labor (x_t) is shown along the horizontal axis. The decomposition of the commodity balance (8.13) is shown along the vertical axis. Production, $y(x)$, is represented by curve ABC. The capital formation, $(\nu + \zeta)x$, required to maintain unchanged the level of capital invested per efficiency unit of labor is the straight line OH; its slope with the horizontal axis is $\nu + \zeta$. By definition, for each value x_t, the vertical distance between this straight line and curve ABC measures $y(x_t) - (\zeta + \nu)x_t$. Equation (8.13) states that this difference is equal to $z_t + \dot{x}_t$. The problem is to allocate optimally the sum $z_t + \dot{x}_t$ between consumption (z_t) and net investment per efficiency unit of labor $\dot{x}_t$.

An allocation between consumption and investment through time can be defined by the function $z(x_t)$. The corresponding growth path is represented by the movement of the point with coordinates x_t and z_t in the (x, z) space. Curve DBE of Figure 8.5 illustrates such a growth path. Consider any point along this path: for example, D. The value x_t is the abscissa read along the horizontal axis. The value z_t is the vertical

Figure 8.5 Time Path of Consumption and Production

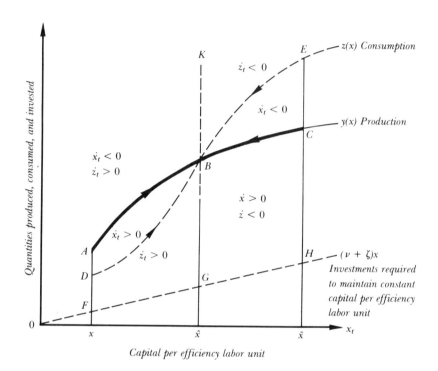

Capital per efficiency labor unit

distance (DF) between point D and the straight line OH. For x_t and z_t to be positive, any path must remain inside the space bounded by the vertical axis and straight line OH.

If the optimal path converges, it must lead to the point ($\hat{x}$, $\hat{z}$) at which $\dot{x}_t$ and $\dot{z}_t$ are equal to zero. Equation (8.14) shows that $\dot{z}_t = 0$ requires either $\hat{z}_t = 0$ (which can be disregarded since it corresponds to zero consumption) or:

$$(8.18) \qquad\qquad \hat{r} = \nu + \delta + \zeta/\sigma.$$

This equality is satisfied for the value $\hat{x}$ measuring the abscissa of point B, where the slope of the tangent ($\dot{r} = dy/dx$) to the production curve $y(x)$ takes the value given in (8.18). Equation (8.14) can then be rewritten in the form:

$$(8.14') \qquad\qquad \frac{\dot{z}_t}{z_t} = \sigma(r_t - \hat{r}).$$

With declining marginal productivity of capital ($y''(x) < 0$):

$$x_t \lessgtr \hat{x} \Rightarrow r_t \gtrless \hat{r} \Rightarrow \dot{z}_t \gtrless 0.$$

The vertical going through B therefore divides the (x_t, z_t) space in two regions. To the left, $\dot{z}_t$ is positive; to the right, $\dot{z}_t$ is negative.

Similarly, equation (8.13) shows that $\dot{x}_t = 0$ requires:

(8.19) $$z_t = y(x_t) - (\zeta + \nu)x_t = \phi(x_t),$$

which is the equation of the *ABC* curve in the (x_t, z_t) space. Equation (8.13) can then be rewritten:

(8.13') $$\dot{x}_t = \psi(x_t) - z_t.$$

Curve *ABC* also divides the (x_t, z_t) space in two regions. Below it ($z_t < \phi[x_t]$), $\dot{x}_t$ is positive; above it, $\dot{x}_t$ is negative. The convergence point B is at the intersection of the two frontiers (*G3K* and *ABC*). The optimal path must remain interior to subregion *ABG* if the convergence point B is reached from below. It must remain interior to subregion *CBK* if convergence is reached from above. The path $z(x)$ of Figure 8.5 satisfies these conditions. If the economy is initially capital poor (point D), x_t and z_t increase monotonically from D until they reach B. If the economy were originally capital rich, x_t and z_t would decline monotonically from E to B. Equation (8.14') shows that the growth rate of consumption (per efficiency unit of labor) per unit of time ($\dot{z}_t/z_t$) declines as one gets closer to the convergence point B.

The conditions for convergence can be read easily from Figure 8.4:

(8.20) $$\hat{r} > \delta + \nu + \frac{\zeta}{\sigma} > \underline{r}, \quad \text{and}$$

(8.20') $$\delta + \nu + \frac{\zeta}{\sigma} \geq \nu + \zeta.$$

The first condition is that the equilibrium point B must be between the two extreme points A and C. In numerical models, these two extreme points are identified by the minimum and the maximum values allowed for the capital-output ratio.

The second condition is that the asymptotic value of the marginal productivity of capital cannot be lower than the asymptotic value of the rate of capital accumulation. If it were, consumption would have to become negative; the sum of the claims of future generations would be infinitely larger than the claim of the present one and the integral would be unbounded. When the elasticity of substitution of consumption (σ) is less than unity, the existence condition (8.20') is always satisfied for positive values of the discount rate (δ). The latter could even take negative values satisfying $\delta > -(1/\sigma - 1)\zeta$.

The asymptotic values can now be summarized:

Consumption per capita $\hat{\gamma} = \zeta$ from (8.12)

Consumption $\hat{g} = \hat{\gamma} + \nu = \zeta + \nu$ by definition

Interest rate $\hat{r} = \delta + \nu + \dfrac{\zeta}{\sigma}$ from (8.18)

Capital-output ratio $\hat{k} = k_0 \left(\dfrac{\hat{r}}{r_0}\right)^{-\bar{\sigma}} = k_0 \left(\dfrac{r_0}{\delta + \nu + \zeta/\sigma}\right)^{\bar{\sigma}}$

from (8.17)

Saving ratio[8] $\hat{s} = (\zeta + \nu)\hat{k} = k_0(\zeta + \nu) \left(\dfrac{r_0}{\delta + \nu + \zeta/\sigma}\right)^{\bar{\sigma}}$

With labor-augmenting technical progress ($\zeta > 0$), the asymptotic value of the interest rate ($\hat{r}$) declines when the elasticity of substitution of consumption (σ) rises. The asymptotic values of the capital-output ratio ($\hat{k}$) and of the saving ratio ($\hat{s}$) increase when either of the two elasticities of substitution (σ and $\bar{\sigma}$) rises. The modification in the capital-output ratio $\hat{k}/k_0$ is an increasing function of the two elasticities of substitution.

The asymptotic value of the growth rate of consumption, $\hat{g}$, defines the "golden-age path." It is generally lower (never higher) than the asymptotic interest rate, $\hat{r}$, which defines the "golden utility path" in Phelps terminology (see Phelps 1966, p. 96). The equality $\hat{g} = \hat{r}$ occurs only at the limit of convergence. This case, which defines the borderline between existence and nonexistence, has been of major interest to growth theorists. It is of no particular interest to practical economists. In the numerical applications of the model, $\hat{r}$ is about twice as large as $\hat{g}$.

Before reaching convergence the growth rate of consumption and the capital-output ratio are related to the difference between the prevailing and the asymptotic values of the marginal productivity of capital:

$$g_t - \hat{g} = \frac{1}{\sigma}(r_t - \hat{r}) \quad \text{from (8.14'), and}$$

$$k_t/\hat{k} = (r_t/\hat{r})^{-\bar{\sigma}} \quad \text{from (8.17).}$$

8. $\hat{s} = \left[\dfrac{\hat{K}}{Y}\right] = \left[\dfrac{\hat{K}}{K}\right]\left[\dfrac{\hat{K}}{Y}\right]$, where $\left[\dfrac{\hat{K}}{K}\right] = \left[\dfrac{\hat{C}}{C}\right] = \zeta + \nu$ and $\left[\dfrac{\hat{K}}{Y}\right] = \hat{k}$.

Starting with a capital-poor economy, the level of consumption per labor-efficiency unit and the capital-output ratio increase monotonically, while the saving ratio declines monotonically.[9]

Knowing the model asymptotic properties, an approximate solution of the infinite-time–horizon model can be computed by truncating the time horizon $(t = 1, \ldots, \infty)$ at time T. The value of the objective function during the preterminal period $(t = 0, \ldots, T)$ is computed exactly. The value during the postterminal period $(t = T, \ldots, \infty)$ is approximated by assuming that the growth rate of per capita consumption is equal to the asymptotic growth rate $(\hat{r})$. It is always possible to find a value of the terminal time T sufficiently high to satisfy any specified level of accuracy.

The value of the objective function is computed in two parts:

(8.5″)
$$V = V_T + V_T^\infty,$$

where
$$V_T = \int_{t=0}^{t=T} e^{-\delta t} U(c_t)\,dt, \quad \text{and:}$$

(8.5‴)
$$V_T^\infty = e^{-\delta T} U(c_T) \int_{\tau=0}^{\tau=\infty} e^{-\delta \tau} \left(\frac{c_{T+\tau}}{c_T}\right)^{1-1/\sigma} d\tau.$$

The integral appearing in equation (8.5‴) is approximated by neglecting the term ϵ_T in $c_{T+\tau}/c_T = (1 + \epsilon_T)e^{\zeta \tau}$, since it is always possible to find a value of T sufficiently large for ϵ_T to be smaller than any prespecified number ϵ. This gives:

$$V_T^\infty \simeq e^{-\delta T} U_T \int_{\tau=0}^{\tau=\infty} e^{-[\delta + \zeta(1/\sigma - 1)]\tau}\,d\tau,$$

where
$$\delta + \zeta\left(\frac{1}{\sigma} - 1\right) = \hat{r} - \hat{g}.$$

For $\hat{r} > \hat{g}$, which is the condition for convergence (8.20′), the postterminal value of the objective function is approximated by:

(8.5⁗)
$$V_T^\infty \simeq \frac{e^{-\delta T} U_T}{\hat{r} - \hat{g}}.$$

9. This property can be established when the elasticities of substitution σ and $\bar{\sigma}$ (for consumption and production) are both less than unity. The derivative ds/dk is expressed as a function of dz/dx, which is replaced by its value from equations (8.13) and (8.14). The first and second derivatives, ds/dk and d^2s/dk^2, are both negative. The optimal path must therefore satisfy $\dot{s} < 0$ with $\dot{k} > 0$ (starting with a capital-poor economy) or $\dot{s} > 0$ with $\dot{k} < 0$ (starting with a capital-rich economy). The computation, which is somewhat lengthy, has not been reproduced.

Table 8.4. The One-Good Yearly Model

Year	Consumption activity	Year 1			Year T−2			Year T−1			Year T			Right-hand side	Dual value
		$Y_{s,1}$	I_1	C_1	$Y_{s,T-2}$	I_{T-2}	C_{T-2}	$Y_{s,T-1}$	I_{T-1}	C_{T-1}	Y_T	I_T	C_T		
	Maximand		–	–			–			–		–	–	–	
1	CC_1	$+1$	-1	-1										$=0$	Π_1
	CK_1	$-k_s$												$\geq -\bar{K}$	$\Pi_{k,1}$
	CL_1	$-(1+\zeta)^{-1}l_s$												$\geq -\bar{L}_1$	$\Pi_{\lambda,1}$
T−2	CC_{T-2}				$+1$	-1	-1								Π_{T-2}
	CK_{T-2}		$+1$		$-k_s$										$\Pi_{k,T-2}$
	CL_{T-2}				$-(1+\zeta)^{2-\eta}l_s$										$\Pi_{\lambda,T-2}$
T−1	CC_{T-1}							$+1$	-1	-1				$=0$	Π_{T-1}
	CK_{T-1}		$+1$			$+1$		$-k_s$						$\geq -\bar{K}$	$\Pi_{k,T-1}$
	CL_{T-1}							$-(1+\zeta)^{1-\eta}l_s$						$\geq -\bar{L}_{T-1}$	$\Pi_{\lambda,T-1}$
T	CC_T										$+1$	-1	-1	$=0$	Π_T
	CK_T		$+1$			$+1$			$+1$		$-k_s$			$\geq -\bar{K}$	$\Pi_{k,T}$
	CL_T										$-(1+\zeta)^{-\eta}l_s$			$\geq -\bar{L}_T$	$\Pi_{\lambda,T}$
ΔT	$CK_{\Delta T}$										$-\bar{g}k_s$	$+1$		≥ 0	$\Pi_{k,\Delta T}$
	$CL_{\Delta T}$										$-(\bar{g}-\zeta)(1+\zeta)^{-\eta}l_s$			$\geq -\Delta\bar{L}_T$	$\Pi_{\lambda,\Delta T}$

This property is used for truncating the time horizon of the linear programming model.

The Simplified Programming Model

The algebraic model of the preceding section is translated into programming terms in Table 8.4. Time becomes a discrete variable taking the values $t = 1, 2, \ldots, T$. For the sake of simplicity, the year is taken as the time unit.[10] An investment made in year t generates a capacity which can be used in year $t + 1$ and does not depreciate thereafter.

At each point in time, there is a single consumption activity, C_t, and a single investment activity, I_t. Both activity levels are assumed to be positive. Because labor can be substituted for capital, a series of production activities is available; each activity is characterized by a different capital-labor ratio identified by subscript s. The level of the particular production activity, $Y_{s,t}$, shown in the tableau is always assumed to be positive.

In each year t, three equalities (or inequalities) have to be satisfied. The first (CC_t) is the single commodity balance existing in a one-commodity economy. The second (CK_t) is the balance for reproducible capital. The third (CL_t) is the balance for labor, which is assumed not to be reproducible.

The three equations are shown for the terminal year, T, and for the two preterminal years, $T - 1$ and $T - 2$. For the first optimization year, $t = 1$, the capital balance (CK_1) defines the initial conditions. Since technological progress is labor augmenting, labor requirements per unit of production are measured by $(1 + \zeta)^{-t}l_s$, where $\zeta(>0)$ is the annual rate of technological progress.

The three other rows which appear in Table 8.4 deserve more attention. They define the maximand and the postterminal conditions $(CK_{\Delta T})$ and $(CL_{\Delta T})$. The maximand is decomposed into two components, as in equation (8.5″). Each component is expressed in the form of a summation instead of an integral:

$$(8.21) \qquad \text{MAX} = \left[\sum_{t=1}^{t=T-1} (1 + \delta)^{-t} U_t \right] + \frac{(1 + \delta)^{-T} U_T}{1 - a},$$

where

$$0 < 1 - a < 1.$$

---

10. These simplifying assumptions, which facilitate the algebraic presentation, are removed in the numerical model (see below).

The factor $1 - a$ in (8.21) is the equivalent of the factor $\hat{r} - \hat{g}$ in (8.5''''). Its value can be calculated by approximating the growth of per capita consumption in the postterminal period as:

$$c_{T+\tau}/c_T \approx (1 + \zeta)^\tau,$$

and writing the sum of the discounted utilities of consumption from year T till infinity as:

$$(8.22) \quad \sum_{t=T}^{t=\infty} (1 + \delta)^{-t}U_t = (1 + \delta)^{-T}U_T \sum_{\tau=0}^{\tau=\infty} (1 + \delta)^{-\tau}(1 + \zeta)^{(1-1/\sigma)\tau}.$$

For $\delta > 0$, $\zeta > 0$, and $0 < \sigma < 1$, the summation converges toward $(1 - a)^{-1}$, where a is defined by:

$$(8.23) \quad a = (1 + \delta)^{-1}(1 + \zeta)^{1-1/\sigma}.$$

Consider now the dual variables in preterminal years $(t < T)$. The dual equation of the consumption activity, C_t, defines the marginal contribution of a unit of consumption to the value of the objective function:

$$(8.24) \quad \Pi_t = (1 + \delta)^{-t}\frac{dU_t}{dC_t},$$

where total consumption (C_t) is linked to per capita consumption (c_t) by the relation:

$$(8.25) \quad C_t = (1 + \nu)^t \bar{N}_0 c_t.$$

The combination of (8.24) and (8.25) gives:

$$(8.26) \quad \Pi_t = \bar{N}_0^{-1}(1 + \delta)^{-t}(1 + \nu)^{-t}u_t,$$

where the marginal utility of per capita consumption is:

$$(8.27) \quad u_t = \frac{dU_t}{dc_t} = \left(\frac{c_t}{c_0}\right)^{-1/\sigma}.$$

From the combination of (8.26) and (8.27), it follows that:

$$(8.28) \quad \frac{\Pi_{t-1}}{\Pi_t} = (1 + \delta)(1 + \nu)(1 + \gamma_t)^{1/\sigma},$$

where

$$\gamma_t = \frac{c_t - c_{t-1}}{c_{t-1}}$$

is the growth rate of per capita consumption.

Turn now to the investment activities. Subtracting the dual equation of investment activity I_t from that of investment activity I_{t-1} gives:

(8.29) $$\Pi_{t-1} - \Pi_t = \Pi_{k,t}, \quad \text{for} \quad t < T.$$

The dual equation of the production activity can be written:

(8.30) $$\Pi_t = k_s \Pi_{k,t} + (1 + \zeta)^{-t} l_s \Pi_{\lambda t} \quad \text{for} \quad t < T,$$

$$= \left[1 + (1 + \zeta)^{-t} \frac{l_s}{k_s} \frac{\Pi_{\lambda t}}{\Pi_{k,t}} \right] k_s \Pi_{k,t},$$

$$= [\text{share going to capital}]^{-1} k_s \Pi_{k,t}.$$

Calling, as before, r_t the marginal productivity of capital:

$$\frac{\partial Y}{\partial K} = [\text{share going to capital}] k_s^{-1} = r_t,$$

equation (8.30) may be rewritten:

(8.30′) $$\Pi_t = r_t^{-1} \Pi_{k,t}.$$

Dividing (8.29) by (8.30′) gives:

(8.31) $$\frac{\Pi_{t-1} - \Pi_t}{\Pi_t} = r_t.$$

Finally, the combination of (8.28) and (8.31) gives:

(8.32) $$(1 + \delta)(1 + \nu)(1 + \gamma_t)^{1/\sigma} = 1 + r_t.$$

When the time interval tends toward zero, equation (8.32) tends toward:

$$\delta + \nu + \gamma_t/\sigma = r_t,$$

which is the dynamic equation (8.8) established earlier from the Euler equality when time was treated as a continuous variable.

Let us now come to the truncation of the time horizon. In defining the objective function (8.22) with (8.23), it was assumed that per capita consumption would grow, during the postterminal period, at the asymptotic rate ζ. Production was therefore assumed to grow at the asymptotic rate:

(8.33) $$\hat{g} = (1 + \nu)(1 + \zeta) - 1,$$

where ν is the population growth rate. If this is true throughout the postterminal period, it must also be true between years T and $T + 1$.

Hence:

(8.34) $$Y_{T+1} = (1 + \hat{g})Y_T.$$

The capital constraints at time T and time $T + 1$ can therefore be written:

(CK_T) $$\sum_{t=1}^{t=T-1} I_t - k_s Y_T \geq - \bar{K},$$

(CK_{T+1}) $$\sum_{t=1}^{t=T} I_t - k_s(1 + \hat{g})Y_T \geq - \bar{K}.$$

Replacing (CK_{T+1}) by its difference with (CK_T) gives the constraint on terminal investment:

$(CK_{\Delta T})$ $$I_T - k_s\hat{g}Y_T \geq 0.$$

Since capital and labor are substitutable, a postterminal constraint $(CL_{\Delta T})$ must also be imposed upon labor. Otherwise, it would always be optimal in year $T + 1$ to select the technology with the lowest capital-output ratio, since labor would become a free good. In Table 8.4, the last two rows $(CK_{\Delta T})$ and $(CL_{\Delta T})$ define the postterminal conditions for capital and labor.

Assume that the truncation of the time horizon does not affect the primal solution for $t \leq T$ nor the dual solution for $t < T$. How does it affect the dual variables of terminal and postterminal years?

Calling Π'_t the dual values of the nontruncated model for $t \geq T$ and Π_t those of the truncated model, the relations are as follows:

(8.35) $$\Pi_T = \sum_{\tau=0}^{\tau=\infty} \frac{C_{T+\tau}}{C_T} \Pi'_{T+\tau} = \frac{\Pi'_T}{1 - a} = \frac{1 + \hat{r}}{\hat{r} - \hat{g}} \Pi'_T,$$

(8.36) $$\Pi_{k,T} = \Pi_{T-1} = (1 + r_T^{-1})\Pi'_{k,T},$$

where

(8.37) $$\hat{r} = (1 + \delta)(1 + \nu)(1 + \hat{\gamma})^{1/\sigma} - 1, \quad \text{and}$$

$$\hat{g} = (1 + \nu)(1 + \zeta) - 1,$$

$$\Pi_{k,\Delta T} = \Pi_T = \frac{1}{\hat{r} - \hat{g}} \frac{1 + \hat{r}}{1 + r_{T-1}} \Pi_{k,T}.$$

The truncation procedure may be summarized as follows:
• The economy is assumed to have reached its asymptotic growth in the terminal year.
• A value $\tilde{\gamma}$ of the asymptotic growth rate of per capita consumption

is selected before solving the model. In the simple model described in this section, this asymptotic value is the growth rate of labor productivity ($\bar{\gamma} = \hat{\gamma} = \zeta$). With the exogenously given rate of population growth (ν), the asymptotic growth rate of the economy is $\bar{g} = (1 + \nu)(1 + \bar{\gamma}) - 1$.

- The sum of the discounted utility of consumption V_T^∞ from year T onward is obtained by multiplying the discounted utility in the terminal year $(1 + \delta)^{-T}U_T$ by the factor $(1 - a)^{-1} > 1$, with $a = (1 + \delta)^{-1}(1 + \bar{\gamma})^{1-1/\sigma}$ and $0 < a < 1$.

- Investment in the terminal year (I_T) must generate between years T and $T + 1$ the capacity increment ($K_{T+1} - K_T$) allowing the production increment $Y_{T+1} - Y_T = \bar{g}Y_T$.

- The impact of the truncation is to increase the dual values of consumption and capacities in the terminal year. Equation (8.35) shows that the dual value of terminal consumption is multiplied by the factor $(1 - a)^{-1} > 1$. Equation (8.36) shows that the dual value of terminal capacity is multiplied by the factor $1 + r_T^{-1} > 1$, where r_T is the marginal productivity of capital in the preterminal year (8.30'). Equation (8.37) shows that the dual value of the postterminal constraint on capacities is equal to the dual value of terminal consumption; it is approximately equal to the dual value of terminal capacities multiplied by $(\hat{r} - \hat{g})^{-1}$, where $\hat{r} - \hat{g} = (1 + \nu)(1 + \bar{\gamma})[(1 + \delta)(1 + \bar{\gamma})^{1/\sigma-1} - 1]$.

The truncation procedure does not significantly affect the primal solution for $t \leq T$ nor the dual solution for $t < T$ under two conditions: First, with the nontruncated model the asymptotic growth rate would have almost been reached by year T. Second, the value $\bar{\gamma}$ selected before solving the model is a good approximation of the asymptotic growth rate ($\hat{\gamma}$).

In simple models such as the one described in this section, the exact value of the asymptotic growth rate can be computed algebraically ($\hat{\gamma} = \zeta$). In complex models such as the one of the Ivory Coast, the exact value of the asymptotic rate cannot be solved analytically. An approximate value is selected ex ante and the accuracy of this estimate is improved by solving the model iteratively on the computer. The convergence is rapid.

The iterative procedure is illustrated in Figure 8.6. Consumption path *ABCDE* is the solution which would have been obtained with an infinite time-horizon model. It defines the asymptotic growth rate $\hat{\gamma}$. It is assumed that T is sufficiently large for the growth rate γ_{T+1} between years T and $T + 1$ to be sufficiently close to the asymptotic rate $\hat{\gamma}$.

Figure 8.6. Iterations on the Value Selected for the Postterminal Growth Rate

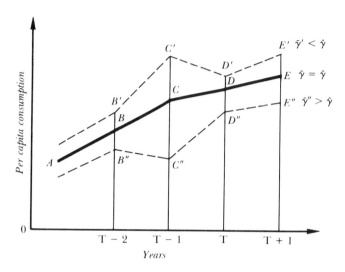

Figure 8.7. The Impact of the Value Selected for the Terminal Capital Stock

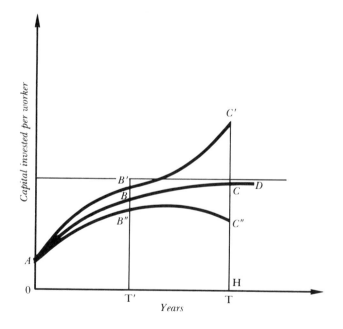

Suppose that the initial value selected for the asymptotic rate is too high $\bar{\gamma}' > \hat{\gamma}$. The combination of (8.22) and (8.23) shows that the multiplicative factor $(1 - a)^{-1}$ applied to the utility of consumption in the terminal year is too low.[11] Hence, the dual value of terminal consumption Π_T is also too low. On the other hand, for a given level of production in terminal year Y_T, the postterminal capacity constraint $I_T \geq \bar{g}kY_T$ shows that more investment is required in the terminal year. Selecting a postterminal growth rate $\bar{\gamma}' > \hat{\gamma}$ simultaneously undervalues terminal consumption and overstates the requirements for terminal investment. Consequently, in the terminal year, too much is invested and not enough consumed. This leads to the consumption time path $B'C'D'E'$. Conversely, with a postterminal growth rate $\bar{\gamma}'' < \hat{\gamma}$ that is too low, too much would have been consumed and not enough invested in the terminal year. This would lead to time path $B''C''D''E''$. By iterations, a monotonic path such as $ABCDE$ is reached. This search for monotonicity is based on the algebraic relation between the growth rates γ_{T-1}, γ_T, and γ_{T+1} during the three consecutive periods of time $(T - 2$ to $T - 1; T - 1$ to $T; T$ to $T + 1)$:

$$(8.38) \quad (1 + \hat{r}) \left(\frac{1 + \gamma_{T-1}}{1 + \bar{\gamma}}\right)^{1/\sigma} - (\hat{r} - \hat{g}) \left(\frac{1 + \gamma_T}{1 + \bar{\gamma}}\right)^{1/\sigma}$$

$$= 1 + \hat{g} + r_{T-1} - r_T.$$

For $r_{T-1} = r_T$, monotonic growth requires $\gamma_{T-1} = \gamma_T = \bar{\gamma}$. Assume that the start is made from the time path $ABCDE$ of the nontruncated model and that the capital-output ratio remains constant. Deriving equation (8.38) shows that a modification $d\bar{g}$ in the asymptotic growth rate is associated with a variation $dg_T = [(1 + \hat{g})/(\hat{r} - \hat{g})] \, d\bar{g}$ in the opposite direction. This leads to the nonmonotonic growth paths $B'C'D'E'$ or $B''C''D''E''$ of Figure 8.6.

The truncation procedure followed does not eliminate the need for iterations, but it reduces it to the minimum. Assume that the length of the truncated horizon (T) is sufficiently large so that, throughout any set of experiments, the postterminal growth rate can be approximated by the asymptotic one. Iterations are needed only to reach a good approximation of the asymptotic rate. Once the proper value $\bar{\gamma}$ has been found, there is no need to adjust this value during the course of the experiments. This is not the case with the simpler truncation procedures described below.

---

11. $\dfrac{d[(1 - a)^{-1}]}{d\bar{\gamma}} = a(1 - a)^{-2}(1 + \bar{\gamma}) \left(1 - \dfrac{1}{\sigma}\right) < 0$, since $1 - \dfrac{1}{\sigma} < 0$ for $\sigma < 1$.

Two simple truncation procedures are frequently used. One consists in specifying ex ante the level of terminal investment (I_T) or terminal capacities (K_T). The other is to specify ex ante the price (Π_T') at which the terminal capital stock is valued. In the latter case, the objective function measures the sum of the discounted utility of consumption for $t = 1, \ldots, T$, plus the value of the endogenous terminal capital stock:

$$\Pi_T' \sum_{t=1}^{t=T} I_t.$$

Truncating the time horizon in this way does not affect the optimal solution for $t \leq T$ if one condition is fulfilled. The value Π_T' selected ex ante must be identical to the dual value of consumption in year T, which would have been obtained from the optimal solution of the nontruncated model. Guessing the right value Π_T' is equivalent to guessing to the right value of consumption c_T. In the optimal solution of the infinite-time–horizon model, Π_T' is linked to c_T by:

$$\Pi_T' = \bar{N}_0^{-1}(1 + \delta)^{-T}(1 + \nu)^{-T} \left(\frac{c_T}{c_0}\right)^{-1/\sigma}.$$

These simple truncation procedures are fairly similar. They consist in selecting ex ante the levels of either terminal investment (I_T) or terminal capacity (K_T) or terminal consumption (c_T) from which Π_T' is derived. Clearly, the optimal values of consumption, investment, and capacity in year T do not remain constant throughout a set of experiments. Differences between the value selected ex ante and the optimal value (of the nontruncated model) generate "horizon effects" in preterminal years.

Figure 8.7, borrowed from the Turnpike theorem of Samuelson (1965) illustrates the horizon effects. Path $ABCD$ corresponds to the solution of the infinite-time–horizon model. Path $AB'C'$ is the solution of the truncated model, when the prespecified terminal capital stock per worker (HC') exceeds the optimal level (HC) for that year in the nontruncated model. Path $AB''C''$ corresponds to the case when the level of terminal stock was underestimated. The horizon effect is reduced as one goes backward in time: $B''B' < C''C'$ for $T' < T$. The horizon effect $B''B'$ in year T' can be smaller than any prespecified value provided the time horizon is extended for a sufficiently long period, $T - T'$.

Horizon effects can be eliminated in two ways. The first is by iterating toward monotonic path ABC. This is not, however, very convenient, because the iterative procedure has to be repeated throughout the experiments. The second is to extend the time horizon beyond of the year T' in which there is interest. The period T' through T is used as a buffer for dampening the horizon effects. It is an expensive procedure for large-scale programming models. When the length of the time horizon doubles, the cost of computation may increase fivefold. This explains why a more complex but less sensitive truncation procedure has been selected.

The Actual Programming Model

In the Ivory Coast model, the preterminal period consists of twenty years (1970–1990). This twenty-year period is divided into four subperiods of five years each. The model is optimized for the terminal years of each of the five-year subperiods (1975, 1980, 1985, and 1990), subject to terminal constraints. Those ensure that investment in the terminal year (1990) is sufficient to permit production increasing at the annual growth rate $(1 + \bar{\gamma})(1 + \nu) - 1$ during the decade following the terminal year (1990–2000).

The objective function takes the following form:

$$\text{MAX} = \sum_{\tau=1}^{\tau=3} (1 + \delta)^{-5\tau} U_{5\tau} + \frac{(1 + \delta)^{-20} U_{20}}{1 - a}$$

where $a = (1 + \delta)^{-5}(1 + \zeta)^{-5(1/\sigma - 1)}$, and the postterminal capacity constraints become:

$$\psi_{\Delta 20} I_{20} - k_s[(1 + \nu)^{10}(1 + \bar{\gamma})^{10} - 1]Y_T \geq 0.$$

Coefficient $\psi_{\Delta 20}$ measures the capacity increment generated in the year 2000 from the investment activities made through the ten-year period starting in the year 1990–p, where p is the gestation lag of investments. The value of coefficient ψ is related to the growth rate of investments and to the lengths of the gestation lag and of the life span of capacities. The nature of these relationships is analyzed in Chapter 10.

Altogether, there are twenty-three postterminal constraints.[12] They refer to physical capacities (by origin and destination), to human capital (by skill categories), and to foreign exchange. The latter has to be included in the terminal conditions because fourteen goods can be supplied either from domestic production or from imports. Without postterminal constraint on foreign exchange, the latter

12. For the calculation of the coefficients in the postterminal constraints, see Chapter 16.

would become a free good in the year 2000. It would then be always optimal to replace domestic production by imports for the fourteen commodities that can be either produced domestically or imported.

The analysis of the relationships between dual values was simplified in the previous sections of this chapter. At each point in time, it was necessary to deal only with two dual values. One, Π_t, referred to the single commodity of the model. The other, Π_{kt}, referred to the single renewable capital stock. In the actual model, there are more than twenty different capital stocks, each with its own dual values. There are capital goods (such as vehicles and machinery) which can be invested into capital stocks for specified uses. There are eight different types of consumer goods which can be transformed into utility of consumption. Each of these goods has its own dual value.

To simplify the analysis of the choice between consumption and savings, the existence of a single aggregate called consumption has been assumed in this chapter. Such an aggregate does not exist in the model. The time path of consumption and the composition of consumption are simultaneously optimized. Optimal choice among consumer goods is the object of the next chapter.

Chapter 9

The Choice among Consumer Goods

A DISTINCTION IS MADE in the model among three types of consuming agents, as was explained in Chapter 7: public administration, foreigners, and nationals. This chapter is concerned only with nationals. Private consumption by nationals is the only type of consumption which, in this model, enters into the utility function and responds to variations in prices and income.

The treatment of consumption by nationals takes into account two types of exogenous factors (population and urbanization) and two types of endogenous factors (income and prices). Population growth does not affect the composition of consumption; the demand for all types of consumer goods increases proportionately with the size of the total population, which is taken as exogenous. A modification in the distribution of the population among rural and urban areas does affect the pattern of consumption; thus, urbanization increases the demand for housing and reduces the demand for traditional foods. The combined effects of population and urbanization are treated as a time-trend factor. The endogenous income and price effects are measured net of this time trend.

The income effect reflects the observed variations in the values of income elasticities (η_i) for commodities i along the Engel path. Along this path, the utility of aggregate consumption, which can there be treated as a single good, is defined as an isoelastic function $U_t = -A(\Sigma_i\ c_{it})^{1-1/\sigma}$. Consequently, all the formulas given in the preceding chapter apply along the Engel path.

The system of utility functions $U = \Sigma_i\ U_i$ is identical to Houthakker's system of addilog utilities (see Houthakker 1960) only when all income elasticities remain constant—that is, when they are all identical to unity. In the neighborhood of the equilibrium, where varia-

[207]

tions in income elasticities can be neglected, all formulas for direct and cross price elasticities established by Frisch (1959) apply.

The assumption of separable utilities presents two principal limitations. First, no inferior goods ($\eta_i < 0$) are allowed in the system. Second, the price effect cannot reflect the Hicksian substitution effect between margarine and butter. These limitations are not too serious for broad commodity groups. This was the reason for limiting the level of disaggregation to eight commodity groups.

The first section of the chapter defines the system of utility functions, while the second analyzes the mechanism of price formation. Appendix A deals with the impact of urbanization taken as exogenous in this demand system. Appendix B describes the procedure of piecewise linear approximation.

The notations used in this chapter are the following:

Indexes

t	time
$i = 1, \ldots, n$	commodity
*	superscript characterizing the point at the intersection of the isoutility curve and the Engel path

Endogenous variables

C	consumption
c	per capita consumption
U	utility
u	marginal utility
$x = \log(c_t/\bar{c}_t)$	increase in per capita consumption net of trend factors
p_{it}	price of commodity i at time t ($p_{i0} = 1$)
$\eta_i = a_i + b_i x$	income elasticity
$\sigma_i = \eta_i \sigma$	own elasticity of substitution
ϵ_{ii} and ϵ_{ij}	direct and cross-price elasticities

Fixed parameters

σ	overall elasticity of substitution
a_i, b_i	parameters of the income elasticity function
$\bar{c}_{it}$	per capita consumption, including the exogenous impact of urbanization

Appendix A: rural and urban patterns of consumption

V	variance
VW	variance within groups
VB	variance between groups

Appendix B: linear interpolation

$s = 1, \ldots, m$ subscript defining interpolation steps

W_s variable interpolation weight

The Disaggregated Utility Function

In Chapter 8, consumption was treated as an aggregate; utilities of consumption at different points in time were assumed to be separable and additive. In this chapter, consumption is disaggregated into n commodity groups $(i = 1, \ldots, n)$; utilities derived from each commodity group are again assumed to be separable and additive:

$$(9.1) \qquad U_t = \sum_i U_{it}(c_{it}) \quad \text{and}$$

$$(9.1') \qquad \frac{\partial U_{it}}{\partial c_{it}} = \frac{dU_{it}}{dc_{it}} = u_{it},$$

where

$$u_{it} > 0 \quad \text{and} \quad \frac{du_{it}}{dc_{it}} < 0.$$

For defining the utility function (9.1), it is sufficient to specify the Engel path and the marginal utility of consumption along this path. Because utilities $U_i(c_i)$ are separable among commodities, the utility function validated along the Engel path must apply outside this path as well.

Along the Engel path, all prices remain constant over time and all marginal utilities vary proportionately over time. Taking prices as unity in the base year,[1] the Engel path is therefore defined by:

$$(9.2) \qquad u_{it} = u_t \quad \text{for all } i \text{ and all } t \text{ and}$$

$$p_{it} = 1 \quad \text{for all } i \text{ and all } t.$$

Because quantities and expenditures remain identical along the Engel path, aggregate consumption is unequivocally defined as the sum of the quantities consumed for each item i:

$$c_t = \sum_i p_{it}c_{it} = \sum_i c_{it} \text{ for all } t.$$

---

1. The unit of quantity is the bundle of goods which could be bought with a unit of expenditure (CFAF1 million) at base-year prices. All prices are therefore taken as unity during the base year.

The elasticity of demand for a given commodity group, c_i, in relation to total consumption, c, will be called below the income elasticity, η_i. It is defined as:

(9.3) $d(\ln c_{it}/\bar{c}_{it}) = \eta_i d(\ln c_t/\bar{c}_t)$ or

(9.3′) $dx_i = \eta_i dx$, with $\eta_i > 0$ for $i = 1, \ldots, n$,

where $\bar{c}_{it}$ and $\bar{c}_t$ are the exogenous values of per capita consumption reflecting the urbanization effect at time t, and where x_{it} and x_i measure in logarithmic form the endogenous variations in per capita consumption:

(9.4) $x_i = \ln(c_{it}/\bar{c}_{it})$,

(9.4′) $x = \ln(c_t/\bar{c}_t)$.

Trend factors being eliminated from the x variables, time subscript t is omitted from these variables for the sake of simplicity.

Not all the income elasticities η_i defined in (9.3′) can remain constant over time, except in the trivial case in which they are all identical to unity. It has been assumed here that income elasticities vary linearly with the level of income. For $n - 1$ commodities, elasticity is defined as:

(9.5) $\eta_i = a_i + b_i x$ with a_i and b_i being constant for $i = 1, \ldots, n - 1$,

for the nth commodity, the elasticity η_m is derived as:

(9.5′) $\eta_m c_{nt} = c_t - \sum\limits_{i=1}^{i=n-1} \eta_i c_{it}$, with $\eta_i > 0$ for all i.[2]

Replacing in (9.3′) η_i by its value from (9.5) gives:

(9.3″) $dx_i = (a_i + b_i x)dx$.

Integrating (9.3″) between 0 and x gives, in turn:

(9.6) $x_i = a_i x + (b_i/2)^{x^2}$, for $i = 1, \ldots, n - 1$.

---

2. Marginal utility, given in equation (9.9), is always positive, as it should be. Because its derivative has to be negative, inferior goods ($\eta_i < 0$) must be excluded:

$$\frac{du_{it}}{dc_{it}} = \frac{du_{it}}{dx} \frac{dx}{dx_i} \frac{dx_i}{dc_{it}}$$

$$= -\frac{1}{\sigma}(a_i + b_i x)^{-1} c_{it}^{-1} e^{-x/\sigma}$$

$$= -(\sigma \eta_i c_{it})^{-1} e^{-x/\sigma} < 0,$$

if $\eta_i > 0$,   for $\sigma > 0$ and $c_{it} > 0$.

Since per capita consumption, c_{it}, was defined in (9.4) as:

$$c_{it} = \bar{c}_{it} e^{x_i},$$

it can be rewritten from (9.6') as:

(9.7) $\qquad c_{it} = \bar{c}_{it} e^{a_i x + b_i (x^2/2)}$ for $i = 1, \ldots, n - 1$.

Calling N_t as the size of the population, total consumption is given by:

(9.8) $\qquad C_{it} = N_t \bar{c}_{it} e^{a_i x + b_i (x^2/2)}$, for $i = 1, \ldots, n - 1$.

(9.8') $\qquad C_{nt} = N_t \bar{c}_t e^x - \sum_{i=1}^{i=n-1} C_{it}$.

Along the Engel path defined by (9.2), utility of consumption can be expressed, as in Chapter 8, in the form of an isoelastic function of total per capita consumption c_t. Marginal utility, which had been defined by equation (8.1), can be rewritten with the notations specified in (9.4') as:

(9.9) $\quad u_{it} = u_t = \left(\dfrac{c_t}{\bar{c}_t}\right)^{-1/\sigma} = e^{-x/\sigma}$, with u_0

$$= 1, \text{ for } x = 1 \text{ at time } t = 0.$$

The marginal utility, u_i, derived from the consumption of commodity i and the increase in utility dU_i, can be written as:

$$\frac{dU_{it}}{dc_{it}} = u_{it} \quad \text{and}$$

(9.10) $\qquad\qquad\qquad dU_{it} = u_{it} c_{it} \dfrac{dc_{it}}{c_{it}}.$

In equation (9.10), c_{it} can be replaced by its value from (9.7) and $dc_{it}/c_{it} = dx_i$ by its value from (9.3''). Along the Engel path, moreover, the marginal utility u_{it} can be replaced by its value from (9.9). Proceeding to these three substitutions, equation (9.10) can be rewritten in relation to variable x as follows:

(9.11) $\qquad dU_{it} = (e^{-x/\sigma})(\bar{c}_{it} e^{a_i x + b_i (x^2/2)})(a_i + b_i x)dx$

The distance from bliss associated with the level of consumption $c_{it}(x)$ is calculated by integrating (9.11) from x to infinity as:

(9.12) $\qquad\qquad U_\infty - U_{it} = \int_x^\infty U_{it}(x)dx.$

It is unnecessary, however, to integrate (9.11) until an infinite income level is reached. It is sufficient to integrate it until an income level, x, has been reached which is sufficiently high that it will not have been reached during the terminal year in any solution of the model. Calling $\bar{U}_{it}$ the level of utility associated with $\bar{x}$, the utility reached along the Engel path for the income level $x(<\bar{x})$ can be written:

$$(9.13) \qquad U_{it} - \bar{U}_{it} = -\int_{x}^{\bar{x}} U_{it}(x)\,dx.$$

Replacing, in (9.13), $U_{it}(x)dx$ with its value from (9.11) finally gives:

$$(9.14) \qquad U_{it} - \bar{U}_{it} = -\bar{c}_{it}\int_{x}^{\bar{x}} (a_i + b_i x)e^{[a_i - (1/\sigma) + b_i(x/2)]x}dx.$$

Since $\bar{U}_{it}$ is a constant term in the maximand, its particular value does not affect the optimization process, and constant $\bar{U}_{it}$ can as well be taken as zero. For each commodity group i and each decision year t, equations (9.14) and (9.8) define two monotonic functions, $C_{it}(x)$ and $U_{it}(x)$. Eliminating the intermediate variable x from these two functions gives the utility function $U_{it}(C_{it})$ incorporated into the model through the utility matrix described in Appendix B.

When the income elasticity η_i remains constant for commodity i ($b_i = 0$), (9.14) takes the simplified form:[3]

$$U_{it} - \bar{U}_{it} = -\bar{c}_{it}\int_{x_i}^{\bar{x}_i} e^{[1-(1/\eta_i\sigma)]x_i}dx_i,$$

which can be integrated and expressed as an explicit function of consumption:

$$(9.14') \qquad U_{it} - \bar{U}_{it} = -A_i c_{it}^{1-(1/\sigma_i)},$$

where A_i and $\sigma_i = \eta_i\sigma$ are positive constants. This is the familiar isoelastic utility function, which is a special case ($b_i = 0$) of the more general function (9.14) with (9.7). The algebraic expression of the latter appears much more complicated than that of the former. With the interpolation procedure used in this model (see Appendix B), it is not, however, more difficult to compute the general form (9.14) with (9.8) than to compute the special form (9.14').

The variability in the values of income elasticities may be illus-

---

3. In (9.14), x and dx are replaced by their values from (9.6) and (9.3″) for $a_i = \eta_i$ and $b_i = 0$.

trated by a simple numerical example with two commodities and two time periods. At time 0, commodity A accounts for a third of total consumer expenditures, and commodity B for the remaining two-thirds; if the income elasticity is equal to 2 for commodity A, it must be equal to 0.5 for commodity B, since $(1/3)(2) + (2/3)(0.5) = 1$. Suppose that income (or, more precisely, aggregate consumption) doubles between times 0 and t. In one case, the elasticity is assumed to remain equal to 2.0 for commodity A, which implies that the elasticity for commodity B is reduced to -2.5 at time t. In the other case, the elasticity is assumed to remain equal to 0.5 for commodity B, which implies that the elasticity for commodity A declines to 1.45 at time t.

| | | | Time t | | | |
| | Time 0 | | η_A constant | | η_B constant | |
	c	η	c	η	c	η
Commodity A	$1/3$	2.0	$4/3$	2.0	1.06	1.45
Commodity B	$2/3$	0.5	$2/3$	-2.5	0.94	0.50
Aggregate	1	1.0	2	1.0	2.00	1.00

Assuming that $n - 1$ elasticities remain constant and deriving the nth elasticity as a residual could clearly lead to unreasonable implications. In particular, if the residual elasticity were to become negative, the maximand would become unbounded. There is ample statistical evidence, moreover, that the income elasticity for some commodity groups, such as all food, declines when income rises.

In this model, for seven of the eight commodity groups, elasticity was taken as a linear function $\eta_i = a_i + b_i x$ (with $i = 1, \ldots, 7$) and the values a_i and b_i were selected on the basis of data available for the Ivory Coast and results of intercountry comparisons. The consistency between the coefficients selected for the first seven commodity groups and those implied for the eighth group was checked in a side model, taking the growth rate of income as exogenous. Appropriate adjustments were made to reach a reasonable elasticity pattern for all elasticities throughout the planning period.

Price Formation

The system of utility functions has been defined by equations (9.1), (9.8), and (9.14). It remains now to explain how optimal prices are

Figure 9.1. Price Equilibrium

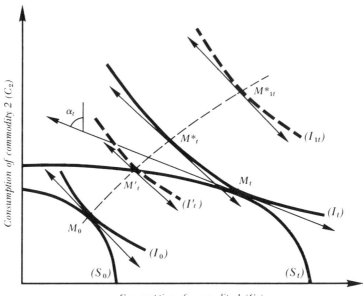

Consumption of commodity 1 (C_1)

derived from the dual solution obtained by maximizing utility subject to resource constraints. This will first be illustrated diagrammatically with a model composed of two commodities and two time periods. For the sake of simplicity, the choice between investment and consumption (which was discussed in Chapter 8) will be taken here as given, and the trend factors will be neglected.

As the size of the population is assumed to remain constant, it can be taken as unity. No distinction needs to be made, therefore, between per capita consumption and consumption by the total population. Consumption levels of commodities 1 and 2 are measured along the axes of Figure 9.1. The efficiency frontiers for supplying these two commodities are represented by (S_0) at time 0 and (S_t) at time t. The frontier defines the most efficient combinations of commodities 1 and 2 among which consumers may choose. The three isoutility curves (I_0), (I_t'), and (I_t) define the combinations of commodities 1 and 2, providing consumers with levels of total utility equal, respectively to U_0, U_t' and U_t, with $U_0 < U_t' < U_t$. At time 0, with optimal resource allocation, the equilibrium is at point M_0 where isoutility curve (I_0) is tangent to supply efficiency frontier (S_0). Since prices in the base year are taken as unity, the tangent in point M_0 makes a 45-degree angle with the axes. At time t, the equilibrium point is at point M_t, where isoutility curve (I_t) is tangent to the new efficiency frontier (S_t). In Figure 9.1, the angle made by the tangent in M_t with the vertical axis happens to be greater than 45 degrees, which means that, between times 0 and t, the price of commodity 2 increases in relation to that of commodity 1. The Engel path is represented by curve $M_0M_t'M_t^*$; along each point of this path, the tangent to the isoutility curve makes a 45-degree angle with the axes, and the relative prices of commodities 1 and 2 remain constant.

The modification in the pattern of consumption between times 0 and t is represented by M_0M_t. It may be decomposed into the pure income effect $M_0M_t^*$ along the Engel path and the substitution effect $M_t^*M_t$ along the isoutility curve (I_t). If no substitution had been possible between the consumption of commodities 1 and 2, the equilibrium point would have been at M_t' instead of M_t. The gain from substitution represented by $M_t'M_t^*$ corresponds to the utility gain $U_t - U_t'$.

The pure income effect $(M_0M_t^*)$ and the Slutsky effect of substitution $(M_t^*M_t)$ can actually be computed from the optimal solution of the model, and numerical values were given in Table 3.5 of Chapter 3. From the level of utility, U_t, arrived at in the optimal solution the value x^*, corresponding to point M_t^* of the Engel path, can be calculated by solving:

$$(9.15) \qquad \sum_i U_{it}(x) - \bar{U}_t = 0.$$

Since $U_{it}(x)$, as defined in (9.14), is a monotonic function, (9.15) has a single solution, x_t^*. The consumption levels C_{it}^* corresponding to point M_t^* are computed from the demand function (9.8) by replacing x with its value x_t^* from (9.15). The marginal utility u_t^* can be computed similarly from (9.9). Since prices remain equal to unity along the Engel path, the prices p_{it} can be derived from the dual values Π_{it} of the optimal solution as:

$$(9.16) \qquad p_{it} = \frac{u_{it}}{u_t^*} = \frac{\Pi_{it}}{(1 + \delta)^{-t}N_t^{-1}u_t^*}.$$

Reintroducing the time trend, it is possible now to identify the four factors influencing consumption. Changes in the consumption of commodity i between times 0 and t can be decomposed as follows:

(9.17)
$$\ln \frac{C_{it}}{C_{i0}} = \ln \frac{N_t}{N_0} + \ln \frac{\bar{c}_{it}}{\bar{c}_{i0}} + \ln \frac{c^*_{it}}{\bar{c}_{it}} + \ln \frac{c_{it}}{c^*_{it}}.$$

$$\begin{bmatrix} Consumption \\ change \end{bmatrix} = \begin{bmatrix} Population \\ effect \end{bmatrix} + \begin{bmatrix} Urbanization \\ effect \end{bmatrix} + \begin{bmatrix} Income \\ effect \end{bmatrix} + \begin{bmatrix} Price \\ effect \end{bmatrix}.$$

The population and the urbanization effects are exogenous, while the income and the price effects are endogenous. From equation (9.7), the income effect can be written:

(9.18)
$$\ln \frac{c^*_{it}}{\bar{c}_{it}} = a_i x^* + b_i \frac{x^{*2}}{2}.$$

In equation (9.18), $x_t^* = \ln c_t^*/\bar{c}_t^*$ measures the increase in total consumption along the segment $M_0 M_t^*$ of the Engel path, while $a_i = \eta_{i0}$ and $a_i + b_i x^* = \eta_{it}$ measure the values of the income-elasticity coefficients, respectively, at points M_0 and M_t^* of the Engel path. The income effect can therefore be rewritten as:

(9.18′)
$$\ln \frac{c^*_{it}}{\bar{c}_{it}} = \frac{\eta_{i0} + \eta_{it}}{2} \ln \frac{c_t^*}{\bar{c}_t^*}.$$

From equation (9.7), the price effect can be expressed similarly as:

(9.19)
$$\ln \frac{c_{it}}{c^*_{it}} = a_i(x_i - x^*) + \frac{b_i}{2}(x_i^2 - x^{*2}),$$

$$= \left(a_i + b_i \frac{x^* + x_i}{2} \right)(x_i - x^*).$$

By combining equations (9.9) and (9.16), the second terms of the RHS of (9.19) can be rewritten as:

(9.20)
$$x_i - x^* = -\sigma \ln p_{it}.$$

From equation (9.5) defining the income elasticity, the first term can be expressed as:

(9.21)
$$a_i + b_i \frac{x^* + x_i}{2} = \frac{a_i + b_i x^* + a_i + b x_i}{2} = \frac{\eta_{it} + \eta_{iti}}{2},$$

where η_{it} and η_{iti} are the values of the income-elasticity corresponding to, respectively, points M_t^* and M_{ti}^* along the Engel path. At point M_t^*, the level of utility from total consumption is the same as in the optimal solution, M_t, but the pattern of consumption is different. At point M_{it}^*, the consumption of commodity i is the same as in the optimal solution but the level of utility is different (see Figure 9.1).

Combining equations (9.19), (9.20) and (9.21), the price effect can finally be written:

$$(9.19') \qquad \ln \frac{c_{it}}{c_{it}^*} = -\frac{\eta_{it} + \eta_{iti}}{2} \ln p_{it}.$$

When the price effect (9.19') exactly offsets the income effect (9.18'), consumption of item i remains at its initial trend values. In that case, $\eta_{iti} = \eta_{i0}$ and the combination of (9.18') and (9.19') gives:

$$\ln \frac{c_{it}^*}{\bar{c}_{it}} = \sigma \ln p_{it}.$$

The overall elasticity of substitution, σ, then becomes the ratio between the absolute value of the price elasticity and the value of the income elasticity.

Suppose now that, for a particular commodity i, income elasticity η_i remains constant along the Engel path. By combining equations (9.17), (9.18') and (9.19'), the demand function can be written in the familiar form:

$$(9.22) \qquad \ln \frac{C_{it}}{C_{i0}} \quad = \quad f_i(t) \quad + \quad \eta_i \ln \frac{c_i^*}{\bar{c}_t^*} - \quad \eta_i \sigma \ln \frac{p_{it}}{p_{i0}}.$$

[*Change in consumption*] = [*Trend effect*] + [*Income effect*] + [*Price effect*].

Income elasticities η_i cannot, however, remain constant for all commodities i, except in the trivial case in which all elasticities are identical to unity. This is why, in the system of demand functions used in this model, variations in the values of income-elasticity coefficients have been allowed for.

In the neighborhood of the equilibrium, where variations in the values of the income elasticities can be neglected, the implied values of the direct- and cross-price elasticities can be derived from Frisch's relations (see Frisch 1959):

$$(9.23) \qquad \epsilon_{ii} = -\sigma \eta_i + (c_{it}/c_t)(\sigma \eta_i - 1)\eta_i \quad \text{and}$$

$$(9.24) \qquad \epsilon_{ij} = (c_{jt}/c_t)(\sigma \eta_j - 1) \text{ for } i \neq j.$$

Equation (9.23) shows that the direct price elasticity ϵ_{ii} is approximately equal to the Slutsky elasticity $-\sigma_i(= -\eta_i\sigma)$ when the budget share (c_{it}/c_t) of commodity i is small. Equation (9.24) shows that cross-price elasticities ϵ_{ij} are positive for $\eta_j > \sigma^{-1}$ and negative for η_j

$< \sigma^{-1}$. Taking $\sigma = 0.5$, all commodities with income elasticities less than 2 are gross complements, only those commodities with elasticities greater than 2 are gross substitutes. This is a limitation of additive utility functions.

When total consumption is divided into n groups, $i = 1, \ldots, n$, the system of n equations (9.22) may be used to estimate simultaneously parameter σ and the n elasticity coefficients η_i. The fact that coefficients η_i should not remain constant may not, in practice, raise much more serious problems than the choice of appropriate deflators. Sato (1972) recommends deflating aggregate expenditure by a price index based on average shares as weights and prices by an index based on marginal shares.

In most numerical solutions of the model, aggregate consumption at base year prices $c_t = \Sigma_i\, c_{it}$ exceeds only by a small percentage (0.5 to 1.5) the consumption bundle $c_t^* = \Sigma_i\, c_{it}^*$, which would have provided consumers with the same level of total utility at constant prices. This suggests that practical planners can ignore the distinction between c_t and c_t^* and that econometricians can be satisfied with any reasonable cost-of-living index to estimate σ and η_i.

Appendix A. Rural and Urban Patterns of Consumption

Throughout this chapter, reference has been made to the pattern of consumption of the average Ivorian. In a rapidly changing society, what does the Engel path of the average consumer mean?

The relative sizes of the effects of income level and socioprofessional category can be analyzed from the results of nationwide consumption surveys. This has been done elsewhere for a large number of countries (see Goreux 1960, 1972). Differences between Engel coefficients estimated within and among groups may be analyzed as follows:

	Elasticity	*Variance*
Within group j	η_j	VW_j
Average within groups	η_a	$VW = \Sigma_j\, (VW_j)$
Between groups	η_m	VB
Total	η_0	$V = VB + VW$

where $\eta_a(VW) = \Sigma_j\, [\eta_j(VW_j)]$,
and $\eta_0 V = \eta_m(VB) + \eta_a(VW)$.

If elasticities within groups (η_j) do not differ significantly, the best

Figure 9.2. The Positive Urbanization Effect ($\eta_m > \eta_0 > \eta_a$, Where η_a is the Average of η_u and η_R).

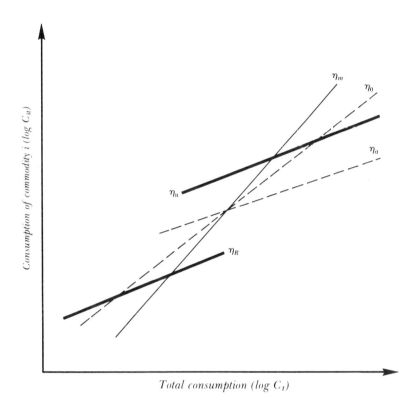

estimate is provided by η_a. If η_a does not differ significantly from the elasticity between groups η_m, the best estimate is given by η_0 computed from the nonstratified sample. In such a case, differences in patterns of consumption between groups can be attributed to income differentials between groups; a single demand function is applicable to the entire population. In this study, such an assumption was assumed to be valid both within the urban population and within the rural population, but not between the two. For a given item (say, housing) there is a positive urbanization effect if, for that item, the elasticity between groups (η_m) is higher than the elasticity within groups (η_a); this case is illustrated in Figure 9.2. Assume, for the sake of simplicity, that income per capita increases by the same percentage in urban and rural areas. Projecting the demand for housing for the average consumer on the basis of elasticity η_a without taking urbanization into account would mean underestimating the national demand for housing. As has been shown elsewhere, it would be generally preferable to project the demand of the average consumer by using elasticity η_0 instead of η_a (see Goreux 1969).

Ideally, national demand should be projected by adding up the projections of the rural and urban demands and treating the share of the urban population as a variable. Since this could not be done, national demand was measured by making two simplifying assumptions: first, the percentage growth in per capita income is the same in rural and urban areas; second, the rate of urbanization is known.

The first step was to project the share of the urban population N_{ut}/N_t. The average per capita demand, $\bar{c}_{it}$, which would be reached without any change in per capita income within the urban and rural populations, was then computed as:

$$\bar{c}_{it} = c_{iu0} \frac{N_{ut}}{N_t} + c_{iR0} \left(1 - \frac{N_{ut}}{N_t}\right),$$

where c_{iu0} (or c_{iR0}) is the average per capita expenditure on item i during the base year in urban (or rural) areas.

If the share of the urban population were to remain constant, $\bar{c}_{it}$ would be equal to $\bar{c}_{i0}$. The pure urbanization effect is therefore measured by $\bar{c}_{it}/\bar{c}_{i0}$. The pure population effect is measured by N_t/N_0. The combined impact of the endogenous price and income effects is measured by $c_{it}/\bar{c}_{it}$, which is the ratio entering into the utility functions (9.7) and (9.14). The income elasticity entering into these functions is the weighted average of the elasticities in rural and urban areas. The intermediate variable $x = \log(c_t/\bar{c}_t)$ defines the increase in per capita aggregate consumption, which is assumed to be the same in rural and urban areas.

Variations in total consumption are measured by:

$$\frac{C_{it}}{C_{i0}} = \frac{N_t}{N_0} \cdot \frac{\bar{c}_{it}}{\bar{c}_{i0}} \cdot \frac{c_{it}}{\bar{c}_{it}}.$$

$$\begin{bmatrix} Total \\ variation \end{bmatrix} = \begin{bmatrix} Population \\ effect \end{bmatrix} \cdot \begin{bmatrix} Urbanization \\ effect \end{bmatrix} \cdot \begin{bmatrix} Income \ and \\ price \ effects \end{bmatrix}.$$

Because consumption by Ivorians is computed through an open loop with endogenous price and income effects, the urbanization effect had to be introduced exogenously. If consumption had been computed through a closed loop, the urbanization effect would have been measured endogenously. Thus, consumption by Europeans was computed by multiplying a set of propensities to consume (taken as exogenous data) by their wage bill (which is an endogenous variable). The same was done for consumption by non-Ivorian Africans with a different set of propensities. In neither case, however, was consumption affected by variations in prices and incomes.

Appendix B. The Piecewise Linear Approximation

Nonlinear functions can easily be incorporated into a linear programming model provided that the nature of the nonlinearities is either increasing costs or diminishing returns. (With either decreasing costs or increasing returns linear programming cannot be used; mixed-integer programming must be used instead; see, for example, Hadley and Kemp 1971.) The piecewise linear approximation procedure described below relates to the utility of consumption, which enters into the maximand. For all other nonlinear functions entering into the constraints of the model, the same procedure was applied.

Consider the utility derived from the consumption of commodity i at time t. The utility function $U_{it}(C_{it})$ is represented by a nonlinear curve in the (U_{it}, C_{it}) space. Since subscripts i and t apply to all points in this space, they can be omitted. Call (U) the utility curve and A_s a point of this curve. The nonlinear curve (U) can be approximated by a series of $m - 1$ linear segments $(A_1A_2, A_2A_3, \ldots, A_{m-1}A_m)$ connecting m consecutive points A_s on curve (U). In Figure 9.3, only three such segments have been shown.

The piecewise linear approximation $A_1A_2, \ldots, A_m$ is incorporated into the model in the form of three equations:

$$(9.25) \qquad \sum_{s=1}^{s=m} \overline{U}_s W_s - U = 0,$$

$$(9.26) \qquad \sum_{s=1}^{s=m} \overline{C}_s W_s - C = 0, \text{ and}$$

$$(9.27) \qquad \sum_{s=1}^{s=m} W_s = 1,$$

where $$W_s \geq 0.$$

The m pairs of coefficients, $\overline{C}_s$ and $\overline{U}_s$, define the coordinates of the

Figure 9.3. The Piecewise Linear Approximation

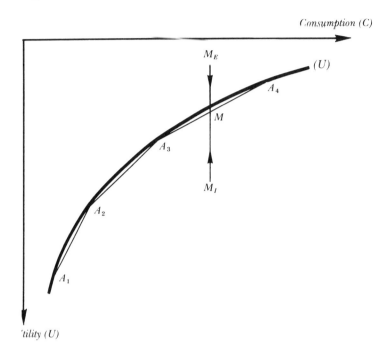

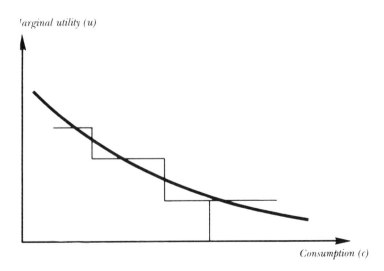

m points A_s. The interpolation weights are the m positive variables W_s. Any set of values given to these m variables defines from (9.25) and (9.26) a pair of values of C and U that, in turn, defines a point of the (C, U) space. It will be shown below that the optimal solution of the model can only lead to a point on the piecewise linear approximation $A_1, A_2, \ldots, A_m$.

First, because the interpolation variables W_s are nonnegative, the point must be in the quadrant containing curve (U). Second, because of diminishing returns ($U'' < 0$ implied by $\eta > 0$ and $\sigma < 1$), the convexity constraint (9.27) excludes any exterior point such as M_E. Third, because utility is maximized, any interior point such as M_I is excluded. With the same level of consumption, and therefore with the same resource requirements, utility could always be increased by moving upward along the vertical drawn from M_I to the point M located on the piecewise linear approximation $A_1, A_2, \ldots, A_m$.

In summary, the point defined by the coordinates C and U found in the optimal solution must belong to the piecewise linear approximation $A_1, A_2, \ldots, A_m$, since it can be neither exterior nor interior to it. $A_1, A_2, \ldots, A_m$ can be called the consumption-efficiency frontier. Any vertex A_s on this frontier is defined by $W_s = 1$ and $W_{s'} \equiv 0$ for $s' \neq s$. Any point M interior to linear segment $A_s A_{s+1}$ is defined by two positive interpolation weights satisfying $W_s + W_{s+1} = 1$ and $m - 2$ zero weights $W_{s'}$ for $s' \neq s$ and $s' \neq s + 1$. Thus, point M halfway between A_2 and A_3 is defined by $W_2 = W_3 = 0.5$ and $W_s = 0$ for all other s.

By increasing the number of points A_s, curve U can be approximated to any prescribed level of accuracy. This requires adding up interpolation variables W_s, but does not require the addition of any constraint. This is the main computational advantage of this method.

In the approximation procedure more frequently used, utility of consumption would have been measured as the area below the marginal utility curve. This curve would have been approximated with a step function by imposing an upper bound on the value of consumption at each step. An additional step would then have required an additional constraint. This addition is avoided in the procedure described earlier.

Having dealt with the linear-approximation principle, it remains to describe the construction of the utility matrix linking the maximand to the commodity balances. This matrix, outlined in Table 9.1, is the matrix U shown in summary form in Figures 7.3 and 7.4.

In a given year t, consider a particular commodity i. The utility function $U_{it}(C_{it})$ is defined, as in Figure 9.3, by m pairs of coefficients

Table 9.1. The Utility Submatrix for Year t[a]

Balance or constraint	Weight by commodity (W_{ist})[b]			Consumption by commodity (C_{it})		Total utility (U_t)	Right-hand side
	$i = 1$ $s = 1,\ldots,m$	$\cdots$ $\cdots$	$i = 8$ $s = 1,\ldots,m$	$i = 1$	$\ldots, \quad i = 8$		
Utility balance	$-\ldots-$	$-\ldots-$	$-\ldots-$			-1	$= 0$
Commodity balances							
$i = 1$	$+\ldots+$			-1			$= 0$
$\cdots$		$+\ldots+$					$= 0$
$i = 8$					-1		$= 0$
Convexity constraints							
$i = 1$	$+1\ldots+1$						$= 1$
$\cdots$		$+1\ldots+1$					$= 1$
$i = 8$			$+1\ldots+1$				$= 1$

a. $\sum_i \sum_s (\bar{U}_{ist}) W_{ist} - U_t = 0$

   $\sum_s (\bar{C}_{ist}) W_{ist} - C_{it} = 0$

   $\sum_s W_{ist} = 1$, with $W_{ist} \geq 0$.

b. i = commodity group; s = interpolation step.

$(\bar{C}_{ist}, \bar{U}_{ist})$. Those are computed by solving the consumption functions $C_{it}(x)$ given in (9.8) and the utility function $U_{it}(x)$ given in (9.14) for m values of x called $\bar{x}_1, \ldots, \bar{x}_s, \ldots, \bar{x}_m$. These values must be selected so as to cover the relevant range of the utility curve of commodity i at time t.

Assume, initially, that relative prices remain constant, and call γ the average yearly growth rate of per capita consumption between years 0 and t. The coordinates of the point M_{ist} reached at time t are the solutions of (9.8) and (9.14) for the value of x given by $x = \ln(1 + \gamma)^t \approx \gamma t$.

Although the optimal value of γ is unknown before solving the model, its likely range of variations may be identified by lower and upper limits, $\underline{\gamma}$ and $\bar{\gamma}$, for which the relevant range for x can be derived as $\underline{\gamma}t$ and $\bar{\gamma}t$.

Assume now that, starting from unity in the base year, prices may increase to $p(> 1)$ or decline to $1/p(< 1)$. The relevant range for x becomes $\underline{x}_t = \underline{\gamma}t - \sigma \ln p, \bar{x}_t = \bar{\gamma}t + \sigma \ln p$.

When t rises from 5 in the first decision year to 20 in the last one, the upper and lower limits ($\underline{x}_t$ and $\bar{x}_t$) as well as the range between them ($\bar{x}_t - \underline{x}_t$) increase. For a given year t, a set of m_t values was selected for x within the range ($\underline{x}_t, \ldots, \bar{x}_t$). The same set of values was used for all commodities i because it was not possible to make a commodity price forecast that would be applicable to all experiments. The number of values selected for x within the range $\underline{x}_t \leq x \leq \bar{x}_t$ was raised from $m_5 = 14$ for the first decision year to $m_{20} = 30$ for the last one.

In year t, the utility functions $U_{it}(C_{it})$ are defined by the n pairs of equations (9.8) and (9.14), where $i = 1, \ldots, n$. Each pair of equations was solved for the m_t values selected for x in year t. This led to nm_t pairs of values $(\bar{C}_{ist}, \bar{U}_{ist})$, which are the coefficients of the activity columns W_{ist} represented in Table 9.1 by $+$ in the case of $\bar{C}_{ist}$ and $-$ in the case of $\bar{U}_{ist}$. Because utilities derived from all commodities are assumed to be additive, there is a single utility balance, but there are one commodity balance and one convexity constraint for each commodity. Combining the T decision years, the utility matrix consists of $(2n + 1)T$ equations and $(n + 1)T + n \sum_{\tau=1}^{\tau=T} m_\tau$ variables.

If substitution between commodities had not been allowed, the optimal solution would have been constrained to remain on the Engel path. The interpolation weights and the convexity constraints would have ceased to be commodity-specific; therefore, the number of equations would have been reduced to $(n + 2)T$ and the number of variables to $(1 + n)T + \sum_{\tau=1}^{\tau=T} m_\tau$.

If the propensities to consume had been taken as given and if the objective function had been expressed in terms of quantities consumed (instead of utility of consumption), the number of columns would have been reduced to the T variables C_t. This formulation, which is frequent in dynamic programming models, does assume that the intertemporal elasticity of substitution is infinity while the intratemporal one is zero. Assumed, instead, has been a common overall elasticity of substitution $0 < \sigma < 1$ for intertemporal and intratemporal choices. In programming terms, it consists in interposing the utility matrix just described between the maximand and the commodity balances.

Chapter 10

Savings and Physical Investments

TWO TYPES OF INTERTEMPORAL LINKAGE are present in the model. The first occurs through the utility maximand; it was analyzed in Chapter 8 in connection with the tradeoff between consuming more today and consuming more tomorrow. The second occurs through investment activities, which withdraw resources from consumption today in order to create stocks of capital for the future. The second type of intertemporal linkage, illustrated in Figure 7.3 by matrices K, E, and H, are dealt with in Chapters 10 and 11.

The first section of this chapter describes the balance between investments and savings for the economy as a whole. The following three sections deal with physical investments in the urban sector.

The Balance between Investments and Savings

In the simplified model of Chapter 8, domestic savings were always equal to investments. The level of investments (and thus of savings) was optimized by equalizing the marginal utility of the last unit of consumption forgone today to that of the additional consumption generated for tomorrow. Savings were optimized in an open loop in the absence of any institutional constraint. A departure is now made from this simple formulation in three ways. First, domestic investment is now equal to the sum of domestic savings and of the net inflow of capital from abroad. Second, each of these three variables is disaggregated. Third, the model can be solved with and without institutional constraint on savings.

The savings-investment balance is written:

(10.1) $S + F = I$,

with $F = \bar{F} + F_c$ Net inflow of capital from abroad, where $\bar{F}$ = exogenous flow resulting from servicing and repayment of initial debts, and receipts (net of repayments) from soft loans contracted during the optimization period, and F_c = endogenous flow resulting from borrowing at commercial rates during the optimization period;

$$I = I_u + I_S + I_E + \bar{I}_G \qquad \text{Total investments,}$$

where I_u = physical investments in the urban sector, I_S = physical investments in the rural sectors and in the two large projects (the iron mine and Riviera), I_E = human investment in education, and $\bar{I}_G$ = public "nonproductive investments" given exogenously; and

$$S = S_p + S_G + S_S \qquad \text{Total domestic savings,}$$

where S_p = private savings linked to private consumption, S_G = linked public savings, and S_S = public savings treated either as a slack or as a linked variable.

Private savings, S_p, are derived from private consumption by a behavioral relationship defining the private propensity to consume. Linked public savings, S_G, are given by the difference between government receipts and government expenditures, both of which are linked to production and trading activities.[1] The additional component of public savings, S_S, is either a slack or a linked variable.

When the level of domestic savings is optimized without institutional constraint, as discussed in Chapter 8, variable S_S is treated as a slack. From the optimal value $\hat{S}_S$ found for the slack, the optimal rate of taxation, $t\hat{a}x$, is derived ex post from:

$$(10.2) \qquad t\hat{a}x = \hat{S}_S/GNP.$$

When the model is solved with an institutional constraint on savings, variable S_S is linked to the level of GDP by the constraint:

$$(10.2') \qquad S_S = (t\bar{a}x)GNP,$$

where $t\bar{a}x$ is a coefficient lower than the optimal rate of taxation, $t\hat{a}x$, found in the open-loop solution.

The impact of the savings constraint on the dual solution is shown in Table 10.1. The matrix of coefficients is presented in triangular form. The dual value Π_s of the savings-investment constraint appears in the first row. The dual values of the other rows are derived recursively. The algebraic formulas are followed by the numerical values of the coefficients. When the savings constraint is relaxed, all dual values becomes equal to zero.

---

1. The values of these coefficients vary with the tariff policies.

Capital Goods and Capital Stocks in the Urban Sector

There are three capital goods (vehicles, machinery, and construction) which are identified by subscript q. These three capital goods can be invested into nine types of urban capital stocks, which are identified by subscript k. For each capital good q, there is a commodity balance expressed in terms of annual flows. This commodity balance ensures that in year $\bar{t}$, total uses (consumption + investments) do not exceed available supplies (domestic production + imports − exports). For each capital stock k, there is a capacity balance. This balance ensures that the sum of the capital stocks of type k required by all production activities in year t does not exceed the total stock accumulated by that year, net of depreciation.

The two capital stocks identified only by the origin of the capital good invested—vehicles or construction—can be used for any urban production activity. The other seven capital stocks consist of machinery equipment installed for specialized purposes. Thus, the capital good called machinery can be invested in a textile plant or in six other types of plants. Once the choice of investment has been made, the seven types of capital stocks are not fungible. Excess machinery capacity may prevail in some types of plants and not in others.

When the capital good q is invested, a corresponding amount is subtracted from the commodity balance at time $\bar{t}$. The productive life of the invested capital thus generated starts at time $\bar{t} + p_q$ and ends at time $\bar{t} + p_q + lf_q$. Parameters p_q and lf_q measure the lengths of the gestation lag and the life span of the capital stock, respectively. The numerical values retained are shown in Table 10.2.

Time Aggregation

In the central model, there is a five-year interval between each two consecutive optimization years (1975, 1980, 1985, and 1990); the postterminal period (1990–2000) covers ten years. This creates a problem of time aggregation, which is illustrated in Figures 10.1 and 10.2.

Start with the simplest case of Figure 10.1, where time is treated as a continuous variable.[2] Call θ the interval between two consecutive

---

2. This procedure was suggested by Charles R. Blitzer of the Development Research Center of the World Bank.

Table 10.1. *The Effect of a Savings Constraint on the Dual Values of Selected Contraints*

| | Activities | | | | | | | Dual values[a] $\Pi_j = a\Pi_s + b\Pi_f$ | |
| | | | | | | | | a | b |
Constraint	Private savings	Public expendi- tures	Public receipts	GNP	Physical invest- ment	Human invest- ment	Private consump- tion	Net flow of foreign capital	Formula	Numerical value in 1980
Balance defining										
1. Private savings	+1						−1		−1	−1
2. Investment as the sum of domestic savings and net capital flow	+1	−1	+1		−1	−1		1 − f	+1	+1
3. Public expenditures		−1	γ	e					−1	−1
4. Public receipts			−1	ρ				f	$+\dfrac{1-(1+e)\gamma}{1-\rho\gamma}$	0.899

	(1)	(2)	(3)	(4)	(5)	Algebraic value of a	Numerical value of a	b
5. GNP	γ	-1	$+1$	$+1$		$+\dfrac{\rho(1-\gamma)-\varepsilon}{1-\rho\gamma}$	0.062	
6. Physical investment		-1				$-\dfrac{1-\rho+\varepsilon}{1-\rho\gamma}$	-0.938	
7. Human investment			-1			$-\dfrac{1-\rho+\varepsilon}{1-\rho\gamma}$	-0.938	
8. Private consumption				-1		$+\dfrac{s+\rho(1-\gamma-s\gamma)-\varepsilon}{1-\rho\gamma}$	0.232	
9. Net flow of foreign capital					-1	$+1-f\gamma\dfrac{1-\rho+\varepsilon}{1-\rho\gamma}$	0.960	$+1$
10. Balance of payments					$+1$		-1	

Note: The dual equations, which are read along the columns, include all the nonzero coefficients. The primal equations, which are read along the rows, include the nonzero coefficients relating only to the eight activities listed.

The dual values of constraints 1, 4, 9, and 10 were shown in rows 1–4 of Table 5.3 in cases T1, T3, and T4. The numerical values of the parameters for the year 1980 are $\gamma = 0.4$, $\varepsilon = 0.1077$, $\rho = 0.0458$, $s = 0.12$, $s = 0.17$, $f = 0.4$.

a. The dual value of constraint j ($= 1, \ldots, 10$) can be expressed as a linear function of the dual values of savings (Π_s) and foreign exchange (Π_f) as $\Pi_j = a\Pi_s + b\Pi_f$. The penultimate and antepenultimate columns give, respectively, the algebraic and numerical values of coefficient a, the last column that of coefficient b.

*Figure 10.1. Interpolation Procedure When Time Is Treated
as a Continuous Variable*

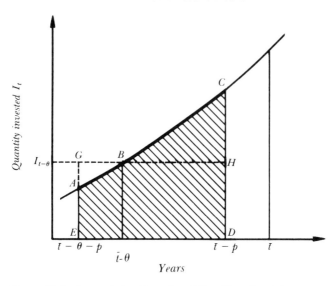

*Figure 10.2. Interpolation Procedure When Time Is a Discrete Variable
Characterizing the Year*

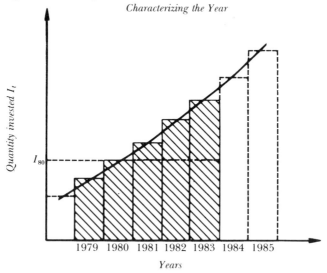

Five-year interpolation period ($\theta = 5$)

One-and-a-half-year lag ($p = 1.5$)

Table 10.2. *Characteristics of Three Capital Goods*
(Number of years)

Period	Vehicles	Machines	Buildings
Gestation lag between investment and availability of capacity, p_q	1	1	2.5
Life span of the capital stock, lf_q	10	15	25

points in time, $\bar{t}$ and $\bar{t} - \theta$, for which the model is optimized and omit, for the sake of simplicity, the subscript q, which characterizes the origin of the capital stock. Capital stock available at time $\bar{t}$ originates from investments made over the period, defined by the following range:

$$(10.3) \qquad \bar{t} - lf - p \leq t \leq \bar{t} - p.$$

Three simplifying assumptions will be made: (a) the life span, lf, of the capital stock is an integer multiple of the time interval θ; (b) the gestation lag, p, is smaller than the time interval θ; and (c) the growth rate of investments remains constant and equal to g throughout the investment period defined by (10.3).

Combining the assumptions (a) and (b), the period of time defined by (10.3) can be decomposed into lf/θ subperiods, each having the same length θ. The first and the last subperiods are defined by the following ranges of the time variable:

$$t = \bar{t} - lf + \tau \text{ with } -p \leq \tau \leq \theta - p, \text{ and}$$

$$t = \bar{t} - \theta + \tau \text{ with } -p \leq \tau \leq \theta - p.$$

The capital accumulated from investments made during the last subperiod corresponds to the shaded area of Figure 10.1. Because investments have been assumed in (c) to grow at the constant rate g, the capital accumulated during the last subperiod is measured by:

$$\int_{\tau=-p}^{\tau=\theta-p} I_{\bar{t}-\theta+\tau} = I_{\bar{t}-\theta} \int_{\tau=-p}^{\tau=\theta-p} e^{g\tau} d\tau.$$

Since the integral is a constant which remains the same for all subperiods, the capital stock available at time $\bar{t}$ is given by:

$$(10.4) \qquad K_{\bar{t}} = \psi \sum_{t=\bar{t}-lf}^{t=\bar{t}-\theta} I_t, \text{ with}$$

$$(10.5) \qquad \psi = \frac{e^{g\theta} - 1}{g e^{gp}}.$$

Table 10.3. Values of the Interpolation Coefficient
ψ for Five-Year Time Periods ($\theta = 5$)

Gestation lag (p)	Growth rate of investments (g)			$\dfrac{\psi_{0.07}}{\psi_{0.15}}$
	0.0	0.07	0.15	
0.5	5.0	5.79	6.77	0.86
1.5	5.0	5.37	5.86	0.92
2.5	5.0	5.06	5.11	0.99
3.5	5.0	4.70	4.43	1.06
4.5	5.0	4.42	3.87	1.14

Suppose now that time is a discrete variable and that all empirical data are measured on a yearly basis, as shown in Figure 10.2. The relevant investment period and the interpolation coefficient become:

(10.3′) $\bar{t} - lf - p + 0.5 \le t \le \bar{t} - p - 0.5$ and

(10.5′) $$\psi = \frac{(1+g)^{\theta} - 1}{g(1+g)^{p-0.5}},$$

where g now defines the yearly growth rate of investments.

With an annual model and a one-half–year gestation lag ($\theta = 1$ and $p = 0.5$), equation (10.5′) shows that the interpolation coefficient is equal to unity ($\psi = 1$). This is the familiar assumption which was made in Chapter 8 with the annual model outlined in Table 8.4.

Equation (10.5′) can be rewritten in the form of a MacLaurin series:

$$\psi = \theta \, \frac{1 + \dfrac{g\theta}{2} + \dfrac{(g\theta)^2}{6} + \dots}{1 + gp + \dfrac{(gp)^2}{2} + \dots}.$$

It follows that: $\psi \simeq \theta$ for g small, for $p = \theta/2$, and for $(g\theta)^2$ and $(gp)^2$ small; and that $\psi \gtrless \theta$ for $p \lessgtr \theta/2$ and $g > 0$ (since $\partial\psi/\partial p < 0$ for $g > 0$).

In Table 10.3 numerical values of ψ are shown in the case of $\theta = 5$ for three values of $g(= 0.0, 0.07$ and $0.15)$ and five values of $p(= 0.5, \dots, 4.5)$.

Figure 10.2 illustrates the case $\theta = 5$ and $p = 1.5$. With a ten-year life span, the capital stock available in year 1985 results from the investments made in the two subperiods 1979–83 and 1974–1978. It is computed as:

$$K_{85} = \psi(I_{75} + I_{80}),$$

where the last term of the righthand side (RHS) corresponds to the shaded area of Figure 10.2. Clearly, the shaded area exceeds five times the level of investment made in the year 1980, if investments increase at a positive rate during the subperiod 1979–83. With a 2.5-year gestation lag, the decision year 1980 would have come in the middle of the interpolation period. The shaded area would have been exactly equal to five times the investments made in the year 1980, if investments had grown linearly during the interpolation period 1978–82. Because investments have been assumed to grow exponentially and not linearly, the value of ψ shown in Table 10.3 for $p = 2.5$ slightly exceeds $\theta = 5$ for $g > 0$, but the difference is small.

In the case of construction ($p = 2.5 = \theta/2$), the choice of the growth rate of investment did not significantly affect the value of the interpolation coefficient. In the case of vehicles and machinery ($p = 1$), it did. For this reason, the value of the interpolation coefficient was adjusted according to the growth rate of investment found in the optimal solution. The values thus selected were kept constant throughout the experiments.

Dual Values

The dual equation of the investment activity is:

$$(10.6) \qquad \Pi_{q,\bar{\imath}} + \Pi_{inv,\bar{\imath}} = \left[\sum_{t=\bar{\imath}+5}^{t=\bar{\imath}+lf_q \leq 20} \psi_g \Pi_{k,t} \right] + (\Delta \psi) \Pi_{k,\Delta T}.$$

The lefthand side (LHS) measures the cost of the investment activity as the sum of the value of the capital good invested ($\Pi_{q,\bar{\imath}}$) and of the penalty on investment ($\Pi_{inv,\bar{\imath}}$), if there is a binding constraint on savings. The RHS measures the return on investments as the sum of ψ_g times the rental values of the capital accumulated during each decision year ($\Pi_{k,t}$) and the sum of $\Delta \psi$ times the dual value of the postterminal constraint ($\Pi_{k,\Delta T}$).[3]

3. $\Delta\psi_{g,\bar{\imath},lf_q} = \psi_{g,\bar{\imath},30} - \psi_{g,\bar{\imath},20}$,

$\quad \psi_{g,\bar{\imath},30} = 0$ for $\bar{\imath} < 30 - lf_q$, and

$\quad \psi_{g,\bar{\imath},20} = 0$ for $\bar{\imath} < 20 - lf_q$.

For construction $\Delta\psi = 7.13$ for a growth rate of investments equal to 7 percent a year.

Without any constraint on savings and with an infinite time horizon, the difference between the dual equations of the investment activities in years t and $t - \theta$ can be written:

$$(10.7) \qquad \psi_g(\Pi_{k,t} - \Pi_{k,t+lf}) = \Pi_{q,t-\theta} - \Pi_{q,t}.$$

The difference between dual values at two points in time is defined as $\Pi_{k,t+lf} = (1 + r_k)^{-lf}\Pi_{k,t}$ and $\Pi_{q,t} = (1 + r_q)^{-\theta}\Pi_{q,t-\theta}$, where $r_{q,t}$ = own yearly average rate of interest on capital good q between years $t - \theta$ and t, and $r_{k,t}$ = own yearly average rate of interest on capacity k between years t and $t + lf$.

Equation (10.7) may then be rewritten:

$$(10.8) \qquad \Pi_{k,t}/\Pi_{q,t} = \psi_g^{-1}\frac{(1 + r_{q,t})^{\theta} - 1}{1 - (1 + r_{k,t})^{-lf}}.$$

The numerator of the RHS of (10.8) can in turn be rewritten:

$$(10.9) \qquad (1 + r_{q,t})^{\theta} - 1 = \frac{(1 + r_{q,t})^{\theta} - 1}{r_{q,t}(1 + r_{q,t})^{p_q - 0.5}}\, r_{q,t}(1 + r_{q,t})^{p-0.5}.$$

The first term of the RHS of (10.9) is the formula (10.5′) which defines the interpolation coefficient ψ. Hence (10.8) can be rewritten:

$$(10.10) \qquad \frac{\Pi_{k,t}}{\Pi_{q,t}} = \frac{\psi_r}{\psi_g}\frac{(1 + r_{q,t})^{p_q - 0.5}}{1 - (1 + r_{k,t})^{-lf}}\, r_{q,t}.$$

In Chapter 8, this equation was written in the simplified form:

$$(8.30') \qquad \Pi_{k,t} = r_t\Pi_t.$$

This simplification was based on the following assumptions: (a) Depreciation can be neglected ($lf \simeq \infty$); (b) the gestation lag of investments is half a year ($p_q = 0.5$); (c) the model is annual ($\theta = 1$, hence, with $p_q = 0.5$ the ψ coefficients are the same); and (d) the rate of interest on the capital good q is equal to the rate of interest on consumption ($r_{q,t} = r_t$), either because there is a single good in the economy or because the price of capital good q remains equal to unity.

Under these four assumptions, the marginal productivity of capital is equal to the rate of interest on consumption (r_t), taking the dual value of consumption (Π_t) as the numéraire. This is why r_t could be interpreted as the marginal productivity of capital in dynamic equation (8.32). These simplifying assumptions will now be relaxed one by one.

The denominator of the second term of the RHS of (10.10) accounts for capital depreciation. For a rate of interest of 15 percent on capital ($r_k = 0.15$), the value $[1 - (1 + r_{k,t})^{-lf}]^{-1}$ is equal to 1.33 for vehicles that have a ten-year life span. It is equal to 1.12 for machinery that has a fifteen-year life span. It becomes equal to 1.02 in the case of construction which has a twenty-five-year life span. When the rate of interest and the length of the life span are both high, the cost of depreciation becomes negligible ($1.02 \approx 1.0$).

In the numerator of (10.10), the term $(1 + r_{q,t})^{p_q - 0.5}$ is greater than unity when the gestation lag (p_q) exceeds half a year. Because the lag in construction was taken as two and a half years instead of half a year, the term $(1 + r_{q,t})^{p_q - 0.5}$ was equal to approximately 1.3. This explains why a high cost was found for housing in the first part of this book. This cost may have been overestimated for two reasons. First, the length of the gestation lag may be less than two and a half years. Second, the entire cost of construction is not disbursed two years before occupancy, as is assumed implicitly in the model.

The rate of interest on capital good ($r_{q,t}$) can be expressed in relation to the rate of interest on consumption (r_t) and the price of the capital good (p_q). By definition:

$$p_{q,t} = \Pi_{q,t}/\Pi_t$$

where $p_{q,0} = 1.0$, $\Pi_t = (1 + r_t)^\theta \Pi_{t-\theta}$, and $\Pi_{q,t} = (1 + r_{q,t})^\theta \Pi_{q,t-\theta}$. Hence:

$$\frac{p_{q,t}}{p_{q,t-\theta}} = \left(\frac{1 + r_{q,t}}{1 + r_t}\right)^\theta \text{ and}$$

$$r_{q,t} = (1 + r_t)\left(\frac{p_{q,t}}{p_{q,t-\theta}}\right)^{1/\theta} - 1.$$

Clearly, if the price of capital good q remains constant, $r_{q,t}$ is identical to r_t.

Turn now to the ratio between the interpolation coefficients in the RHS of (10.10). In the denominator, the interpolation coefficient ψ_g is based on the growth rate of investments at which capacities accumulate in the primal solution. In the numerator, the interpolation coefficient ψ_r is based on the rate of interest at which dual values decline in the dual solution. As already noted, the rate of interest is of the order of 15 percent, whereas the rate of growth of investment is only of the order of 7 percent. The ratio between the interpolation coefficients, therefore, is approximately equal to unity only for $p_q = \theta/2$, which is the case with construction. It is greater than unity when the gestation lag is less than half the time interval $p_q < \theta/2$, which is the case with vehicles and machinery.

The ratio between the interpolation coefficients appears also from the comparison between a time-aggregated model and a yearly model. The dual equation of the time-aggregated model is:

$$\Pi_{q,\bar{\iota}} = [\psi_g][\Pi_{k,\bar{\iota}+\theta} + \Pi_{k,\bar{\iota}+2\theta} + \ldots].$$

Characterizing with a prime the dual values of the corresponding annual model, the corresponding dual equation can be written:

$$\Pi'_{q,t} = \sum_{t=\bar{\iota}+p+0.5}^{t=\bar{\iota}+\theta+p-0.5} \Pi'_{k,t} + \ldots.$$

With a constant rate of interest on capital, the dual equation of the yearly model would become:

$$\Pi'_{q,\bar{\iota}} = \Pi'_{k,\bar{\iota}+\theta} \sum_{\tau=-p+0.5}^{\tau=\theta-p-0.5} (1+r)^\tau + \ldots,$$

$$\Pi'_{q,\bar{\iota}} = [\psi_r][\Pi'_{k,\bar{\iota}+\theta} + \Pi'_{k,\bar{\iota}+2\theta} + \ldots..$$

Dividing the dual equation of the annual model by that of the aggregated model gives:

$$\frac{\Pi_{k,\bar{\iota}+\theta} + \ldots}{\Pi_{q,\bar{\iota}}} = \frac{\psi_r}{\psi_g} \frac{\Pi'_{k,\bar{\iota}+\theta} + \ldots}{\Pi'_{q,\bar{\iota}}}.$$

With $p < \theta/2$ and $r > g > 0$, it follows that $\psi(r) > \psi(g)$. In that case, time aggregation results in an overstatement of the dual values of the capacities in relation to the dual values of the capital goods. With $p \neq \theta/2$ and $r \neq g$, the aggregation procedure described cannot be fully satisfactory for both the primal and dual solutions. This was the reason for adopting a more elaborate aggregation procedure in the case of education, where the time-lag structure is considerably more complex.

Chapter 11

Human Investments

BECAUSE OF THE COMPLEXITY of the lag structure, the starting point is a full-fledged annual model of the postprimary educational sector. Each educational activity is represented by a cohort of students who enroll in the first grade of a given cycle of studies. Each year some of the students belonging to this cohort are promoted, others repeat the same grade, and the remainder drop out of school. The cost per student in a given grade is expressed in terms of labor inputs of given skills (professors and students) and of physical inputs (school buildings, administrative expenses, and so forth). The benefit per student success-fully completing a study cycle is the increment of labor productivity resulting from the upgrading of his skills. No utility is ascribed to the purely cultural benefits of education.

Once an educational activity is initiated in a given year, a cohort of students is constituted. The net impact of this cohort on the labor balances and the commodity balances for nonlabor educational inputs is computed year by year in a first step and aggregated for the representative years of the central model in a second step. This operation is repeated for each type of educational activity in each of the interpolation periods. The net impacts thus computed for all educational activities define the educational matrix incorporated into the central model. All labor balances for intermediate grades (which are strict equalities) are eliminated from this reduced-form matrix. The choice among alternative educational technologies is preserved, since the levels of the educational activities become investment variables in the central model.

Converting the full-fledged educational model into its reduced form would not introduce any error if the central model were annual. Converting an annual model into a multiannual one does introduce errors, however, thus bringing up the general problem of aggregation over time in dynamic models. On the one hand, the optimization model should be annual to take into account the wide variety in time lags attached to the various educational activities. On the other hand, the planning horizon should extend until the year 2000 in order to analyze the problem of Ivorization. Since a dynamic programming model covering thirty individual years would be unmanageable, a shortcut is required.[1]

The selection of the time-interpolation periods is such that the middle of each period coincides with a decision year of the central model. Within each interpolation period, an exogenous growth rate is selected for each educational activity. The particular values selected for these growth rates have little effect on the coefficients of the reduced-form matrix incorporated into the central model; the error introduced by time aggregation is therefore small.

Although the educational matrix was computed primarily to become a component of the central model, it was also used to solve a deterministic model of the educational sector alone. The latter has been an efficient instrument for testing various changes in the educational system before incorporating the educational matrix into the central optimizing model. The combination of a simple deterministic model for the sector with a more complex optimizing model for the economy as a whole may be a promising form of multilevel programming.

The first section of this chapter describes the educational activities, while the second section outlines the computation of the reduced-form matrix. The third section illustrates the linkage between the educational sector and the rest of the economy. The last section compares the solution of the educational model incorporated in the central one with the solution of the educational model alone.

Educational Activities

The educational system is represented by a series of activities through which professional skills can be acquired. In each decision year, there is a choice among the fifteen different educational activities shown in Figure 11.1. Some of these activities are alterna-

---

1. Solving for thirty periods of time rather than five would mean multiplying the number of equations by six and the cost of computation by more than fifty. In such a case, it might be preferable to replace the linear programming model with a control-theory model.

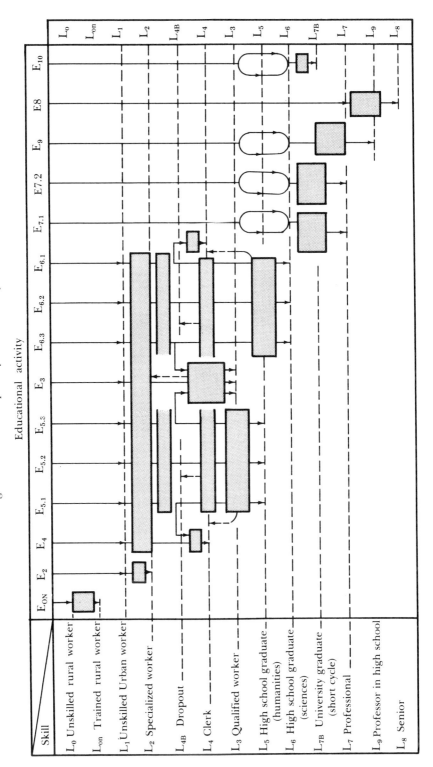

Figure 11.1. The Postprimary Educational System

tive ways of acquiring the same qualifications. For example, a high-school graduate (qualification λ = 5 or 6) can become a university graduate (qualification λ = 7) by attending a university in the Ivory Coast (activity E7.1) or abroad (activity E7.2).

Each educational activity defines a sequence of cycles of studies; these cycles are represented by the boxes shown in Figure 11.1. Each study cycle, in turn, defines a sequence of years of study; a sequence is characterized by a common set of parameters (rates of promotion and repetition, student-teacher ratio, and so forth). The full specifications of the system are contained in Tables 11.1 and 11.2.

Table 11.1 defines the characteristics of each of the fourteen cycles. Row 1 gives the length of the study cycle; rows 2 and 3, the rates of promotion and repetition; rows 4–13, the educational inputs.

Consider cycle C, which corresponds to the last three years of high school and leads to the *baccalauréat lettres*. The rates of promotion and repetition are π = 0.86 and ρ = 0.11. Take a cohort of 100 students who, in year $\bar{t}$, enroll for the first time in a given grade. In year $\bar{t}$ + 1, 86 of these students are in the next higher grade of the cycle; 11 are repeating the same grade; 3 have dropped out. The cost per student enrolled is shown in terms of labor inputs in rows 4, 6, and 10. Row 4 accounts for the labor supply forgone by sending a student to school. A student attending cycle C is counted as 0.9 male adult equivalent of a worker with the qualification λ = 1. There is one "professor of qualification" λ = 9 for 17.5 (=1/0.057) students; this corresponds to the Unesco (1973) recommendation of 1.7 professors per class of 30 students (1.7/30 = 0.057). In addition, there is one administrator of qualification λ = 5 for 250 (=1/0.004) students. Physical costs per student are shown in rows 11 and 12. They are expressed in row 11 in terms of current consumption by public administration (CFAF60 thousand a year for paper, electricity, and so forth). They are expressed in row 12 in terms of requirements for building capacity (CFAF180 thousand worth of school buildings).

Turn now to Table 11.2, which defines the fifteen educational activities. Rows 1–4 specify the sequence of cycles; row 5, the qualifications required for enrollment; rows 6–9, the qualifications of the dropouts; row 10, the qualifications after graduation. The last row, 11, gives the number of years of productive life after graduation.

Consider educational activity E5.2. It consists of a two-year cycle, A, two one-year cycles, B_1 and B_2, and a three-year cycle, C. After a student receives his *baccalauréat lettres*, he can be employed for thirty-eight years in the skill category λ = 5. Alternatively, he can enroll in one of the five educational activities, E7.1 through E10, in order to obtain a higher qualification.

With educational activities E5.1 and E5.3, the dropouts from B_2 are recycled. In one case, they go through cycle G and become clerks; in the other, they go through cycle F and become specialized workers.

The system of fourteen cycles and fifteen activities defined in Tables 11.1 and 11.2 provides a fairly realistic picture of the actual educational system in the Ivory Coast. The technical specifications of the cycles are based on historical series, recommendations presented in the Unesco report, and discussions with Ivorian officials. A distinction is made between the "old" and the "new" regimes. The old regime, based on historical coefficients (shown within parentheses in Table 11.1), applies to students enrolled in 1972 or earlier. The new regime applies to students enrolled in 1973 and later. The new regime assumes a substantial reduction in the student-teacher ratio as well as in the rates of repetition and dropping out.

The Reduced Form of the Educational Model

The choice variable $(E_{\lambda,\nu,\bar{t}})$ is the number of students newly enrolled in decision year $\bar{t}$ in educational activity λ, ν. The first subscript defines the skill of graduation, λ; the second subscript defines the particular way, ν, followed to acquire skill λ; the third subscript defines the year, $\bar{t}$, in which students newly enroll in activity λ, ν. Once the level $(E_{\lambda,\nu,\bar{t}})$ has been chosen, a cohort has been formed and the distribution of this cohort by cycle of study and category of labor skills is determined year by year till the last member of this cohort has retired from the labor force.[2] For all years $t \geq \bar{t}$, the effects of educational activity $E_{\lambda,\nu,\bar{t}}$ on promotions and costs are therefore also determined.

2. This does not apply to a particular individual. Consider the classical high school educational activity (E5.2). An individual belonging to cohort 5.2, $\bar{t}$ and graduating with the qualification λ = 5 may remain in this skill category or may enroll in a new study cycle to acquire qualification λ = 7. Whether this individual is employed in the active labor force at skill λ = 5 or is used as an input in educational activity E7.1 is not of interest. In either case, he is recorded as a unit of labor input (−) in the labor balance for skill λ = 5. The only concern here is with labor balances. All members of a given skill category are assumed to be interchangeable.

Table 11.1. Cycles of Study[a]

Characteristic		A	B1	B2	C	D	E	F
						Activity		
1.	Number of grades	2	1	1	3	3	1	3
2.	Promotion rate	0.81	0.75	0.70	0.86	0.86	1.0	0.90
		(0.74)	(0.75)	(0.40)	(0.80)	(0.80)	(1.0)	(0.85)
3.	Repeating rate	0.12	0.13	0.14	0.11	0.11	0.0	0.08
		(0.17)	(0.10)	(0.14)	(0.12)	(0.12)	(0.0)	(0.10)
	Labor inputs							
4.	L1		0.5	0.8	0.9	1.0	0.7	1.0
5.	L3						0.005	0.010
6.	L5	0.004	0.004	0.004	0.004	0.004		
7.	L6							
8.	L7							
9.	L8							
10.	L9	0.035	0.035	0.035	0.057	0.067	0.110	0.101
		(0.025)	(0.025)	(0.025)	(0.035)	(0.040)	(0.110)	(0.067)
	Other inputs							
11.	Public consumption	0.030	0.030	0.030	0.060	0.120	0.180	0.220
12.	Capacities of school buildings	0.174	0.174	0.174	0.180	0.200	0.320	0.320
13.	Foreign exchange							

Characteristic		Activity						
		G	H	I	J	K	L	M
1.	Number of grades	1	5	4	4	3	2	2
2.	Promotion rate	1.0	0.60	0.82	0.84	0.85	1.0	0.85
		(1.0)	(0.60)	(0.55)	(0.84)	(0.85)	(1.0)	(0.85)
3.	Repeating rate	0.0	0.20	0.15	0.16	0.15	0.0	0.12
		(0.0)	(0.20)	(0.45)	(0.16)	(0.15)	(0.0)	(0.12)
	Labor inputs							
4.	L1	0.7						
5.	L3							
6.	L5	0.004		$(\alpha_t)1.04^b$	$(\alpha_t)^b$	$(\alpha_t)1.04^b$		$(\alpha_t)1.04^b$
7.	L6			$(1-\alpha_t)$	$(1-\alpha_t)$	$(1-\alpha_t)$		$1-\alpha_t$
8.	L7			0.10		0.09	0.003	0.07
9.	L8			0.05		0.03		0.03
10.	L9	0.042					0.005	
		(0.042)						
	Other inputs							
11.	Public consumption	0.100		0.325		0.20	0.005	0.20
12.	Capacities of school buildings	0.250		0.900		0.30	0.100	0.30
13.	Foreign exchange				1.0			

a. Figures in parentheses are historical parameters.
b. $(\alpha_t = 0.75 - 0.01t)$ proportion of students with classical baccalaureat enrolling at university.

Table 11.2. *Educational Activities*

Characteristic	Activity									
	E0N	E2	E3	E4	E5.1	E5.2	E5.3	E6.1	E6.2	E5.3
1. First cycle	L	E	A	A	A	A	A	A	A	A
2. Second cycle			F	G	B1	B1	B1	B1	B1	B1
3. Third cycle					B2,G	B2	B2,F	B2,G	B2	B2,F
4. Fourth cycle					C	C	C	D	D	D
5. Qualifications at entry	L0	L1	L1	L1	L1	L1	L1	L1	L1	L1
Qualifications on dropping out from:										
6. First cycle	L0	L1	L1	L1	L1	L1	L1	L1	L1	L1
7. Second cycle			L2	L4B	L1	L1	L1	L1	L1	L1
8. Third cycle					L4B	L4B	L4B,L2	L4B	L4B	L4B,L2
9. Fourth cycle					L4	L4	L4	L4	L4	L4
10. Qualifications at graduation	L0N	L2	L3	L4	L5,L4	L5	L5,L3	L6,L4	L6	L6,L3
11. Length of professional career after graduation	45	45	40	42	38	38	38	38	38	38

Characteristic	Activity				
	E7.1	E7.2	E8	E9	E10
	I	J	H	K	M
1. First cycle					
2. Second cycle					
3. Third cycle					
4. Fourth cycle					
5. Qualifications at entry	(α_t)L5+$(1-\alpha_t)$L6	(α_t)L5+$(1-\alpha_t)$L6	L7	(α_t)L5+$(1-\alpha_t)$L6	(α_t)L5+$(1-\alpha_t)$L6
Qualifications on dropping out from:					
6. First cycle	(α_t)L5+$(1-\alpha_t)$L6	(α_t)L5+$(1-\alpha_t)$L6	L7	(α_t)L5+$(1-\alpha_t)$L6	(α_t)L5+$(1-\alpha_t)$L6
7. Second cycle					
8. Third cycle					
9. Fourth cycle					
10. Qualifications at graduation	L7	L7	L8	L9	L7B
11. Length of professional career after graduation	30	30	25	30	32

For a unitary level of activity ($E_{\lambda,\nu,\bar{t}} \equiv 1$), these effects are measured by the coefficients of column $E_{\lambda,\nu,\bar{t}}$ in the rows of the central model affected by educational activities. These rows are the labor balances and the three balances in which educational costs other than labor are expressed. The latter are the commodity balance for consumption by public administration, the capacity balance for school buildings, and the foreign-exchange balance. The matrix of these coefficients is the reduced form of the educational model, which is incorporated into the central optimizing model.

If the optimizing model were annual, the use of the reduced form would not introduce any error. (The reduced form is computed by solving a system of equations for which there is no degree of freedom.) Because there is a five-year interval between any two decision years of the central model, an interpolation procedure is required. This introduces an approximation error which has to be minimized.

The computation of the reduced form is described in two steps, the first dealing with the case of an annual model, the second, with the problem of time aggregation.

THE ANNUAL MODEL

Consider, in Figure 11.2, an educational activity consisting of a single cycle with three years of study. The first three columns record the number of students enrolled in each of the three grades, I, II, and III; the last column records the number of graduates. In the first row, $t = \bar{t}$, we start with a cohort of size unity enrolled in grade I.[3] The distribution of this cohort in years $t > \bar{t}$ is shown in the lower rows. The cohort is distributed among the four columns according to the binomial distribution $(\pi + \rho)^{t-\bar{t}}$ from year $\bar{t}$ till year $\bar{t} + 3$. After that year, the binomial distribution is truncated to the right by the departure of students from school. If students are not allowed to repeat indefinitely, the distribution is also truncated to the left. Thus, when students are not allowed to repeat more than twice, the distribution starts being truncated to the left in year $\bar{t} + 3$.

Table 11.3 gives a numerical illustration in the case of cycle C, which corresponds to the last three years of classical high school education. The coefficients $\pi = 0.8$ and $\rho = 0.12$ correspond to the old regime; they are measured from recent high school records. Students can repeat only twice. Table 11.3 shows that in year $\bar{t} + 5$,

---

3. In the model unity corresponds to 1,000 students.

Figure 11.2. Distribution of a Cohort of Students First Enrolled in Year Ī (Three-Year Study Cycle)

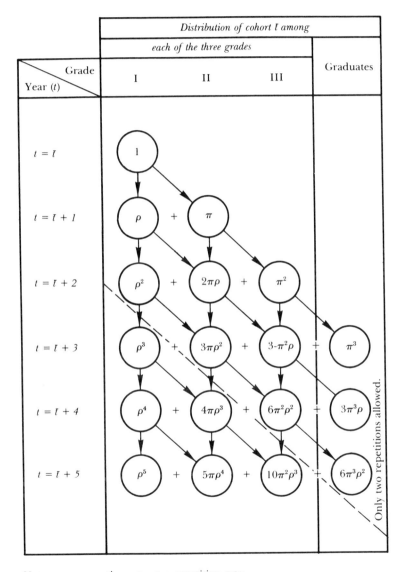

Note: π = promotion rate; ρ = repetition rate.

Table 11.3. *Cycle C (Last Three Years of High School;*
Historical Parameters $\pi = 0.8$, $\rho = 0.12$, *Repeating Allowed*
Only Twice)
Percent

| | | Cumulated number of | | |
Year	Student population	Graduates	Dropouts	Total
$t = \bar{t}$	1.00			
$t = \bar{t} + 1$	0.920		0.080	1.00
$t = \bar{t} + 2$	0.846		0.154	1.00
$t = \bar{t} + 3$	0.267	0.512	0.221	1.00
$t = \bar{t} + 4$	0.055	0.696	0.239	1.00
$t = \bar{t} + 5$		0.740	0.260	1.00

no student remains in school, 74 percent of the students have
graduated, and the remaining 26 percent have dropped out.

Suppose now that the educational cycle comprises two cycles. In
Figure 11.2, the fraction π^3 of the initial cohort $(\bar{t})$ promoted in year
$\bar{t} + 3$ from the third grade of cycle 1 defines a subcohort entering
cycle 2 in that year. The fraction $3\pi^3\rho$ promoted from the third
grade of cycle 1 in year $\bar{t} + 4$ defines a second subcohort. The
fraction $6\pi^3\rho^2$ promoted in year $\bar{t} + 5$ defines the third subcohort,
which enrolls for the first time in cycle 2 in year $\bar{t} + 5$. The analysis
presented in Figure 11.2 for the single cohort of size unity enrolling
in cycle 1 at time $\bar{t}$ can be repeated for each of the three subcohorts
enrolling in cycle 2 in years $\bar{t} + 3$, $\bar{t} + 4$, and $\bar{t} + 5$. The distribution
of the initial cohort among the various grades and the graduates of
cycle 2 is obtained by summation of the three subcohorts. The
process involved in going from cycle 1 to cycle 2 can be repeated to
go from cycle 2 to cycle 3, and so on.

From this long series of operations, two types of data are ultimately required. The first is the cumulated number of students
having graduated from the last cycle with qualification λ in year t;
this number is the increment to the labor supply of skill λ in year t.
The second is the student population per cycle in year t; this number
is required to compute educational costs in that year. The exact
formulas permitting computation of these numbers are given in
Tables 11.10 and 11.11.

THE TIME-AGGREGATED MODEL

The levels of enrollment in the annual model must now be
expressed in relation to the levels of enrollments in years 1975,

1980, 1985, and 1990, which are the four decision years of the central model. This is done by defining four interpolation periods, 1972–77, 1978–82, 1983–87, and 1988–2000. An interpolation period in the annual model is associated with each educational activity of the central model $(E_{\lambda,\nu,\bar{t}})$. The growth rate of enrollments is assumed to remain equal to $g_{\lambda,\nu,\bar{t}}$ within each interpolation period.

Instead of starting, as in Figure 11.2, with a single cohort of size unity in year $\bar{t}$, we now start with five cohorts of size $(1 + g_{\lambda,\nu,\bar{t}})^{\tau}$ in each of the five years $\bar{t} + \tau$, where τ is an interpolation variable taking the values -2, -1, 0, $+1$, and $+2$. The problem is to compute from the annual model the impact of these five cohorts on the labor balances and on the three physical balances in each of the five years 1975, 1980, 1985, 1990, and 2000.

Table 11.4 illustrates the computational procedure in the case of vector $\mathbf{E}_{5.2.05}$, which corresponds to the classical high-school educational activity initiated in year $\bar{t} = 5$. This vector is taken from the first version of the model, where activity 5.2 was composed of only three cycles.[4] Both A and B are two-year cycles; C is a three-year cycle. Students cannot repeat more than twice in each cycle. New enrollments are assumed to increase 12 percent a year between years 3 and 7. The first column measures new enrollments. The next three measure, for each cycle, the students promoted in the upper part and the student population in the lower one.

In the upper part, the column giving the number of students promoted from the last grade of cycle C measures the number of graduates who receive their *baccalauréat lettres*. It shows that the combination of the five cohorts begins to produce graduates in year 10 and continues to do so until year 20. The students graduating in year 10 are those who belong to the cohort enrolled in year 3 and never repeat. The students graduating in year 20 are those who belong to the cohort enrolled in year 7 and repeat twice in each cycle; their number is so low that it disappears when the figures are rounded. The students graduating in the other nine years are a mix between students originating in various cohorts and subcohorts.

In year 10, 0.2507 labor units are added to the labor balance for skill $\lambda = 5$, and the same number are subtracted from the labor balance $\lambda = 1$, which corresponds to the skill of entry. In year 20, the number added (or subtracted) to the labor balances is the cumulated number of graduates from year 10 to year 20. In the case of dropouts, a similar operation is performed when the qualification

4. Cases listed in Table 6.16.

Table 11.4. Vector $\mathbf{E}_{5,2,05}$, *Classical Secondary Education: Graduates and Student Population by Cycle and Coefficients of the Reduced Form*

Individual year T	New enrollment in 1st grade with enrollments increasing by 12 percent a year	Cycle A	Cycle B	Cycle C	Cumulative increment to labor supply of skill λ = 5 in representative years t
		Students Promoted			
3	0.7972				
4	0.8929				
5	1.0000	0.6033			5
6	1.1200	0.7796			
7	1.2544	0.8865	0.3394		
8		0.9929	0.5044		
9		1.1121	0.5933		
10		0.1821	0.6676	0.2507	0.2507 (t=10)
11		0.0211	0.7480	0.4448	
12			0.2396	0.5595	
13			0.0494	0.6401	
14			0.0052	0.7189	
15			0.0003	0.3634	2.9774 (t=15)
16				0.1180	
17				0.0241	
18				0.0034	
19				0.0003	
20				0.0000	3.1232 (t=20)

Current administrative expenditures in representative years

Individual year T	New enrollment in 1st grade with enrollments increasing by 12 percent a year	Cycle A	Cycle B	Cycle C	
		Student Population			
3	0.7972	0.7972			
4	0.8929	1.6550			
5	1.0000	1.9788	0.6034		0.08104 (t=5)
6	1.1200	2.2316	1.2907		
7	1.2544	2.4994	1.6403	0.3394	
8		1.3944	1.8773	0.8438	
9		0.2186	2.1069	1.4371	
10		0.0242	1.2966	1.8537	0.18195 (t=10)
11			0.3686	2.1556	
12			0.0696	1.8324	
13			0.0071	1.2375	
14			0.0004	0.5190	
15				0.1511	0.03172 (t=15)
16				0.0292	
17				0.0039	
18				0.0003	
19				0.0000	
					20

of the dropout differs from the qualification required for initial enrollment in the educational activity $(\lambda = 1$ in this example).

The upper part of Table 11.4 is used to compute upgradings. The lower part is used to compute educational costs. For each year, the size of the student population in each cycle is multiplied by the corresponding input vector of Table 11.1; the products are summed up over cycles. The cost in a decision year is computed by multiplying the sum of the costs in each year of the interpolation period by an interpolation coefficient; this coefficient is calculated by assuming that the student population increases at a constant exponential rate during each interpolation period.[5]

The cost vector thus computed is composed of labor and nonlabor inputs. The figures shown in the last column of the lower part of Table 11.4 refer to a nonlabor input called "consumption by public administration." These figures appear with a minus sign in the reduced-form matrix under the activity column $\mathbf{E}_{5,2,05}$ and the rows defining the commodity balances for consumption by public administration for the years $t = 5$, 10, and 15.[6] The coefficients of column $\mathbf{E}_{5,2,05}$ in the labor-balance rows for years t (= 5, 10, 15, 20, and 20/30) measure the net contribution of the educational activity initiated in year 5. This net contribution is computed by combining the impacts of promotions (from the upper part of Table 11.4) and of labor inputs (which are derived from the size of the student population in the lower part of the table). Labor inputs are counted as minus; upgradings of labor from skill 1 to skill 5 are counted as plus in the balance for labor skill 5 and minus in the balance for labor skill 1.

Repeating the operation just described for each of the fifteen educational activities and for each of the four decision years gives the reduced form, $\mathbf{E}$, of the educational model. Approximately twenty rows of the central model are affected by educational activities in each of the four decision years and in the year 2000;

---

5. Costs in decision year $\bar{t}$ are calculated as:

$$(\text{Cost}_{\bar{t}})(1 + g'_{\lambda,\nu,\bar{t}})^\tau = \sum_\tau (\text{Cost}_{\bar{t}+\tau})$$

Thus, to compute costs in year 15, the sum of the costs in years 13–17 is multiplied by an interpolation coefficient. This coefficient declines from 0.2 to 0.193 when the assumed growth rate of the student population rises from 0 percent to 20 percent a year.

6. Requirements are expressed in terms of quantities per student. The unit is the volume of consumption by the public administration worth CFAF1 million at 1970 prices.

Table 11.5. Sensitivity of the Matrix Coefficients to the Rate of Interpolation

Hypotheses of enrollment

A. Classical secondary education

Year	12 percent (1)	20 percent (2)	Difference (2) − (1)	Percentage $100\frac{(2)-(1)}{(1)}$
1972	0.797	0.694	−0.103	−13.1
1973	0.893	0.833	−0.060	−7.3
1975	1.000	1.000	0.000	0.0
1976	1.120	1.200	0.080	7.1
1977	1.254	1.440	0.186	14.8
Total	5.064	1.167	0.103	2.0

B. University (Abidjan)

Year	17.5 percent (1)	25 percent (2)	Difference (2) − (1)	Percentage $100\frac{(2)-(1)}{(1)}$
1972	0.724	0.650	−0.074	−10.2
1973	0.851	0.800	−0.051	−6.0
1975	1.000	1.000	0.000	0.0
1976	1.175	1.250	0.075	−6.4
1977	1.381	1.562	0.181	13.1
Total	5.131	5.262	0.131	2.5

Coefficients of the aggregate matrix

Costs

Administrative expenditures

Year	(1)	(2)	Difference (2) − (1)	Percentage $100\frac{(2)-(1)}{(1)}$
1975	0.0810	0.0771	−0.0039	−4.9
1980	0.1820	0.1829	0.0009	0.5
1985	0.0317	0.0348	0.0031	9.5

Public expenditures

Year	(1)	(2)	Difference (2) − (1)	Percentage $100\frac{(2)-(1)}{(1)}$
1975	4.3228	4.1780	−0.1448	−3.4
1980	2.0817	2.2316	0.1499	7.2

Stocks

High school graduates

Year	(1)	(2)	Difference (2) − (1)	Percentage $100\frac{(2)-(1)}{(1)}$
1980	0.2194	0.1911	0.0283	−13.0
1985	2.4714	2.5117	0.0403	1.6

University graduates

Year	(1)	(2)	Difference (2) − (1)	Percentage $100\frac{(2)-(1)}{(1)}$
1980	4.2894	4.3281	0.0387	0.9
1985	4.9945	5.1127	0.1182	2.4

matrix **E** therefore consists of approximately 100 (= 20 × 5) rows and 60 (= 15 × 4) columns. Representing by vector **x** the levels of the sixty endogenous educational activities, the impact of these activities on the rows of the central model is measured by:

$$(11.1) \qquad \mathbf{z} \quad = \quad \mathbf{E} \quad \mathbf{x}.$$

$$(100{\cdot}1) \quad (100{\cdot}60) \quad (60{\cdot}1).$$

The computation of the reduced form, **E**, of the educational model was not simple. The final equation (11.1) is, however, extremely simple. The labor balances and the three physical balances in which educational costs other than labor are expressed were already part of the central optimizing model. The educational model is therefore integrated in the central optimizing model by adding to it the sixty educational columns without adding any rows.[7] Unlike the Leontief matrix, the educational matrix **E** is not square, and choices among various educational technologies are preserved. The only source of error is the selection of the growth rates within in each interpolation period. It remains to consider the sensitivity of the results to the selection of these rates.

In the example of Table 11.4, the coefficients of the reduced-form matrix belonging to column $\mathbf{E}_{5,2,05}$ were computed by assuming that enrollments increase 12 percent annually between years 3 and 7. The left part of Table 11.5 shows what occurs when the interpolation growth rate for enrollments in high schools is raised from 12 percent to 20 percent. The right part shows the impact of raising the interpolation rate for university enrollments from 17.5 percent to 25 percent. The upper part of the table indicates that, in both cases, enrollments are reduced approximately 10 percent in 1972 and increased slightly more than 10 percent in 1977; cumulated enrollments increase approximately 2 percent, while high-school costs are reduced in 1975 and increased in 1985; total costs are hardly affected, however. The number of high school graduates is reduced in 1980, and the cumulated number of graduates increases 1.6 percent in 1985. In the case of university graduates (lower righthand corner), the impact of a change in growth rates is also small. These two comparisons relate to very high rates of growth. For low rates of growth, the differences are much smaller. As was noted in Chapter 10, in the section dealing with physical investments, the interpolation procedure is quite efficient when the interpolation period is centered on the decision year, as is the case here.

7. A number of rows were actually added for accounting and policy purposes.

The set of coefficients $g_{\lambda,\nu,\bar{\imath}}$ was adjusted iteratively in the initial stage of computations. The set selected was kept unchanged throughout the experiments. Except for the postterminal year 2000, this time-aggregation procedure does not introduce significant errors.[8]

Labor Balances

Equation (11.1) has shown how to compute the impact of the endogenous educational activities. This section will cover the linkage between education and the rest of the economy by considering the overall equilibrium between demand for and supply of labor according to skill category. The presentation will be simplified here by ignoring migrations from rural areas to urban, disguised unemployment, and substitution between skills. With these simplifications and by retaining from the educational matrix only the labor rows, the labor balances may be expressed in the following form:

(11.2)
$$\mathbf{f} \quad + \quad \mathbf{Ex} \quad + \quad \overline{\mathbf{Ex}} \quad + \quad \overline{\mathbf{n}} \quad = \quad \mathbf{d} \quad + \quad \overline{\mathbf{d}}.$$

$$\underbrace{\begin{bmatrix} Foreign \\ labor \end{bmatrix} + \overbrace{\begin{bmatrix} Net\ impact\ of\ educational \\ activities \end{bmatrix}}^{[endogenous]\ +\ [exogenous]} + \begin{bmatrix} Exogenous \\ labor \\ supply \end{bmatrix}}_{[Supply\ of\ labor]} \underbrace{=}_{=} \underbrace{\begin{bmatrix} Endogenous \\ linked\ to \\ production \\ and\ trade \end{bmatrix} + \begin{bmatrix} Exogenous \\ civil \\ servants \end{bmatrix}}_{[Demand\ for\ labor]}$$

Vectors $\mathbf{x}$ and $\bar{\mathbf{x}}$ define the levels of the educational activities; $\mathbf{x}$ relates to the four decision years 1975, 1980, 1985, and 1990 and $\bar{\mathbf{x}}$ to the four preceding decision years, 1970, 1965, 1960, and 1955. Matrix $\overline{\mathbf{E}}$ is computed from the historical values of the educational parameters and matrix $\mathbf{E}$ from the revised parameters. The model, by shifting backwards the initial year, can be used to project the number of graduates and the size of the student population in the recent past (early 1970s). These data are known much more accurately than enrollments or promotion rates ten or fifteen years earlier. Consequently, the initial estimates of $\bar{\mathbf{x}}$ and $\overline{\mathbf{E}}$ were adjusted iteratively until the projections made for the recent past coincided with the actual numbers of graduates and students, which were accurately known for recent years.

---

8. The year 1990, in which terminal investments are made, is not in the middle of the interpolation period (1988–2000).

Vector **f** defines the numbers of foreigners employed in the various skill categories. The actual size of the foreign labor force and its distribution are known reasonably well for the base year.

The demand for labor consists of two components. The exogenous component, $\overline{\mathbf{d}}$, accounts for civil servants in public administration and for primary school teachers. The endogenous component, **d**, is computed by multiplying requirements for skilled labor per activity (at the unit level) by the endogenous levels of the production and trading activities. Neither the labor norms (on the demand side), nor the rate of participation of the population in the active labor force (on the supply side) are precisely known. Ensuring the equilibrium of the labor balances during the base year is a way of offsetting the errors made in the estimation of supply and demand. During the course of this adjustment, it appeared that, in the base year, a number of skilled jobs were filled by nationals who had not acquired the requisite skills through the educational system (which includes university abroad). It was assumed that these nationals would be progressively replaced by others who had the required skills. For this reason, the exogenous vector $\overline{\mathbf{n}}$ includes, in addition to the new entrants in the labor force with skill $\lambda = 1$, a stock of pseudoskilled labor which declines linearly from the 1970 level to zero in 1990.

Starting from labor balances adjusted by skill categories for the year 1970, the model projects **f, Ex,** and **d** in the years 1975, 1980, 1985, 1990, and 2000. Tables 11.6a through 11.6c illustrate for three skill categories the projected labor balances.

Table 11.6a shows the balance between the demand and the supply of professionals ($\lambda = 7$). Row 7 measures the combined impact of all endogenous educational activities on the net supply of professionals. This supply is measured net of the demand for professors with qualification $\lambda = 7$ and net of professionals promoted to the qualification $\lambda = 8$. In the year 1975, there is a shortage of 300 professionals (-0.3). The explanation is simple. On the one hand, none of the students who entered the university during the years 1973, 1974, and 1975 have graduated in 1975. On the other hand, the students newly enrolled in postprimary educational activities during the years 1973, 1974, and 1975 need 300 professors of qualification $\lambda = 7$ during the year 1975.

Row 6 measures the combined impact of the exogenous educational activities; it therefore refers to students having enrolled in the year 1972 or before. In 1975, 1,300 such students have graduated from the university, but only 500 are available on the labor market in the skill category $\lambda = 7$. On the other hand, the students enrolled before 1973

Table 11.6. Labor Balances for Three Skill Categories (Case F1)

Component of the balance	1970	1975	1980	1985	1990	2000
Professionals, long university cycle, $\lambda = 7$ *(thousands of persons)*						
Demand						
1. Professors required by the educational sector		0.5	0.8	1.2	1.3	1.8
$\bar{d}$ 2. Exogenous requirements for civil servants[a]		4.0	5.4	7.2	9.6	16.4
d 3. Requirements linked to economic activities		8.0	10.4	13.7	17.4	30.6
$d+\bar{d}$ 4. Demand outside the educational sector[b]		12.0	15.8	20.9	27.0	47.0
Supply						
$\bar{n}$ 5. Nationals who did not go through the educational sector		4.0	3.0	2.0	1.0	0.0
Nationals who went through the educational sector (net of educational requirements and promotions)						
$\overline{\text{Ex}}$ 6. Enrolled before 1973		0.5	1.0	1.0	1.0	0.6
Ex 7. Enrolled after 1972		−0.3	1.0	9.4	24.0	46.4
f 8. Deficit		7.8	10.8	8.5	1.0	0.0
Senior professionals, $\lambda = 8$ *(thousands of persons)*						
Demand						
9. Professors required by the educational sector		0.2	0.4	0.6	0.7	1.0
$\bar{d}$ 10. Exogenous requirements for civil servants[c]		1.3	1.6	2.1	2.7	4.3
d 11. Requirements linked to economic activities		3.4	4.4	5.8	7.4	12.9
$d+\bar{d}$ 12. Demand outside the educational sector[d]		4.7	6.0	7.9	10.0	17.2
Supply (net of educational requirements)						
$\bar{n}$ 13. Nationals who did not go through the educational sector		1.6	1.2	0.8	0.4	0.0
Ex+ 14. Professionals who were						
$\overline{\text{Ex}}$ promoted		0.6	4.4	7.1	9.6	17.2
f 15. Deficit		2.5	0.4	0.0	0.0	0.0

Table 11.6. (Continued)

Component of the balance	1970	1975	1980	1985	1990	2000
High school teachers, λ = 9 *(thousands of persons)*						
16. Demand for high-school teachers[e]	1.92	4.46	6.11	6.46	7.12	10.11
Graduates from the Ecole normale						
Ex 17. Enrolled before 1973[f]	0.15	0.77	0.85	0.85	0.85	0.70
Ex 18. Enrolled after 1972	0.0	0.40	1.33	4.13	6.25	9.41
f 19. Deficit	1.77	3.29	3.92	1.42	0.00	0.00

a. Figures given in rows 2, 5, and 6 are exogenous data; those given in all other rows are derived from the optimal solution.

b. Row 2 + row 3 = row 4 = row 5 + row 6 + row 7 + row 8.

c. Figures given in rows 10 and 13 are exogenous data; figures given in all other rows are derived from the optimal solution.

d. Row 10 + row 11 = row 12 = row 13 + row 14 + row 15.

e. Row 16 = row 17 + row 18 + row 19.

f. Figures given in row 17 are exogenous data; figures given in all other rows are derived from the optimal solution.

need 200 professors with qualification $\lambda = 7$ in the year 1975. This is why the total demand for professors of qualification $\lambda = 7$ shown in row 1 is equal to 500 (= 200 + 300). On the other hand, by the year 1975, 600 professionals ($\lambda = 7$) have already been promoted to qualification $\lambda = 8$.

All the students who enrolled in the university in 1972 or before have graduated or have dropped out in 1980. Since the exogenous educational activities do not produce graduates after 1980, the 1,000 new professionals ($\lambda = 7$) who have entered the labor market by 1980 remain in the market in 1985 and 1990. In the year 2000, however, because the students who enrolled before 1965 have since retired from the active labor force, the supply of professionals drops to 600.

The balance for senior professionals ($\lambda = 8$) given in Table 11.6b is very similar to the previous one. Promotion to the qualification $\lambda = 8$ requires at least five years of experience but no educational inputs. There is a repeating rate because some professionals take more than five years to be promoted. There is a dropout rate because some professionals are never promoted.

The balance for high school teachers in Table 11.6c is simpler than the previous two. Graduates from the *École Normale* are employed only as teachers in high schools. The deficit between demand and supply is met by expatriates.

General versus Partial Equilibrium

The labor balances of Table 11.6 refer to the free-market solution. With other policies, the labor balances would be different. As already noted in Chapter 6, the demand for labor is affected by import-substitution policies. Thus, tariffs on imports of competing manufactures stimulate domestic production of those goods and reduce production of agricultural goods for export. Because the production of $1 million worth of manufactured goods requires more skilled labor and less unskilled labor than $1 million worth of agricultural exports, total demand for skilled labor rises and total demand for unskilled labor declines.

Because the length of the gestation lag is large for most educational investments, the profitability of these investments is highly sensitive to variations in the interest rate. As was noted in Chapter 5, when this rate is raised through institutional constraints on savings or restrictions on inflows of capital from abroad, the replacement of expatriates with nationals becomes less profitable. In contrast, when the shadow price of foreign exchange increases in the 1980s, the replacement of expatriates by nationals becomes more profitable; in the 1970s, therefore, it becomes optimal to increase the level of enrollments. As in a true general-equilibrium model, everything depends on everything else.

The general-equilibrium approach is appropriate for the central planner who has to formulate a development policy for the economy as a whole. A simpler, partial-equilibrium approach can be followed by the educational planner, who needs to know the demand for labor by skill categories outside of the educational sector. With those data he can draw his educational plan.

THE CONSISTENCY MODEL

Table 11.7 shows the demand for labor by skill categories, net of requirements by the educational sector. This is the optimal demand computed for the free-market case. It corresponds, in the central model, to the endogenous demand vector $\mathbf{d}$ of equation (11.2). It becomes, in the educational model, the exogenous demand vector $\bar{\mathbf{d}}_c$:

$$(11.3) \qquad \mathbf{f} + \mathbf{Ex} = -\bar{\mathbf{n}} + \bar{\mathbf{d}}_c + \bar{\mathbf{d}}.$$

The sectoral model for education is summarized by equation (11.3). It has been solved by selecting given values of the enrollment vector, $\mathbf{x}$, and by computing as a residual the demand for expatriates, $\mathbf{f}$. Sensitivity analysis has been conducted in relation to the

Table 11.7. Demand for Labor (Nationals plus Foreigners minus Teachers and Students—Case F1)

Skill category		1970	1975	1980	1985	1990	2000
	Skilled labor (absolute numbers, thousands of workers)						
$\lambda=2$	Specialized workers	45	62	83	110	137	211
$\lambda=3$	Qualified workers	18	24	31	42	53	83
$\lambda=4$	Clerks	23	33	46	62	81	114
$\lambda=2-4$	Total, medium-skilled workers	86	119	160	214	271	408
$\lambda=5$	High school graduates (humanities)	17	22	29	37	47	86
$\lambda=6$	High school graduates (sciences)	12	15	18	23	30	47
$\lambda=7B$	University graduates (short cycle)		1	2	4	5	9
$\lambda=7$	Professionals (long university cycle)[a]	9	12	16	21	27	47
$\lambda=8$	Senior professionals[b]	4	5	6	8	10	17
$\lambda=5-8$	Total, highly skilled workers	42	55	71	93	118	205

		1970–80	1980–90	1990–2000
	Growth rates (average yearly percentage)			
$\lambda=0$	Unskilled rural workers	1.9	2.8	. . .
$\lambda=1$	Unskilled urban workers[c]	6.3	5.3	. . .
$\lambda=2-4$	Medium-skilled workers	6.4	5.4	4.2
$\lambda=5-8$	Highly skilled workers	5.3	5.3	5.7

a. Figures correspond to those given in row 4 of Table 11.6.
b. Figures correspond to those given in row 12 of Table 11.6.
c. Formal and informal.

levels of enrollments, **x**, and to the values of some of the educational parameters (such as promotion rates and ratios of students to teachers).

Equation (11.3) can also be treated as a Leontief model provided that three conditions are fulfilled: The supply of foreign labor by skill categories, **f**, is given exogenously; technological choices among educational activities are eliminated; and postterminal conditions are removed (which can be done by increasing the number of decision years).

Having removed the postterminal conditions, the number of years becomes the same in the columns and the rows of matrix **E**. Consider a given year, say 1975, and call $\mathbf{E}_{75}$ the submatrix corresponding to that year. Submatrix $\mathbf{E}_{75}$ contains $n + q$ rows and $n + p$ columns. The first group of n rows defines the labor balances for each of the n skill categories. The second group of q rows measures nonlabor inputs; it also measures various accounting variables, such as the number of students in high school or public expenditures on education. The first n educational activities are those for which the level of enrollments is treated as a variable in the sectoral model; the last p activities are those for which levels of enrollments are treated as exogenous data. Submatrix $\mathbf{E}_{75}$ and vector $\mathbf{x}_{75}$ are partitioned as:

$$
\begin{array}{cc}
 & n \quad | \ p \qquad 1 \\
\begin{array}{c} n \\[6pt] q \end{array} &
\left[\begin{array}{c|c} \mathbf{E}_\lambda & \mathbf{E}_{\bar\lambda} \\ \hline \mathbf{E}_q & \mathbf{E}_{\bar q} \end{array}\right]
\left[\begin{array}{c} \mathbf{x}_\lambda \\ \bar{\mathbf{x}}_{\bar\lambda} \end{array}\right]
\begin{array}{c} n \\[6pt] p \end{array}
\end{array}
$$

Equation (11.3) can then be rewritten:

$$
(11.4) \qquad
\underset{(n\cdot n)\cdot(n\cdot 1)}{[\mathbf{E}_\lambda]\ \mathbf{x}_\lambda}
\; = \; \underset{(n\cdot n)\cdot(n\cdot 1)}{-[\mathbf{E}_{\bar\lambda}]\ \bar{\mathbf{x}}_{\bar\lambda}} \underset{(n\cdot 1)}{- \bar{\mathbf{f}}} \underset{(n\cdot 1)}{- \bar{\mathbf{n}}} \; + \; \underset{(n\cdot 1)}{\bar{\mathbf{d}}_c} \; + \; \underset{(n\cdot 1)}{\bar{\mathbf{d}}}.
$$

$$
\text{(Endogenous supply)} = \ -(\text{Exogenous supply}) + (\text{Exogenous demand}).
$$

On the righthand side [RHS], the net demand for labor can be expressed in the form of a row vector:

$$
(11.5) \qquad\qquad \bar{\mathbf{d}}_n = -[\mathbf{E}_{\bar\lambda}]\ \bar{\mathbf{x}}_{\bar\lambda} - \bar{\mathbf{f}} - \bar{\mathbf{n}} + \bar{\mathbf{d}}_c + \bar{\mathbf{d}}.
$$

Since matrix $\mathbf{E}_\lambda$ is square, the value of $\mathbf{x}_\lambda$ can be computed from the combination of (11.4) and (11.5) as:

$$
(11.6) \qquad\qquad \mathbf{x}_\lambda = [\mathbf{E}_\lambda]^{-1}\ \bar{\mathbf{d}}_n.
$$

$$
(n\cdot 1) = (n\cdot n)\ (n\cdot 1)
$$

Using the value x_λ derived from (11.6), nonlabor costs are computed as:

$$
(11.7) \qquad\qquad [\mathbf{E}_q \mathbf{E}_{\bar q}] \quad \left[\begin{array}{c} \mathbf{x}_\lambda \\ \bar{\mathbf{x}}_{\bar\lambda} \end{array}\right] \quad = \text{nonlabor costs.}
$$

$$
[(q)(n+p)\,][(n+p)(1)] \qquad\qquad (q\cdot 1)
$$

Equations (11.5) through (11.7) can be solved for all decision years at once. As is the case with a Leontief model, consistency is ensured but optimality is not reached.

The profitability of the educational activities can be analyzed in two ways. The first corresponds to the conventional project analysis: Given exogenous prices and wage levels, the internal rate of return is determined endogenously. The second corresponds to a long-term equilibrium of the Von Neuman type: wages are determined endogenously by equalizing the rates of returns for all educational activities.

THE INTERNAL RATE OF RETURN

Consider a given educational activity defined by a column of matrix **E**. Because prices are known, all costs incurred and all benefits accruing in a given year may be aggregated in the form of a single number. The own rate of interest on consumption (which is the numéraire) is used as the time-discount rate; this rate is assumed to remain constant over time. The present value of the investment activity is:[9]

(11.8) Present value in year $\bar{t}$

$$= \sum_{\tau=0}^{\tau=\theta+lf} (1 + r)^{-\tau}(-\text{cost}_{\bar{t}+\tau} + \text{benefits}_{\bar{t}+\tau}).$$

The internal rate of return, r_λ, of investment activity λ is the value of r in the RHS of (11.8), which leads to a zero present value in the lefthand side [LHS]. This rate, r_λ, is higher or lower than the general rate of economic return, r, depending on whether the present value computed in the LHS of (11.8) for r given is positive or negative. Present value and rate of internal return are two different manners of measuring the same thing. In either case, it is assumed that the investment activity does not affect prices that are given exogenously.

LONG-TERM WAGE EQUILIBRIUM

Prices of all nonlabor inputs, wages of unskilled labor, and the general rate of economic return are still treated as exogenous data. The problem is to find the wage structure (w_λ, with $\lambda > 1$) ensuring equal profitability of all educational activities ($r_\lambda \equiv r$ for all $\lambda > 1$).

With n skill categories and with the wage of unskilled workers ($\bar{w}_1$) given, the number of variables is $n - 1$ (w_λ, with $\lambda > 1$). With these $n - 1$ variables are associated $n - 1$ educational activities by which unskilled labor may be upgraded. Technological choice is eliminated and repeating is not allowed. The present value (at the time of enrollments) of each of the $n - 1$ educational activities is expressed as a linear function of the $n - 1$ wage variables (w_λ, with $\lambda > 1$). The wage structure (w_λ) and the rate of return (r) are assumed to remain

9. The length of professional career after graduation is represented by lf and the length of studies by θ.

Table 11.8. Wage Structure Corresponding to Alternative Rates of Returns (Basic Case: New Regime, Market Rate for Nonqualified Workers, Repeaters Promoted) (Millions of CFAF a man-year)

Equilibrium wage (W_λ)	Percentage rate of returns a year					Prevailing market wage
	10	12.5	15	17.5	20	
$\lambda = 1$ Nonqualified	0.10	0.10	0.10	0.10	0.10	0.10
$\lambda = 2$ Specialized worker	0.14	0.16	0.19	0.22	0.29	0.25
$\lambda = 3$ Qualified worker	0.41	0.55	0.76	1.11	1.80	0.95
$\lambda = 4$ Clerk	0.21	0.25	0.32	0.42	0.62	0.45
$\lambda = 5$ Bachelor of Letters	0.88	1.27	1.88	2.91	4.97	1.30
$\lambda = 6$ Bachelor of Sciences	0.94	1.36	2.00	3.07	5.22	1.60
$\lambda = 7$ Professional	1.40	2.04	3.02	4.70	8.13	3.00

constant. The system of $n - 1$ equations and of $n - 1$ variables is:[10]

(11.9)

$$\underset{(1)(n-1)}{\mathbf{w}} \quad \underset{\cdot (n-1)(n-1)}{\mathbf{E}} \quad = \underset{(1)(n-1)}{[\text{costs at exogenously given prices}]}.$$

The row vector **w** defines the $n - 1$ endogenous wage variables (w_λ for $\lambda > 1$). The row vector on the RHS defines the costs of each of the $n - 1$ educational activities in terms of nonlabor inputs and unskilled workers (the prices of both are given exogenously). **E** is a square matrix, the coefficients of column λ define the sum of the discounted net contributions of activity λ to the labor balances of the $n - 1$ skill categories ($\lambda = 2, \ldots, n$). The equilibrium wage structure is:

$$(11.10) \quad \underset{(1)(n-1)=}{\mathbf{w}} \quad = \underset{(1)(n-1)}{[\text{cost exogenous}]} \quad \underset{(n-1)(n-1)}{\mathbf{E}^{-1}}.$$

Table 11.8 shows the solution of (11.10) for five different values of the rate of return, r. When this rate rises, all salaries increase (except, of course, wages of unskilled workers, which are given). The salary increase is greater for workers with higher skills. For example, when the rate of return is raised from 10 percent to 20 percent a year, the wage ratio between skill levels $\lambda = 7$ and $\lambda = 1$ increases from 14 to 81; between skill levels $\lambda = 7$ and $\lambda = 2$, it increases from 10 to 28. If the rate of return were to rise from 20 percent to 25 percent, the wage of skill level $\lambda = 7$ would reach infinity, and there

---

10. The formula used for computing one such equation is given in Table 11.13, in the appendix to this chapter.

Table 11.9. Rates of Return on Educational Activities for Approximating the Prevailing Wage Structure (Variations on the Basic Case)
(Percent a year)

Equilibrium wage for nonqualified worker ($\lambda = 1$)	Old regime		New regime	
	Repeaters dropped	Repeaters promoted	Repeaters dropped	Repeaters promoted
Market rate ($W_1 = 0.10$)	4.0	12.5	12.0	15.0
Zero ($W_1 = 0.00$)	5.5	16.0	15.0	20.0

would be no solution unless some wages could become negative. A 15 percent rate of return leads to a wage structure similar to the one now prevailing in the labor market (right-hand column). The sensitivity of this rate of return to three types of factors is shown in Table 11.9.

The first experiment deals with the replacement of the old regime by the new. As will be recalled from the beginning of this chapter, this reform leads to a higher rate of promotion at the expense of a higher teacher-student ratio. The second experiment deals with repeaters. Because repeaters could not be accounted for properly in this simplified model, two extreme assumptions were made. Under the first, repeaters are treated as dropouts, thereby understating the profitability of the educational system. Under the second, repeaters are promoted, thereby leading to the opposite bias. Finally, the opportunity cost of unskilled labor is taken as equal to the market price in one case and to zero in the other.

Although unskilled labor is the primary input of education, the wage of unskilled workers has little effect on the rate of return (last two rows of Table 11.7). With a ratio of thirty to one between wages of professionals and wages of unskilled labor, what matters is the wages forgone by students who have already reached some qualification, the wages of teachers, and the costs of some physical inputs.

The model is rather sensitive to the assumption made with respect to repeaters, especially under the old regime. This was the reason for taking repeaters into consideration in the optimizing model.

Table 11.10. Notations

Subscripts and parameters	

μ Cycle of study

$\theta(= 1, 2, \ldots, p_\mu)$	Grades in the cycle (sequence of years of study).
ρ_μ	Number of grades in cycle μ.
π_μ	Average promotion rate for each grade.
ρ_μ	Average repeating rate for each grade.
ζ_μ	Maximum number of repeats allowed in the cycle.
λ_μ	Skill category reached by dropouts.
	Requirements proportional to the size of the student population in cycle λ.
$c_{\mu,\lambda}$	For labor of skill category λ.
$c_{\mu,q}$	For nonlabor input of type q.

λ, ν, $\bar{\iota}$ *Educational activity*

λ	Skill category to which students are upgraded.
lf_λ	Length of productive life after promotion to skill λ.
ν	Educational route defined as an ordered combination of cycles $(\mu 1, \mu 2, \mu 3, \ldots)$.
$\bar{\iota}$ (time subscript of the column)	Time at which a student is withdrawn from the labor balance for skill category. λ to be first enrolled in the educational route λ, ν.
t (time subscript of the row affected)	Time at which resources are withdrawn or capacity is created.

Activity levels

$E_{\lambda,\nu,\bar{\iota}}$	Number of students (in thousands) newly enrolled in type of activity λ, ν at time $\bar{\iota}$.

Intermediate variables (**Tables 11.11 and 11.12**)

$SP_{\lambda,\nu,\bar{\iota},\mu,t}$	Student population in cycle μ at time t from vintage λ, ν, t (total number of students enrolled) (in thousands).
$GD_{\lambda,\nu,\bar{\iota},\mu,t}$	Number of students (in thousands) from vintage λ, ν, $\bar{\iota}$ graduating from cycle μ at time t.

Long form equilibrium (Table 11.13)

W_λ	Wage for skill λ (λ entry, $\bar{\lambda}$ exit).
r	Rate of interest

Table 11.11. *Annual Model: Student Population and Graduates in Year t Belonging to Cohort Originating in Year $\bar{t}$*

Item	Coefficients and variables	Years t with Nonzero Elements
Vintage Coefficients (Cycle μ) [a]		
In school	$(sp_{\mu,\bar{t},t}) = \displaystyle\sum_{\theta=t-\bar{t}-\zeta_\mu+1}^{\theta=p_\mu} \frac{(t-\bar{t})!}{(\theta-1)![t-\bar{t}-(\theta-1)]!}\,\rho_\mu^{t-\bar{t}-(\theta-1)}\pi_{\tau_\mu}^{\theta-1}$	$\bar{t} \le t \le \bar{t} + p_\mu + \zeta_\mu - 1$
Graduating	$(grd_{\mu,t}) = \pi_\mu^{p_\mu}\dfrac{(t-\bar{t}-1)!}{(p_\mu-1)!(t-\bar{t}-p_\mu)!}\,\rho^{t-\bar{t}-p_\mu}$	$p_\mu + \bar{t} \le t \le \bar{t} + p_\mu + \zeta$
Cycle 1		
Student population	$(SP_{\lambda,v,\bar{t},\mu1,t}) = (sp_{\mu1,\bar{t},t})(E_{\lambda,v,\bar{t}})$	$\bar{t} \le t \le \bar{t} + p_{\mu1} + \zeta_{\mu1} - 1$
Graduates	$(GD_{\lambda,v,\bar{t},\mu1,t}) = (grd_{\mu1,\bar{t},t})(E_{\lambda,v,\bar{t}})$	$p_{\mu1} + \bar{t} \le t \le \bar{t} + p_{\mu1} + \zeta_{\mu1}$
Cycle 2		
Student population	$(SP_{\lambda,v,\bar{t},\mu2,t}) = \displaystyle\sum_{t=\bar{t}+p_{\mu1}}^{t=\bar{t}+p_{\mu1}+\zeta_{\mu1}} (sp_{\mu2,\bar{t},t})(GD_{\lambda,v,\bar{t},\mu1,t})$	$p_{\mu1} + \bar{t} \le t \le \bar{t} + p_{\mu1} + p_{\mu2} + \zeta_{\mu1} + \zeta_{\mu2} - 1$
Graduates	$(GD_{\lambda,v,\bar{t},\mu2,t}) = \displaystyle\sum_{t=\bar{t}+p_{\mu1}}^{t=\bar{t}+p_{\mu1}+\zeta_{\mu1}} (grd_{\mu2,\bar{t},t})(GD_{\lambda,v,\bar{t},\mu1,t})$	$p_{\mu2} + p_{\mu1} + \bar{t} \le t \le \bar{t} + p_{\mu1} + p_{\mu2} + \zeta_{\mu1} + \zeta_{\mu2}$

a. For 1,000 students newly enrolled in year $\bar{t}$, number (in thousands)

Table 11.12. Time Aggregation

Columns

Definition of interpolation variables

$\hat{t} = 5\hat{t}' + \hat{\tau}$ with $-2 \leq \hat{\tau} \leq +2$ for $-3 \leq \hat{t}' \leq 3$

Exogenous investments for $-3 \leq \hat{t}' \leq 0$

Endogenous investments for $1 \leq \hat{t}' \leq 4$

$-2 \leq \hat{\tau} \leq +10$ for $\hat{t}' = 4$

Rows

$t = 5\hat{t}' + \hat{\tau}$ with $-2 \leq \tau \leq +2$ for $-1 \leq t' \leq 4$

$-7 \leq \tau \leq 0 \qquad t' = 6$

Hypotheses

Students entering

$(E_{\lambda,\nu,5\hat{t}'+1}) = (1 + g_{\lambda,\nu,\hat{t}'})^{\hat{\tau}}(E_{\lambda,\nu,5\hat{t}'})$

Implications

Number of students

$(SP_{\lambda,\nu,5\hat{t}'+\hat{\tau}\mu1,t}) = (E_{\lambda,\nu,5\hat{t}'}) \sum_{\hat{\tau}=-2}^{\hat{\tau}=+2} (sp_{\mu1,5\hat{t}'+\hat{\tau},t})(1 + g_{\lambda,\nu,\hat{t}'})^{\hat{\tau}}$

Nonzero elements for t contained within the interval

$-2 + 5\hat{t}' \leq t \leq 5\hat{t}' + p_{\mu1} + \zeta_{\mu1} + 1$ for $-3 \leq \hat{t}' \leq 3$

$-2 + 5\hat{t}' \leq t \leq 5\hat{t}' + p_{\mu1} + \zeta_{\mu1} + 9$ for $\hat{t}' = 4$

Promotions

$(GD_{\lambda,\nu,5\hat{t}'+\hat{\tau}\mu1,t}) = (E_{\lambda,\nu,5\hat{t}'}) \sum_{\hat{\tau}=-2}^{\hat{\tau}=-2} (gd_{\mu1,5\hat{t}'+\hat{\tau},t})(1 + g_{\lambda,\nu,\hat{t}'})^{\hat{\tau}}$

$-2 + p_{\mu1} + 5\hat{t}' \leq t \leq 5\hat{t}' + p_{\mu1} + \zeta_{\mu1} + 2$ for $-3 \leq \hat{t}' \leq 3$

$-2 + p_{\mu1} + 5\hat{t}' \leq t \leq 5\hat{t}' + p_{\mu1} + \zeta_{\mu1} + 10$ for $\hat{t}' = 4$

Table 11.13. Long-Term Wage Equilibrium (Dual Equations of the Educational Activities Used in Equation 11.9)

Period	Present Value at Time $\bar{t}$ of Costs and Benefits
Cycle 1 $\bar{t} \leq t \leq \bar{t} + p_{\mu 1} - 1$	$-\left[\dfrac{1 - (r\pi_{\mu 1})^{p_{\mu 1}}}{1 - r\pi_{\mu 1}}\right]\left[c_{\mu 1} + \displaystyle\sum_{\lambda}(c_{\mu 1,\lambda})(W_{\lambda})\right]$
Cycle 2 $p_{\mu 1} + \bar{t} \leq t \leq \bar{t} + p_{\mu 1} + p_{\mu 2} - 1$	$-\left[(r\pi_{\mu 1})^{p_{\mu 1}}\right]\left[\dfrac{1 - (r\pi_{\mu 2})^{p_{\mu 2}}}{1 - r\pi_{\mu 2}}\right]\left[c_{\mu 2} + \displaystyle\sum_{\lambda}(c_{\mu 2,\lambda})(W_{\lambda})\right]$
Cycle 3 $p_{\mu 2} + p_{\mu 1} + \bar{t} \leq t \leq \bar{t} + p_{\mu 1} + p_{\mu 2} + p_{\mu 3} - 1$	$-\left[(r\pi_{\mu 1})^{p_{\mu 1}}\right]\left[(r\pi_{\mu 2})^{p_{\mu 2}}\right]\left[\dfrac{1 - (r\pi_{\mu 3})^{p_{\mu 3}}}{1 - r\pi_{\mu 3}}\right]\left[c_{\mu 3} + \displaystyle\sum_{\lambda}(c_{\mu 3,\lambda})(W_{\lambda})\right]$
Productive life in skill λ $p_{\mu 3} + p_{\mu 2} + p_{\mu 1} + \bar{t} \leq t \leq \bar{t} + p_{\mu 1} + p_{\mu 2} + p_{\mu 3} + U_{\lambda} - 1$	$+\left[(r\pi_{\mu 1})^{p_{\mu 1}}\right]\left[(r\pi_{\mu 2})^{p_{\mu 2}}\right]\left[(r\pi_{\mu 2})^{p_{\mu 3}}\right]\left[\dfrac{1 - r^{(U_{\lambda} - 1)}}{1 - r}\right]\left[W_{\lambda}^{-} - W_{\underline{\lambda}}^{-}\right] = 0$

Chapter 12

Intrasectoral and Intersectoral Linkages

THE UTILITY MAXIMAND was related to the growth path and to the composition of final consumption in Chapters 8 and 9. The relationship between investment in a given year and availability of additional capital in later years was the subject of Chapters 10 and 11. It remains to be shown how physical and human capital can be used to produce consumer goods and investment goods.

When all production and import activities are explicitly specified, the economywide model is very easy to describe but too large to solve. It is therefore necessary to transform the sectoral components into a more compact form before integrating them into the central model. In some cases, the size of the sectoral components can be considerably reduced without losing any information. In other cases, some information is lost in the transformation. This chapter first considers those cases for which no information is lost.

The Reduced Form of the Urban Model

The full form of the urban model is outlined in Table 12.1. All supply activities are shown at the left and all demand activities at the right. In specified branches, domestic production is the source of supply; in all other branches, the entire supply has to be imported. There is no make-or-buy choice.

The supply activities may be illustrated by two examples: branch 1 supplies automobiles and branch 2 supplies trucks. Domestic production is the source of supply in the first case and imports are the source in the second. In branch 1, all automobiles must be assembled locally; none can be imported already assembled. In branch 2, all trucks have to be imported; none can be assembled locally. The activity called "assembling automobiles" requires a variety of intermediate inputs and resources; these are represented in the first column by minus coefficients. The second activity, "importing trucks," requires a single intermediate input (commercial services from branch n) and a single resource (foreign exchange from resource row r). The set of n supply activities is fully defined by the coefficients of the input-output matrix, $I - A$, and by those of the resource requirements matrix, R.

Turn now to the demand activities shown on the right side of Table 12.1. Investment in the form of vehicles is the first demand activity. It requires automobiles and trucks in fixed proportions. Consequently, there is a coefficient with a minus sign in the commodity balance for automobiles and another in that for trucks; the sum of these two coefficients is -1. The contribution of the investment activities to the capacity balances does not appear in Table 12.1, because this table is limited to a single year.[1]

The second set of demand activities deals with exports. Various baskets of urban goods can be exported. The composition of each basket is defined by the minus coefficients appearing in the different commodity balances; again, for each export activity, the sum of the input coefficients is -1. Each export activity has two additional nonzero coefficients: a unity coefficient in the constraint defining the maximum amount that can be exported and a plus coefficient in the foreign exchange balance.

The last set of demand activities deals with consumption. A distinction is made among three types of consuming agents: foreigners, public administration, and nationals. In the case of foreigners, a distinction is made between Europeans and non-Ivorian Africans. For each group, the sum of the coefficients appearing in the n commodity balances defines the propensity to consume local goods and services; the coefficient appearing in the foreign-exchange balance defines the fraction of the foreigner's salary repatriated in the form of savings abroad. For public administration, the $+1$ coefficient ensures that the exogenously given consumption requirements are satisfied; the minus coefficients shown in the commodity balances define the consumption propensities by type of goods and services. In the case of Ivorians, a distinction is made among five different baskets of urban goods and

---

1. The measurement of this contribution was described in Chapter 10; it was represented by matrix K in Figures 7.3 and 7.4.

Table 12.1. Full Form of the Urban Model

Constraint	Supply of Urban Goods by domestic production and non-competing imports	Consumption by						Right-hand side
		Investments Exports 1,...,5 1,...,5	Europeans	Africans	Public administration	Ivorians 1,...,5	Utility	
Constraint	$\mathbf{x}_1, \quad \mathbf{x}_2, \ldots, \quad \mathbf{x}_n$	$\mathbf{y}_1, \ldots$	$\ldots$	$\ldots$	$\ldots$	$\ldots, \mathbf{y}_q$	$\mathbf{u}$	

Maximand 　　+

$\mathbf{U}$	-1

$= \mathbf{0}$
$= \mathbf{1}$

Transforming consumption into utility

[272]

Requirements of the public
administration $\geq \bar{\mathbf{G}}$

Upper limit on urban exports $\leq \overline{\mathbf{EX}}$

Commodity balances

		C	
	+1		+1

1 Domestically assembled automobiles $+1$ $-$ $-$ $-$ $-$ $\cdots$ $-$ $+1$ $= 0$

2 Imported trucks $+1$ $-$ $-$ $-$ $-$ $\cdots$ $-$ $-$ $= 0$

   I − A   **F**

$n-1$ $-$ $+$ $-$ $-$ $-$ $\cdots$ $-$ $-$ $= 0$

n Commerce $-$ $-$ $+1$ $-$ $-$ $\cdots$ $-$ $-$ $= 0$

Resource balances

	R		**Γ**

1 Labor by skill $-$ $-$ $-$ $-$ $-$ $\cdots$ $-$ $-$ $\leq -\bar{\mathbf{L}}_{\lambda}$

Capacities by type k $-$ $+$ $+$ $+$ $+$ $\cdots$ $-$ $\leq -\bar{\mathbf{K}}_{k}$

r Foreign exchange $-$ $-$ $-$ $+$ $+$ $\cdots$ $-$ $\leq -\bar{\mathbf{F}}$

services. Within each basket, the composition is fixed; no substitution is
allowed. Between baskets $(i = 1, \ldots, 5)$, substitution is allowed; it
occurs through the utility matrix **U**, which was described in Chapter 9.

The n commodity balances and r resource balances of Table 12.1 can
be written in matrix form as:

$$(12.1) \quad \underset{(n \cdot n)}{(I - A)} \; \underset{(n \cdot 1)}{x} \; - \; \underset{(n \cdot q)}{F} \; \underset{(q \cdot 1)}{y} \; = \underset{(n \cdot 1)}{0} \; \text{ and}$$

$$(12.2) \quad \underset{(r \cdot n)}{R} \; \underset{(n \cdot 1)}{x} \; - \; \underset{(r \cdot q)}{\Gamma} \; \underset{(q \cdot 1)}{y} \; \leq \; \underset{(r \cdot 1)}{-\bar{K}}.$$

Because the Leontief matrix $I - A$ is square, it can be inverted.
Replacing **x** in (12.2) by its value from (12.1) gives:

$$(12.2') \quad \underset{(r \cdot n)}{R} \; \underset{(n \cdot n)}{(I - A)^{-1}} \; \underset{(n \cdot q)}{F} \; \underset{(q \cdot 1)}{y} \; - \; \underset{(r \cdot q)}{\Gamma} \; \underset{(q \cdot 1)}{y} \; \leq -\underset{(r \cdot 1)}{\bar{K}}.$$

This is the form in which the urban sector has been incorporated
in the central model. Instead of $n + r$ rows and $n + q$ columns in
equations (12.1) and (12.2), there are only r rows and q columns in
equation (12.2'). This is a worthwhile simplification, particularly
when there are about seventy urban branches $(n = 70)$.[2] In the
absence of choices among alternative sources of supply in the urban
sector, no error is made, nor is any information lost. After the
central model has been solved, the implied levels of the urban
supply activities $(x_1, \ldots, x_n)$ can be derived from the final demand
vector, y, found in the optimal solution as:

$$\underset{(n \cdot 1) =}{x} \; \underset{(n \cdot n)}{(I - A)^{-1}} \; \underset{(n \cdot q)}{F} \; \underset{(q \cdot 1)}{y}.$$

In the rest of this chapter, the reduced form of the urban model
will be referred to as "matrix **D**":

$$\underset{(r \cdot q) =}{D} = \underset{(r \cdot n)}{R} \; \underset{(n \cdot n)}{(I - A)^{-1}} \; \underset{(n \cdot q)}{F}.$$

It measures direct and indirect resource requirements by type of
final demand.

2. Many economywide optimizing models are based on the Leontief technology. It
is therefore somewhat surprising that the "reduced form," first used by Bruno (1967)
in an optimizing model of the economy of Israel, has not been applied more widely.

Intersectoral Deliveries

The previous section dealt with the deliveries between the branches of the urban sector. This section deals with the deliveries between the urban and the other sectors. It is illustrated with the problem of intersectoral deliveries between the urban sector and one of the rural sectors. The latter is referred to below as "the rural sector." The urban deliveries to the rural sector are in the form of electricity, fertilizers, commercial services, and the like. The rural deliveries to the urban sector are in the form of internationally traded commodities—wood, cotton, coffee, and so forth.

In the first step, the problem of urban deliveries will be considered and that of rural deliveries ignored. In Table 12.2, the urban model of Table 12.1 is summarized in matrix form; the rural model consists of activity vector $\mathbf{x}^*$ and the four matrices $\mathbf{C}^*$, $\mathbf{A}^*$, $\mathbf{\Gamma}^*$, and $\mathbf{R}^*$. Matrix $\mathbf{C}^*$ accounts for the contribution of the rural activities to final consumption. Matrix $\mathbf{A}^*$ defines the requirements of the rural sector for goods and services originating from the urban sector— electricity, fertilizers, and so forth. Matrix $\mathbf{\Gamma}^*$ defines the direct rural requirements for (or contributions to) resources used (or produced) jointly by the urban and the rural sectors; most important among them are skilled labor, public funds, and foreign exchange. Finally, matrix $\mathbf{R}^*$ defines the rural requirements for resources such as land and water, which are used exclusively by the rural sector, as well as upper bounds on exports of commodities originating exclusively from the rural sector.

Consider the commodity balances for the goods and services originating from the urban sector. Those balances can be written:

$$(12.3a) \quad \underset{(n \cdot n)}{(\mathbf{I} - \mathbf{A})} \underset{(n \cdot 1)}{\mathbf{x}} - \underset{(n \cdot n^*)}{\mathbf{A}^*} \underset{(n^* \cdot 1)}{\mathbf{x}^*} - \underset{(n \cdot q)}{\mathbf{F}} \underset{(q \cdot 1)}{\mathbf{y}} = \underset{(n \cdot 1)}{\mathbf{0}}.$$

Taking the level of rural activities, $\mathbf{x}^*$ and of the final demand activities, $\mathbf{y}$, as given, the required level of urban activities can be derived as:

$$(12.3') \quad \mathbf{x} = (\mathbf{I} - \mathbf{A})^{-1}(\mathbf{A}^*\mathbf{x}^* + \mathbf{F}\mathbf{y}).$$

The resource constraints common to the urban and the rural sectors are:

$$(12.4a) \quad -\mathbf{R}\mathbf{x} - \mathbf{\Gamma}^*\mathbf{x}^* - \mathbf{\Gamma}\mathbf{y} \geq -\bar{\mathbf{k}}.$$

Replacing $\mathbf{x}$ by its value from $(12.3')$, the common resource con-

Table 12.2. Urban-Rural Linkage

[12.2a] Full form

Constraint	Urban $\mathbf{x}$	Rural $\mathbf{x}^*$	Final demand $\mathbf{y}$	Utility $\mathbf{u}$	Maximand
Objective function				+	Maximand
Final demand		$+\mathbf{C}^*$	$+\mathbf{C}$	$-\mathbf{U}$	≥ 0
Urban commodity balances	$(\mathbf{I}-\mathbf{A})$ $(n \cdot n)$	$-\mathbf{A}^*$ $(n \cdot n^*)$	$-\mathbf{F}$ $(n \cdot q)$		$=\mathbf{0}$
Common resources	$-\mathbf{R}$ $(r \cdot n)$	$-\mathbf{\Gamma}^*$ $(r \cdot n^*)$	$-\mathbf{\Gamma}$ $(r \cdot q)$		$\geq -\bar{\mathbf{k}}$
Resources used only by rural		$-\mathbf{R}^*$ $(r^* \cdot n^*)$			$\geq -\bar{\mathbf{k}}^*$

[12.2b] Reduced form

Constraint	Rural $\mathbf{x}^*$	Final demand $\mathbf{y}$	Utility $\mathbf{u}$	Maximand
Objective function			+	Maximand
Final demand	$+\mathbf{C}^*$	$+\mathbf{C}$	$-\mathbf{U}$	≥ 0
Common resources	$-(\mathbf{\Gamma}^*+\mathbf{D}^*)$ $(r \cdot n^*)$	$-(\mathbf{\Gamma}+\mathbf{D})$ $(r \cdot q)$		$\geq -\bar{\mathbf{k}}$
Resources used only by rural	$-\mathbf{R}^*$ $(r^* \cdot n^*)$			$\geq -\bar{\mathbf{k}}^*$

[276]

straints can be rewritten:

(12.4b) $\qquad -(\Gamma + \mathbf{D})\mathbf{y} - (\Gamma^* + \mathbf{D}^*)\mathbf{x}^* \geq -\bar{\mathbf{k}},$

where
$$\begin{array}{cccc} \mathbf{D} = & \mathbf{R} & (\mathbf{I} - \mathbf{A})^{-1} & \mathbf{F}, \text{ and} \\ (r \cdot q) & (r \cdot n) & (n \cdot n) & (n \cdot q) \end{array}$$

$$\begin{array}{cccc} \mathbf{D}^* = & \mathbf{R} & (\mathbf{I} - \mathbf{A})^{-1} & \mathbf{A}^*. \\ (r \cdot n^*) & (r \cdot n) & (n \cdot n) & (n \cdot n^*) \end{array}$$

On the lefthand side of Table 12.2, the model is expressed in the form of constraints (12.3a) and (12.4a). On the righthand side, these two sets of constraints are replaced by the single set of constraints (12.4b). With this substitution, the n rows and columns corresponding to the n urban branches are eliminated from the central model. In Table 12.2a on the left, urban capacities in vehicles, machinery, and construction were resources specific to the urban sector. In Table 12.2b on the right, they become resources common to the urban and the rural sectors, because of the nonzero coefficients of matrix $\mathbf{D}^*$.

Because the urban model follows a Leontief technology, it is possible to eliminate the rows delivering urban goods to the rural sectors. While the rural sectors do not follow a Leontief technology, it is nonetheless possible to eliminate the rows delivering rural goods to the urban sector, provided that two conditions are fulfilled. First, these deliveries must take the form of internationally traded commodities, such as coffee, cocoa, and wood. Second, for each commodity, it must be known in advance whether the country will have a net import deficit or a net export surplus.

Assume that $\alpha + \beta$ commodities are sold by the rural sector to the urban sector and that it is known that the country will have a net import deficit for the first α commodities and a net export surplus for the last β commodities. Call $\mathbf{t}_m$ the import activity vector $(\alpha \cdot 1)$ and p_m the c.i.f. price vector $(1 \cdot \alpha)$ for the first α commodities. Similarly, call $\mathbf{t}_x$ the export activity vector $(\beta \cdot 1)$ and $\mathbf{p}_x$ the f.o.b. price vector $(1 \cdot \beta)$; Table 12.3 shows, on the left, the impact of the $\alpha + \beta$ trading activities on the $\alpha + \beta$ commodities balances and on the foreign exchange balance. It shows, on the right, the impact of the urban and rural activities (x and x^*) on the $\alpha + \beta$ commodity balances. Because there is no choice between importing and exporting, the trade matrix is square and can be inverted. Since the inverse of the identity matrix is the identity matrix, the results are particularly simple. For the α commodities, urban purchases are counted as positive imports at c.i.f. prices in the $\mathbf{R}$ matrix and rural sales as negative imports at c.i.f. prices in the Γ^* matrix. For the β commodi-

Table 12.3. Internationally Traded Commodities Produced by the Rural Sector and Delivered to the Urban Sector

		Trading		Urban	Rural
		t_m	t_x	x	x^*
Constraint		$1\cdots\alpha$	$1\cdots\beta$	$1\cdots n$	$1\cdots n^*$
Commodity balances with net import deficit	1 · · · α	$+\mathbf{I}$		$-\mathbf{M}_m$	$-\mathbf{M}_m{}^*$
Foreign exchange with net export surplus	1 · · · β		$-\mathbf{I}$	$-\mathbf{M}_x$	$+\mathbf{M}_x{}^*$
Foreign exchange		$-\mathbf{p}_m$	$+\mathbf{p}_x$		

ties, urban purchases are counted as negative exports at f.o.b. prices in the **R** matrix and rural sales as positive exports at f.o.b. prices in the **Γ*** matrix. Urban commercial services delivered to the international trading activities are counted as intermediate activities of the urban purchasing activities in the **I** − **A** matrix. This transformation is in the spirit of Little and Mirrlees (1968), who express tradable goods in terms of world prices.

When the future trading position of the country is uncertain and when the difference between c.i.f. and f.o.b. prices is significant, the commodity balance for that product must be treated as a central row. This was the case with cotton, for which a row was introduced in the resource matrix, **R**, and therefore in the reduced-form matrix, **D**. With this row is associated a central adjustment activity having a cost equal to the difference between the c.i.f. and f.o.b. prices. The level of this activity is positive only when urban requirements exceed rural supply.

Competing Imports in the Urban Sector

The results obtained in the two preceding sections were particularly simple because no make-or-buy choice existed in the urban sector. How these results are modified by the introduction of make-or-buy choices will now be considered.

In Table 12.1, all trucks had to be imported. Now there is a choice between assembling trucks locally (which is the production activity) and importing them already assembled (which is the importing activity). An activity column defining the domestic assembly of trucks must be added to the $I - A$ and R matrices of Table 12.1. With the full form of the urban model, this does not present any problems. With the reduced form, there is a problem: matrix $I - A$ is now composed of n rows and $n + 1$ columns; it can no longer be inverted. This difficulty is overcome by using a linear combination of two reduced-form matrices. With the first, D_m, trucks must be imported, while with the second, D_p, trucks must be assembled locally; in the $I - A$ and R matrices of Table 12.1, the truck-importing activity is replaced with the truck-production activity. More generally, if a make-or-buy choice exists for s branches,[3] import is the source of supply for these s branches in matrix D_m, while production is the source of supply for the same s branches in matrix D_p. The two matrices, D_m and D_p, which describe the two extreme ways of satisfying final demands, are incorporated simultaneously into the optimizing model:

$$(12.5) \qquad \underset{(r \cdot 2q)}{D} = \underset{(r \cdot q)}{D_m} \ \underset{(r \cdot q)}{D_p}, \text{ with}$$

$$(12.5m) \qquad \underset{(r \cdot q)}{D_m} = \underset{(r \cdot n)}{R_m} \ \underset{(n \cdot n)}{(I - A_m)^{-1}} \ \underset{(n \cdot q)}{F}, \text{ and}$$

$$(12.5p) \qquad \underset{(r \cdot q)}{D_p} = \underset{(r \cdot n)}{R_p} \ \underset{(n \cdot n)}{(I - A_p)^{-1}} \ \underset{(n \cdot q)}{F}.$$

The final demand vector, y, contains $2q$ elements. It can be decomposed into two subvectors, y_m and y_p; each of them contains q elements that correspond to the types of final demand identified by subscript $d(=1, \ldots, q)$. For a given type of final demand d, the total demand, y_d, is the sum of two components. The first, y_{dm}, measures the demand satisfied by importing the s commodities directly or indirectly needed for final demand d. The second, y_{dp}, measures the demand satisfied by

---

3. In the model, there are fourteen such branches.

producing the s commodities which are directly or indirectly needed for final demand d:

(12.6) $$y_d = y_{dm} + y_{dp} \text{ for all } d.$$

For each branch $i(=1, \ldots, n)$ of the urban sector, total supply is given by:

(12.7) $$x_i = x_{im} + x_{ip} \text{ for all } i,$$

where x_{im} and x_{ip} are components of vector $\mathbf{x}_m$ and $\mathbf{x}_p$ computed as:

(12.8m) $$\underset{(n \cdot 1)}{\mathbf{x}_m} = \underset{(n \cdot n)}{(\mathbf{I} - \mathbf{A}_m)^{-1}} \ \underset{(n \cdot q)}{(\mathbf{F})} \ \underset{(q \cdot 1)}{\mathbf{y}_m}, \text{ and}$$

(12.8p) $$\underset{(n \cdot 1)}{\mathbf{x}_p} = \underset{(n \cdot n)}{(\mathbf{I} - \mathbf{A}_p)^{-1}} \ \underset{(n \cdot q)}{(\mathbf{F})} \ \underset{(q \cdot 1)}{\mathbf{y}_p}.$$

Total supply $x_i = x_{im} + x_{ip}$ defines the level of imports in the case of commodities that cannot be locally produced, while it defines the level of domestic production in the case of commodities that cannot be imported. In the case of the commodities h that can be both imported and locally produced, x_{hm} defines the level of imports and x_{hp} the level of domestic production.[4]

Resource requirements can be calculated by postmultiplying the reduced form matrices given in equations (12.5m) and (12.5p) by final demand vectors $\mathbf{y}_m$ and $\mathbf{y}_p$. Alternatively, they can be calculated by premultiplying the level of gross output given in equations (12.8m) and (12.8p) by resource matrices $\mathbf{R}_m$ and $\mathbf{R}_p$. These two different ways of expressing resource costs are equivalent:

(12.9) $$\underset{(r \cdot n)}{\mathbf{D}_m} \ \underset{(q \cdot 1)}{\mathbf{y}_m} + \underset{(r \cdot q)}{\mathbf{D}_p} \ \underset{(q \cdot 1)}{\mathbf{y}_p} = \underset{(r \cdot n)}{\mathbf{R}_m} \ \underset{(n \cdot 1)}{\mathbf{x}_m} + \underset{(r \cdot n)}{\mathbf{R}_p} \ \underset{(n \cdot 1)}{\mathbf{x}_p} \ .$$

The righthand side (RHS) of equation (12.9) may be rearranged by noting that matrices $\mathbf{R}_m$ and $\mathbf{R}_p$ have $n - s$ columns in common. Call $\mathbf{R}$ the common part that relates to the $n - s$ branches without make-or-by choices and partition the matrices as:

$$\mathbf{R}_m = \mathbf{R} \ \mathbf{R}_m^*, \text{ and}$$

$$\mathbf{R}_p = \mathbf{R} \ \mathbf{R}_p^*.$$

---

4. This was the procedure used to compute the level of competing imports given in Table 6.9.

Table 12.4. Distribution Matrix Δ: Direct and Indirect Requirements for Competing Import Goods (h) by Type of Final Demand (d)

Urban branches with make-or-buy choices	Type of final demand (d)		
	1	$\cdot$ $\cdot$ d $\cdot$ $\cdot$	q
1	c_{11}	c_{1d}	c_{1q}
$\cdot$			
h	c_{h1}	c_{hd}	c_{hq}
$\cdot$			
$\cdot$			
s	c_{s1}	c_{sd}	c_{sq}

Call $\mathbf{x} = \mathbf{x}_m + \mathbf{x}_p$ the supply vector corresponding to the $n-s$ branches without make-or-by choice, and $\mathbf{x}_m^*$ and $\mathbf{x}_p^*$ the import and production vectors relating to the other s branches. Equation (12.9) can then be rewritten as:

$$(12.10) \quad \underset{(r \cdot q)\,(q \cdot 1)}{\mathbf{D}_m \quad \mathbf{y}_m} + \underset{(r \cdot 1)\,(q \cdot 1)}{\mathbf{D}_p \quad \mathbf{y}_p} =$$

$$\underset{(r \cdot n - s)\,(n - s \cdot 1)}{\mathbf{R} \quad \mathbf{x}} + \underset{(r \cdot s)\,(s \cdot 1)}{\mathbf{R}_m^* \quad \mathbf{x}_m^*} + \underset{(r \cdot s)\,(s \cdot 1)}{\mathbf{R}_p^* \quad \mathbf{x}_p^*}.$$

When the model is solved in its reduced form, resource costs are linked to $2q$ activity variables, which are those represented on the lefthand side (LHS) by final demand vectors $\mathbf{y}_m$ and $\mathbf{y}_p$. Knowing the values of these variables, the levels of commodity production and imports ($\mathbf{x}$, $\mathbf{x}_m^*$, and $\mathbf{x}_p^*$) can be derived from equations (12.8m) and (12.8p). Alternately, when the model is solved in its full form, resource costs are linked to the $n+s$ activity variables that define the levels of gross output and imports by commodities and are represented by vectors $\mathbf{x}$, $\mathbf{x}_m^*$, and $\mathbf{x}_p^*$ on the RHS. The discrepancy between the two sets of results characterizes the error attached to the use of the reduced form.

Replacing the gross output vector $\mathbf{x}_p$ by the final demand vector $\mathbf{y}_p$ consists of premultiplying vector $\mathbf{y}_p$ by matrix $(\mathbf{I}-\mathbf{A}_p)^{-1}\mathbf{F}$, which defines the inputs of each branch required (directly and indirectly) to supply a unit of final demand. Call Δ the part of that matrix that corresponds to the s branches with a make-or-buy choice and that is illustrated in Table 12.4. The level of gross output in these *s* branches can be written as:

$$(12.11) \qquad\qquad \begin{array}{ccc} \mathbf{x}_p^* &=& \boldsymbol{\Delta} & \mathbf{y}_p \, . \\ (s \cdot 1) && (s \cdot q) & (q \cdot 1) \end{array}$$

When the model is solved in its reduced form, imports can be replaced by domestic production in q different ways that are associated with the q types of final demand. Each way is defined along the columns of the matrix $\boldsymbol{\Delta}$ as a specified mix of the s commodities. When the model is instead solved in its full form, imports can be replaced by production by combining the s commodities in any possible way.

If there is a make-or-buy choice for a single commodity, solving the reduced form or the full form of the model leads to identical results; increasing the production of that commodity is the only way to replace imports by production in either case. If there is a make-or-buy choice for several commodities ($s > 1$), the solution of the reduced form of the model is generally suboptimal since this form allows for only q ways of replacing imports by production. The loss of optimality generally increases with the ratio s/q, but depends on the structure of distribution matrix $\boldsymbol{\Delta}$. At one extreme, the column rank of matrix $\boldsymbol{\Delta}$ could be equal to unity; final demand could be then treated as a single composite good and a single way of replacing imports by production would remain available. At the other extreme, all elements of matrix $\boldsymbol{\Delta}$ could be identical to zero, except along the diagonal ($c_{11}, c_{22}, \ldots, c_{ss}$, with $s \leq q$). For the s commodities with a make-or-buy choice, production activities could be combined in any possible way, and the reduced form would lead to the exact solution. In that case, the s commodities then could be treated as final demand activities and, therefore, excluded from the input-output matrix (see the appendix to this chapter).

With the full form of the model, quantities produced and imported ($\mathbf{x}_m^*$ and $\mathbf{x}_p^*$) are the activity variables, and no more than one commodity is simultaneously produced and imported in most optimal solutions. This extreme specialization does not occur with the reduced form of the model because the same commodity generally enters into several types of final demand. The entire supply of commodity h should be imported only if optimal activity levels y_{dp} were equal to zero for all types of final demand with a nonzero coefficient in row h of matrix $\boldsymbol{\Delta}$.[5]

---

5. In most optimal solutions of the reduced form of the model, activities levels y_{dm} and y_{dp} are both positive for a single type of final demand d; for the other types, either y_{dm} or y_{dp} is positive.

The difference from Bruno

When Bruno (1967) treats import substitution as an export activity, he makes two simplifying assumptions. First, he assumes that replacing imports with production for commodity h does not affect the resource-cost vectors for other commodities; this is strictly true only if commodity h is a final consumer good which does not enter in the production of any other goods. Second, he assumes that upper bounds to import-substitution activities are not affected by the level of final demand, and he treats the import-substitution bounds as exogenous data.

In the present formulation, there is no need for such bounds; import-substitution activities are introduced as alternative technologies for satisfying various types of final demands. Replacing imports of commodities h by production does affect the resource-cost vectors for other commodities, as it should. Not all possible ways in which these costs could be affected are taken into account, however. When the reduced form consists of the two matrices, $\mathbf{D}_m$ and $\mathbf{D}_p$ corresponding to the two extreme import-substitution possibilities, only $q(=18)$ different ways of combining the replacement of the $s(=14)$ commodities are considered; these ways are defined by the weights shown in the columns of matrix $\boldsymbol{\Delta}$. (See Table 12.4.) When a matrix corresponding to an intermediate import-substitution activity is added, twice as many combinations are considered, $(2q = 36)$.

Urban deliveries to other sectors

In an earlier section, rural purchases of urban goods were expressed in terms of requirements for central resources, because no make-or-buy choice existed in the urban sector. When such choices exist, the commodity balances for the goods sold to the rural sectors might have to be treated as central rows. Whether or not it is important to add such rows to the central model depends on two types of considerations. The first is the importance of substitution among central resources on account of rural purchases in relation to the scope for substitution on account of other types of final demands. The second is the share of the rural purchases of urban goods in the total costs of the rural sector. On the basis of these considerations, four commodity balances for urban goods delivered to other sectors were treated as central rows. These are the balances for each of the three capital goods (vehicles, machinery, and construction) and the balance for commercial services.[6]

Rural to Center Linkage

Sectoral models have been linked to the central model in two different ways depending on the number of constraints specific to the sector. The urban and educational models are fully integrated; the rural models are not.

In the case of education, apart from monotonicity constraints on enrollments, the only resource constraints specific to the sector are those on school buildings and high school teachers. In the case of the urban sector, capacities in the form of urban capital stocks of vehicles, machinery, and buildings are treated as central resources, because urban deliveries to other sectors are expressed in terms of their requirements for urban resources, which include urban capital stocks. Consequently, the upper bounds on urban exports are the only constraints which remain specific to the urban sector. Few rows need to be added to the central model, therefore, in order to integrate the educational and urban models into it fully. The columns which need to be added to the central model for each decision year are the fifteen educational activities and the fifty-four (= 18 × 3) activities supplying the eighteen different types of urban goods and services with three different import-substitution techniques.

The story of the rural models is quite different. Each rural model contains several hundred rows specific to the sector. This high number of sectoral constraints is the result of the decomposition by districts and by seasons. Fully integrating the three rural models into the central one would probably have exceeded the capacity of the computer; it would surely have exceeded the computational budget allocated to this study. A shortcut had to be devised. The one used here is derived from the decomposition principle of Dantzig and Wolfe (1961).

Consider an optimal solution of the rural model identified by subscript s. Call $\mathbf{q}_s$ the vector defining the quantities of central goods

---

6. In a given decision year there is one commodity balance for machinery. There are three supply activities which are the columns of the $\mathbf{D}$ matrices corresponding to the three different urban import-substitution activities. There are twelve demand activities which define the seven different destinations of investment in machinery in the urban sector and the demands originating from the two large projects, the iron mine and Riviera.

produced by the rural sector and the quantities of central resources required to produce these goods in sectoral solution s. Any convex combination of several sectoral solutions defined as $\Sigma_s(\mathbf{q}_s)W_s$ with $W_s \geq 0$ and $\Sigma_s\ W_s \leq 1$ satisfies the constraints specific to the sector. Those constraints, therefore, do not need to be included in the central model. The optimal combination of the sectoral solutions is selected in the central model, which assigns the optimal set of weights W_s.

Table 12.5 illustrates the linkage procedure in the case of a single rural model. The rural model is fully integrated in the master model outlined in Table 12.5a. Solving the master model with the simplex algorithm will be called "the direct solution." Instead, the indirect solution consists in solving iteratively the sectoral and the central models outlined in Tables 12.5b and 12.5c. With the algorithm of Dantzig and Wolfe, the center sends shadow-price signals and the sector responds in terms of quantities.

Consider the optimal solution of the central model (12.5c) at iteration $s - 1$. The dual values found for the consumer goods produced by the rural sector and for the central resources used by that sector are represented by column vectors $\boldsymbol{\pi}_{i,s-1}$ **and** $\boldsymbol{\pi}_{r,s-1}$. These are the price signals addressed by the center to the sector at the end of iteration $s - 1$. It is on the basis of these prices that the sector values its production of central goods and its use of central resources at iteration s. Consequently, the vector defining the coefficients of the rural objective function in the rural model 12.5b at iteration s is:

$$
\begin{array}{cccc}
(12.13) & \boldsymbol{\rho}_s & = \boldsymbol{\pi}_{i,s-1} & \mathbf{C}^* & - \boldsymbol{\pi}_{r,s-1}\ (\boldsymbol{\Gamma}^* + \mathbf{D}^*), \\
& (1 \cdot n^*) & (1 \cdot c) & (c^* \cdot n^*) & (1 \cdot r^*) & (r^* \cdot n^*)
\end{array}
$$

where $\mathbf{C}^*$ and $\boldsymbol{\Gamma}^* + \mathbf{D}^*$ are the matrix coefficients of the rural activities in the central rows of the master model 12.5a.

At iteration s, the rural model is solved with the coefficient vector $\boldsymbol{\rho}_s$. The optimal sectoral solution defines the level of rural activities, $\mathbf{x}_s^*$, the quantity of central goods produced, $\mathbf{C}^*\mathbf{x}_s^*$, and the quantities of central resources used, $(\boldsymbol{\Gamma}^* + \mathbf{D}^*)\mathbf{x}_s^*$. These last two sets of numbers define the quantity vector, $(\mathbf{q}_s)$, which is the sectoral response at iteration s to the price signal, $(\boldsymbol{\pi}_{s-1})$, which was addressed by the center at iteration $s - 1$. This quantity response, $(\mathbf{q}_s)$, is the new column vector added to the rural matrix of the central model, 12.5b, before solving it at iteration s.

The sum of the weights applied in the central model to each of the rural solutions $(\mathbf{q}_1, \ldots, \mathbf{q}_s)$ is constrained not to exceed unity. Consequently, the linear combination of the rural solutions which is selected must satisfy the constraints specific to the rural sector (those

Table 12.5. Rural-Center Linkage

12.5a. Master Model

Direct solution	Dual solution	Rural $\mathbf{x}^*$	Central y	Central u	
Objective functions	1		+	+	Maximand
Final consumer goods					
Rural	$\pi_i{}^*$	$\mathbf{C}^*$ $(c^* \cdot n^*)$	$-\mathbf{U}^*$		≥ 0
Urban	π_i		$\mathbf{C}$ $(c \cdot q)$	$-\mathbf{U}$	≥ 0
Common Resources	π_r	$-[\mathbf{\Gamma}^* + \mathbf{D}^*]$ $(r \cdot n^*)$	$-[\mathbf{\Gamma} + \mathbf{D}]$ $(r \cdot q)$		$\geq -\bar{\mathbf{k}}$
Rural Resources	$\pi_r{}^*$	$-\mathbf{R}^*$ $(r^* \cdot n^*)$			$\geq -\bar{\mathbf{k}}^*$

12.5b. Rural Model (Iteration s)

Dual solution	Activities $\mathbf{x}_s{}^*$	
1	$\boldsymbol{\rho}_s$ $(1 \cdot n^*)$	Maximand
$\pi_{r,s}^*$	$-\mathbf{R}^*$ $(r^* \cdot n^*)$	$\geq -\mathbf{k}^*$

12.5c. Central Model (Iteration s)

Dual solution	Rural $\mathbf{w}_s{}^*$	Central y	Central u	
1		+	+	Maximand
$\pi_{i,s}^*$	$\mathbf{C}^* \ \mathbf{X}^*$ $(c^* \cdot n)(n^* \cdot s)$	$-\mathbf{U}^*$		≥ 0
$\pi_{i,s}$		$\mathbf{C}$ $(c \cdot q)$	$-\mathbf{U}$	≥ 0
$\pi_{r,s}$	$(\mathbf{\Gamma}^* + \mathbf{D}^*)\mathbf{X}^*$ $(r \cdot n^*)(n^* \cdot s)$	$-\mathbf{D}$ $(r \cdot q)$		$\geq \bar{\mathbf{r}}$
	1			≤ 1

do not appear in the central model). Because the sectoral vectors, q_s, are accumulated from one iteration to the next, the value of the objective function of the central model cannot decline; it must increase monotonically from one iteration to the next, until convergence. At that point, the solution reached by solving the sectoral and the central models (12.5b and 12.5c) iteratively is identical to the one which could have been reached by solving the master model (12.5a) directly with the simplex algorithm.

Instead of starting in the first iteration with a single sectoral vector as with the Dantzig and Wolfe algorithm, it is possible to start with several vectors at once to accelerate convergence, as suggested by Kornai (1969). This study started with three vectors for each of the three rural models at the first iteration. A second iteration could be made but no more. The linkage between the rural and central models is therefore rigid.

Assessment of Alternative Decomposition Procedures

Various linkage procedures have been used in the Ivory Coast model. What lessons have been learned?

Incorporating several rural solutions into the central model at the first iteration is a device for accelerating convergence. It does not dispense with the need for further iterations between the rural and the central models. When a series of policy experiments is conducted in the manner described in Chapter 6, shadow prices vary from one experiment to the other. A new series of iterations between sector and center would therefore be required for each policy experiment if optimality were to be reached. This would be quite time consuming. With the algorithms available at the time of writing, it would have been easier and cheaper to solve the master model directly with the simplex algorithm, after having reduced the rural models to more manageable sizes.

Reducing the size of the rural models introduces errors of aggregation. The indirect solution described earlier is a particular type of aggregation procedure. This procedure may be an efficient one if the sectoral model covers a single period.

To return to the linkage outlined in Table 12.5. When the rural sector is solved alone the price vectors π_i^* and π_r^* are the unknowns. Call p the number of common products and resources. Since the price of one product can be used as the numéraire, the true number of unknowns is p 1. In a one-period model, the number of possible combinations between a high and a low value for each unknown is 2^{p-1}. Solving the rural model for these 2^{p-1} price combinations and incorporating the corresponding 2^{p-1} rural solutions into the central model would give a reasonable flexibility to the linkage. The procedure is manageable if p is sufficiently small.

It has been seen that the value of p can be substantially reduced by expressing rural purchases of urban goods and services in terms of primary resources. If the rural sector produces several types of final consumer goods, the number p can be further reduced by incorporating the utility matrix for these goods in the rural model.[7] Finally, a single value has to be selected for the shadow price of a resource if the scope for substituting this resource in the rural sector is small in relation to the scope for substituting it in the rest of the economy.

The complications arise in moving from a static to a dynamic sectoral model. With T decision years, the number of possible combinations rises to $2^{T(p-1)}$. This number can be enormous and the decomposition problem formidable.

One way to surmount this difficulty would have been to reduce the choices available in the rural sector by restricting the dynamic analysis to the problems of tree crops and livestocks. The problem of annual crops would have been analyzed separately in a one-period model. Consider now how the rural activities could have been linked to the central model under this alternative.

In the case of tree crops and livestocks, as in that of education, an annual model could have been constructed to deal with time lags and life spans of various lengths. The reduced form of the agricultural investment activities (planting cocoa trees in industrial estates or in small holdings, for example), would have been incorporated into the central model in the same way as educational activities were (enrolling students in a university in the Ivory Coast or abroad). The levels of agricultural investments would have become activity variables for each of the decision years of the central model. This would have increased the flexibility of intertemporal tradeoffs greatly.

In the case of annual crops, a static model would have been constructed in much the same way as the agricultural model of the Mexico study (Duloy and Norton 1973b). This model could have been solved sequentially for each time period and incorporated into

7. In the case of three final goods, the number of variables would be reduced by two.

the central model in the form of a matrix of sectoral solutions as outlined in the preceding section. The intertemporal linkage would have been more flexible because a different set of weights, (W_{st}), would have applied for each decision year of the central model. Instead, in the case of a dynamic sectoral model, the same set of weights applies to all decision years. Intertemporal adjustments occur only through a modification of the mix, W_s, between sectoral solutions which have different time profiles.

With this alternative procedure, the flexibility of intertemporal adjustments would have been greatly improved on the one hand; on the other, the competitive claims of annual and tree crops on the supply of labor by seasons would have been overlooked. This interdependence is an important aspect of seasonal unemployment and migrations of labor.

Finally, a parallel may be drawn between the decomposition procedures applied to the rural and urban sectors. The choice among agricultural technologies in the rural sector and the make-or-buy choice in the urban sector present basically the same problem. In both cases, a choice has to be made between different ways of supplying the same good.

In the case of the rural sector, there is no restriction on the choice among the many technologies available. By contrast, the choice among the values of the shadow prices of the p central resources is severely restricted. For the shadow prices of each of these p resources, a start is made with two extreme values. Among the 2^{p-1} possible price combinations, we select three. The rural solutions corresponding to the three selected price combinations become the three rural activities of the central model.

In the case of the urban sector, the opposite applies. There is no restriction on the variations of the shadow prices of the central resources. The restrictions affect the technological choices. For each of the s branches in which there is a make-or-buy choice, a start is made from the two extreme supply technologies (importing or producing locally). Among the 2^{s-1} possible combinations of the make-or-buy choice, the two extreme combinations (producing in the s branches, importing in the s branches) and an intermediate one are selected. The reduced forms of the urban model corresponding to these three different ways of supplying urban goods and services are the three urban matrices incorporated into the central model.

Because there are eighteen different types of final demand for urban goods and services, there are eighteen urban supply activities, each providing a particular way of replacing imports with domestic production. Because different make-or-buy choices can be made in each of the four decision years, the number of urban activities in the central model is multiplied by four. Although in both cases there are three different combinations at the start, the result comprises three rural vectors in one case and $3 \times 18 \times 4 = 216$ urban supply vectors in the other. This is why the intertemporal linkage is much more flexible in the case of the urban model than in the case of the rural model.

Appendix. Import Substitution

The total resource cost of final demand can be decomposed into two parts:

$$(12.14) \quad \begin{matrix} \mathbf{D}_m & \mathbf{y}_m & + & \mathbf{D}_p & \mathbf{y}_p \\ (r \cdot q) & (q \cdot 1) & & (r \cdot q) & (q \cdot 1) \end{matrix} \qquad \begin{array}{l} \textit{Total resource cost of final} \\ \textit{demand} \end{array}$$

$$\begin{matrix} = & \mathbf{D}_m & (\mathbf{y}_m + \mathbf{y}_p) \\ & (r \cdot q) & (q \cdot 1) \end{matrix} \qquad \begin{array}{l} \textit{Resource cost of supplying} \\ \textit{final demand by importing} \\ \textit{when there is a make-or-buy} \\ \textit{choice} \end{array}$$

$$\begin{matrix} + & (\mathbf{D}_p - \mathbf{D}_m) & \mathbf{y}_p \\ & (r \cdot q) & (q \cdot 1) \end{matrix} . \qquad \begin{array}{l} \textit{Net resource cost of import-} \\ \textit{substitution} \end{array}$$

The net resource cost of import-substitution defines the additional amounts of domestic resources that are required to save a given amount of foreign exchange. This cost, $(\mathbf{D}_p - \mathbf{D}_m) \, \mathbf{y}_p$, may be decomposed into two parts. The first part is the direct resource cost of producing instead of importing the s commodities for which there is a make-or-buy choice:

$$(12.15) \quad \begin{matrix} (\mathbf{R}_p^* - \mathbf{R}_m^*) & (\mathbf{I} - \mathbf{A}_p)^{-1} & \mathbf{F} & \mathbf{y}_p & = & (\mathbf{R}_p^* - \mathbf{R}_m^*) & \mathbf{x}_p^*; \\ (r \cdot s) & (s \cdot n) & (n \cdot q) & (q \cdot 1) & & (r \cdot s) & (s \cdot 1) \end{matrix}$$

in the righthand side, the columns of matrix $\mathbf{R}_p^* - \mathbf{R}_m^*$ define the resource cost of import-substitution in the s branches, while vector $\mathbf{x}_p^*$ measures the levels of gross domestic production in these branches.

The second part is the indirect resource cost corresponding to the additional gross outputs required when imports are replaced by domestic production:

$$(12.16) \quad \begin{matrix} \mathbf{R}_m & [(\mathbf{i} - \mathbf{A}_p)^{-1} - (\mathbf{I} - \mathbf{A}_m)^{-1}] & \mathbf{F} & \mathbf{y}_p \\ (r \cdot n) & (n \cdot n) & (n \cdot q) & (q \cdot 1) \end{matrix} .$$

If none of the s commodities with a make-or-buy choice is used in the production of any other good, matrices $(\mathbf{I} - \mathbf{A}_p)^{-1}$ and $(\mathbf{I} - \mathbf{A}_m)^{-1}$ have $n-s$ columns in common and the difference between them is a matrix with only s columns containing nonzero elements. Consequently, indirect resources requirements can be calculated, as in (12.15), by multiplying a matrix r rows and s columns $\mathbf{R}_m[(\mathbf{I} - \mathbf{A}_p)^{-1} - (\mathbf{I} - \mathbf{A}_m)^{-1}]$ by a vector of s elements defining the final demand for the final demand for the s commodities with a make-or-buy choice.

Chapter 13

Trade Policies

THE METHOD USED FOR SIMULATING alternative tariff, tax, and subsidy policies is described in this chapter, which also analyzes the similarities and dissimilarities between the concept used in the Ivory Coast programming model and the effective protection concepts used by Balassa (1965) and Corden (1966) or the concept of domestic resource cost used by Bruno (1967).

The Free-Trade and Tariff Solutions

In an economywide model, the balance of payments is one of the most important constraints. It expresses the fact that the deficit (or surplus) of foreign exchange on current account (+ imports, − exports) cannot exceed the surplus (or deficit) on capital account. In the absence of such a constraint, the solution would be unbounded; it would always be possible to increase consumption by importing and consuming more. The balance of payments being expressed in foreign exchange equivalent, imports are measured at c.i.f. prices and exports at f.o.b. prices. Since the foreign exchange constraint is always binding, choices are based on prices exclusive of tariffs and subsidies. This solution of the optimizing model is called the "free-trade solution," because all choices are made on the basis of prices c.i.f. and f.o.b.

The free-trade solution provides a useful basis of reference for allocation of resources. If it is known that not all tariffs and subsidies will not be removed, however, this "best" solution is not a realistic one. The shadow prices found in the free-market solution may differ widely from actual market prices, which are the ones that motivate private consumers and producers in their actual choices. For this reason, the "second-best" solution, which takes tariffs and subsidies into account has also been computed.

In the tariff solution, imports and exports must be measured at prices inclusive of tariffs and subsidies in the binding constraint. The balance on current account with tariffs and subsidies differs from the one at c.i.f. and f.o.b. prices by the amount of government receipts from tariffs on imports net of export subsidies. This amount must therefore be deducted (in the form of a constant term) from the foreign exchange constraint in order to ensure the equilibrium of the balance of payments. The value of the constant term is determined by iterations.

Accounting Procedure

In the Ivory Coast, as in most other countries, national accounts are expressed at domestic retail prices. The relations between world border prices ($p_j{}^w$) and domestic retail prices ($p_j{}^d$) are shown in Figure 13.1 in the case of imported goods and of exported manufactured goods. Start with the case of a good which is simultaneously imported and produced domestically. As shown in the left of Figure 13.1, the factory gate price in the Ivory Coast plus the commercial margin on domestic production is equal to the price paid by consumers at retail. This price must at the same time be equal to the price c.i.f. plus tariffs plus commercial margins on imported goods.

Turn now on the right side of Figure 13.1 to the case of goods manufactured locally, which are simultaneously consumed in the country and exported. The difference between domestic retail and factory prices remains equal to the commercial margin on domestic production. The factory gate price is equal to the price f.o.b. minus export subsidies, if there are any. Commercial margins are assumed to be zero, in conformity with the accounting practice of the Ivory Coast. There is no retail cost and the transportation cost is negligible; most manufacturing industries are located in the vicinity of the port of Abidjan.

In the case of agricultural exports, the price f.o.b. minus export tax (if any) exceeds the farm gate price by the amounts spent on transportation and processing. These costs are accounted for in the rural models, which include transportation and processing activities.

The pricing procedure for agricultural goods is straightforward; quantities are expressed in terms of tons of coffee or cocoa. For manufactured goods, quantities are measured in terms of quantity indexes. The unit of quantity is the bundle of goods worth CFAF1 billion in 1970; the price index is by definition equal to unity in the base year, 1970. For that year, the relation between domestic retail prices and

Figure 13.1. Domestic and World Prices

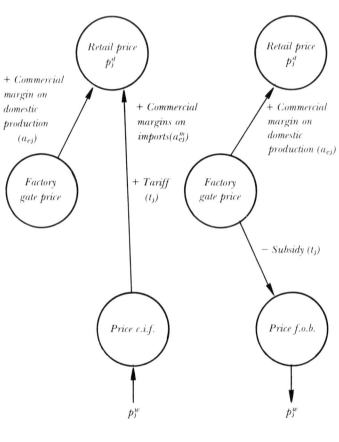

Imported goods   Manufactured goods exported

world prices can be described as follows:

$p_j{}^d$ = Domestic retail price in national currency ($=1.0$ in base year),

$p_j{}^w$ = World border price in foreign currency,

r = Exchange rate per unit of foreign currency,

a_{cj} = Commercial margin on domestically produced good j, measured as a fraction of domestic market price,

a_{cj}^m = Commercial margin on imported commodity j, measured as a fraction of domestic market price,

τ_j = Ad valorem tariff (or subsidy) measured as a fraction of the price c.i.f. (or f.o.b.),

$t_j = 1 - (1 + \tau_j)^{-1}$ = Ad valorem tariff (or subsidy) measured as a fraction of price c.i.f. plus tariff (or price f.o.b. plus subsidy).[1]

In the case of imported commodities, the domestic market price can be decomposed into three elements:

$$(13.1) \quad p_j{}^d = 1 = a_{cj}^m + (1 - a_{cj}^m)t_j + (1 - a_{cj}^m)(1 - t_j).$$
$$[domestic = [commer- + [Tariff] + [Value\ c.i.f.]$$
$$retail \qquad cial$$
$$price] \qquad margin]$$

In the case of nonagricultural exports, the factory gate price can be decomposed into two elements:

$$(13.1') \quad 1 - a_{cj} = (1 - a_{cj})t_j + (1 - a_{cj})(1 - t_j)$$
$$[Domestic\ value\ at = [Export\ subsidy\ (for + [Value\ f.o.b.]$$
$$factory\ gate] \qquad t_j > 0)\ or\ export$$
$$tax\ (for\ t_j < 0)]$$

The last term on the righthand side (RHS) measures the world price in terms of local currency $r^{-1}p_j{}^w$. If commodity ($j = 1$) is imported while commodity ($j = 2$) is exported, the world price ratio is given by:

$$\frac{p_1{}^w}{p_2{}^w} = \frac{1 - t_1}{1 - t_2} \cdot \frac{1 - a_{c1}^m}{1 - a_{c2}}.$$

The world price ratio and the domestic price ratio are the same

---

1. An export tax (or an import subsidy) can be treated as a negative export subsidy (or a negative import tariff) $t_j < 0$.

under two conditions:[2] first, the subsidy on exports (t_1) is equal to the tariff on imports (t_2); second, the commercial margin (a_{c1}^m) on imported good, 1, is equal to the commercial margin (a_{c2}) on the locally produced good, 2, which is exported.

Programming Technique

Having specified the units of measurement, the free-market and tariff solutions can now be expressed in the form of Tables 13.1 and 13.2. For the sake of simplicity, the economy is supposed to consist of only three sectors. Sector 3 produces commercial services which serve as intermediate inputs; they can be neither exported nor imported. Sectors 1 and 2 produce tradable goods for intermediate use and for final consumption (private and public). Commodity 1 can be imported and commodity 2 can be exported. Primary resources are represented by labor of various skill categories (λ); labor availabilities are given $(\bar{L}_\lambda)$. The foreign exchange balance on current account must be in equilibrium. The levels of public consumption $(\bar{G}_1$ and $\bar{G}_2)$ are given exogenously. The objective is to maximize the utility derived from the private consumption of commodities 1 and 2.

Start with the free-trade solution, which is shown in Table 13.1. In the foreign exchange constraint (FF), the coefficient of the import activity is the last term of equation (13.1) with a minus sign; it measures the cost of importing a unit of commodity 1 at c.i.f. prices. The coefficient of the export activity is the last term of (13.1') with a plus sign; it measures the receipt from a unit of commodity 2 at f.o.b. prices. If it is optimal to import commodity 1 and to export commodity 2, the dual equations of the trading activities are:

(13.2) $\Pi_1^F - a_{31}^m \Pi_3^F = (1 - a_{31}^m)(1 - t_1)\Pi_f^F = r^{-1}p_1^w$ and

(13.2') $\Pi_2^F - a_{32} \Pi_3^F = (1 - a_{32})(1 - t_2)\Pi_f^F = r^{-1}p_2^w,$

where superscript F is used to identify the free-market solution. With this solution, the ratio between the price paid by the importer at the port and the price received by the exporter, which is the factory gate price of the exported good, is equal to the world price ratio:

$$\frac{\Pi_1^F - a_{31}^m \Pi_3^F}{\Pi_2^F - a_{32} \Pi_3^F} = \frac{p_1^w}{p_2^w}.$$

2. These conditions are sufficient but not necessary.

Table 13.1. The Free-Trade Solution

Row	Production			Import I_1	Export E_2	Consumption		Right-hand side	Dual values
	Q_1	Q_2	Q_3			C_1	C_2		
Maximand						$+$	$+$		
Commodity balances									
(CC_1) importable	$+1$	–	–	$+1$		-1		$\geq \bar{G}_1$	Π_1^F
(CC_2) exportable	–	$+1$	–		-1		-1	$\geq \bar{G}_2$	Π_2^F
(CC_3) commercial margins	$-a_{31}$	$-a_{32}$	$+1$	$-a_{31}^m$	$+a_{32}$			≥ 0	Π_3^F
Factor balances									
(DL_λ) Labor	$-l_{\lambda 1}$	$-l_{\lambda 2}$	$-l_{\lambda 3}$					$\geq -\bar{L}_\lambda$	Π_λ^F
Trade balance									
(FF) prices c.i.f. and f.o.b.				$-(1 - a_{31}^m)(1 - t_1)$	$+(1 - a_{32})(1 - t_2)$			≥ 0	Π_f^F

Table 13.2. The Tariffs Solution[a]

Iteration on $\bar{T}$

Row	I_1	E_2	C_1	C_2	SF	Right-hand side	Dual value
Maximand			$+$	$+$			
Commodity balances							
(CC_1) importable	$+1$		-1			$\geq \bar{G}_1$	Π_1^T
(CC_2) exportable		-1		-1		$\geq \bar{G}_2$	Π_2^T
(CC_3) commercial margin	$-a_{31}^m$	$+a_{32}$				≥ 0	Π_3^T
Trade balances							
(FT) at prices c.i.f. + tariff and prices f.o.b. + subsidies	$-(1 - a_{31}^m)$	$+(1 - a_{32})$			-1	$\geq -\bar{T}$	Π_f^T
(FF) at prices c.i.f. and f.o.b.	$-(1 - a_{31}^m)(1 - t_1)$	$+(1 - a_{32})(1 - t_2)$				$= 0$	0

Iteration on $\bar{\Pi}_g$

Row	I_1	E_2	C_1	C_2	GT	Right-hand side	Dual value
Maximand[b]			$+$	$+$	$-\bar{\Pi}_g$		
(FF) at prices c.i.f. and f.o.b.	$-(1 - a_{31}^m)(1 - t_1)$	$+(1 - a_{32})(1 - t_2)$				≥ 0	Π_f^T
(GT) proceeds of tariffs net of subsidies	$-(1 - a_{31}^m)t_1$	$+(1 - a_{32})t_2$			$+1$	$= 0$	Π_g^T

a. Production activities Q_1, Q_2, and Q_3 as in Table 13.1.
b. Commodity balances CC_1, CC_2, and CC_3 as above.

If marketing costs are proportional to world prices, domestic retail prices are also proportional to world prices:

$$\frac{a_{31}^m}{a_{32}} = \frac{p_1{}^w}{p_2{}^w} \rightarrow \frac{p_1{}^d}{p_2{}^d} = \frac{p_1{}^w}{p_2{}^w}.$$

The price structure found in the dual of the optimal solution may differ significantly from the price structure observed in the base period. The differences may be accounted for by any combination of three factors: The equilibrium was not optimal in the base year; the structure of world prices (which is given exogenously) has changed; or the tariff rate on commodity 1 was not equal to the subsidy rate on commodity 2 in the base year.

Turn now to the tariff solution outlined in Table 13.2. The production activities Q_1, Q_2, and Q_3 have not been reproduced, since their coefficients remain unchanged. There is a new binding constraint (FT); imports (and exports) are valued there at prices c.i.f. plus tariffs (and prices f.o.b. plus subsidies); a constant term $-\bar{T}$ is introduced in the RHS in order to account for government receipts from tariffs (net of subsidies). The foreign exchange constraint (FF) of Table 13.1 becomes a free row; its slack, SF, measures the foreign exchange surplus $(+)$ or deficit $(-)$. Since constraint (FT) is always binding, subtracting primal equation (FT) from primal equation (FF) gives:

$$(13.4) \qquad (1 - a_{31}^m)t_1 I_1 - (1 - a_{32})t_2 E_2 = SF + \bar{T}.$$

The value of $\bar{T}$ is modified iteratively till the slack variable, SF, becomes equal to zero. The corresponding value of the constant term, $\bar{T} + \Delta\bar{T}$, measures government revenues from tariffs net of government expenditures on export subsidies:

$$(13.4') \quad (1 - a_{31}^m)t_1(I_1 + \Delta I_1) - (1 - a_{32})t_2(E_2 + \Delta E_2) = \bar{T} + \Delta\bar{T}.$$
$$\quad\; [\textit{Receipt from tariffs} \quad - [\textit{Outlays on} \qquad\qquad = [\textit{Net govern-}$$
$$\quad\qquad \textit{on imports}] \qquad\qquad \textit{export subsidies}] \qquad\qquad \textit{ment}$$
$$\qquad\qquad\qquad\qquad\qquad\qquad\qquad\qquad\qquad\qquad\qquad\quad \textit{revenue}]$$

Subtracting (13.4) from (13.4′) gives:

$$(13.5) \qquad (1 - a_{31}^m)t_1 \Delta I_1 - (1 - a_{32})t_2 \Delta E_2 = \Delta\bar{T} - SF.$$

Similarly, subtracting the foreign exchange balance (FF) corresponding to the first iteration $(\bar{T})$ from that corresponding to the last iteration $(\bar{T} + \Delta\bar{T})$ gives:

$$(13.6) \quad -(1 - a_{31}^m)(1 - t_1)\Delta I_1 + (1 - a_{32})(1 - t_2)\Delta E_2 = -SF.$$

Finally, the combination of (13.5) and (13.6) gives:

(13.7) $$\Delta \bar{T} = \frac{SF}{1 - t_1} + (1 - a_{32})\left(t_1 \frac{1 - t_2}{1 - t_1} - t_2\right)\Delta E_2.$$

In the absence of export subsidies, the second member of the RHS is very small. The modification required in the constant term ($\Delta \bar{T}$) can be approximated by $(SF)(1 - t_1)^{-1}$, where SF is the value of the slack found in the first iteration and t_1 is the tariff rate applied to the marginal import activity. In the Ivory Coast model, convergence was very fast. At the second iteration, the slack did not exceed 1 percent of the value of export earnings in any year (the four decision years plus the postterminal period).

Another procedure outlined in the lower part of Table 13.2 could have been used to solve the model with tariffs. With this alternative, the slack variable SF is removed from the foreign exchange constraint at world prices (FF). Constraint (FT), at prices with tariffs and subsidies, is replaced by constraint (GT) which measures the amount, GT, of tariffs paid net of subsidies received. Tariffs and subsidies are valued at a predetermined shadow price $\bar{\Pi}_g$; it is the coefficient of the tax activity GT entering into the maximand with a minus sign. With the previous formulation the binding constraint was (FT). With this alternative formulation the constraints (FF) and (GT) are both binding. The dual equations of the import activities with the first and the second formulations, respectively, are:

(13.8) $$\Pi_1{}^T - a_{31}^m \Pi_3{}^T = (1 - a_{31}^m)\Pi_f{}^T \text{ and}$$

(13.8') $$\Pi_1{}^T - a_{31}^m \Pi_3{}^T = (1 - a_{31}^m)(1 - t_1)\Pi_f{}^T$$
$$+ (1 - a_{31}^m)t_1 \bar{\Pi}_g.$$

For $\bar{\Pi}_g = \Pi_f{}^T$, the two equations are identical. In the first case, iterations are made on the RHS of the (FT) constraint. In the second, they are made on the coefficient $-\bar{\Pi}_g$ entering the maximand. In both cases, the dual solution corresponds to prices inclusive of tariffs or net of subsidies.

Equation (13.8) shows that if the shadow price of the nontraded commodity (Π_3) is equal that of the traded commodity, all dual values are the same:

$$\Pi_1 = \Pi_2 = \Pi_3 = \Pi_f{}^T = \Pi.$$

Since domestic prices are all taken as unity in the base year, the price structure of the dual solution is identical to that of the base year in that particular case. The foreign exchange balance is cleared with the existing rate of exchange (r) and the prevailing levels of tariffs and subsidies (t_1 and t_2). Factor prices are derived from the dual equations of the production activities:

$$1 - \sum_j a_{ij} = \sum_\lambda l_{\lambda j}(\Pi_\lambda / \Pi).$$

Effective Protection and Domestic Resource Costs (DRC)

The rate of effective protection can easily be derived from the combination of the free-market and tariff solutions outlined in Tables 13.1 and 13.2 if two simplifying assumptions are made. First, all goods are tradable (the coefficients a_{31} and a_{32}^m, which in Tables 13.1 and 13.2 measure the contributions of commercial services to import and export activities, can then be neglected). Second, for all commodities j used as intermediate inputs in the production of commodity i, either import is the marginal source of supply or the commodity is produced locally and exported. In both cases, the level of the trading activity j is positive and its dual equation can be written:

(13.9) $\quad \Pi_j^T = (1 - t_j)\Pi_f^F \quad$ with free trade, and

(13.9') $\quad \Pi_j^T = \Pi_f^T \quad\quad\quad$ with tariff and subsidies.

If it were optimal to produce domestically a given commodity i, the dual equation of that production activity would be:

(13.10) $\quad \Pi_i^F - \sum_j a_{ij}\Pi_j^F = \sum_\lambda l_{\lambda i}\Pi_\lambda^F \quad$ with free trade, and

(13.10') $\quad \Pi_i^T - \sum_j a_{ij}\Pi_j^T = \sum_\lambda l_{\lambda i}\Pi_\lambda^T \quad$ with tariffs and subsidies.

In (13.10) and (13.10'), replacing the dual values of the products with those derived from (13.9) and (13.9') gives:

(13.11) $\quad \{(1 - t_i) - \sum_j a_{ij}(1 - t_j)\}\Pi_f^F = \sum_\lambda l_{i\lambda}\Pi_\lambda^F$

$$\text{with free trade, and}$$

(13.11') $\quad\quad\quad\quad (1 - \sum_j a_{ij})\Pi_f^T = \sum_\lambda l_{i\lambda}\Pi_\lambda^T$

$$\text{with tariffs and subsidies.}$$

Dividing (13.11') by (13.11) gives the familiar formula of net effective protection:[3]

$$(13.12) \qquad \frac{1 - \sum_j a_{ij}}{(1 - t_i) - \sum_j a_{ij}(1 - t_j)} \Big/ \frac{\Pi_f^F}{\Pi_f^T} = \frac{\sum_\lambda l_{i\lambda} \Pi_\lambda^T}{\sum_\lambda l_{i\lambda} \Pi_\lambda^F}.$$

The RHS is the ratio between domestic resource costs (or value added) with tariffs cum subsidies and with free trade. The lefthand side (LHS) is composed of two parts. The first defines the *gross* rate of effective protection:

$$1 + e = 1 + \frac{\text{net tax on the import of } i}{\text{net foreign exchange saved}}.$$

The second term Π_f^F/Π_f^T is the adjustment for the increase in the dual value of the foreign exchange following the removal of tariffs and subsidies (see below). Imagine that all tariffs on imports and all subsidies on exports are the same ($t_i = t_j = t > 0$). The common rate t defines the rate of devaluation required to keep the trade balance in equilibrium with free trade:

$$(1 + t)^{-1} = 1 + \tau = \Pi_f^F/\Pi_f^T.$$

Although the gross rate of protection is equal to τ (the common rate of tariff and subsidies); the net rate is equal to zero. Comparative advantages among industries are not affected by removing all tariffs and subsidies, because all rates are the same.

Consider now the case of nontradable goods. To measure effective protection Balassa (1965) and Corden (1966) express nontradable goods and services in terms of tradable goods and primary resources by "traveling back" through the input-output matrix. Alternatively, the input-output matrix can be inverted as is done here and is done by Bruno (1967) for computing the DRC. As long as there is a make-or-buy choice for only one commodity, i, there is no basic difference between the three approaches.[4] The primary resource cost of producing commodity i is compared with that of importing it when

---

3. If tariffs and subsidies were measured in relation to c.i.f. and f.o.b. prices, $1 - t_i$ would be replaced by $(1 - \tau_i)^{-1}$. Labor by skill category could be interpreted in the same way as any kind of domestic primary resource.

The shadow price of foreign exchange with free trade is divided by the shadow price with tariff. The latter is equal to the shadow price of consumption only if all nontariff barriers can be simulated by quasi tariffs and if the balance of payments can be equilibrated at the official exchange rate.

4. All commodities and services $j \neq i$ fall into two groups. Some must always be produced locally; others must always be imported.

the marginal source of supply in every branch, j, other than i is the same with the three methods.[5] A difference occurs when a make-or-buy choice exists in several sectors i.

Balassa and Corden measure effective protection in industry i from equation (13.12) by assuming that, in all industries other than i with a make-or-buy choice, import is the marginal source of supply. Bruno assumes instead that domestic production remains the marginal source of supply whenever the commodity is produced locally during the base year. In present terminology, Balassa uses as reference the reduced-form matrix, D_m (import whenever there is a choice), whereas Bruno uses the D_p matrix (continue to produce whenever you have already done so). This difference led to the controversy over the appropriate source of marginal supply for the steel entering into the production of machine tools (see Balassa and Schydlowsky 1968).

In the Ivory Coast model, allowance is made for simultaneous make-or-buy choices. Any combination of supply activities corresponding to the D_m and D_p matrices can be used (see Chapter 12). The number of simultaneous choices is, however, limited by the number of reduced-form matrices corresponding to given combinations of make-or-buy choices. This limitation would have been removed if the model had been expressed in its full form as in Tables 13.1 and 13.2. One production and one importing activity would have been available for each of the fourteen sectors in which a make-or-buy choice existed. These twenty-eight ($=2 \times 14$) activities could have been combined in any possible way. This is the approach which has been followed by Evans (1972) in the programming model of the Australian economy.

Protection with the Reduced Form

The free-trade and tariff solutions were outlined in Tables 13.1 and 13.2 by considering the full form of the model in the case of a three-sector economy. Table 13.3 shows how these solutions are expressed with the two reduced-form matrices D_m and D_p. The first column

5. Even in this case, however, the three methods are not identical. Effective protection differs from the other two methods in not allowing for variations in the relative prices of primary resources. The method used by Bruno differs from mine because Bruno defines the upper bound of the import-substitution activity exogenously, while, as explained in Chapter 12, no upper bound is needed in the present model.

Table 13.3. Two Alternative Formulations of the Reduced Form [a]

	Row	By import-ing (y_{dm})	By produc-ing (y_{dp})	Only by import-ing (y_d)	Replacing imports with production (s_d)	Dual value
			Supplying final demand d			
	Final demand	+1	+1	+1		Π
(DL_λ)	Domestic primary resources	$-l_{\lambda dm}$	$-l_{\lambda dp}$	$-l_{\lambda dm}$	$\Delta l_{\lambda d}$	Π_λ
(FF)	Foreign exchange	f_{dm}	f_{dp}	f_{dm}	Δf_d	Π_f
(GT)	Tariffs net of subsidies	θ_{dm}	θ_{dp}	θ_{dm}	$\Delta \theta_d$	$\mu \Pi_f$
	Matrix used	$\mathbf{D}_m$	$\mathbf{D}_p$	$\mathbf{D}_m$	$\mathbf{D}_p - \mathbf{D}_m$	

a. $\mu = 0$ with free trade; $\mu = 1$ with tariffs and subsidies.

corresponds to the activity supplying a given type of final demand d when all commodities for which there is a make-or-buy choice are imported. The second column corresponds to the supply activity when all the commodities for which there is a choice are produced domestically. The levels of these two activities are defined by variables y_m and y_p. The coefficients +1 in the first row measure the contribution of these two activities to final demand.

In the domestic resource row (DL_λ), coefficient $-l_{\lambda dm}$ measures the amount of primary domestic resource λ required directly and indirectly to supply a unit of final demand of type d; import is the source of supply in the fourteen sectors for which a choice exists. Coefficient $-l_{\lambda dp}$ measures the corresponding requirements when domestic production is the source of supply in these fourteen sectors.

In the foreign exchange row (FF), coefficient f_{dm} is positive when final demand d refers to exports and negative otherwise. In the former case, the foreign exchange gained in exporting a commodity normally exceeds the import content of the intermediate goods used in producing that export commodity. In the latter case, coefficient f_{dm} accounts for the import content of all production and importing activities contributing to the supply of a unit of final demand d.

In the last row (GT), coefficients θ_{dm} and θ_{dp} measure the amounts paid directly and indirectly in the form of tariffs net of subsidies received. Clearly, the value of these coefficients depends on the levels of tariffs and subsidies and therefore on the trade policy applied. In the tariff solution, constraint (GT) is binding and its dual value Π_f is equal to that of the *(FF)* constraint.[6] In the free-trade solution, the *(GT)* constraint is not binding; it has a zero dual value and could be deleted.[7]

The resources required to satisfy final demand **y** can be expressed in two different ways:

(12.10) $$\mathbf{D}_m\mathbf{y}_m + \mathbf{D}_p\mathbf{y}_p = \mathbf{D}_m\mathbf{y} + (\mathbf{D}_p - \mathbf{D}_m)\mathbf{s} \text{ with}$$

$$\mathbf{y} = \mathbf{y}_m + \mathbf{y}_p \text{ and } \mathbf{s} = \mathbf{y}_p.$$

The first two columns of Table 13.3 correspond to the LHS of equation (12.10) and the next two to the RHS. The coefficients of the third column are identical to those of the first. The coefficients of the fourth column are equal to the difference between those of the second and first columns; they define the resource cost of import substitution. The rates of gross effective protection can be derived directly from the coefficients shown in the penultimate column and in the last two rows of Table 13.3

To start with the two simple cases described in Chapter 12: assume that beer is the only commodity which can be either imported or produced domestically. Beer for domestic consumption defines a given type of final demand $\bar{d}$. Beer is not used as an intermediate input in any industry. The coefficients of matrix $\mathbf{D}_p - \mathbf{D}_m$ are equal to zero in all columns, except in the one corresponding to the final demand for beer $(\bar{d})$. In that column, coefficient $\Delta l_{\lambda\bar{d}}$ measures the net domestic resource cost of producing beer instead of importing it; coefficient $\Delta f_{\bar{d}}$ measures the net foreign exchange saved by producing beer locally instead of importing it; coefficient $\Delta \theta_{\bar{d}}$ measures the government proceeds forgone from the tariffs on imported beer minus the government proceeds from tariffs on the intermediate goods used in producing beer. The import-substitution activity s_d is treated in the fourth column exactly as an export activity y_x is treated in the first column. This is the procedure used by Bruno (1969).

In the case of an export activity $(d = x)$, the gross rate of effective protection is defined as:

(13.14) $$e_x = \theta_{mx}/f_{mx}.$$

This rate can be negative, if there is no subsidy on exports and if there are tariffs on the import of the intermediate products used in the production of the export good.

---

6. The formulation outlined in the lower part of Table 13.2 with iteration on the penalty coefficient in the objective function is referred to here.

7. The formulation is given in Table 13.1.

The gross rate of effective protection on the production of beer $(d - \bar{d})$ is defined unequivocally as:

(13.15) $e_{\bar{d}} = \Delta\theta_{\bar{d}}/\Delta f_{\bar{d}}.$

What was done for beer could be repeated for any other commodity that is not used as an intermediate product.

Suppose now that commodity i is an intermediate input for other industries but that there is a single such commodity i for which a make-or-buy choice exists. Call c_{id} the direct and indirect use of commodity i in each type of final demand d. All columns of matrix $\mathbf{D}_p - \mathbf{D}_m$ can be derived from a single one of these $\bar{d}$ by multiplying that column by $c_{id}/c_{i\bar{d}}$. The ratio $\Delta\theta_d/\Delta f_d$ is the same for all d. Again, the gross rate of effective protection for industry i can be defined unequivocally by (13.15). If there is a make-or-buy choice for fourteen commodities i, the operation could be repeated fourteen times with fourteen different matrices $\mathbf{D}_m$. In each of these matrices, import would be the marginal source of supply for thirteen of the branches in which there is a make-or-buy choice. (Each time, domestic production would be the marginal source of supply in a different branch.) This is the standard measurement of effective protection.

When there are fourteen commodities i which are used as intermediate inputs, the import substitution activities s_d shown in the last column of Table 13.3 can no longer be identified with particular industries. A rate of effective protection can actually be defined only for the group of fourteen industries in which a make-or-buy choice exists. The overall rate of gross effective protection for the fourteen industries as a whole is:

(13.15′) $e_m = \sum_d (\Delta\theta_d)(y_d)/\sum_d (\Delta f_d)(y_d),$

where y_d is the level of final demand for each type d. This rate computed for 1980 with the base-year tariff rates was equal to 63 percent. This can be compared with the 55 percent rate estimated by Garry Pursell from data collected at the level of the firm.[8]

Suppose now that, in addition to the two extreme combinations corresponding to matrices $\mathbf{D}_m$ and $\mathbf{D}_p$, an intermediate combination has been retained. With the intermediate combination corresponding to matrix $\mathbf{D}_i$, six commodities are imported and eight are produced domestically. The overall rate of effective protection for

---

8. Effective protection domestic market (Pursell, Stryker, and Monson 1975, Appendix Table A1).

the first six industries can be derived from the coefficients $\Delta\theta$ and Δf of the $\mathbf{D}_p - \mathbf{D}_i$ matrix. The rate for the last eight industries can be derived from those of the $\mathbf{D}_i - \mathbf{D}_m$ matrix.

The Case of Agricultural Exports

Nonagricultural imports and exports are expressed in the central model through the reduced form of the urban sector. Agricultural exports are treated differently. Because a variety of agricultural technologies can be applied, the production of an agricultural export good can be raised at increasing costs. It is assumed, moreover, that prices f.o.b. are not affected by the volume of Ivorian exports (small-country assumption) for any export goods (manufactured and agricultural) except coffee and cocoa. For these two commodities, the demand for Ivorian exports is taken as less than infinitely price elastic. Consequently, it is optimal for the Ivory Coast to impose an export tax on cocoa and coffee.

The price elasticity of the demand for Ivorian exports of coffee and cocoa was derived from the price elasticity of the world import demand and from the share of Ivorian exports, as has been explained elsewhere (Goreux 1972) by:

$$(13.16) \qquad \epsilon = \frac{\epsilon_w - (1 - \alpha)\zeta}{\alpha},$$

where ϵ_w = price elasticity of world import demand, ϵ = price elasticity of demand for Ivorian exports, α = share of Ivorian exports in world exports, and ζ = price elasticity of export supply in the rest of the world.

For cocoa, $\epsilon_w = -0.35$, $\zeta = +0.6$ and $\alpha = 0.17$ give $\epsilon = -5.0$. For coffee, the price elasticity calculated was $\epsilon = -3.5$. The lower absolute value for coffee is accounted for by the fact that the Ivorian share of exports was estimated in relation to world exports on the subsidiary market outside quota. This was done at the time the international coffee agreement was in effect.

Neglecting constant terms, the demand function for Ivorian exports is:[9]

$$q = p^\epsilon,$$

where q = quantity exported by the Ivory Coast and p = price f.o.b.

---

9. Call $\bar{q}_0$ the quantity exported and $\bar{p}_0$ the f.o.b. price in the base period. Call $\bar{q}_t$ the quantity which could be exported at time t at the same deflated price $\bar{p}_0$. The demand function is $q_t/\bar{q}_t = (p_t/\bar{p}_0)^\epsilon$.

Foreign exchange earnings are related to quantities exported by:

$$pq = q^{1+\epsilon^{-1}}.$$

The marginal foreign exchange return (MR) per unit of quantity exported is related to prices f.o.b. by:

(13.18) $\text{MR} = d(pq)/d(q) = (1 + \epsilon^{-1})p.$

With a demand infinitely price elastic ($\epsilon = \infty$), the marginal return is equal to the price f.o.b. With a price elasticity of demand equal to unity ($\epsilon = -1$), the marginal return is equal to zero. With a price elasticity higher than unity in absolute value, the equality between marginal cost and marginal revenue requires:

(13.19) $\begin{array}{ccc} marginal\ cost\ + & |\epsilon^{-1}|p & = & p. \\ [Domestic\ price] + & [Optimal\ export\ tax] & = & [Price\ f.o.b.] \end{array}$

The optimal rate of the export tax is $-\epsilon^{-1}$ in relation to the price f.o.b. and $(-\epsilon^{-1})(1 + \epsilon^{-1})^{-1}$ in relation to the domestic price. Thus, for $\epsilon = -5$ in the case of cocoa, the optimal rate of taxation is 20 percent in relation to prices f.o.b. and 25 percent in relation to domestic prices. For coffee, with $\epsilon = -3.5$, the rates are, respectively, 29 percent and 40 percent. The optimal rates of 25 percent and 40 percent do not differ greatly from the actual tax rates of 41 percent and 43 percent during the base period. The discrepancy between actual and optimal rates may be interpreted as a repayment by farmers of government investments made earlier in the form of subsidies on plantings. For this reason, the solution of the model with official tax rates may be considered a satisfactory approximation of the solution equalizing marginal costs and revenues with free trade.

The decreasing rate of transformation of cocoa into foreign exchange may be combined with the increasing cost of producing cocoa. For the sake of simplicity, scarce primary domestic resources used in the production of cocoa are identified below with labor. The DRC of producing a unit of cocoa is measured by the labor requirement, l_q, which increases with the level of cocoa production, q:

$$l_q = \bar{l}q^{\eta^{-1}} \text{ with } \eta > 0.$$

At the limit, for $\eta = +\infty$, labor requirements per unit of output remain constant ($l_q = \bar{l}$).

Marginal labor requirements are related to the volume of production by:

$$d(ql_q)/d(q) = (1 + \eta^{-1})\bar{l}q^{\eta^{-1}}.$$

The equality between marginal costs and revenues thus becomes:

$$\bar{l}(1 + \eta^{-1})q^{\eta^{-1}}\Pi_\lambda = (1 + \epsilon^{-1})q^{\epsilon^{-1}}\Pi_f.$$

The domestic cost of earning foreign exchange through exports is:

(13.20)
$$\text{DRC} = \frac{\Pi_f}{\Pi_\lambda} = \bar{l}\,\frac{1 + \eta^{-1}}{1 + \epsilon^{-1}}\,q^{(\eta^{-1} - \epsilon^{-1})}.$$

If the elasticities of supply (η) and the demand (ϵ) are both equal to infinity, the DRC remains constant ($\bar{l}$). In the normal case ($0 < \eta < \infty$ and $-\infty < \epsilon < 0$), the DRC increases with the quantity exported. With linear programming, exporting coffee (or cocoa) is represented by a sequence of activities the profitability of which declines as the volume of coffee (or cocoa) exports rises.

The Impact of Tariffs

When tariffs and subsidies are removed, the balance of trade is adjusted through a modification of the price of foreign exchange in relation to the prices of domestic primary resources. With the partial-equilibrium analysis, the problem is simplified by assuming that relative prices among primary domestic resources remain unchanged. Domestic resource costs can then be expressed in the form of a quantity index at constant factor prices. For the sake of simplicity, the case of a single resource, labor, will be referred to be low. Labor requirements could as well be visualized as a quantity index of primary domestic resource requirements at constant factor prices.

With a single factor, import substitution and export activities can be ranked unequivocally according to increasing domestic resource costs. With tariffs, these activities define the import-demand curve (M^T) and the export supply curve (X^T) of Figure 13.2. The assumptions made are the same as those made in Figure 5.1. At the equilibrium point, T, the domestic resource cost of foreign exchange must be the same for the marginal export and import-substitution activities. The ordinate z of point T is therefore given by:

(13.21)
$$z^T = \frac{\Pi_f{}^T}{\Pi_\lambda{}^T} = \frac{l_{\lambda xm}}{(1 + e_x)f_{xm}} = \frac{\Delta l_{\lambda d}}{(1 + e_d)\Delta f_d} = HT.$$

With free trade, the gross rate of effective protection becomes equal

Figure 13.2. The Effects of the Removal of Tariffs and Subsidies on the Volume of Trade and the Price of Foreign Exchange

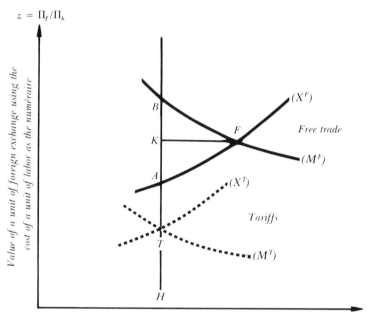

Values of imports (I) and exports (E) measured c.i.f. and f.o.b. at the official rate of exchange in the base period

to zero. The ordinate of point F thus becomes:

$$(13.21')   z^F = \frac{\Pi_f^F}{\Pi_\lambda^F} = \frac{l_{\lambda xm}}{f_{xm}} = \frac{\Delta l_{\lambda d}}{\Delta f_d} = HK.$$

In Figure 13.1, it was assumed that $e_m > e_x > 0$. Hence, the supply and demand curves are shifted upwards from point T to points A and B defined by:

$$HA = (1 + e_x)HT = (1 + e_x)z^T \text{ and}$$

$$HB = (1 + e_m)HT = (1 + e_m)z^T.$$

With free trade, it becomes optimal to export and to import more $(e_m > e_x)$. The volumes of exports (E) and imports (I) must increase by equal amounts ΔE and ΔI.[10] The ratio between the relative

10. It is assumed that the other components of foreign exchange remain unaffected.

increase in the quantities traded and the relative changes in the values of foreign exchange are equal to the price elasticities of the export supply (or the import demand):

(13.22)
$$\frac{\Delta E}{E^T} = \eta_x \frac{z^F - (1 + e_x)z^T}{(1 + e_x)z^T} \text{ and}$$

(13.22′)
$$\frac{\Delta I}{I^T} = \eta_m \frac{z^F - (1 + e_m)z^T}{(1 + e_m)z^T},$$

where $\eta_x > 0$ and $\eta_m < 0$ are the elasticities measured from points A and B corresponding to the levels of exports E^T and imports I^T with tariffs.

From the equality $\Delta E = \Delta I$, the increase in the relative value of foreign exchange can be derived from equations (13.21) through (13.22′):

(13.23)
$$\frac{z^F}{z^T} = \frac{\Pi_f^F}{\Pi_\lambda^F} \Big/ \frac{\Pi_f^T}{\Pi_\lambda^T} = \frac{-\eta_m I^T + \eta_x E^T}{-\eta_m (1 + e_m)^{-1} I^T + \eta_x (1 + e_x)^{-1} E^T}.$$

If elasticities had been measured from point F, corresponding to the free trade solution, E^F and I^F, the relation would have become:

(13.23′)
$$\frac{z^F}{z^T} = \frac{-\eta_m (1 + e_m) I^F + \eta_x (1 + e_x) E^F}{-\eta_m I^F + \eta_x E^F}$$

This formula differs somewhat from equation (26.a) in Balassa and Associates (1971). It makes use of the coefficients of effective protection and draws a distinction between competing and noncompeting imports. As shown in Table 5.1, in our model the volume of noncompeting imports is insensitive to variations in the price of foreign exchange, while the volume of competing imports is highly sensitive to it. The income effect has been neglected because the welfare gain from free trade is relatively modest.

When the assumption of constant factor prices is relaxed, the formula (13.23) is no longer applicable. A modification in tariff policies affects the value of the DRC and the rate of effective protection may not continue to be a reliable indicator of the resource pull. There is no alternative to solving the model with different tariff policies. The resulting variations in relative factor prices were illustrated in the first part of this volume (Chapters 5 and 6). Treating factor prices as endogenous variables is an improvement, provided the variations of the dual solution reflect true economic relations and not peculiarities of the programming model.

The Excise Tax and Consumers' Subsidies

When the rates of tariffs and subsidies are uniform, the domestic and foreign rates of transformation are the same for all commodities (apart from the difference between c.i.f. and f.o.b. prices). Full advantage can be taken of the substitution possibilities in domestic production and in world trade. This is no longer the case when the rates of tariffs and subsidies differ widely.

Tariffs can be used to discourage the consumption of goods of low social value, such as alcoholic beverages, or as a source of government revenues. These functions can also be performed by excise taxes. The latter do not create distortions between the rates of domestic and foreign transformation. If the cost of raising tariffs on imports and excise taxes on domestic consumption were the same, the latter would be more efficient in terms of social welfare. For this reason, the impact of excise taxes (on beverages) and consumer's subsidies (on housing) has been simulated in the Ivory Coast model.

Excise taxes are treated in Table 13.4 in much the same way as tariffs were treated in Table 13.2. A subsidy on consumption is treated as a negative excise tax. In the absence of any excise tax (or subsidy) on commodity i, the entry of consumption activity i is equal to unity in both the commodity balance i belonging to the utility matrix and the material balance ensuring the equilibrium between demand and supply; the dual values of these two rows are the same. With excise tax τ_i, the entry of consumption activity i in material balance i becomes $1 + \tau_i$, the ratio between the price paid by consumers (dual value Π_i of commodity balance i in the utility matrix) and the marginal cost of supply [dual value $(1 + \tau_i)^{-1}\Pi_i$ of material balance i] is equal to $1 + \tau_i$. The consumer pays (or receives) the ad valorem tax (or subsidy) τ_i at the ultimate stage of retailing. The proceeds of taxes net of subsidies are measured in an account-

Table 13.4. Solution with Excise Tax or Subsidy on Consumption

Row	Consumption activity C_i	Righthand side	Dual value
Utility matrix, commodity i	-1	$= 0$	Π_i
Material balance between supply and demand, commodity i	$-(1 + \tau_i)$	$= \bar{G}_i - \tau_i\bar{C}_i$	$(1 + \tau_i)^{-1}\Pi_i$
Government proceeds from taxes	$-\tau_i$	$= 0$	0

ing row with entry τ_i in the column corresponding to consumption activity i.

Without excise tax, the RHS of material balance i was the exogenously given level of government consumption $\bar{G}_i$. With the excise tax τ_i, the RHS becomes $\bar{G}_i - \tau_i\bar{C}_i$, where $\bar{C}_i$ is an iterative constant approximating the level of consumption C_i found in the optimal solution. If $\bar{C}_i \equiv C_i$ for all i, demand and supply are balanced for all commodities i, and there is no problem. In general, this condition is not fulfilled at the first iteration, and a commodity surplus or deficit arises. The total surplus (+) or deficit (−) is measured by:

$$\Delta C = \sum_i \tau_i(\bar{C}_i - C_i)\Pi_i,$$

and the level of total consumption by:

$$C = \sum_i C_i\Pi_i,$$

where subscript i covers all commodities, whether or not there is a nonzero tax (or subsidy) rate τ_i.

A small variation $\tau_i\Delta\bar{C}_i$ in the value of the iteration constant has little impact on the structure of the production costs and, therefore, on the relative values of the dual prices Π_i. Neglecting the substitution effects caused by variations in the dual prices, the optimal level of consumption can be approximated by adding to the value C_i found in the preceding iteration the income effect:

$$\Delta C_i/C_i = \eta_i\,\Delta C/C,$$

where η_i is the income elasticity for commodity i. The value of the constant to be selected in the second iteration, therefore, is:

(13.24) $\qquad \tau_i(\bar{C}_i + \Delta\bar{C}_i) = \tau_iC_i(1 + \eta_i\,\Delta C/C).$

The constant $\bar{C}_i + \Delta\bar{C}_i$ calculated in (13.24) from the values found in the first iteration approximated very closely the optimal level of consumption found in the second iteration, so a third iteration was not required.

As in the case of tariffs, the impact of the excise tax could have been measured by introducing in the objective function a penalty coefficient on the consumption of good i. Iterations should then have been conducted on the value of the penalty coefficient, which would have to equate the dual value of the material balance. Since those values are not the same for all commodities i, the penalty coefficients in the objective function have to be commodity specific. Otherwise, the taxes would not be ad valorem.

A comparison between the impact of the tariff and of the excise tax is shown in Figure 13.3, which refers to a two-commodity economy. Along the axes are measured the quantities of commodities 1 and 2 which can be produced domestically, traded, and consumed. With free trade, the quantities produced are the coordinates of point F. At this point, the slope of the tangent to the production-efficiency frontier is equal to the ratio between the price f.o.b. of commodity 1 and the price c.i.f. of commodity 2. The quantities consumed are the coordinates of point F', where the tangent to the production-efficiency frontier is tangent to an isoutility curve. The quantity of commodity 1 which is exported is the

Figure 13.3. *The Effects of Tariffs and Excise Taxes on Production, Consumption, and Utility*

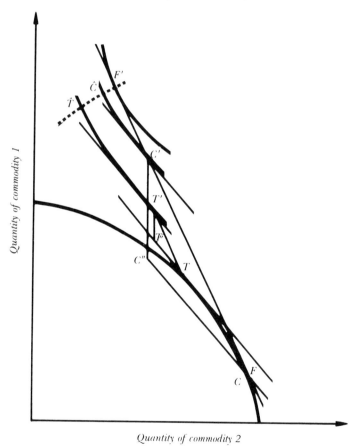

Quantity of commodity 1

Quantity of commodity 2

difference between the abscissas of points F and F'. The quantity of commodity 2 which is imported is the difference between the ordinates of points F' and F. With free trade, the foreign rate of transformation (slope of FF') is equal to the domestic rate of transformation (tangent to the production-efficiency frontier in F) and to the domestic rate of substitution by consumers (tangent to the isoutility curve in F').

With tariffs, the quantities produced are the coordinates of point T; the quantities consumed are the coordinates of point T'. The rate of domestic transformation (tangent to the production efficiency frontier in T) and the rate of domestic substitution by consumers (tangent to the isoutility curve in T') are both equal to the ratio between domestic prices inclusive of tariffs. They differ from the rate of foreign transformation (slope of TT') at which commodities 1 and 2 can be exchanged on the world market. Using commodity 2 as the numéraire, the proceeds of the tariffs perceived in importing commodity 2 is represented by $T''T'$.

If the tariff is replaced by an equal excise tax, the quantities produced are the coordinates of point C that are identical to those of point F, the equilibrium with free trade. The quantities consumed are the coordinates of point C'. This point must belong to linear segment FF', and the tangent to an isoutility curve in C' must be equal to the ratio of consumer prices inclusive of the excise tax (equal in this case to the tariff). The rate of domestic and foreign transformation are both equal to the ratio between prices c.i.f. and prices f.o.b. But they differ from the rate of domestic substitution by consumers. The proceeds of the excise tax are measured by $C'C''$.

With the excise tax, the private welfare loss is represented by $\hat{C}F'$, where $\hat{C}$ is the point of intersection between the isoutility curve going through C' and the Engel curve going through F'. With tariffs, the welfare loss is $\hat{T}F'$, where $\hat{T}$ is similarly defined. This welfare loss is measured in the Ivory Coast model by the variation in the value of the maximand.

When all tariffs on manufactured imports are removed, the comparison between solutions F1 and T1 reported in Table 6.8 shows that the volume of exports and imports increases approximately 50 percent in 1980 and 1985, while the value of the discounted utility of consumption rises 4.4 percent. The impact of a 30 percent excise tax on beverages and a 30 percent subsidy on housing was illustrated in Table 6.11 from the comparison between cases $F3$ and $F1$, both with free trade. During 1980 and 1985, consumption of housing services was raised approximately 20 percent while that of beverages was reduced 11 percent. The discounted utility of private consumption was reduced 1.1 percent.

Government Revenues

As described in Chapter 10, the Ivory Coast model can be solved with an open loop for government revenues. Special sources of revenues, such as tariffs on imports and excise taxes, are identified in the equation *GT* referred to in Tables 13.2–13.4. This equation contains a slack variable, which measures the level of additional government resources required to optimize the level of government savings. Government revenues have a zero dual value. It is assumed that the additional government revenue (defined by the slack variable) can be raised without cost and without introducing price distortions. With this formulation, the loss of government revenues resulting from the removal of tariffs is compensated for by an increase in the rate of neutral taxation (expressed in Chapter 10 as a fraction of the GDP); the level of savings remains optimal. There is no tradeoff between liberalizing the import policy and reducing public savings.

When the model is solved with a closed savings loop, the slack variable disappears from the government revenue equation. If this constraint is binding, government revenues have a nonzero dual value. This value rises when the proceeds of tariffs decline. There is a tradeoff between a more liberal import policy and a higher level of public savings. Unfortunately, this tradeoff cannot be measured correctly in this model. The tariff is treated as a penalty imposed on the user of the imported commodity. At the same time, there is a premium on the proceeds from the tariffs accruing to government. The original penalty is thereby reduced. At the limit, if the dual value of government revenues and foreign exchange were the same, the free-trade and tariff solutions would also be the same. The loss of the user of the imported good would be equal to the government gain. The treatment of tariffs and excise taxes described in this chapter, therefore, is strictly correct only with an open loop for public savings.

Chapter 14

Employment and Wages

THERE IS SIMULTANEOUSLY a large influx of foreign labor and a serious problem of underemployment among nationals in the Ivory Coast. Foreign labor belongs to two categories.[1] The first consists of professionals coming mainly from Europe, the second of unskilled agricultural workers migrating from neighboring countries, particularly those of Sahel. There are three critical types of underemployment. The first is seasonal unemployment in agriculture; the second is disguised unemployment of unskilled urban workers; the third is underemployment of school dropouts who wish to occupy clerical positions and do not want blue-collar jobs.

The object of this chapter is to describe the ways in which these particular features of the labor market are represented in the Ivory Coast model. The first section deals with foreign labor and its effect on shadow wages. The second deals with the problem of underemployment of nationals.

Foreign Labor

Assume that it is optimal to import foreign labor belonging to a given skill category λ. The shadow wage, $\Pi_{\lambda t}$, of nationals belonging to that skill category is equal to the marginal cost of hiring the foreign worker divided by an equivalence coefficient, $equ_{\lambda t}$. The marginal cost of hiring the foreigner is equal to his wage, $iw_{\lambda t}$, measured in millions of CFAF at base-year prices, multiplied by the dual value, $\Pi_{L\lambda t}$, of supplying a basket of foreign exchange, goods, and services worth CFAF1 million at

---

1. There is also a group of non-African and non-European immigrants, most of whom come from Lebanon. These, who seem to be permanently settled, are treated as nationals in the model.

[317]

base-year prices. Foreign exchange accounts for repatriated savings, while domestic goods and services account for consumption in the country. There is one basket for European expatriates and another for unskilled workers migrating from neighboring African countries. The shadow wage, $\Pi_{\lambda t}$, of a national is therefore related to the marginal cost, $iw_{\lambda t}\Pi_{L\lambda t}$, of hiring a foreigner belonging to the same skill category by the following relation:

$$(14.1) \qquad \Pi_{\lambda t} = (iw_{\lambda t}/equ_{\lambda t})\Pi_{L\lambda t}.$$

Consider, for example, the free-market solution $F1$. In 1975, the dual value $\Pi_{L\lambda t}$ of the foreign basket exceeds that of Ivorian consumption (which is used as the numéraire) by 10 percent for European expatriates and by 9 percent for African migrants. These percentages are reduced to 7 and 6, respectively, in 1980. It might have been expected that the dual value of the African basket would be substantially lower than that of the European basket, but such is not the case.[2] The gain on account of the lower import content of the African consumption basket is almost offset by two factors. First, agricultural workers do not pay direct taxes; second, the fraction of their salaries repatriated is even higher for Africans than for Europeans (0.4 against 0.3).

EXPATRIATES

For expatriates, wages are taken as exogenous. They are treated as prices c.i.f. in the case of imported goods. For all high skill categories ($\lambda \geq 5$), the coefficients defining the labor-productivity equivalence between foreigners and nationals are the same. The dual values $\Pi_{L\lambda t}$ are also the same. If it is optimal to import expatriates in all high skill categories, therefore, the shadow wage ratios between skill categories are the same for nationals and foreigners:

$$\Pi_{\lambda t}/\Pi_{\lambda't} = \Pi_{L\lambda t}/\Pi_{L\lambda't}, \text{ with } \lambda \text{ and } \lambda' \geq 5.$$

On the other hand, if it is optimal not to import expatriates of a given skill category, the shadow wage of nationals belonging to that skill is lower than the one which would have been derived from (14.1). The shadow wage must, in that case, be derived from the dual equation of the appropriate educational activity; as explained in Chapter 11, this equation discounts the costs and benefits attached

2. The foreign exchange premium is 35 percent in 1980 in the free-market solution, $F1$.

to the educational activity throughout the time horizon of the model.

The values of the equivalence coefficient equ_{xt} have been selected in relation to observed wage ratios. Whether wage ratios are a good proxy for labor productivity ratios remains an open question. For high-skill categories, it has been assumed that the equivalence coefficient declines from 1.75 in 1970 to 1.00 in 1990. The productivity of the nationals follows a learning curve; by the end of the planning period, nationals have caught up with expatriates. Because marginal costs reflect marginal productivity, a fairly substantial improvement in the labor productivity of nationals is implicitly assumed.[3] This may have led to some underestimation of the demand for highly skilled nationals.

Because the demand for expatriates was minimal in relation to the size of the European labor market, the small-country assumption was applicable; the wages of expatriates could be taken as given for the Ivory Coast. The same does not apply to agricultural workers from neighboring countries. As shown in Figure 14.1, the supply curve (*GE*) is rising. More migrants can be employed at increasing costs.

In a perfectly competitive market with a multitude of buyers and sellers, the equilibrium would be reached at point *H* of Figure 14.1. At this point, marginal cost and marginal productivity would both be equal to the prevailing market wage (*KH*). The same equilibrium could be reached in the model by maximizing the utility of consumption by nationals if the wage bill paid to foreigners was limited to the area (*AKHG*) below the supply curve. In such a case, the marginal cost of a foreign worker would remain *KH*; the Ivory Coast economy would act as a discriminatory monopsonist. This hypothesis, which is not very realistic, has been rejected.

In the Ivory Coast model, all foreign migrants receive the same wage at any given point in time. It follows that the marginal-cost curve (*GC*) represented in Figure 14.1 is above the average-cost curve (*GH*) and that the optimal solution corresponds to point *C*. Importing at rising costs and exporting at decreasing prices raise basically the same problem. As was shown in Chapter 13, it was optimal for the Ivory Coast to impose an export tax on cocoa

---

3. When a national is appointed to a position held previously by an expatriate, the expatriate may remain for some time as advisor; labor productivity may thus increase more slowly than has been assumed here.

Figure 14.1. Import of Unskilled Labor

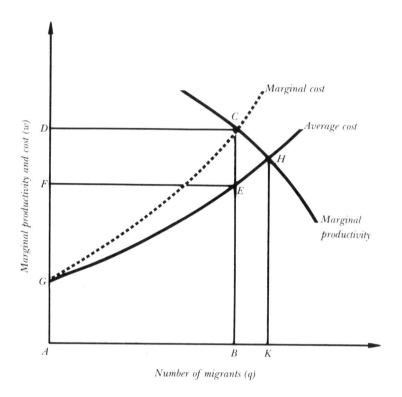

because the world demand for Ivorian exports was less than infinitely price elastic. Similarly, because the supply of migrants is less
than infinitely price elastic, it would be optimal for the Ivory Coast
to impose an import tax (*EC*); this tax could be paid either by the
migrants or by their employers. The tax would restrict the number
of migrants (from *AK* to *AB*). It would ensure a higher wage to
nationals than to foreigners performing the same task (*BC* compared
with *BE*). The rent (*FECD*) would be perceived by the state; it would
ultimately be redistributed among nationals.

In actuality, there is no tax on the employment of foreign
migrants; there is, however, a wage differential in favor of nationals.
As in most countries under similar conditions, this differential
results from a complex of sociological and ethnic considerations.
Those factors are not taken into account in the model, but the
optimization procedure applied leads to the same result: the shadow

wage of nationals is slightly above the shadow wage of foreign migrants performing similar tasks.

Consider now how the difference between marginal and average costs appears in the model. In a given year, the number of migrants (q) and their wage (w) are related to the interpolation variable (x) by:[4]

(14.2) $$q = \bar{q}x \text{ and}$$

(14.3) $$w = \bar{w}f(x),$$

where $f(0) = 1$ and $f'(x) > 0$.

Since the wages received by all migrants are assumed to be the same at any time, the wage bill is:

(14.4) $$qw = (\bar{q}\bar{w}) \, x f(x).$$

The ratio between marginal and average cost is:

$$\frac{\text{marginal cost}}{\text{average cost}} = \frac{d(qw)}{wd(q)} = 1 + x \frac{f'(x)}{f(x)} > 1 \text{ for } x > 0.$$

The interpolation procedure is the same as the one described in Appendix B of Chapter 9. For each decision year, eight different values are selected for the interpolation variable x. The corresponding values $\bar{q}_{xt}$ and $\bar{q}_{xt}\bar{w}_{xt}$ computed from (14.2) and (14.4) are the coefficients shown in Table 14.1 for a given interpolation activity. The variable of the model is the level W_{xt} of the interpolation activity in decision year t; it defines the weight placed on the coefficients $\bar{q}_{xt}$ and $\bar{q}_{xt}\bar{w}_{xt}$ in the labor and wage-bill balances.

The dual value ($\Pi_{\lambda t}$) of the labor balance measures the shadow wage of Ivorian unskilled agricultural workers; it is equal to the marginal cost of importing a foreigner. It corresponds to BC on Figure 14.1 and can be written:

(14.3') $$\Pi_{\lambda t} = \bar{w}_t[f(x) + xf'(x)]\Pi_{LAt}.$$

Table 14.1. Importing Workers at Rising Costs

Row	W_{xt}	Righthand side	Dual value
Labor balance	$+\bar{q}_{xt}$	$\geq -\bar{L}_{\lambda t}$	$\Pi_{\lambda t}$
Wage bill	$-\bar{q}_{xt}\bar{w}_{xt}$	$= 0$	Π_{LAt}
Weight constraint	$+1$	≤ 1	$-\Pi_{At}$

4. For the sake of simplicity, subscript t is not shown in equations 14.2–14.4

The second row of Table 14.1 measures the wage bill. Its dual value (Π_{LAt}) is the marginal cost of supplying a given mix of foreign exchange and domestic goods or services worth CFAF1 million at 1970 prices. This is the numéraire used to measure wages along the vertical axis of Figure 14.1.

The last row of Table 14.1 states that the sum of the interpolation weights cannot exceed unity, which constrains the optimal solution to remain on the marginal-cost curve (see Appendix 9.2). Assuming the interpolation weight to be unity ($W_{xt} = 1$), the dual equation of the interpolation activity can be interpreted in terms of the demand and supply curves of Figure 14.1 as:

$$(14.5) \quad \begin{array}{l} \bar{q}_{xt}\Pi_{\lambda t} - \bar{q}_{xt}\bar{w}_{xt}\Pi_{LAt} = \Pi_{At}. \\ [ABCD] - [ABEF] = [FECD] \end{array}$$

The first term of the lefthand side measures what would be the total cost of employing migrants if each migrant were paid at his marginal cost to the Ivorian economy. The second term measures what migrants actually receive (it includes the traditional producer's rent, *GEF*). The righthand side is equal to the difference between marginal and average cost multiplied by the number of migrants. This is a rent which remains in the hands of the Ivorians; it accrues to the employers (public or private) who transmit it ultimately to the Ivorian consumer. (It is interesting to note that the government of the Upper Volta believes that the Ivory Coast benefits from a rent and asked, without success, for an indemnity.)

In the free-market case (*F*1), the shadow wage of foreign migrants is 3.4 percent below the shadow wage of nationals. In case *F*2, with a rural employment program in the north (see Chapter 6), the differences are 7.7 percent in 1975, 5.2 percent in 1980, and 4.7 percent in 1985.

Underemployment

In the model, underemployment can take the form of seasonal unemployment in rural areas and disguised unemployment in urban areas.

SEASONAL AGRICULTURAL UNEMPLOYMENT

In a given rural district, different reservation prices for labor are assigned to different population groups. (The reservation price could be interpreted as the utility of leisure forgone by working.) This defines a step function which may be taken as the labor supply curve (*GH*) of Figure 14.1. The area under the supply curve (*AKHG*) enters with a minus sign into the objective function of the rural model. The marginal labor productivity is therefore equal to the marginal disutility of labor (*KH*). For each quarter, there is a different labor supply curve. At peak seasons, the local labor force is fully employed and migrants may be needed. At other seasons, only part of the local labor force is employed.

The introduction of quarterly labor constraints affects the choice of the cropping pattern and that of the technology used (tractors as opposed to traditional methods). This is of particular importance in the savanna region (see Chapter 17). When the rural models are linked to the central model, quarterly labor requirements are translated into yearly requirements, taking one year as the equivalent of three full quarters.[5]

DISGUISED URBAN UNEMPLOYMENT

In the industrial countries, the concept of urban unemployment is clear because welfare payments are provided to the unemployed. In the Ivory Coast, as in most other developing countries, such payments do not exist and the concept of unemployment is unclear. No attempt was made to measure open urban unemployment. Instead, an attempt was made to measure a form of disguised unemployment called here "employment in the informal urban sector." Unskilled urban workers who do not succeed in obtaining employment in the formal sector have to find some other means of subsistence. They may render various types of services which are paid for in cash or in kind within the context of the "extended family" system. These types of services represent the output of the informal urban sector.

In the model, an urban unskilled worker is employed either in the formal or in the informal sector. The formal sector covers branches of urban activities which are identifiable in the national accounts of the Ivory Coast. With each branch j is associated a labor norm, l_{jt}, which defines the number of unskilled workers required to produce a unit of gross output in year t. The labor requirement of the formal sector is measured by $\Sigma_j l_{jt}X_{jt}$, where X_{jt} is the activity level of branch j in year t.

---

5. It would have been preferable to introduce quarterly labor balances for agricultural labor in the central model. This, however, is only one of the problems in the linkage of the rural models to the central model, which was discussed in Chapter 12.

The labor balance for unskilled urban workers can therefore be expressed as:

$$(14.6) \qquad S_t \quad = \quad \sum_j l_{jt} X_{jt} \quad + \quad D_t.$$

[*Supply of unskilled* = [*Labor requirements* + [*Labor employed*
urban workers]   *of the formal sector*]   *in the*
                                    informal sector]

In the base year, employment in the informal sector was computed as a residual by replacing S_t and X_{jt} by their actual values in (14.6). The number of workers (D) implicitly employed in the informal sector was 15 percent of the total number of urban unskilled workers (S). This percentage was considerably higher than the one obtained by dividing the number of workers officially registered as unemployed by the total number of unskilled urban workers.

The informal sector transforms labor of urban unskilled workers into services. These services can replace some of the goods and services produced by the formal sector; between the products of the two sectors the rate of substitution becomes less favorable to the informal sector as its output rises. More specifically, labor productivity (w_t) in the informal sector declines linearly with the fraction (x_t) of the labor force employed in that sector:

$$(14.7) \qquad \frac{w_t}{\bar{w}_t} = \frac{1 - ax_t}{1 - a\bar{x}},$$

where $a = 1.666$, $\bar{x} = 0.5$, and x_t defined as:

$$(14.8) \qquad D_t = x_t S_t.$$

Taking the labor supply as exogenous, the output of the informal sector is measured by integrating (14.7) as:

$$(14.9) \qquad QD_x = \int_0^{x_t} w_t \bar{S}_t dx_t = \bar{w}_t(1 - a\bar{x})^{-1}\bar{S}_t(x_t - 0.5\,ax_t{}^2).$$

The coefficients of the interpolation activity shown in Table 14.2 are obtained by solving equations (14.8) and (14.9) for selected values of x. In commodity balance i, coefficient α_{Di} (with $\Sigma_i\,\alpha_{Di} = 1.0$) defines the share of the output of informal services provided in the form of consumer goods and services i. The shadow wage of an unskilled urban worker is a function of the dual values Π_{it} of the urban consumer goods and services as well as of the fraction x_t of the

Table 14.2. Supply of Informal Services at Decreasing Returns

Row	W_{Dxt}	Righthand side	Dual value
Commodity balance for group of final consumer goods i	$+\alpha_{Di}\overline{QD}_{xt}$	$\geq -\tilde{G}_i$	Π_{it}
Labor balance for unskilled urban workers	$-\bar{D}_{xt}$	≥ 0	$\Pi_{\lambda t}$
Interpolation constraint	$+1$	≤ 1	$-\Pi_{Dt}$

labor force employed in the informal sector:

$$(14.7') \qquad \Pi_{\lambda t} = \bar{w}_t \frac{1 - ax_t}{1 - a\bar{x}} \sum_i (\alpha_i \Pi_{it}).$$

If the time subscript is dropped and the interpolation weight is assumed to be unity, the dual equation of the interpolation activity may be written:

$$(14.10) \qquad \overline{QD}_x \sum_i (\alpha_{Di}\Pi_i) \quad - \quad \bar{D}_x\Pi_\lambda \quad = \quad \Pi_D.$$

$$[ABEG] \quad - \quad [ABEF] \quad = \quad [EGF] = [FECD]$$

This equation may be interpreted in relation to the average and marginal labor productivities shown on Figure 14.2.[6] The first term of the lefthand side of (14.10) measures the value of informal services; it corresponds to the area *ABEG* below the marginal-productivity curve. The second term measures the return to workers employed in the informal sector. The righthand side measures the rent, which is equal to the difference between the average and marginal productivities multiplied by the number of workers employed in the informal sector. Surfaces *FEG* and *FECD* are the same, since the equations of the average and marginal productivity curves, respectively, are:

$$\text{average productivity} = \frac{\bar{w}}{1 - a\bar{x}}\left(1 - \frac{a}{2}x\right) \text{ and}$$

$$\text{marginal productivity} = \frac{\bar{w}}{1 - a\bar{x}}(1 - ax).$$

In Figure 14.3, the value of informal services is shown along the vertical axis.[7] The average and marginal productivities at point *M*

6. Labor productivity is measured along the vertical axis, using $\Sigma_i \alpha_{Di}\Pi_i$ as the numéraire.

7. As in Figure 14.2, $\Sigma_i \alpha_{Di}\Pi_i$ is used as the numéraire.

Figure 14.2. Labor Productivity in the Informal Sector

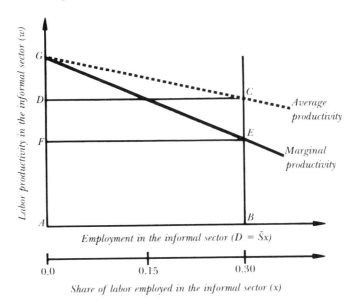

Figure 14.3. Output of the Informal Sector

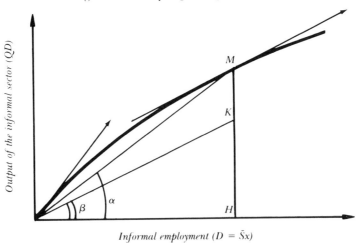

are measured by *tan* α and *tan* β, respectively. The value of informal services (*HM*) is equal to the return imputed to labor (*HK*) plus a rent (*KM*), which is the dual value of the interpolation constraint. In the free-market case, *F*1, the rent (*KM*) accounts for 5 percent of the return imputed to workers (*HK*) in 1975; this proportion increases to 15 and 17 percent, respectively, in 1980 and 1985. In those two years, the value (*HM*) of the services provided by the informal sector accounts respectively for 5.1 and 4.6 percent of the total value of urban consumer goods and services.

RURAL-URBAN MIGRATIONS

Shadow wages of unskilled workers are affected, in rural areas, by migrations from neighboring countries and in urban areas by the level of disguised unemployment. In turn, the difference between urban and rural wages determines the rate of migration from rural to urban areas.

When a worker migrates from a rural to an urban area, he needs additional services in the form of urban infrastructure and public facilities. In the optimal solution of the model, the cost of these additional services per migrant is equal to the difference between urban and rural wages. The elasticity of migrations in relation to the wage differential reflects the increasing cost of urbanization.

Start from a given migration path characterized by the number of migrants, $\bar{M}_t$, and the associated cost of urbanization per migrant, $\Delta\bar{w}_t$. When the number of migrants increases from $\bar{M}_t$ to M_t, the cost of urbanization per migrant rises from $\Delta\bar{w}_t$ to Δw_t according to the linear relation:

$$(14.11) \qquad \frac{\Delta w_t - \Delta\bar{w}_t}{\Delta\bar{w}_t} = a\,\frac{M_t - \bar{M}_t}{\bar{M}_t}, \text{ with } a > 0.$$

It follows from (14.11) that the elasticity of migrations in relation to the wage differential is equal to $1/a$, taken here as 2.5.

Calling x_t the change in the migration rate:

$$(14.12) \qquad x_t = \frac{M_t - \bar{M}_t}{\bar{M}_t},$$

the cost of urbanization per migrant can be written as follows:

$$(14.13) \qquad \Delta w_t = \Delta\bar{w}_t(1 + ax_t).$$

When the number of migrants increases from $\bar{M}_t$ to M_t, the total cost of urbanization rises by:

(14.14)
$$CM_t = \int_{\bar{M}_t}^{M_t} (\Delta w_t) dM_t$$

$$= \int_0^{x_t} (\Delta \bar{w}_t)(1 + ax_t)(\bar{M}_t dx_t)$$

$$= \bar{M}_t(\Delta \bar{w}_t)x_t \left(1 + \frac{a}{2} x_t\right).$$

The increment, CM_t, in the cost of urbanization is shared in fixed proportions, α_{Mi} with $\Sigma_i\ \alpha_{Mi} = 1$, among various groups of urban goods and services i. Calling Π_{it} the dual value of these goods and services, the difference, $\Delta\Pi_{\lambda t}$, between urban and rural wages measured from the dual of the optimal solution can be written as follows:

(14.13′)
$$\Delta\Pi_{\lambda t} = \Delta\bar{w}_t \left(1 + a\ \frac{M_t - \bar{M}_t}{\bar{M}}\right) \sum_i \alpha_{Mi}\Pi_{it}.$$

As in the case of the informal sector, the coefficients of the interpolation activities are obtained by computing from (14.12) and (14.14) the values of M_t and CM_t corresponding to selected values of x. The entries of these activities are $-\alpha_{Mi}\overline{CM}_{xt}$ in commodity balances i, $-\bar{M}_{xt}$ in the labor balance for unskilled agricultural workers, and $+ \bar{M}_x$ in the labor balance for unskilled urban workers. The dual value of the interpolation constraint is equal to the number of migrants multiplied by the difference between average and marginal costs of urbanization.

SKILL SUBSTITUTION

Migration of unskilled workers from rural to urban areas has a real cost in additional urbanization services. Upgrading the skill category of a worker has a real cost in educational inputs during the time the worker attends school.[8]

Consider a fall in the demand for skilled labor with a given qualification. Supply can be adjusted by reducing the number of expatriates employed in that year. If no expatriate is employed, the supply of nationals has to be reduced by cutting school enrollments in earlier years. As the levels of educational activities are optimized simultaneously for all decision years, a surplus of professionals is

---

8. These inputs are listed in Table 11.1.

unlikely to be shown in a solution of the model. It would rarely be optimal to enroll a student in the university today if it were known that no job could be found for him later. This does not apply, however, to clerks. Many dropouts from school become clerks, and dropouts are only by-products of educational activities.

In the absence of any substitution possibility, the shadow wage for skill λ would fall to zero whenever supply exceeded demand for that skill category. If one worker of qualification λ, however, could replace one worker having a lower qualification, λ^-, for performing a task requiring qualification λ^-, the shadow wage for skill λ could not, however, fall below the shadow wage for skill λ^{-9}. Instead of assuming that one worker of qualification λ can replace one worker of qualification λ^-, the rate of substitution between the two workers could be expressed as a function of the number of workers of skill category λ performing tasks requiring qualification λ^-. This procedure was followed with respect to several skill categories, in particular those affected by dropouts. Such a procedure recognizes that the elasticity of substitution may be high between skill categories for which the qualifications required are not too different. It brings some flexibility into the formulation of the labor norms and smooths variations in shadow wages.

Using x_{λ_t} as the interpolation variable, the number of workers with qualification λ performing tasks requiring the lower qualification λ^- is:

$$(14.15) \qquad q_{\lambda t} = \bar{q}_{\lambda t} x_{\lambda t}.$$

The ratio between the marginal productivities of workers having qualifications λ and λ^- (both performing tasks requiring qualification λ^-) is assumed to be a linear function of $q_{\lambda t}$ and therefore of the interpolation variable $x_{\lambda t}$. It is expressed as:

$$(14.16) \qquad w_{\lambda t}/w_{\lambda^- t} = (1 + a_{\lambda t})(1 - x_{\lambda t}) + x_{\lambda t};$$

it takes the values $1 + a_{\lambda t}$ for $x_{\lambda t} = 0$, and 1 for $x_{\lambda t} = 1$.

The corresponding ratio between average productivities is:

$$(14.17) \qquad s_{\lambda \lambda^- t} = (1 + a_{\lambda t})(1 - 0.5 x_{\lambda t}) + 0.5 x_{\lambda t}.$$

Solving (14.15) and (14.17) for selected values of $x_{\lambda t}$ gives the coefficients of the interpolation activity $-\bar{q}$ in the labor balance for skill λ and $+\bar{q}/\bar{s}$ in the labor balance for skill λ^-, as is shown in Table

9. If supply exceeded demand for skill category λ^-, the shadow wage for that skill would fall to the level of that of the lower skill. Ultimately it could become equal to the shadow wage for unskilled workers in the informal sector.

Table 11.3. Skill Substitution

Row	Interpolation weight W_{xt}	Righthand side	Dual value
Labor balances			
Qualification λ	$-\bar{q}_{\lambda xt}$	$\geq -\bar{L}_{\lambda t}$	$\Pi_{\lambda t}$
Qualification λ^-	$+\bar{q}_{\lambda xt}/\bar{s}_{\lambda\lambda^- xt}$	$\geq -\bar{L}_{\lambda^- t}$	$\Pi_{\lambda^- t}$
Interpolation constraint	$+1$	≤ 1	$-\Pi_{st}$

14.3. The dual value of the interpolation constraint is equal to the difference between average and marginal rates of substitution multiplied by the number of workers of skill category λ performing tasks requiring qualification λ^-. Figures 14.4 and 14.2 are very similar. The ordinate of the average productivity curve (*AB*) measures the ratio between the coefficients of the skill substitution activity in the labor balances λ and λ^-. The ordinate of the marginal productivity

Figure 14.4. Skill Substitution

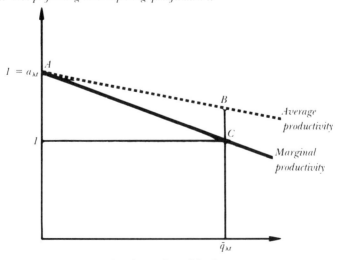

Productivity ratio between workers with qualifications λ and λ^- both performing tasks requiring qualification λ^-

Number of workers with qualification λ performing tasks requiring qualification λ^-

curve (*AC*) measures the ratio between the shadow wages for skills λ and λ^- when some workers with qualification λ are performing tasks requiring the lower qualification λ^-.

Conclusion

With the various facets of the labor market having now been analyzed one by one, it is possible to conclude with the problem of interactions.

Start with the market for unskilled workers and consider two examples. In the first, the demand for unskilled urban workers falls in the formal sector. More urban workers join the informal sector; the level of urban wages falls. The wage differential between urban and rural wages is reduced; migrations from rural to urban areas decline. The number of Ivorians available for agricultural employment rises; fewer workers are imported from neighboring countries; the level of rural wages declines, but less than urban wages did.

In the second, the demand for agricultural workers increases.[10] More agricultural workers are imported from neighboring countries and agricultural wages rise. The differential between urban and rural wages declines, causing fewer workers to migrate to the cities. The supply of urban unskilled workers is reduced. Fewer urban workers are employed in the informal sector; urban wages for unskilled workers increase, but less than agricultural wages did.

The markets for skilled and unskilled labor are linked in two ways. In one way, unskilled labor is the primary input of education. In the other way, dropouts from school fall into labor categories with low-level skills. As supply may exceed demand in those categories, dropouts may find themselves performing the same tasks as unskilled workers.

The ratio between the shadow wages of professionals and those of unskilled workers is largely determined by the ratio between the wages paid to Europeans expatriates and those paid to migrants from neighboring countries. This is the case because foreign labor is the marginal source of supply at both ends of the skill spectrum during a large part of the planning period.

---

10. This could result from an employment program in the north; see Tables 6.3, 6.4, and 6.5.

Part Four

Multilevel Programming

Chapter 15

Formal Linkages

ONCE THE CENTRAL MODEL has been solved under alternative policy options, the choice made by policymakers among these options should define the plan and the set of shadow prices associated with it. These shadow prices would be the signals needed by the project analyst to evaluate and select new proposals in accordance with government policies. If the economywide model provided a perfect representation of the real world, the story would end there.

Unfortunately, a mathematical model can provide no more than an approximation of the real world. The quality of this approximation has to be progressively improved if the model is to be of practical use. Production possibilities can be accurately assessed only after investment proposals have been analyzed. The knowledge progressively accumulated by the project analyst must be transmitted to the sector analyst, who, in turn, must transmit the results of his sectoral analysis to the economist concerned with nationwide issues. The system of models used here provides a logical framework for this exchange of information.

Ideally, the planning process could be visualized as a two-way flow of information. The technological data would be transmitted from the project to the sector and from the sector to the center. The policies would be made at the center. The corresponding shadow prices would be sent from the center to the sectors and, in turn, from the sector to the project analyst. This two-way flow of information is generally the weakest link in the actual planning process.

In practice, sectoral and economywide analyses are usually linked in one of two ways. In one case, the central planner uses the analyses conducted for various sectors only as background information. He constructs his own central model for allocating resources among sectors. The representation of a sector in the central model is not linked to the model built by the sector analyst in any formal way. In the other

[335]

case, the economywide plan is constructed by adding up sectoral plans or project proposals. This addition normally leads to a trade gap and a budget gap that are too large. They have to be reduced by scaling down some of the proposals through appropriate negotiations. This adjustment process is normally conducted on the basis of quantities valued at fixed prices. There is no formal price adjustment between the national plan and the sectoral proposals.

In the present system, there is a formal linkage in terms of both quantities and prices. At the time that sectoral models are completed, upward linkages consist in incorporating the aggregated sectoral matrices into the central model. After the central model has been solved, the impact of the policy package selected can be assessed in disaggregated terms by returning to the sectoral models. For each branch of the urban sector, production and imports can be derived from the final demand vectors computed in the central model.[1] For every year, the number of students and teachers employed in any part of the educational system can be calculated by solving the annual educational model with the optimal growth rates of new enrollments found in the central model.[2] For each rural district, patterns of land use and mixes of techniques can be computed by solving the rural models with the set of shadow prices found in the central model.[3]

When the cycle from the sectors to the center and back to the sectors has been completed, a feasible solution of the nonaggregated economywide model has been obtained—reference is made here to the 5,000-row model of Chapter 7, the one which was too large to be solved. The true optimal solution of the nonaggregated model has not been achieved, because the replacement of the sectoral models by aggregated sectoral matrices has introduced some errors. Nevertheless, this "nearly optimal" solution may be satisfactory for practical purposes. Errors of aggregation may be less serious than the errors made in estimating the basic data, in forecasting world prices for the main export crops, or even in assessing the subjective preferences of policymakers.

At the time of revising the plan, a further cycle of iterations (sector-center-sector) will be made. In the meantime, something can be done to improve central and sectoral models, and this will be our main concern in the last three chapters of this volume. Chapter 15 illustrates diagrammatically and numerically the errors made in the formal linkage. Chapter 16 shows how the disaggregated urban model has

---

1. Equations 12.7, 12.8, and 12.13.
2. Tables 11.3 and 11.4.
3. This consists in recomputing the coefficients of the sectoral objective function, as shown in equation (12.14).

been constructed and how its aggregated form can be used at the sectoral level to perform consistency tests and to project urban requirements under specified assumptions. Chapter 17 deals with the rural sector. It shows that a series of models have been experimented with, some of them at a very disaggregated level.

Diagrammatic Representation

The starting point will be a two-sector model, where labor and foreign exchange are the only two primary resources, and where there is no choice between alternative production technologies, nor a make-or-buy choice. The first sector produces consumer goods; it requires labor and foreign exchange in fixed proportions. The second sector produces export goods and transforms labor into foreign exchange at increasing costs. The availability of labor resources is given and there is an upper bound to the trade gap. The utility of consumption is maximized, and labor must be allocated optimally between the two sectors.

Such an optimizing model can be solved without any iterations. This is illustrated in Figure 15.1, where the vertical part of the diagram is the same as an Edgeworth-Bowley box.[4] Labor requirements are measured from point 0 upward for the sector producing consumer goods; they are measured from point B downward for the export sector; the distance $(0B)$ between these two points defines the size of the labor force shared between the two sectors. The horizontal part of the diagram differs from the Edgeworth-Bowley box in that foreign exchange is treated here as a variable rather than as a constant.

The first sector may consist of any number of branches, provided that the sector follows a Leontief technology. It can produce any number of consumer goods, provided that they are combined in fixed proportions. All sectoral activities can be summarized through the "reduced form" by vector $0M$ (see Chapter 12). The length $(0M)$ of this vector defines the level of consumption. Its projections along the axes $(0N$ and $0L)$ define the quantities of foreign exchange and labor required for producing the amount $(0M)$ of consumer goods.

The export sector is represented in Figure 15.1 by the three vectors, A_1A_2, A_2A_3, and A_3A_4. Each export vector is computed, through the "reduced form," in much the same way as the consumption vector. The horizontal projection of the export vector measures the export earnings

4. In an Edgeworth-Bowley diagram, foreign-exchange requirements would be measured along the horizontal axis in the manner in which labor requirements are measured along the vertical axis of Figure 15.1. An algebraic statement is given in the appendix to this chapter.

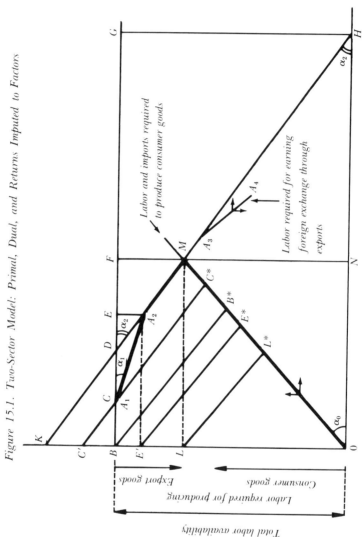

Figure 15.1. Two-Sector Model: Primal, Dual, and Returns Imputed to Factors

valued f.o.b., net of any indirect imports valued c.i.f. Its vertical projection measures direct and indirect labor requirements. Its slope measures the domestic resource cost of earning a unit of foreign exchange. The three export activities are ordered by increasing domestic resource cost ($tan\ \alpha_1 < tan\ \alpha_2 < tan\ \alpha_3$). It is always optimal to exhaust the possibilities of earning foreign exchange through the first activity before starting to use the second. As import requirements in the rest of the economy increase, the equilibrium point moves southeast, starting from A_1, along the efficiency frontier ($A_1A_2A_3A_4$) of the export sector.

In this particular example, it is optimal to use the first export activity fully (A_1A_2), to use the second only in part (A_2M), and not to use the third at all. The maximum level of consumption attainable is equal to $0M$. With this level is associated the volume of imports $0N$, which is measured at c.i.f. The foreign exchange ($0N$) required to pay for these imports is provided for by the exogenous foreign-exchange allocation (BC) plus the earnings (CF) of the export sector.

The slope of the marginal export activity ($tan\ \alpha_2$) defines the ratio between the shadow prices of foreign exchange and labor. As usual, the shadow price of a unit of consumption can be selected as the numéraire. With this convention, it follows that the shadow prices of labor and foreign exchange are measured respectively by the ratio between $0M$ and $0K$ and by the ratio between $0M$ and $0H$ (see demonstration in the appendix). It also follows that the value of the maximand is equal to $0M$ (which measures the number of consumption units) and can be allocated among factors as follows:[5]

$0L^*$ = Returns imputed to labor employed in the sector producing consumer goods,

L^*E^* = Returns imputed to labor employed in second export activity,

E^*B^* = Returns imputed to labor employed in the first export activity,

B^*C^* = Returns imputed to the exogenous allocation of foreign exchange,

C^*M = Rent accruing to the first export activity, and

$0M$ = Value of the maximand = quantity consumed.

5. Points L^*, E^*, B^*, and C^* (along vector OM) are the projections of points, L, E', B, and C' (along the vertical axis). The projection rays make with the horizontal angle α_2; $tan\ \alpha_2$ defines the domestic resource cost (DRC) per unit of foreign exchange earned from the marginal export activity.

From Figure 15.1, therefore, the primal solution, the dual solution, and the decomposition of the minimand can be read at once. Consider, for example, the workers employed in the sector producing consumer goods. The number of these workers (primal) is measured along the vertical axis by $0L$. The efficiency wage of a worker (dual) is equal to $0M$ over $0K$. The return on these workers (component of the minimand) is equal to $(0L)(0M/0K)$, which is itself equal to $0L*$ since $LL*$ parallel to KM implies:

$$\frac{0M}{0L*} = \frac{0K}{0L}, \frac{0M}{0K} = \frac{0L*}{0L} \text{ and } 0L* = 0L \frac{0M}{0K}.$$

Consider now the first export activity. The foreign exchange earned (primal) is measured, along the upper horizontal axis, by CE, which can be decomposed in two parts. The first, DE, accounts for the foreign exchange opportunity cost of the labor employed; its contribution to the maximand is $B*E*$ (number of workers BE' projected on the consumption vector). The second part, CD, is the rent accruing to this activity and its contribution to the maximand is $C*M$. This rent may result from market limitations which do not permit expanding the export activity. Alternatively, it may account for returns imputed to the resources specific to the first export activity—that is, to resources which cannot be used elsewhere in the economy.

When the shadow price of labor is used as the numéraire, the decomposition of the minimand is read along the vertical axis $(0LE'BC'K)$. When the shadow price of foreign exchange is used as the numéraire, it is read along the horizontal axis:

BC = Return imputed to exogenous allocation of foreign exchange,

CD = Rent on the first export activity,

DE = Return imputed to labor employed in the first export activity,

EF = Return imputed to labor employed in the second export activity, and

FG = Return imputed to labor employed in the sector producing consumer goods.

───────

BG = $0M \dfrac{0H}{0M}$ = Value of the maximand using the shadow price of a unit of foreign exchange as the numéraire.

In Figure 15.1, the origin of the export possibility frontier was set from the upper horizontal axis; from there, movement was southeast as the need for foreign exchange increased. Instead, the origin can be set from the consumption vector; movement then is northwest, as shown by dotted lines in Figure 15.2. In this case, the export-possibility frontier is represented by a family of curves convex to the origin. A given level of consumption ($0A$ or $0A'$ or $0A''$) and a given trade gap (BM or BM' or BM'') are associated with each curve, as shown in Figure 15.3. These two types of representations will be combined in later sections.

The Project as a Component of the Sector

In Figure 15.1, the profitability frontier of the export sector ($A_1A_2A_3A_4$) is constructed by ordering export activities according to the increasing domestic resource cost (DRC) of earning a unit of

Figure 15.2. Two Different Representations of Export Sector 2

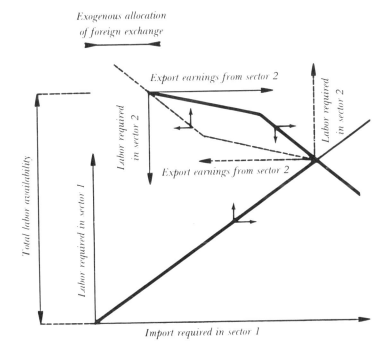

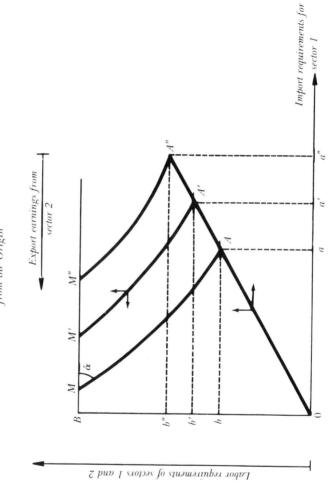

Figure 15.3. Two-Sector Model with Export-Possibility Frontier Concave from the Origin

foreign exchange. The solution of the economywide model defines the marginal export activity and the DRC (*tan* $\hat{\alpha}$) associated with it. Any project with a lower (or higher) DRC should be accepted (or rejected).

In the case of a single product (foreign exchange) and a single resource (labor), the DRC can be unambiguously expressed in terms of a single ratio between physical units. In the case of a project producing several commodities and using several resources, the profitability of the project can no longer be expressed by a single ratio between physical units. The social gain or loss attached to the project has to be computed as the algebraic sum of the quantities produced (+) or used (−) multiplied by the corresponding shadow prices. These can be derived from the dual solution of the optimizing model.

The principle of downward linkages is straightforward. Its usefulness depends on the validity of the shadow prices computed from the optimizing model. The upward linkage from the project to the sector (or the center) is a way of improving the estimation of these shadow prices.

Consider a given export activity of the urban sector. It is represented in the optimizing model by a vector of technical coefficients which approximates average input-output relationships. These are derived from the combination of three input-output tables prepared by the Ivorian planners. The one referring to 1970 is based on actual national accounting. Those referring to 1975 and 1980 were derived from the 1970 table by taking into account what was known in 1972 regarding the likely transformation of certain branches. Shortly after the optimizing model has been completed, some of the data on which it is based have become obsolete. More textile projects have been assessed, and decisions regarding the construction of new factories have been made. When sufficient new knowledge has accumulated, it becomes necessary to revise some parts of the optimizing model.

The Project as a New Sector

The textile project is a component of the sectoral model but the iron mine is not. If the iron mine is not implemented, no iron ore will be produced in the economy. Instead of dealing with a problem of aggregation between sector and projects, it is necessary to deal with a problem of substitution; a choice must now be made among different ways of earning foreign exchange.

In Figure 15.4, domestic resource requirements are measured up-

Figure 15.4. Project Producing a New Commodity at Increasing Costs

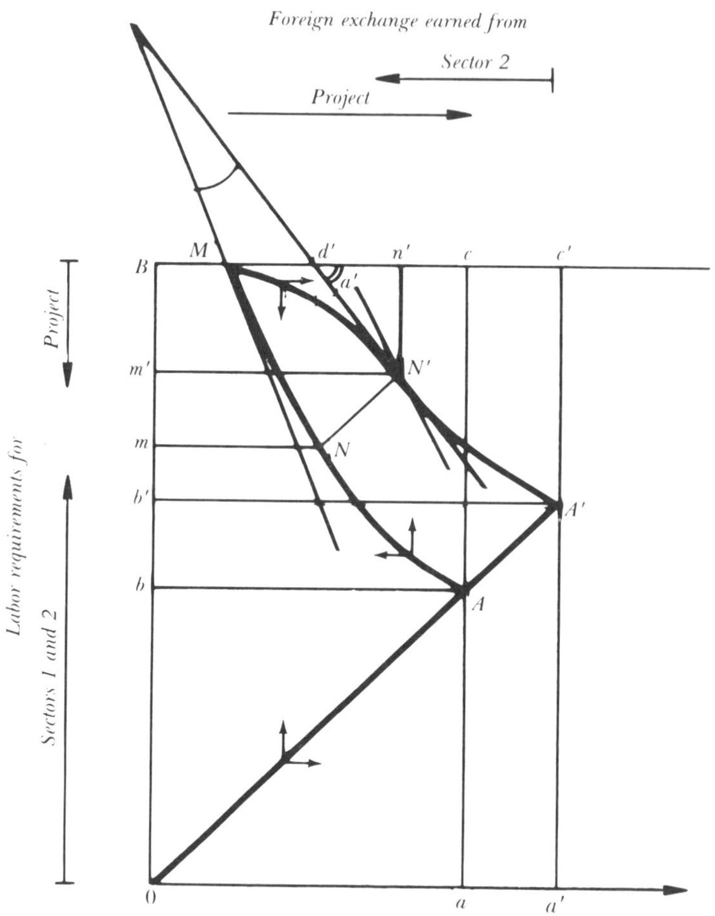

Efficiency frontier without the project (OANM)
Efficiency frontier with the project (OA'N'M)

ward (from *b* to *B*) for the traditional export sector and downward (from *B* to *m'*) for the iron mine; the iron mine is, in fact, a new sector. As in Figure 15.3, the efficiency frontier of the traditional export sector (*AM*) is convex with respect to the origin, 0. As in Figure 15.1, the efficiency frontier of the iron-mining sector (*MN'*) is concave with respect to 0. Without iron ore, the optimal level of consumption is equal to 0*A* and the quantity of foreign exchange *Mc* is earned from traditional export activities. With iron ore, the traditional export activities corresponding to the section *NM* are eliminated and the optimal level of consumption increases from 0*A* to 0*A'*. The quantity of foreign exchange *Mn'* is earned by exporting iron ore, and the quantity *n'c'* by traditional exports. The new efficiency frontier is composed of the curvilinear segment *MN'* (along the iron-ore frontier) and of the curvilinear segment *N'A'* (along the traditional export frontier). The latter is a translation (parallel to *AA'*) of the curvilinear segment *NA*.

When the five-year plan is drawn without including the iron mine, the projects to be implemented are those corresponding to the curvilinear segment *AM*. Suppose that, during the course of the five-year plan, the iron-mining project (*MN'*) is added. With this addition, the plan should be revised, because all projects corresponding to the curvilinear segment *MN* of the traditional export curve have to be deleted in order to release the amount of domestic resources *mB*. These resources are needed not only for the iron mine (*m'B*) but also for the additional requirements (*bb' = mm'*) of the sector producing consumer goods. If no project is deleted, bottlenecks occur and the completion of all projects is delayed; the gestation lags of all investments rise and the overall cost increases. Unfortunately, this occurs all too frequently in countries which are at an early stage of industrialization. In those countries, it is not unusual that a new type of industrial project has to be treated as a new sector.

In the case of a pure enclave project which requires no domestic resource with a positive shadow price, bottlenecks would be avoided. In this extreme case, every factor (or product) would be imported (or exported). The impact of the project on the domestic economy would be limited to its net impact on the balance of payments. Including the project in the model would then be equivalent to modifying the exogenous allocation of foreign exchange (*BM*).

The iron mine is not a pure enclave project. Because the size of the mine is predetermined, the project (*MN'*) is represented in the model by a vector (as in Figure 15.5) and not by a curve (as in Figure 15.4). Because the project uses more than one factor at several points in time, the two-dimensional vector (*MN'*) of Figure 15.5 becomes in the model

Figure 15.5. Efficiency Frontier without Project (OANM) and with Project (OA'N'M)

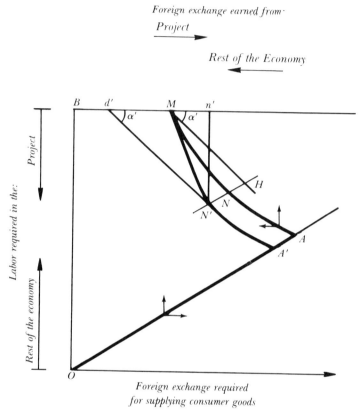

Foreign exchange required
for supplying consumer goods

a vector in a multidimensional space (of approximately 50 dimensions). This vector is the same as the quantity vector used in project analysis. For each year, the outputs of the project are represented by positive numbers and the inputs by negative ones.[6] The gain (or loss) resulting from the project is computed by premultiplying the column vector of quantities by the row vector of prices. In project analysis, the price vector is exogenous; in the model, it is endogenous.[7] This is the basic difference between partial- and general-equilibrium analyses.

Because the time of implementation of the project is a choice

6. In the model, data are aggregated by representative years. The problems raised by time aggregation are discussed in Chapter 10.

7. Project analysts frequently compute the "internal rate of return" leading to a zero profit. The variable becomes the rate of time discount instead of the profit; relative prices at each point in time remain exogenous.

variable, the iron mine is represented by three vectors instead of a single one. With the first vector, investments are made during the five-year period centered on 1975. With the second vector, the time of investment is postponed from 1975 till 1980; with the third, it is postponed till 1985. Since a single mine of a predetermined size has to be built, the sum of the nonnegative weights applied to each of the three vectors must be equal to unity.[8] The dual value of this equality constraint measures the gain (or loss) resulting from the project.

In Figure 15.4, there is a gain (Md') which can be interpreted as the rent imputed to the iron-ore deposit. This rent measures the excess of the foreign exchange earnings (Mn') over the foreign exchange opportunity cost of the domestic resources used ($d'n'$). In Figure 15.5, there is a loss ($d'M$). A policy change is reflected in the model by a modification in the shadow price structure and, consequently, in the gain (or loss) attached to the project. The sensitivity is illustrated by Table 15.1, where the gain (or loss) of the project is expressed as a percentage[9] of the value of the maximand.

As shown in the northwest corner, the project is profitable in the absence of savings constraint and of tariffs on competing imports. When tariffs are imposed, the gain (+0.04) is replaced by a loss

Table 15.1. Profitability of the Iron Mine with and without Tariffs (Sensitivity Analysis)[a]

	Net profit as percentage of maximand	
Tariff situation	*Without constraint on savings*	*With constraint on savings*
No tariffs on competing imports	0.04 (solution 2A)	−0.07 (solution 2)
Tariffs on competing imports and restrictions on foreign capital[b]	−0.03 (solution 3A)	−0.41 (solution 3)
Tariffs on competing imports	. . .	−1.38 (solution 5)
With an increase of 10 percent in export prices of agricultural products in 1975 and 1980		
No tariffs on imports	−0.25 (solution F1)	. . .
Tariffs on all urban imports	−0.30 (solution T1)	−1.1 (solution T5)

a. For a summary of solutions to the central model, see Tables 6.16 and 6.17.
b. With restrictions on capital borrowing and on the entrance of rural workers, employment program in the north.

8. To solve the model without project, unity is replaced by zero.
9. This percentage is defined in Figure 15.5 by the ratio between HN' and $0A'$.

(−0.03). When prices of agricultural exports are raised 10 percent in relation to those of exports of iron ore, the loss increases.

With a constraint on savings, the profitability of the project is substantially reduced. The iron mine is a capital-intensive project. Under the assumptions made, 60 percent of investments are financed by foreign capital which enters into the country only if the project is implemented. The remaining 40 percent must be financed by additional borrowings at increasing costs, by reducing other investments, or both. In case 5, which was reviewed in the penultimate column of Table 6.3, the shadow price of foreign capital is raised by a series of policy measures, and the loss attached to the project reaches 1.38 percent of the value of the maximand. This loss overstates the 1.01 percent gain (see Table 15.2), which would result from the elimination of the project.

The cause of the overestimation is illustrated in Figure 15.5. Without project, the export efficiency frontier is ANM. With project, it becomes $A'N'M$. The project earns the quantity of foreign exchange Mn'. It uses the quantity of labor $N'n'$; the latter is worth $d'n'$ in foreign exchange valued at the shadow price ratio ($tan\ \alpha'$) prevailing with the project. The foreign exchange loss ($Md' = n'd' - n'M$) is equivalent to the consumption loss, $N'H$.[10] The latter exceeds by NH the consumption gain $N'N(= A'A)$ which could be obtained by eliminating the

Table 15.2. *Impact of the Iron Mine*[a]
Percentage change

Economic variable	1980	1985
Physical investments (endogenous)		
Total	17	1
Total without iron mine	−5	1
Exports		
Total	. . .	5
Total without iron mine	. . .	−6
Maximand	−1	
Shadow prices		
Foreign exchange	2	−2
Savings	27	31
Foreign capital	9	6

a. Based on the comparison between solutions 5 and 5A of the central model (with and without the iron mine). See Table 6.16.

10. $N'H$ is parallel to $0A$; and MH is parallel to $d'N'$, which is tangent to the efficiency frontier.

project. The gain, $N'H$, which could be made by deleting the project is overestimated whenever domestic resources can be transformed into foreign exchange at increasing costs, and the extent of the overestimation, NH, increases with the degree of curvature of the export-efficiency frontier.

The impact of the project on selected primal and dual variables is shown in Table 15.2. The changes are expressed as percentages by comparing the optimal solution with project (case 5) to that without project (case 5A). In 1980 (when the iron mine is implemented), total physical endogenous investments increase 17 percent if investments in the iron mine are included; they decline 5 percent if they are excluded. In 1980, exports are not affected. In 1985, total exports increase 5 percent if exports of iron ore are included; they decline 6 percent if they are excluded. The decline occurs in the urban branch exporting processed foods. The shadow price of foreign exchange increases 2 percent when more imports are needed to build the mine; it declines 2 percent when iron ore is exported. The shadow price of savings increases substantially in 1980 and 1985, which raises the shadow price of foreign capital. In this experiment (cases 5 and 5A), a policy of capital Ivorization is pursued (no capital outflow is allowed in the terminal year). With such a policy, a project as capital intensive as the iron mine is not profitable.

Sector Represented by an Optimizing Model

The iron mine was treated as a new sector and was fully incorporated into the central model. The rural sector was treated differently; it was analyzed with a separate optimizing model which is incorporated in an aggregated form into the central model. The process of aggregation, which defines the linkage between sector and center, is illustrated by Figure 15.6.

As in the case of the previous diagrams, it will be assumed that, between sector and center, foreign exchange is the only common product and labor the only common resource. In addition to labor, the rural sector uses several other resources, such as land and water of given specifications in given regions. These other resources are called sector-specific, because they cannot be used outside of the rural sector. The central planner does not need to know about the sector-specific resources. The only information he requires from the sector is the rural efficiency frontier MN_1N_2; this curve defines the quantity of labor needed by the rural sector to earn foreign exchange. With the Dantzig and Wolfe algorithm, this information is acquired through a series of iterations between the sectoral and the central models.

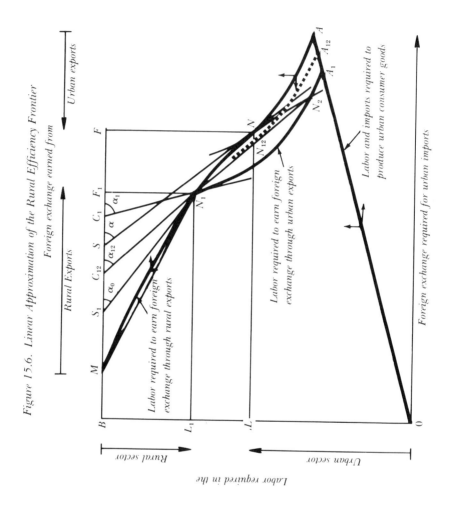

Figure 15.6. Linear Approximation of the Rural Efficiency Frontier

In the first iteration, the sectoral model is solved with a ratio between the shadow prices of foreign exchange and labor equal to *tan* α_0. This sectoral solution defines the coordinates of point N_1. The maximand of the rural model measures the rent accruing to the resources specific to the sector (that is, land and water). Using the shadow price of foreign exchange as the numéraire, this rent is measured by MS_1. It is equal to the value (MF_1) of the foreign exchange earned minus the opportunity cost of labor (S_1F_1).[11]

In the first iteration, of the central model, the rural sector is incorporated into in the form of vector MN_1. The activity of this vector cannot exceed unity, which ensures that the sectoral constraints are satisfied. No more land and no more water can be used than in the optimal solution of the rural model. In the optimal solution of the central model, the efficiency frontier is defined by $0A_1N_1M$. The ratio between the shadow prices of foreign exchange and labor is equal to *tan* α_1. Again using foreign exchange as the numéraire, the cost of labor employed in agriculture is measured by C_1F_1, while the rent accruing to the rural resources is equal to MC_1. The domestic resource cost of earning a unit of foreign exchange is higher in the urban sector (*tan* α_1) than in the rural sector (*tan* α_0). More labor resources should be allocated to the rural sector.

In the second iteration, the sectoral model is solved with a ratio between the shadow prices of foreign exchange and labor equal to *tan* α_1. This leads to a new sectoral solution defining the coordinates of point N_2. The rural sector is now represented in the central model by the old vector MN_1 plus the new vector MN_2. The sum of the weights applied to these two vectors cannot exceed unity, which once more ensures the feasibility of the rural constraints. This is equivalent to approximating the curvilinear rural efficiency frontier by the two linear segments MN_1 and N_1N_2. In the optimal solution of the central model, the shadow price ratio becomes *tan* α_{12} and the rent to rural resources becomes MC_{12}. From the first iteration to the second, consumption has risen by A_1A_{12}.

In the third iteration, the sectoral model is solved with a shadow price ratio equal to *tan* α_{12}. The point corresponding to this solution is not shown in Figure 15.6, because it practically coincides with N, the point of tangency between the rural and urban efficiency frontiers. At this point, the rates of substitution between labor and foreign exchange

---

11. S_1F_1 is equal to the number of workers employed, N_1F_1, multiplied by *cot* α_0, which is the exogenous value selected for the ratio between the shadow prices of labor and foreign exchange; it measures the efficiency wage when the shadow price of foreign exchange is used as the numéraire.

are the same (*tan* α) in the two sectors. Labor is optimally allocated, and consumption is maximized at level 0*A*. In the optimal solution of the central model, the rent accruing to rural resources is measured by *MS*, which is the value of the sectoral maximand arrived at by solving the sectoral model with the optimal shadow price ratio, *tan* α.

With a single resource (labor) and a single factor (foreign exchange), the convergence is quite fast. Instead of proceeding one step at a time as in the Dantzig-Wolfe algorithm, a linear approximation of the entire rural efficiency frontier can be incorporated into the central model from the start. With this procedure, a "nearly optimal" solution is obtained without any iterations.[12]

Suppose now that the sector and the rest of the economy share two resources (labor and capital) instead of a single one. The efficiency frontier of the rural sector becomes a surface in a three-dimensional space. The optimal allocation of labor and capital is reached at the point of tangency between two surfaces in a three-dimensional space. A projection of these surfaces on the two-dimensional space (labor and capital) is shown in the form of isoproduct curves in Figures 15.7 and 15.8. Along each curve, the amount of foreign exchange earned (or spent) remains constant, and the inputs of labor and capital are measured along the axes, which are arranged as in an Edgeworth-Bowley box.

In the case of Figure 15.7, there is a large scope for substitution between labor and capital, both within the sector and within the rest of the economy. The sectoral isoproduct curves (F_1^s), (F_2^s), and (F^s) define the various combinations of labor and capital which are required by the sector to earn the quantities of foreign exchange which were earned at points N_1, N_2, and N of Figure 15.6. For the rest of the economy, the isoproduct curves are represented in Figure 15.7 by broken lines without superscript, such as (F); they define the possibilities of substituting capital by labor without affecting the foreign exchange requirements. With a single common resource, convergence was reached at point N of Figure 15.6 by equalizing the transformation rate between labor and foreign exchange in the sector and in the rest of the economy. With two common resources, this procedure would generally lead to a point, N, of Figure 15.7, where the rates of substitution between labor and capital are not the same. Optimality would now be reached at a different point, N^*, arrived at by adjusting two price ratios simultaneously from one iteration to the next. Clearly the introduction of an additional resource reduces the speed of convergence of the

12. The error results from approximating the curvilinear segment N_1N_2 by a linear one. If the number of linear segments is sufficiently large, the error is negligible.

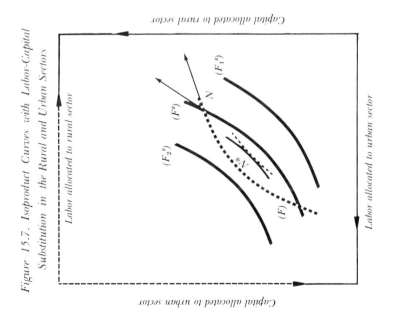

Figure 15.8. Labor-Capital Substitution in the Urban Sector Only

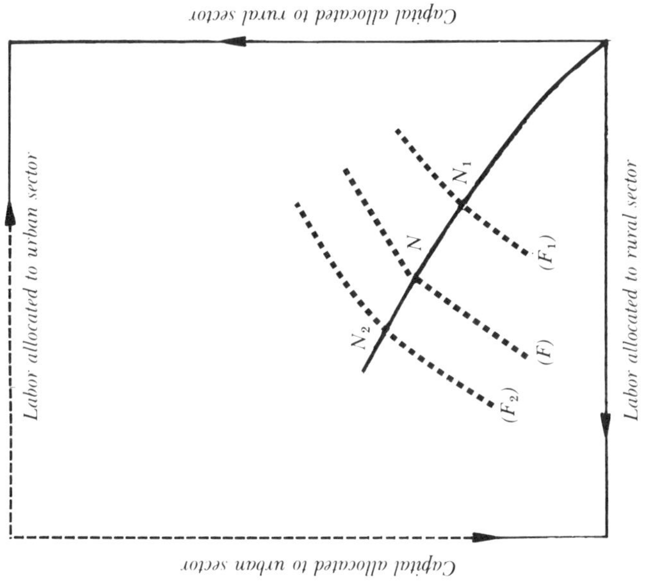

Figure 15.7. Isoproduct Curves with Labor-Capital Substitution in the Rural and Urban Sectors

Dantzig-Wolfe algorithm. Because a new dimension is added to the sectoral efficiency frontier, more points (that is, more sectoral solutions) are required to provide a satisfactory approximation of this frontier.

Turn now to the case of Figure 15.8, where there is no way of replacing capital by labor in the sector. The sectoral isoproduct curve (F_1^s) of Figure 15.7 is reduced to dot N_1 in Figure 15.8. The ratio between the shadow prices of labor and capital is now measured by the tangent to curve (F_1) at point N_1, which characterizes the marginal rate of substitution in the rest of the economy. Because this value does not affect the solution of the sectoral model, the number of iterations between sector and center needed for reaching convergence remains what it was in the case of a single common resource. By analogy, whenever the possibilities of substituting labor for capital in the sector are negligible in comparison with those existing in the rest of the economy, variations in the ratio between the shadow prices of labor and capital can also be neglected in linking the sectoral and central models.

This linkage procedure is efficient under two conditions. First, there are many sector-specific resources and many sectoral production activities; second, between the sector and the rest of the economy there are very few common resources and products, excluding those for which the scope for substitution within the sector is negligible. In this study, the first condition was fulfilled, but the second was not.

The efficiency of the linkage was improved by expressing intersectoral deliveries in terms of primary resources, as explained in Chapter 12. In addition, final consumer goods could have been expressed in terms of utility by incorporating in the rural model the part of the utility matrix dealing with food items. With this procedure, the agricultural model would have taken into account not only the impact of relative prices on the demand for agricultural products, but also the income effect resulting from the contribution of the agricultural sector.[13]

By combining these various devices, the linkage between sector and center can ultimately be expressed only in terms of utility and primary resources (labor, physical capital, savings, and foreign exchange). The number of common variables may nevertheless remain substantial if a distinction is made between various types of labor and capital. Fortunately, the number of independent price variables affecting the linkage is generally lower than the number of common rows, for two reasons: First, variations in some of the price variables are often closely

---

13. Incorporating a utility matrix into the sectoral model defines the numéraire. If there are n agricultural products with separable utilities, the number of price variables is thereby reduced by $n - 1$ (see Chapter 9).

correlated; for example, it could often be assumed for the sake of simplicity that wage variations are proportional for all types of skilled labor and that changes in rental values are also proportional for all types of capital stocks. Second, the scope for substitution between some of the resources may be negligible within a given sector; in such a case, alternative assumptions regarding the relative prices of these resources would not be required, since they would not affect the quality of the linkage.

The general principles of the linkage having been dealt with, its application can be examined by considering the numerical results obtained for two agricultural sectors, one in the south and the other in the north. Table 15.3 shows how sectoral output is divided between export commodities, row 1, and goods for final consumption, row 2. Shares are calculated for each year by combining primal and dual values of the central model solved under free-market policies. Commodities for export account for approximately 80 percent of agricultural production in the south but for less than 20 percent in the north (row 1). In the south, somewhat more than half of total production

Table 15.3. Composition of the Value of the Sectoral Output and of the Cost Imputed to the Resources Used (Free-Market Solution) [a]

	Rural south				Rural north			
Economic variable	*1975*	*1980*	*1985*	*1990*	*1975*	*1980*	*1985*	*1990*
Percentage of value of sectoral output								
1. Foreign exchange	84	86	76	76	9	17	18	18
2. Consumer goods	16	14	24	24	91	83	82	82
3. Output value = imputed returns[b]	100	100	100	100	100	100	100	100
4. Sectoral resources	55	60	50	56	1	23	44	40
5. Central resources	45	40	50	44	99	77	56	60
Percentage of total cost of central resources used by sectors								
6. Total cost of central resources used by sector[c]	100	100	100	100	100	100	100	100
7. Unskilled labor	38	37	33	41	54	43	36	33
8. Skilled labor	25	27	32	22	3	5	8	8
9. Urban capital	6	6	12	8	1	1	2	3
10. Capital goods	23	22	17	22	31	35	35	35
11. Imports	8	8	6	7	11	16	19	21

a. Based on solution $F1$; see Table 6.17.

b. Row 1 + row 2 = row 3 = row 4 + row 5.

c. Row 6 = row 7 + row 8 + row 9 + row 10 + row 11. All minor intermediate inputs are expressed in terms of primary resources in the central model (see Chapter 12) and appear here in rows 7, 8, 9, and 11. Major intermediate inputs, which consist mainly of capital goods, are treated as variables in the linkage (Chapter 12) and appear here in row 10.

costs are returns imputed to resources specific to the sector, such as
land and plantations (row 4); in the north, more than half of production costs are returns imputed to central resources (row 5).[14] The
decomposition of the central resource cost is itself shown in rows 7–11.
In the south, labor accounts for more than 60 percent of central
resource costs (rows 7 and 8). For the central planner, southern
agriculture could therefore be viewed primarily as a means for transforming labor into foreign exchange. This would, however, be a
simplification since capital goods together with rental values of urban
capacities account for almost 30 percent of the central resource cost.

Under free-market policies, the optimal solution of the central model
is a mix between two vectors which represent two different solutions of
the sectoral model of the south. In Figure 15.6, such a mix corresponds
to point N_{12}. In the case of the north, it is optimal to use a single
sectoral solution, which corresponds to the corner solution N_1 of Figure
15.6. When the central model is solved under different assumptions
regarding policies or external events, the optimal mix between sectoral
solutions does not remain the same; the changes are shown in rows 1–4
of Table 15.4. Also, the share of the return imputed to sectoral
resources varies; this share, expressed as a fraction of the maximand, is
given in rows 5 and 6.

The impact of imposing tariffs on manufactures appears from a
comparison between solutions $F1$ and $T1$ shown along the first and the
sixth columns. With tariffs, it is optimal to reduce the weight applied to
the high production vector from 0.71 to 0.11;[15] at the same time, the
rent accruing to southern resources declines from 0.50 to 0.36. The
sum of the weights applied to the north vector falls from 1.00 to 0.98; 2
percent of the resources in the north remain unused, and the imputed
return on the resources of the north falls from 0.019 to zero.

The impact of a reduction of 10 percent in the price of agricultural
exports can be seen by comparing solutions $F4$ and $F8$ along the third

14. This fraction corresponds in Figure 15.6 to the ratio between MS and MF. The
sum of the discounted returns on sector-specific resources for all years is given by the
dual value of the constraint expressing the fact that the sum of the weights applied to
the three sectoral solutions cannot exceed unity. The decomposition of this rent by
years was obtained by premultiplying the selected linear combination of the quantity
column vector of the primal solution by the price row vector of the dual solution. The
rent accruing to the sectoral resources during any given year is obtained as a residual
between the value of the output and that of the central resources. Values referring to
the postterminal period are not shown in Table 15.3.

15. In Figure 15.6, the weight applied to the high-production vector is measured
by the ratio between $N_{12}N_1$ and N_1N_2. The effect of the tariff is to move the
equilibrium point N_{12} toward N_1.

Table 15.4. *Impact of Policies or Events on Weights Applied to Sectoral Vectors and Rent Accruing to Sectoral Resources*[a]

Policy or event	Case							
	F1	F2	F4	F5	F8	T1	T2	T4
Modifications in relation to free market								
Tariffs on imports of manufactures						X	X	X
Employment program in the North		X						
Excise tax and subsidies			X	X	X			
Intermediate import-substitution			X	X	X	X	X	X
Saving constraint				X				
Restriction on borrowing from abroad					X			
Grant							X	
Decline in prices for agricultural exports								
Weight applied to rural vectors								
1. Low production vector in south	0.29	0.26	0.37	0.91	0.50	0.89	1.00	1.00
2. High production vector in south	0.71	0.74	0.63	0.09	0.50	0.11		
3. Low production vector in north	1.00	1.00	1.00	1.00	1.00	0.98	0.99	1.00
4. High production vector in north								
Rent accruing to sectoral resources as fraction of maximand								
5. South	0.501	0.473	0.503	0.501	0.469	0.357	0.328	0.486
6. North	0.019	0.001	0.017	0.009	0.013			0.013
Reduction (−) of the maximand as a fraction of the value in the free market case	0.000	−0.009	−0.008	−0.029	−0.061	−0.046	+0.007	−0.063

a. Based on eight solutions of the central model; see Table 6.17.

and the fifth columns. With lower agricultural prices, less weight is applied to the high production vector in the south (0.50 compared with 0.63) and the rent accruing to rural resources decline both in the south (from 0.503 to 0.469), and in the north (from 0.017 to 0.013).

The impact of a grant can be assumed by comparing solutions $T1$ and $T2$. With the grant, the shadow price of foreign exchange declines; the weight applied to the high production vector of the south falls (from 0.11 to zero) as well as the rent accruing to the southern resources (from 0.357 to 0.328). A constraint on savings (column $T4$ compared with $T1$) also reduces agricultural production in the south; because the capital invested in plantations becomes more valuable, however, this time the rent accruing to southern resources rises.

These few examples show what is gained from the linkage. Without linkage, the sectoral optimizing model is solved for various values of the shadow prices of the central variables. If the price combinations used for solving the sectoral model are not based on an economywide model, there is no clear economic interpretation of the differences found between sectoral solutions. With linkage, the operation is decomposed in three steps. In the first step, the various combinations of central prices are selected only with a view to providing the compact sectoral formulation which is incorporated in the central model. In the second step, the central model is solved for various policy options. A given set of shadow prices for the central resources is associated with each option. In the third step, the sectoral model is solved with these price sets; each sectoral solution then reflects a given policy option.

The Sector Represented by a Consistency Model

The preceding section started from an optimizing model of the sector. The problem was to link it with an optimizing model for the rest of the economy. If the sectoral model had been sufficiently small, it would have been possible to incorporate it directly into the central model. Because the sectoral model was too large, however, only an aggregated version of it was incorporated into the central model. This aggregated version was the multidimensional surface defining the possibilities of substituting central resources (or products) within the sector.

This section starts from an urban model in which there is no choice among alternative production technologies. In fifty-eight branches, there is no make-or-buy choice either. In the remaining fourteen branches, there is a choice between producing and importing. As a result, the input-output matrix consists of seventy-two rows and eighty-six columns for each decision year. If this matrix had been incorporated into the central optimizing model, the exact solution would have been obtained. Because the unaggregated urban matrix has been replaced by its reduced form corresponding to three make-or-buy choices, the solution arrived at is suboptimal. The concern here is to determine the significance of this loss of optimality.

In order to remain with the simple diagrammatical representation, assume that labor and foreign exchange are the only two primary resources used by the urban sector. Assume initially that final demand consists of a single good. The reduced-form matrices corresponding to the two extreme make-or-buy choices define the ratios between labor and foreign exchange requirements (*tan* α_p and *tan* α_m in Figure 15.9). If the same output can be produced with vectors $0A_p$ and $0A_m$, the isoproduct curve corresponding to a linear combination of these two vectors is linear segment A_mA_p. Vector $0A_m$ is the supply activity when import is the source of supply for the fourteen branches in which there is a make-or-buy choice. Vector A_mA_p is the import-substitution activity. Along this vector, imports are replaced by goods produced locally at the same rate in each of the fourteen branches in which there is a choice. The solution of the central model corresponds to point A, where the urban import-substitution line, A_mA_p, is tangent to the rural efficiency frontier, R.

With the unaggregated model, make-or-buy choices could have been combined in all possible ways among the fourteen branches for which such a choice exists. The isoproduct curve would then have been represented by A_mEA_p, which defines the true efficiency frontier of the urban sector. Along frontier A_mEA_p, comparative advantages among the fourteen branches are fully exploited, while along linear segment A_mA_p they are not. The shaded area between the true frontier and the linear segment defines the optimality loss attached to the aggregation procedure. With the unaggregated model, it would have been possible to shift the urban isoproduct curve upward from A_pEA_m to $A_p'E'A_m'$. The optimal level of consumption would then have been measured by $0A_p'$ instead of $0A_p$. The relative loss of consumption caused by our aggregation procedure is measured by $A_pA_p'/0A_p'$.

Because there are eighteen different types of final demand instead of a single one, the optimality loss is smaller than it appears to be in Figure 15.9. This is illustrated in Figure 15.10, in which the existence of two types of final demand, one for clothing (c) and the other for housing (h), is recognized. The maximum-import policy is represented by vector $0A_{mc}^{mh}$; the two types of final demand are satisfied by importing all direct and indirect inputs, whenever there is a make-or-buy choice.

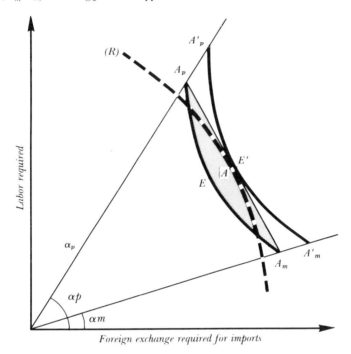

Figure 15.9. True Import-Substitution Frontier (A_pEA_m) and Its Linear Approximation (A_pA_m) with a Single Final Demand, Consumption Loss $(A_mA'_m)$ Resulting from the Approximation

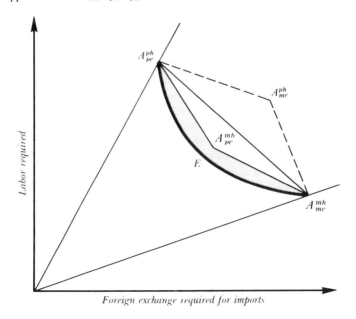

Figure 15.10. True Import-Substitution Frontier $(A_{mc}^{mh}EA_{pc}^{ph})$ and Its Linear Approximation $(A_{mc}^{mh}A_{pc}^{mh}A_{pc}^{ph})$ with Two Final Demands (c and h)

The maximum-production policy corresponds to vector $0A_{pc}^{ph}$; all direct and indirect inputs are produced, whenever there is a choice. In addition to these two extreme policies which were already available in Figure 15.9, there are two new intermediate policies. One is to import all direct and indirect inputs for satisfying the final demand for household goods and to produce all direct and indirect inputs for satisfying the demand for clothing; it corresponds to point A_{pc}^{mh}. The other is to do the opposite (importing in the case of clothing and producing in the case of household goods); it corresponds to point A_{mc}^{ph}.

Vector $A_{mc}^{mh}A_{pc}^{mh}$ is an import-substitution activity; the imports of all direct and indirect inputs used in supplying clothing for final consumption are replaced by domestic production, whenever there is a make-or-buy choice. Vector $A_{mc}^{mh}A_{mc}^{ph}$ defines another import- substitution activity dealing with direct and indirect inputs required for supplying household goods for final consumption. These two import-substitution activities will generally have different domestic resource costs per unit of foreign exchange saved. The one with the lower cost (that is, the vector making the lower slope with the horizontal) defines a section of the efficiency frontier; the other is rejected as being inefficient. The second section of the efficiency frontier is vector $A_{pc}^{mh}A_{pc}^{mh}$; its slope generally differs from that of vector $A_{mc}^{mh}A_{mc}^{mh}$, because the cost of producing a commodity with domestically produced inputs is generally not the same as the cost of producing the same commodity with imported inputs.

With two types of final demand, the true efficiency frontier is approximated by two linear segments in Figure 15.10. With eighteen types of final demand, it is approximated by eighteen linear segments in the central model. For the sake of simplicity, these eighteen segments are represented in Figure 15.11 by smooth curve A_pAA_m, which is inside the true efficiency frontier, A_pEA_m, of Figure 15.12. The optimal solution of the central model corresponds to A, the point of tangency between A_pAA_m (the urban "quasi-efficiency" frontier) and $A_p'AA_m'$ (the rural efficiency frontier). With the shadow price structure prevailing in the optimal solution, the cost of the maximum import-substitution policy exceeds its return $(0A)$ by Ap; the cost of the minimum import-substitution policy exceeds its return $(0A)$ by Am. The curvature of the urban quasi-efficiency frontier can be measured by $Am/0A$ and $Ap/0A$. Table 15.5 provides a numerical illustration based on two solutions of the central model for which only the two extreme import-substitution policies were retained. The curvature is captured by selecting the optimal mix of

*Figure 15.11. Cost Differentials (A_m and A_p) between the Optimal Mix (OA)
and the Two Extreme Import-Substitution Procedures (OA_m and OA_p)*

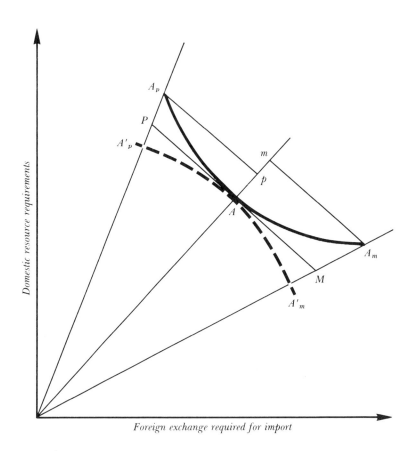

Foreign exchange required for import

import-substitution policies in supplying the eighteen items of final
demand. In both solutions reported in Table 15.5, full import
substitution is optimal for supplying nine items of final demand,
partial import substitution for one, and no import substitution for
the remaining eight.

The cost differential is somewhat higher for the maximum import-
substitution policy than for the minimum one. This implies nothing,
however, about the relative merits of the two policies. If production
were used as the source of supply whenever there was a choice, the

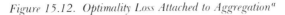

Figure 15.12. Optimality Loss Attached to Aggregation^a

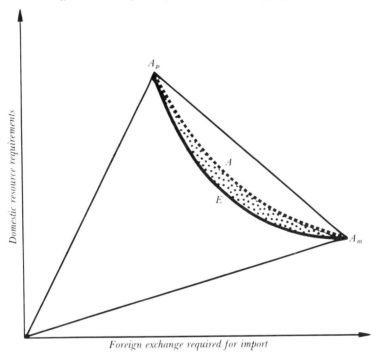

Foreign exchange required for import

a. *Quasi-efficiency frontier in central model (A_mAA_p); true efficiency frontier in unaggregated model (A_mEA_p).*

Table 15.5. Loss Attached to Nonoptimal Make-or-Buy Choices[a]
(Percentage cost increment valued at prices prevailing
with optimal solution)

Activity	Figure 15.11	Case F1	Case 1
		Percentage loss	
Optimal mix	zero	0.0	0.0
Maximum import	$Am/0A$	1.0	1.2
Maximum production	$Ap/0A$	0.7	0.5

a. Losses are measured in relation to optimal solutions of the central model, which correspond respectively to cases F1 and 1 as defined in Tables 6.17 and 6.18.

equilibrium point would move from A to A_p', and the consumption loss would be $A_p'A_p/0A_p$ (instead of the cost increase $PA_p/0A_p$ measured in Table 15.5). Alternatively, if import were selected as the source of supply whenever there was a choice, the consumption loss would be $A_m'A_m/0A_m$. Whether the loss would be greater in one case or in the other would depend on the relative curvatures of the two efficiency frontiers.

A linear combination of the two extreme import-substitution policies captures part of the curvature of the true efficiency frontier when there are many final demand items; it does not, however, capture all of it. The quality of the approximation can be improved (but can never be made worse) by adding an intermediate import-substitution policy, since the efficiency frontier is approximated by thirty-six linear segments instead of eighteen. The comparison between cases $F3$ and $F4$ shows that the quality of the approximation is somewhat improved by adding that intermediate policy; the value of the maximand increases almost 1 percent.

The aggregation procedure followed leads to the quasi-efficiency frontier A_mAA_p of Figure 15.12. In relation to the true efficiency frontier A_mEA_p, it introduces an optimality loss represented by the shaded area. This loss is, however, a small price to pay for reducing the size of the central optimizing model.

Because all resources used by the urban activities are treated as central rows, there is no need to introduce restrictions on the activity levels of the urban vectors in the central model. Such a restriction had to be made in the case of the rural vectors because only some of the resources used by rural activities were included in the central model. The part of the rural model incorporated into the central model may be visualized as the tip of the iceberg; it consists of the central resources inputs and the utility output. The bulk of the iceberg, which accounts for the constraints on the resources specific to the rural sector (land, water, and the like), is replaced by the single constraint placed on the weights applied to the rural vectors; the dual value of that constraint measures the rent imputed to the resources specific to the rural sector.

Conclusion

Decomposing an economywide model into sectoral components can be a programming device for testing each of the components separately before assembling them. More important, it can be an institutional device for decentralizing responsibilities among various planning groups. If the planning unit in charge of a sector can experiment with the sectoral component of the economywide model, this unit is likely to become more involved in the elaboration of the model and in its utilization. If the sectoral component is constructed by the planning unit in charge of the sector, the involvement becomes even greater. The sectoral components can be assembled, however, only if a minimum of uniformity has been enforced. Not all models need to be of the optimizing type simply because the central model is. In this system, a consistency model of the urban sector is incorporated into the central optimizing model. What is essential is to ensure strict uniformity in the treatment of the resources and products linking the various components of the economywide model.

In a system with variable prices, sectoral models can be linked together successfully only if the number of links is sufficiently small. For this reason, the links have been expressed here essentially in terms of primary resources and utility (which is treated here as the final output). Assume, for the sake of illustration, that foreign exchange, labor, capital, and utility are the four links between five sectors. In its simplest form, the central model could be represented by a table of four rows representing the links and five columns representing the sectors. This simple table makes it possible to compute the total output, expressed here in terms of utility, and to compare, for each primary resource, the sum of the sectoral requirements to national availability. If requirements exceed availability for even one resource, the combination of the five sectoral solutions is not feasible and at least one of the sectoral proposals has to be scaled down. By trial and error, a number of feasible combinations can be identified and classified according to their efficiency, which is measured here by the level of utility. The central optimizing model could therefore be visualized as the instrument for proceeding systematically to the selection of the most efficient combination.

In a less simplistic fashion, the central model can be visualized as the aggregated form of an economywide model which is too large to be solved at once. Solving the central model and the nonaggregated economywide models sequentially approximates the solution of the nonaggregated economywide model. This approximation would be satisfactory if the aggregated sectoral matrices used as components of the central model were to represent the possibilities of substitution among central resources within each sector faithfully. In such a case, the shadow prices (or quantities) arrived at by solving the central model under a given set of policies could be used to solve the nonaggregated sectoral models, and the error resulting from this two-level programming procedure would not be of practical significance.

Appendix. The Programming Model Associated with the Diagrammatic Representation

The programming model on which Figure 15.1 was based is specified in Table 15.6. In the northwest corner of the table, the utility matrix links the consumption balance (row 2) to the maximand (row 1) by transforming quantities consumed into utility of consumption. Next to this matrix (which was spelled out in Table 9.1) are four production activities. One ($j = 0$) deals with the production of consumer goods, and the other three ($j = 1, 2,$ and 3) refer to the production of export goods. The penultimate column gives the constant term appearing in the righthand side of the constraint. The last column, which does not belong to the matrix, shows the dual value of the constraint. Row 1 defines the maximand; rows 2, 3, and 4 are the consumption, labor, and foreign-exchange balances; rows 5, 6, and 7 express the fact that exports cannot exceed specified limits. The notations are:

$X_j(j = 0, 1, 2, 3)$	Activity level
$X_0(j = 0)$	Level of activity producing consumer goods
$X_j(j = 1, 2, 3)$	Level of activities producing export goods
$l_j(j = 0, 1, 2, 3)$	Direct and indirect labor required for producing a unit of consumer or export goods
$m_0(j = 0)$	Direct and indirect foreign exchange required for producing a unit of consumer goods
$m_j(j = 1, 2, 3)$	Foreign exchange earned per unit of goods exported, net of the direct and indirect imports associated with the production of the exported goods
$\bar{L}$	Availability of labor resources
$\bar{F}$	Exogenous allocation of foreign exchange

$\bar{X}_j(j = 1, 2, 3)$ Upper bounds to export activities

Π_0 Marginal value of a unit of consumption

Π_λ Marginal return imputed to a unit of labor

Π_f Marginal return imputed to a unit of foreign exchange

$\Pi_j(j = 1, 2, 3)$ Imputed rent per unit of export

where $X_j \geq 0$, $\Pi \geq 0$, $l_j > 0$ and $m_j > 0$.[16]

The three dual equations corresponding to positive activity levels and the equality between maximand and minimand can be written:

Consumption

(15.0) $$-l_0\Pi_\lambda - m_0\Pi_f + \Pi_0 = 0$$

First export activity at its upper bound

(15.1) $$-l_1\Pi_\lambda + m_1\Pi_f - \Pi_1 = 0$$

Second export activity at a positive level below the upper bound

(15.2) $$-l_2\Pi_\lambda + m_2\Pi_f = 0$$

Table 15.6. The Model Associated with Figure 15.1

	Production activities				Right-hand side	Dual values
	Consumer goods	Export goods				
Consumption activities	X_0	X_1	X_2	X_3		
1. $\boxed{\begin{array}{c}+\cdots+\\ \mathbf{U} \\ -\cdots-\end{array}}$						Maximand
2.	$+1$				≥ 0	Π_0
3.	$-l_0$	$-l_1$	$-l_2$	$-l_3$	$\geq -\bar{L}$	Π_λ
4.	$-m_0$	$+m_1$	$+m_2$	$+m_3$	$\geq -\bar{F}$	Π_f
5.		$+1$			$\leq \bar{X}_1$	$-\Pi_1$
6.			$+1$		$\leq \bar{X}_2$	$-\Pi_2$
7.				$+1$	$\leq \bar{X}_3$	$-\Pi_3$

16. In Figure 15.1, the primal and dual variables satisfied

$$X_0 > 0, X_1 > 0, X_2 > 0, X_3 = 0$$

$$\Pi_0 > 0, \Pi_\lambda > 0, \Pi_f > 0, \Pi_1 > 0, \Pi_2 = \Pi_3 = 0.$$

Maximand + minimand = 0

(15.3) $$\bar{L}\,\Pi_\lambda + \bar{F}\,\Pi_f + X_1\Pi_1 - X_0\Pi_0 = 0$$

Angle α_j in Figure 15.1 is defined by:

(15.4) $$tan\ \alpha_j = \frac{l_j}{m_j}.$$

Combination of equations (15.2) and (15.4) shows that, for the marginal export activity ($j = 2$),

(15.2') $$tan\ \alpha_2 = \frac{\Pi_f}{\Pi_\lambda} = \frac{shadow\ price\ of\ foreign\ exchange}{shadow\ price\ of\ labor}$$

The combination of equations (15.0), (15.1), (15.2), and (15.4) gives:

(15.0') $$\frac{\Pi_f}{\Pi_0} = \frac{tan\ \alpha_2}{m_0(tan\ \alpha_0 + tan\ \alpha_2)}\ \text{and}$$

(15.1') $$\frac{\Pi_1}{\Pi_0} = \frac{m_1\ tan\ \alpha_2 - tan\ \alpha_1}{m_0\ tan\ \alpha_0 + tan\ \alpha_2}.$$

With the notations used in Figure 15.1,

$$tan\ \alpha_0 = \frac{NM}{0N}, \qquad\qquad tan\ \alpha_2 = \frac{NM}{NH},$$

$$0N = (m_0)(0M), \quad\text{and}\quad 0H = 0N + NH.$$

It follows that:

$$0H = (m_0)(0M)\left[1 + \frac{tan\ \alpha_0}{tan\ \alpha_2}\right]\ \text{and}$$

$$\frac{0M}{0H} = \frac{tan\ \alpha_2}{(m_0)(tan\ \alpha_0 + tan\ \alpha_2)}.$$

From (15.0') and (15.2'), the result is that:

(15.5) $$\frac{\Pi_f}{\Pi_0} = \frac{0M}{0H}\ \text{and}$$

(15.6) $$\frac{\Pi_\lambda}{\Pi_0} = \frac{0M}{0K}.$$

Dividing (15.1′) by (15.0′) gives:

$$\Pi_1 = (m_1) \left(\frac{\tan \alpha_2 - \tan \alpha_1}{\tan \alpha_2} \right) (\Pi_f), \quad \text{or}$$

$$\Pi_1 = \left(\frac{CE}{A_1 A_2} \right) \left(\frac{CD}{CE} \right) (\Pi_f), \quad \text{or}$$

it follows that:

(15.7) $$\frac{\Pi_1}{\Pi_f} = \frac{CD}{A_1 A_2} .$$

Equation (15.3) giving the decomposition of the value of the maximand into returns imputed to factors can be rewritten as (15f) when the shadow price of foreign exchange is used as the numéraire:

(15f) $$\bar{L} \frac{\Pi_\lambda}{\Pi_f} + \bar{F} + X_1 \frac{\Pi_1}{\Pi_f} = X_0 \frac{\Pi_0}{\Pi_f} .$$

With the notations of Figure 15.1:

$$\bar{L} = HG, \bar{F} = BC, X_1 = A_1 A_2 \quad \text{and} \quad X_0 = 0M;$$

hence, equation (15f) can be rewritten as:

$$HG \frac{DG}{HG} + BC + A_1 A_2 \frac{CD}{A_1 A_2} = 0M \frac{0H}{0M} ,$$

(15f′) $$DG + BC + CD = BG.$$

Using the shadow price of labor as the numéraire, (15.4) can be rewritten as (15λ) and (15λ′):

(15λ) $$\bar{L} + \bar{F} \frac{\Pi_f}{\Pi_\lambda} + X_1 \frac{\Pi_1}{\Pi_\lambda} = X_0 \frac{\Pi_0}{\Pi_\lambda} ,$$

(15λ′) $$0B + BC' + C'K = 0K.$$

Using the shadow price of consumption as the numéraire and projecting $0K$ over $0M$ with *angle* α_2, (15.4) can be rewritten as:

(15.c) $$\bar{L} \frac{\Pi_\lambda}{\Pi_0} + \bar{F} \frac{\Pi_f}{\Pi_0} + X \frac{\Pi_1}{\Pi_0} = X_0,$$

(15.c′) $$0B* + B*C* + C*M = 0M.$$

The decomposition of the value of the maximand by returns imputed to factors can therefore be read along the horizontal axis, the vertical axis, or the consumption vector, depending on whether the shadow price of foreign exchange, labor, or consumption is used as the numéraire.

The relations between the values of the shadow prices and that of *angles* α_j is:

$$\Pi_j \geq 0 \Leftrightarrow \alpha_j \leq \alpha_2,$$

$$\Pi_f \gtrless \Pi_\lambda \Leftrightarrow \alpha_2 \gtrless 45°,$$

$$\Pi_f \gtrless \Pi_0 \Leftrightarrow \alpha_2 \gtrless 90° - \frac{\alpha_0}{2}, \text{ and}$$

$$\Pi_\lambda \gtrless \Pi_0 \Leftrightarrow \alpha_2 \lessgtr 45° - \frac{\alpha_0}{2}.$$

Chapter 16

The Urban Model

WITH PENNY DAVIS

THIS CHAPTER, in which the urban model is described, is divided into four sections. In the first, the three basic matrices of the disaggregated model are reviewed. In the second, the reduced form of the urban model is illustrated numerically. In the third, a consistency model of the urban sector alone is used to conduct a series of consistency tests regarding resource use, commodity balances, and profitability by industries. In the fourth, the solution of the consistency model of the urban sector alone is compared with the optimal solution of the economywide model.

The Disaggregated Matrices

As was explained in Chapter 12 and illustrated in Table 12.1, the disaggregated urban model basically consists of three matrices. The first, final-demand matrix **F**, defines the composition of eighteen types of final demand in terms of goods and services of the urban industries. The second, input-output matrix **I** − **A**, defines interindustry transactions within the urban sector. The third, resource matrix **R**, specifies resource requirements for each urban industry. The construction of the three matrices will be reviewed sequentially.

THE FINAL-DEMAND MATRIX

In the final-demand matrix, the rows correspond to the seventy-two urban industries and the columns to the eighteen types of final demand

*Table 16.1. Types of Final Demand for Urban Products (Columns of the **F** Matrix)*

Consumption by

Ivorians
1. Housing
2. Household durables
3. Transportation
4. Clothing
5. Processed food and beverages

Foreigners
6. Africans
7. Europeans

Public administration
8. Consumption
9. Nonproductive investment

Exports
10. Processed foods
11. Petroleum
12. Textiles
13. Miscellaneous products
14. Transfer products

Investment
15. Vehicles
16. Machinery
17. Construction

Service provided to the rural sector
18. Traditional commerce

listed in Table 16.1. The variables are the levels of the eighteen demand activities, which will be described briefly.

Private demand by Ivorians is optimized among eight groups of consumer goods and services. Only the five of those shown in Table 16.1 enter into matrix **F**. Their composition in products of the urban industries is given by the coefficients of the first five columns of the final-demand matrix. The next two columns (6 and 7) define the consumption patterns of non-Ivorian Africans and of European expatriates. Columns 8 and 9 give the composition of the demand of public administration for consumption and nonproductive investments.

Commodities exported by the urban sector are classified into five groups. The quantum of exports for each group is a variable optimized in the model, while the commodity mix within groups is given by the coefficients of columns 10–14.

The level of investments is also a choice variable in the model; a distinction must be made between the three types of investment goods (vehicles, machinery, and construction) shown under columns 15–17, but none needs to be made according to the destination of the investment (rural sector, urban industries, and so forth). Finally, the coefficients of column 18 define the urban goods and services required per unit of commercial services provided to the rural sector.

The coefficients of the final-demand matrix do not remain time invariant. On the one hand, the share of products originating from modern industries in relation to those from traditional ones increases over time. On the other, the share of noncompeting imports associated with final-demand activities declines linearly over time; it is 40 percent lower in 1990 than in 1975.

THE INPUT-OUTPUT MATRIX

The seventy-two columns of the input-output matrix may be classified into four categories. The first consists of thirty-seven production activities without competing import alternatives. Although a distinction is made between twenty-six modern industries and eleven traditional ones, no substitution is allowed among the products of these two types of industries; it is assumed that modern and traditional activities satisfy different types of demand. The second category covers fourteen commodities which can be produced domestically or imported. Consequently, each of these fourteen commodities can be supplied by either a production activity or an import activity. The third group covers ten commodities which can only be imported. Imports are linked to the level of production for the first eight and to consumption for the other two. The last group of eleven columns characterizes deliveries of agricultural raw materials from the rural to the urban sectors.

Input-output coefficients remain time invariant for fifty-six rows. They increase over time for twelve rows and decline for the eight remaining rows. Thus, industrial development is associated with larger input requirements for energy, chemicals, machinery, and plastics, but with lower requirements for wood and rubber products. The trend coefficients reflect the changes observed in other countries. Because three new industries are expected to be established after 1975, the size of the matrix increases over time.

For each decision year, three different input-output matrices are used (see Table 16.2). With the first, production is always used as the source of supply whenever there is a make-or-buy choice. With the second, import is the source of supply whenever there is a choice. With the third, production is the source of supply for some specified commodities and import for the others.

RESOURCE MATRIX **R**

A given industrial activity requires inputs from other industries; the input requirements per unit of output are the coefficients of the interindustry matrix $[I - A]$. That activity also requires labor, capital, and foreign exchange; the resource requirements per unit of output are the coefficients of the resource matrix **R**.

As shown along the rows of Table 16.3, a distinction is made among

*Table 16.2. Input-Output Activities (**I** − **A** Matrix)*

A. Production activities without competing import alternatives

1. Commercial fisheries
2. Flour milling
3. Bakery products
4. Preserved fish
5. Beer and soft drinks
6. Ice and refrigeration
7. Various food products (excl. sugar)
8. Tobacco and cigarettes
9. Electricity
10. Petroleum products
11. Water and gas
12. Mining (excl. iron ore)
13. Fertilizers
14. Wood products
15. Repair of vehicles
16. Phonograph records[a]
17. Thread and basic material
18. Clothing[a]
19. Leather goods and shoes
20. Plastic products and artificial fibres
21. Miscellaneous plastic articles[a]
22. Construction
23. Transportation
24. Rent
25. Services
26. Commerce
27. Traditional bakery products
28. Traditional furniture
29. Traditional repair of vehicles
30. Traditional machinery
31. Traditional clothing
32. Traditional leather products
33. Traditional handicrafts
34. Traditional construction
35. Traditional transport
36. Traditional services
37. Traditional commerce

B. Supply activities which can be satisfied either by production or by imports

1. First transformation of metals
2. Construction materials
3. Chemicals and pharmaceuticals
4. Furniture
5. Assembly of vehicles
6. Electrical and mechanical equipment
7. Agricultural machinery
8. Fabrics
9. Industrial textiles
10. Clothing
11. Refined vegetable oils
12. Rubber products
13. Paper products
14. Ceramics and glassware

C. Import activities without production alternatives

1. Wheat
2. Crude oil
3. Salt
4. Metals
5. Gypsum
6. Chemicals and drugs
7. Vehicle parts
8. Pulp
9. Alcoholic beverages
10. Miscellaneous products

D. Delivery of agricultural raw materials from the rural sector

1. Wood
2. Sugar
3. Tobacco
4. Maize
5. Cocoa
6. Rubber
7. Tubercule
8. Palm oil
9. Hides
10. Hard fibers
11. Pulp

a. These industries produce exclusively for foreign markets with foreign ownership of all imports except low-skilled labor.

eight skill categories of labor.[1] The coefficients of the labor rows measure for each national of a given skill the thousands of man-years required to produce CFAF1 million worth of output at 1970 prices. The values of these coefficients decline over time as the productivity of labor increases. For the three lowest categories, the productivity of labor rises 2 percent a year. For the other categories, the labor coefficients decline 43 percent between 1970 and 1990. The decline, which follows a learning curve, reflects a progressive closing down of the efficiency gap between nationals and expatriates. In 1970, labor efficiency is 75 percent higher for an expatriate than for a national belonging to the same category. By 1990, the difference has disappeared.

A distinction is made among nine stocks of physical capital. There is a single stock of vehicles, which can be used by any industry. Similarly, there is a single stock of buildings shared among all industries. In the case of machinery, however, a distinction is made among seven types of machinery equipment. Six of them are industry specific; the chemical and vehicles industries, for instance, require two different types of equipment. Because the one cannot be replaced by the other, the production of chemicals may be limited by the availability of installed capacity at a time when part of the equipment available to the vehicles industry remains idle. For all industries other than the six specified in Table 16.3, there is a single stock of equipment which can be used by any of them. The coefficients of the capacity rows are the familiar capital-output ratios which define the number of units of capital stock required per unit of output. These coefficients remain constant over time. As in the simplified model presented in Chapter 8, technological progress is assumed to be labor augmenting and not capital augmenting.

The next five rows deal with foreign exchange. The first two measure, at prices f.o.b., the export earnings forgone by the rural sector when agricultural products are delivered to the urban sector instead of being exported. In the rural sector, no distinction is made between what is sold to the urban sector and what is exported; the entire output is treated as exports valued f.o.b. In the central model, net exports are obtained by deducting the earnings forgone on account of sales to the urban sector from the gross exports of the rural sector. A special row had to be introduced for cotton, because it was not known a priori whether the Ivory Coast would be a net exporter or a net importer. By convention, cotton transactions in each sector are valued at prices f.o.b. If urban purchases exceed rural sales, however, the

---

1. The rows of the resource matrix, **R**, are the same as those of the reduced-form matrix, **D**, which is shown in Table 16.3.

Table 16.3. Supply Patterns of the Aggregated Urban Model, 1980

Row	$\mathbf{D}_p$ (produce whenever there is a choice)				
			Con-sumption by for-eigners	Domestic consumption	
	Invest-ment in vehicles	Export of textiles		House-hold durables	Trans-port
Labor					
1. Unskilled	−0.0506	−0.1545	−0.0725	−0.4709	−0.8852
2. Low-level skilled	−0.0649	−0.1815	−0.0397	−0.1106	−0.0749
3. Middle-level	−0.0412	−0.0297	−0.0266	−0.0311	−0.0526
4. Low-level clerical	−0.0141	−0.0248	−0.0109	−0.0199	−0.0193
5. Middle-level clerical	−0.0217	−0.0381	−0.0168	−0.0306	−0.0296
6. Middle-level technical	−0.0218	−0.0211	−0.0159	−0.0179	−0.0276
7. Professional	−0.0105	−0.0136	−0.0100	−0.0157	−0.0158
8. Senior staff	−0.0059	−0.0067	−0.0047	−0.0075	−0.0067
Capital stocks					
9. Vehicles	−0.0736	−0.0537	−0.0332	−0.0590	−0.1084
10. Construction	−0.2432	−0.4614	−0.4694	−0.4367	−0.3368
11. Machinery for construction	−0.0004	−0.0003	−0.0004	−0.0012	−0.0004
12. Machinery for chemicals	−0.0014	−0.0076	−0.0022	−0.0341	−0.0018
13. Machinery for vehicles	−0.1105	−0.0009	−0.0031	−0.0009	−0.0255
14. Machinery for machinery	−0.0067	−0.0067	−0.0104	−0.0530	−0.0053
15. Machinery for clothing	. . .	−0.1343	−0.0019	. . .	. . .
16. Machinery for rubber goods	−0.0112	−0.0007	−0.0019	−0.0009	−0.0336
17. Machinery for all other goods	−0.1180	−0.6021	−0.2506	−0.4684	−0.2727
Exports					
18. Proceeds (f.o.b.) forgone on cotton	. . .	−0.1145	−0.0026	−0.0003	−0.0001
19. Proceeds (f.o.b.) forgone on other inputs	−0.0259	−0.1651	−0.0176	−0.1173	−0.0169
Imports					
20. Costs (c.i.f.)	0.3902	0.0199	0.0655	0.1815	0.1092
21. Costs + tariffs on noncompeting imports	0.5069	0.0227	0.1017	0.2308	0.1277
22. Costs + tariffs on all imports	0.5069	0.0227	0.1017	0.2308	0.1277
Government revenues					
23. Including tariffs on noncompeting imports	0.1680	0.1132	0.0805	0.1356	0.2059
24. Including tariffs on all imports	0.1680	0.1132	0.0805	0.1356	0.2059

Table 16.3. (continued)

Row	$\mathbf{D}_m$ (import whenever there is a choice)				
				Domestic consumption	
	Invest- ment in vehicles	Export of textiles	Con- sumption by for- eigners	House- hold durables	Trans- port
Labor					
1. Unskilled	−0.0134	−0.0421	−0.0620	−0.4240	−0.0579
2. Low-level skilled	−0.0113	−0.0403	−0.0767	−0.0473	−0.0469
3. Middle-level	−0.0136	−0.0046	−0.0231	−0.0160	−0.0429
4. Low-level clerical	−0.0037	−0.0035	−0.0073	−0.0055	−0.0147
5. Middle-level clerical	−0.0056	−0.0054	−0.0112	−0.0085	−0.0225
6. Middle-level technical	−0.0077	−0.0041	−0.0134	−0.0089	−0.0229
7. Professional	−0.0039	−0.0017	−0.0073	−0.0047	−0.0121
8. Senior staff	−0.0021	−0.0009	−0.0033	−0.0023	−0.0048
Capital stocks					
9. Vehicles	−0.0444	−0.0140	−0.0311	−0.0488	−0.0994
10. Construction	−0.0909	−0.0979	−0.4143	−0.2607	−0.2539
11. Machinery for construction	. . .	. . .	. . .	. . .	. . .
12. Machinery for chemicals	. . .	. . .	. . .	. . .	. . .
13. Machinery for vehicles	. . .	. . .	. . .	. . .	. . .
14. Machinery for machinery	. . .	. . .	. . .	. . .	. . .
15. Machinery for clothing	. . .	. . .	. . .	. . .	. . .
16. Machinery for rubber goods	. . .	. . .	. . .	. . .	. . .
17. Machinery for all other goods	−0.0413	−0.1652	−0.2107	−0.2571	−0.2242
Exports					
18. Proceeds (f.o.b.) forgone on cotton	. . .	−0.0539	−0.0017	. . .	. . .
19. Proceeds (f.o.b.) forgone on other inputs	−0.0001	−0.0540	−0.0064	−0.0300	−0.0006
Imports					
20. Costs (c.i.f.)	0.6271	0.4349	0.1221	0.4859	0.2137
21. Costs + tariffs on noncompeting imports	0.7261	0.4683	0.1618	0.5612	0.2329
22. Costs + tariffs on all imports	0.8303	0.6871	0.1833	0.6696	0.2788
Government revenues					
23. Including tariffs on noncompeting imports	0.0703	0.0179	0.0647	0.0514	0.1730
24. Including tariffs on all imports	0.1743	0.2367	0.8620	0.1598	0.2189

balance must be met by a cotton-importing activity which has a foreign exchange cost equal to the difference between c.i.f. and f.o.b. prices.

There are three import rows because the model can be solved alternatively without tariffs, with the existing tariff structure, or with a different tariff structure. Without tariffs (free-trade policy), the only binding constraint is the row measuring imports at c.i.f. With tariffs, the row measuring imports at c.i.f. plus tariffs becomes the binding constraint, while that measuring imports at c.i.f. only is used to determine the balance of payments surplus or deficit as a slack in the iterative procedure described in Chapter 13. Because two different tariff structures are experimented with, there are two tariff rows, which may be used alternatively. Finally, revenues accruing to the treasury through tariffs and taxes are given in the last two rows, which correspond to the two alternative tariff policies.

All commodity balances are measured in the model at the retail level. The retail price is equal to the border price, plus tariffs and taxes, plus commercial margins (see Chapter 13). It follows that, for any importing activity, the sum of the coefficients in the input-output matrix (unity in the commodity-balance row minus trade margin in the commerce row) is equal to the sum of the coefficients of the resource matrix in the import row at c.i.f. and in the government-revenues row corresponding to the existing tariff structure.

The Reduced-Form Matrix

As explained in Chapter 12, when the input-output matrix is square, it can be inverted, and the resources required by type of final demand can be expressed in the compact form:

$$\mathbf{D} = \mathbf{R}(\mathbf{I} - \mathbf{A})^{-1}\mathbf{F}.$$

$$(r \cdot q) = (r \cdot n)(n \cdot n)(n \cdot q)$$

Because production and imports represent two alternative sources of supply for fourteen commodities, a choice has to be made between the production and the import vectors for supplying these commodities if the matrix $\mathbf{I} - \mathbf{A}$ is to remain square. Three choices, which correspond to three different import-substitution policies, were made. With the policy of maximum import substitution, the production vectors are used to supply the fourteen commodities for which a make-or-buy choice exists; the corresponding input-output and resource matrices are represented by $\mathbf{I} - \mathbf{A}_p$ and $\mathbf{R}_p$. With the opposite policy, the import vectors are used instead of the production vectors to supply fourteen commodities, and the two matrices become $I - A_m$ and R_m. Finally, with the intermediate policy, the production vectors are used for some of the fourteen supply activities and the import vectors for the others; the matrices are then represented by $I - A_i$ and R_i. The three corresponding reduced form matrices are calculated as:

$$D_p = R_p(I - A_p)^{-1}F,$$

$$D_i = R_i(I - A_i)^{-1}F, \text{ and}$$

$$D_m = R_m(I - A_m)^{-1}F$$

Whichever choice is made, the sizes of all matrices remain the same. The coefficients of the reduced-form matrix measure the resources needed directly or indirectly to supply one unit of each type of final demand. Their numerical values are given in Table 16.3 for five of the eighteen types of final demand. Matrix D_p corresponding to the maximum import-substitution policy is shown at the left, and matrix D_m corresponding to the trade opposite policy at the right. The D_p matrix is very dense; zero coefficients appear only in 3 percent of the cells. The D_m matrix is less dense; 28 percent of the coefficients have a zero value. In particular, the six rows measuring the machinery capacity required for six specified industries are all empty. This occurs because the products of these six industries can be either produced or imported. Clearly, if all vehicles are imported, no machinery equipment for producing vehicles is needed.

Per unit of vehicle imported, 0.22 unit of commercial services is needed, and this requires directly and indirectly labor inputs of various skill categories (coefficients in the eight top rows). When vehicles are produced at home instead of being imported, direct and indirect labor input requirements increase; moreover, eight capital stocks (instead of a single one) become directly or indirectly needed. As the foreign exchange cost declines to 0.4161 (= 0.0259 + 0.3902) from 0.6271, only a third of the foreign exchange import cost is saved by producing vehicles at home instead of importing them. If the production activity had been selected only for the vehicle industry, the foreign exchange savings would have been substantially less than a third, because the indirect import content of producing vehicles would have been higher.

The coefficients of the D matrix illustrated in Table 16.3 refer to the year 1980. Their values are different for other years. The variations over time result from labor-productivity gains in the R matrix, technological changes in the $I - A$ matrix, and modifications in the final demand mix in the F matrix. For this reason, the three matrices D_p and D_i and D_m had to be calculated for each of the years 1970, 1975, 1980, 1985, 1990, and 2000. The 1970 matrices were only used for consistency tests, while the matrices referring to the years 1975–90 were incorporated as such into the central model. The matrix referring to the year 2000 was used to calculate the postterminal matrix incorporated into the central model.

As explained in Chapter 8, the time horizon is truncated in 1990 by assuming that the economy will grow after that year at asymptotic rate $\hat{g}$. Investments made in 1990 must generate capacity increments sufficient for sustaining growth rate $\hat{g}$ after 1990. This is expressed in the model by stating that capacity increments between the years 1990 and 2000 must be sufficient to permit an increase in final demand during the same period, which is consistent with asymptotic growth rate $\hat{g}$. Increments in resource requirements are defined as:

(16.1) $$D_{2000}y_{2000} - D_{1990}y_{1990},$$

where y_{1990} and y_{2000}, final-demand vectors for the years 1990 and 2000, are related by:

(16.2) $$y_{2000} = (E\hat{g})y_{1990}.$$

$$(q \cdot 1) = (q \cdot q)(q \cdot 1).$$

The diagonal elements of square matrix $E\hat{g}$ measure, for each type of final demand, the ratio of the 2000 value to the 1990 value; nondiagonal elements are all zero. Replacing in (16.1) y_{2000} by its value from (16.2) gives:

(16.3) $$(D_{2000}E\hat{g} - D_{1990})y_{1990}.$$

$$[(r \cdot q)(q \cdot q) - (r \cdot q)](q \cdot 1).$$

Hence, the y_{1990} vector, which defines the activity variables in year 1990, affects the 1990 resource constraints through the coefficients of the D_{1990} matrix and the postterminal resource constraints through the coefficients of the postterminal matrix.

(16.4) $$D_{1990}^{2000} = D_{2000}E\hat{g} - D_{1990}.$$

$$(r \cdot q) = (r \cdot q)(q \cdot q) - (r \cdot q).$$

The asymptotic growth rate $\hat{g}$ is arrived at iteratively. In the first iteration, the postterminal matrix D is calculated from the E matrix associated with an a priori value $\bar{g}$ for postterminal growth. In the second iteration, calculation is repeated for a different value of the assumed postterminal growth rate.

In calculating the diagonal elements of the **E** matrix, the following assumptions are made: Total private consumption, public consumption, urban deliveries to the other sectors, and all types of investments increase at the given asymptotic growth rate $\bar{g}$; for each of the five commodity groups composed of urban goods and services, final per capita consumption increases according to given income-elasticity coefficients taken as representative for the period 1990–2000; exports increase at the rate $1.15\bar{g}$; the number of foreign agricultural workers remains in 2000 the same as in 1990, and wages increase 2 percent a year; the number of expatriates in 2000 is 75 percent of what it was in 1990.

The Urban Model Solved Alone

The reduced form of the urban sector was constructed to be a part of the central model. The urban model was also solved alone, however, and this led to useful tests of statistical consistency.

When the urban model is solved alone, demands for urban goods by other sectors become final demands for the urban sector. In the **F** matrix, five final-demand columns need to be added, two for the iron ore and Riviera complexes and three for the rural sectors (livestock, north, and south). The coefficients of these additional columns define the composition of the demand by other sectors in terms of goods and services produced by the urban sector.[2] The urban matrix thus expanded may be used to conduct several tests.

RESOURCE REQUIREMENTS

Given the value of the final demand vector, **y**, the resources required by the urban sector are calculated as:

$$\mathbf{Dy} = \mathbf{z}$$

$$(r \cdot q)(q \cdot 1) = (r \cdot 1).$$

For the year 1970, the results are summarized in Table 16.4 for three import-substitution activities. As the intermediate activity for 1970 corresponds approximately to the actual distribution between

---

2. In the central model, these demands are represented by the second term in the lefthand side of equation (12.4b).

Table 16.4. Resource Requirements for Various Urban Import Substitution
Activities, 1970

| Resources | Activity | | | Production/ Import Ratio |
	Production	Intermediate	Import	
Labor	*Thousands of persons*			
Unskilled	283.3	273.2	269.8	1.05
Medium skilled	62.1	43.8	38.5	1.61
High skilled	33.9	22.2	19.9	1.70
Capital	*Millions of CFAF*			
Vehicles	27.2	21.0	19.6	1.39
Construction	212.9	176.0	169.1	1.71
Machinery	131.6	88.6	76.9	1.71
Foreign exchange	65.9	97.3	101.3	.65
Public funds	49.9	53.0	54.9	.91

import and production, any large discrepancy between resource requirements thus calculated and estimates of actual resources used is indicative of statistical inconsistencies which must be corrected.

The possible scope for substitution between resources appears from a comparison of the requirements calculated under the two extreme choices. Thus, the last column of Table 16.4 shows that a third of the foreign exchange cost can be saved at the expense of a 70 percent increase in highly skilled labor and capital stocks (in the form of construction and machinery). Import substitution, on the other hand, hardly affects the demand for unskilled labor (5 percent), because the relevant commodities are produced by modern industries requiring little labor of the lowest category. As the two matrices $\mathbf{D}_p$ and $\mathbf{D}_m$ were postmultiplied by the same demand vector, $\mathbf{y}$, the comparison substantially overstates the scope for saving foreign exchange. Clearly, demand for investments in machinery and demand by expatriates should be higher under the production choice than under the import choice, and the import content of these two types of final demand is above average. Requirements should therefore have been recalculated with two different vectors $\mathbf{y}_p$ and $\mathbf{y}_m$.

CONSISTENCY OF THE COMMODITY BALANCES

The commodity balances for each urban industry are eliminated from the reduced form. Nevertheless, it is useful to ascertain that the implied balances correspond approximately to those observed in the base period by calculating:

(16.5) $(I - A_p)$ $x_p + B_m x_m = $ F   y   +   s.

$$(n \cdot n)(n \cdot 1) + (n \cdot 14)\,(14.1) = (n \cdot q)(q \cdot 1) + (n \cdot 1).$$

In equation (16.5), x_p is the vector of actual gross output by industries, x_m is the vector of actual imports for the fourteen products for which a make-or-buy choice exists, y is the vector of actual final demand, and s is a residual vector. Matrix B_m consists of the fourteen import activities which are replaced by production activities in the $I - A_p$ matrix.

Ideally, the residual vector, s, should consist only of zero coefficients. In practice, the average discrepancy could not be reduced below 1.5 percent, and substantially larger errors were found in some industries. This consistency check has proved quite useful and has permitted the correction of a number of statistical errors.

PROFITABILITY TESTS

By assigning a price to each resource, production costs may be calculated for each product and service of the urban sector from (16.6), and for each type of final demand from (16.7):

(16.6) $$PR(I - A)^{-1} = V.$$

$$(r \cdot r)(r \cdot n)(n \cdot n) = (r \cdot n).$$

(16.7) $$PD = V.$$

$$(r \cdot r)(r \cdot q) = (r \cdot q).$$

P is a square matrix that contains resource prices along the diagonal and zero coefficients elsewhere. The columns of the V matrix show the analysis of production costs. Adding up the coefficients in each column gives total production costs. In the absence of profits and statistical errors, costs would always add up to unity if each resource were paid for at the same price by all industries using it.

The results shown in Table 16.5 provide some idea of relative profitability. Modern commerce is at the top of the list, and mining (which excludes iron), at the bottom. The high profitability of the former does not seem to result from inaccuracy of the data, but rather from the semimonopolistic position of importers in the early 1970s. Part of this commercial margin was treated in the model as quasi tariff, and it was assumed that its level would decline progres-

Table 16.5. Profitability of Seventeen
Selected Industries, 1970

Industry	Private costs [a]
Modern commerce	0.551
Transformation of metals	0.867
Construction materials	0.882
Chemicals and pharmaceuticals	0.897
Fabrics	0.933
Machinery	0.952
Traditional construction	0.954
Refined vegetable oils	0.974
Rubber products	0.992
Clothing	0.996
Industrial textiles	1.034
Furniture	1.045
Modern construction	1.067
Assembly of vehicles	1.068
Paper products	1.084
Traditional commerce	1.210
Mining (excluding iron)	1.579

a. Private costs are calculated from equation (16.6) and expressed as a fraction of the market price, which is taken as unity in 1970.

sively as a result of greater competition. The low profitability of mining is a result of the high capital ratio prevailing in the industry and of the rate of interest selected (10 percent).

Consistency versus Optimization

When an input-output table already exists, it is useful to complement this source of information with a final-demand matrix and a resource matrix. These three matrices together provide a convenient framework for organizing statistical data. By simple matrix operations, a series of consistency tests can be conducted.

The inverted input-output matrix premultiplied by the resource matrix and postmultiplied by the final-demand matrix gives the reduced-form matrix, which expresses in compact form the relations between final demands and primary resources. Postmultiplying the reduced-form matrix by a final-demand vector gives the corresponding resource requirements. These can be calculated easily for many different final-demand vectors.

The traditional input-output table contains only production activities in the columns. There is no reason, however, for not treating import activities the same way as production activities, since the former use commercial services as inputs. If the matrix were to include two alternative activities for supplying the same commodity, the matrix would no longer be square and invertible. This is the reason for constructing several square matrices. With one, production activities are selected whenever there is a choice; with another, import activities are used instead. This leads to two reduced-form matrices. Postmultiplying them by appropriate final-demand vectors provides information on the scope for import substitution and on resource tradeoffs.

All these operations remain fairly simple and they provide a series of useful consistency tests. Going from such a consistency model to an optimizing one is a major step, especially if the optimizing model is dynamic. Because of the sizable number of resources and items of final demand, the idea of constructing an optimizing model for the urban sector alone did not appear to be promising. The required assumptions concerning the shadow prices of the resources and the levels of final demand would have been too numerous. The practical choice was bet•·een the simple urban-consistency model described in this chapter, and the economywide optimizing model described in other chapters of this volume.

A comparison is shown in Table 16.6 between a feasible solution

Table 16.6. *Feasible Solution of the Urban Consistency Model and Optimal Solution of the Central Model, Urban Sector, 1980*

Component of final production and total cost	Solution		Gain from optimization
	Feasible	Optimal	
	(1)	(2)	$100 \dfrac{(2) - (1)}{(1)}$
	(billions of CFAF)		(percent)
Final production of the urban sector (valued at base-year prices)			
Consumer goods for nationals	281.5	295.1	+4.8
Export goods	63.7	72.2	+13.3
Other goods	308.2	298.2	−3.2
Total	653.4	665.5	+1.8
Cost of production (valued at shadow prices of the optimal solution)	637.4[a]	604.3	−5.2

a. Cost calculated from equation (16.8).

of the urban consistency model and the optimal solution of the central model. The final-demand vector **y** is given in the consistency model, while it is optimized in the central model. Final demand is valued at base-year prices in the four top rows of Table 16.6. An analysis is made according to private consumption by nationals, exports, and others (consumption by foreigners and the public administration, investments, and deliveries to other sectors). In the bottom row, costs of production are valued at the shadow prices obtained in the optimal solution of the central model, and the amount of foreign exchange required by the urban sector is the same in both cases. With the urban consistency model, this is achieved by weighting appropriately the final-demand vectors associated with maximum and minimum import substitution as follows:[3]

$$\mathbf{y}_p = x\mathbf{y} \text{ and}$$
$$\mathbf{y}_m = (1 - x)\mathbf{y},$$

and by calculating costs as follows:

(16.8) $$\mathbf{C} = \mathbf{P} \ (\mathbf{D}_p \ \mathbf{y}_p + \mathbf{D}_m \ \mathbf{y}_m).$$
$$(r \cdot 1) = (r \cdot r)[(r \cdot q)(q \cdot 1) + (r \cdot q)(q \cdot 1)].$$

In equation (16.8), **y** is the given final-demand vector; **P** is the diagonal matrix defining the shadow prices; $\mathbf{D}_p$ and $\mathbf{D}_m$ are the reduced-form matrices associated with maximum production and maximum import.

As appears from the last column of Table 16.6, more is produced in the optimal solution (1.8 percent more at base-year prices) at a lower resource cost (5.2 percent less at dual prices). The optimal solution obtained after a few hundred iterations of the central model is more efficient than the consistency solution obtained through a single iteration. Nevertheless, the consistency solution may provide useful information to the planner, even if it is suboptimal.

---

3. Calling F the quantity of foreign exchange required in the optimal solution and F_p and F_m the amounts required for supplying final demand **y** with matrices $\mathbf{D}_p$ and $\mathbf{D}_m$, the weight x is calculated as follows:

$$x = (F_m - F)/(F_m - F_p).$$

Chapter 17

The Rural Sector

WITH RENÉ VAURS

A DESCRIPTION OF TWO REGIONAL MODELS not formally linked with the central model begins this chapter.[1] A one-period model of the north is used to study the relative profitability of animal and mechanical tractions in the savanna zone and to assess the scope for substitution between labor and capital in that region. A dynamic model of the southwest is used to assess relative profitability among tree crops for export and to analyze the optimal timing of planting. The scope of the two former models is then expanded so as to cover the full rural sector, and the chapter concludes with formal linkages between the rural sector and the rest of the economy.

Motorization or Animal Traction in the North

Cotton is one of the most promising speculations in the north of the Ivory Coast, and plans have already been made for expanding the domestic textile industry. Cotton can be grown in rotation with rice, and a good deal of experience has been gained on ways of improving cotton production in the savanna zone, both in the Ivory Coast and in neighboring countries. Without oxen or tractor power, cotton production is limited to the area that farmers can till during the short rainy season. This limitation could be removed by using animal or mechanical traction, which would permit the extension of farm sizes to about

---

1. A detailed description of the components of the agricultural models is given by René Vaurs, Henri Quaix, L. Guinard, and Jacques Loup in working papers listed under World Bank, Development Research Center, 1975 in the bibliography.

twenty hectares. Such a transformation would, however, require substantial public expenditures.

Three alternative technologies for producing cotton and rice have been identified. One is simply an improvement of traditional practices and does not require mechanical or animal traction. The other two use either oxen or tractors as the mode of traction. If the prices of all inputs and outputs were known unequivocally, it would be easy to calculate the costs and benefits attached to each alternative technology and to select the most profitable among them. A difficulty arises, however, from the seasonal nature of the cultural operations. Without traction, labor is fully employed during a few months of the year, but only partly employed during the other months. The use of animal or mechanical traction would substantially modify the seasonal pattern of employment and, consequently, the scarcity price of labor. The cost of using a tractor or a pair of oxen cannot be taken as a constant, however, since the weekly cost depends on the rate of utilization. If tractors or oxen were to be used only a few weeks each year, the average weekly cost could become prohibitive. To reduce costs, the cultivation of cotton has to be combined with that of other crops having peak requirements at different times in the year. Alternative cropping patterns must therefore be investigated before the most profitable way of growing cotton can be selected. Such an investigation is made by solving an optimizing model in which the cropping pattern is treated as a variable.

The objective is to maximize the value added in a given rural area, which is defined as the excess of the value of the commodities produced in that area over the cost of the inputs purchased from outside the area. For purchased inputs, such as fertilizers, the price is given. For resources tied to the area, such as land and water, the imputed rent is the variable which is maximized.

In the absence of labor mobility, the labor residing in the area would be treated in the same way as land. The shadow price of labor would then be equal to zero as long as some workers remained unemployed in the area, while it could become extremely high when all workers were employed. This excessive rigidity is avoided by recognizing the existence of seasonal migrations and introducing a reservation price for labor. For each month of the year, the supply of labor is given by an upward sloping curve. The lower segment of the curve reflects different preferences for leisure among various population groups residing in the area. The middle segment of the curve reflects the choice of the male adults residing in the area between working in their village and migrating seasonally to the south, where salaries are higher. The upper segment of the curve reflects similar preferences on the part of workers from neighboring countries. During peak periods, wages in the area may become high enough to attract foreigners to work there.

Regarding tractors and oxen, the problem of seasonality is solved by considering an imaginary pool. In a given year, the size of the pool can be enlarged by purchasing any number of tractors and oxen at fixed prices. The size of the pool cannot, however, be modified during the course of the year. All tractors (or oxen) belonging to the pool incur a maintenance cost throughout the year, while they incur an operating cost, such as gasoline (or additional feeding), only when they are used.

The northern region is divided into three districts. Within each district, perfect mobility is assumed. Between districts, seasonal mobility is restricted to male adults and to tractors. Taking into account seasonal migrations clearly increases the size of the model. As shown in Table 17.1, the monthly constraints on unskilled labor, tractors, and oxen account for more than 80 percent of the total number of rows.

The results of the model are illustrated by a comparison among three different ways of growing cotton. Rows 1 and 2 of Table 17.2 give the output per hectare; cotton and rice have to be produced jointly because they alternate with fallow years on the same piece of land. Rows 3 to 5 specify the amounts of labor and traction required per hectare. For all inputs other than land, labor and traction, costs

Table 17.1. Static Model of Agriculture in the North
(Number of rows or columns)

Constraint or activity	Rows	Columns
Land	16	15
Labor		
Annual unskilled	24	2
Monthly unskilled	96	180
Skilled	7	7
Investment		
Traction	39	3
Other	5	5
Nonagricultural resources	3	3
Production activities		90
Demand constraints	11	11
Total	191	316

Table 17.2. Alternative Technologies for Producing Cotton and Rice in the North

Item	Human	Oxen	Tractors
		Type of traction	
Output (tons per hectare)			
1. Cotton	0.39	0.51	0.51
2. Rice	1.08	1.20	1.08
Inputs with endogenous prices			
3. Unskilled labor *(working days per hectare)*	258	180	185
4. Oxen *(number per hectare)*	. . .	0.4	. . .
5. Tractors *(hours per hectare)*	. . .	. . .	17
Inputs purchased at fixed prices (thousands of CFAF*)*			
6. Purchased by farmers	10.9	21.4	19.4
7. Purchased by government agencies	3.6	6.0	14.0
8. Purchased by processing firms	27.9	31.9	30.0
Social profit (thousands of CFAF*)* [a]			
9. Exporting cotton and importing rice	62	59	38
10. Importing cotton and rice	69	64	48
11. Importing cotton and exporting rice	59	57	36

a. Output valued f.o.b. or c.i.f. depending on assumptions made in rows 9 to 11, less expenditures on labor, oxen, and tractors (rows 3–5) valued at the shadow prices of the northern model, less other expenditures valued at fixed prices (rows 6–8).

can be aggregated in terms of CFAF since prices are given. In rows 6–8, a distinction is made between the costs covered by the farmers (such as fertilizers and light equipment), those paid by the government in the form of subsidies or salaries to extension agents, and the cost of processing and marketing.

Profits are calculated in rows 9 to 11 by selecting alternatively each of the three ways of growing cotton and making three different assumptions regarding prices of cotton and rice. In row 9, cotton is valued f.o.b. and rice c.i.f., assuming that the Ivory Coast will have (as in the past) an export surplus for the former and an import deficit for the latter. In row 10, cotton is valued c.i.f. on the assumption that production in the north will not increase sufficiently to satisfy the needs of the expanding domestic textile industry. In row 11, cotton is valued c.i.f., but rice is valued f.o.b., which supposes that the trade pattern is reversed.

Tractor technology appears to be the least profitable under any assumption because the average price per tractor-hour is high on account of the low rate of use; it turned out to be 2.7 times as high as the price charged at the time by the state agency. On the other hand, profits scarcely decline with the use of oxen, which are fed to a large extent from fallow crops. Because a fraction of the land has to lie fallow each year, the cost of maintaining oxen is not prohibitive, even if they work only part of the year. In addition, traction by oxen would be a step toward mix farming, which is generally considered desirable for this region.

When cotton can be grown in any of the three ways outlined in Table 17.2, a mix between the three technologies is generally optimal. Without imposing a minimum income target on the north, the optimal number of tractors is low. When a minimum-income target is imposed on the north as a whole, tractor technology is more profitable in the Bouaké area, where there are two rainy seasons, than in the Korhogo area, where there is a single rainy season. A program aiming at a better distribution of income between north and south may therefore raise problems regarding the distribution of income within the north itself.

The Scope for Substitution between Labor and Capital

When the agricultural area is sufficiently small, it can be treated as a price taker for its inputs and its outputs. The area can be treated in this respect as a single farm. When the area is enlarged to cover the entire agricultural sector, the constant price assumption is not any more valid. If the sector absorbs a significant share of some of the central resources, the central planner should know what the possibilities are for replacing one central resource with another within the sector.

The scope for replacing capital with labor is illustrated in Tables 17.3 and 17.4 and Figure 17.1, in which five solutions of the static model of the North are summarized. The annual cost of using a unit of capital stock in the sector is taken as the sum of amortization and interest charges. This sum is calculated by multiplying the value of the capital stock by the capital recovery factor.[2] On the one hand, the capital recovery factor declines with the length of the life expectancy of the capital stock, which remains constant in all

2. The capital recovery factor is calculated as:

$$\left[\sum_{t=1}^{t=lf} \left(\frac{1}{1+r} \right)^t \right]^{-1},$$

where lf is the life expectancy of the capital stock taken as five years for oxen and tractors, ten years for machinery, and twenty years for buildings.

Table 17.3. The Effects of the Interest Rate on the Substitution between Labor and Capital

Exogenous or endogenous variable	Specified rate of interest (percent)				
	20 (case 1)	*15* (case 2)	*10* (case 3)	*20* (case 4)	*30* (case 5)
Volume index					
1. Capital invested	27.0	55.7	100	75.4	60.9
2. Labor employed	91.0	91.0	100	113.2	125.1
3. Commodity output	64.1	84.9	100	97.2	93.6
Value index					
4. Return imputed to land	78.1	88.5	100	67.6	40.0
5. Capital and labor cost[a]	87.4	97.1	100	130.2	155.9
6. Return land, capital, and labor	95.7	92.9	100	100.0	100.0

a. Capital invested in the form of land improvement, machinery, and livestock.

experiments. On the other hand, it increases with the rate of interest, which is modified from one case to the other. In the first series of experiments, the interest rate is reduced progressively from 20 percent in Case 1 to 15 percent and 10 percent in Cases 2 and 3, respectively. As the interest rate declines from 20 percent to 15 percent, commodity output increases by one-third (row 3 of Table 17.3) and the average capital-labor ratio doubles (row 1 over row 2). The projects selected become more capital intensive, but more projects are selected. These two effects offset each other and the level of employment remains unchanged (columns 1 and 2 of row 2). When the interest rate is reduced further from 15 to 10 percent, the employment increases somewhat (columns 2 and 3 of row 2). This time, the increment in the capital-labor ratio is more than compensated for by the increase in activity. If the opportunity cost of capital were equal to 15 percent in the rest of the economy, reducing the rate of interest to 10 percent in the north would increase employment and income in that region, but at some loss for the national economy.

The comparison between Cases 1, 2, and 3 does not permit measurement of the elasticity of substitution between labor and capital, because the value added does not remain the same in the three solutions. This was the reason for conducting a second series of experiments, in which the value added by land, labor, and capital was constrained to remain constant when the interest rate was raised progressively from 10 percent in Case 3 to 20 percent in Case 4 and 30

Figure 17.1. Capital-Labor Substitution

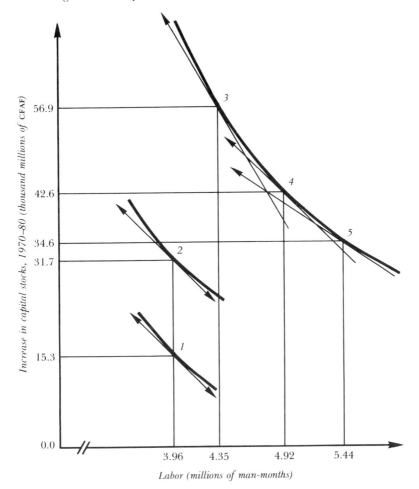

Labor (millions of man-months)

percent in Case 5. In Figure 17.1, uses of labor and capital are measured along the axes; the points corresponding to cases 3, 4, and 5 are located along the same isoquant, while those corresponding to Cases 2 and 1 are located along two lower isoquants.

In a multifactor and multiproduct model, an isoquant may be defined in many different ways. Here, the value added by land, labor, and capital (row 6 of Table 17.3) is constrained to remain constant. When the rate of interest is raised, it becomes optimal to employ more labor and less capital for producing less. As more labor is employed in the north, fewer workers can migrate to the south

Table 17.4. *Earnings Forgone and Savings Made by Replacing Capital with Labor*
(Billions of CFAF at 1970 prices)

	Difference from Case 3	
Component affected	*Case 4*	*Case 5*
Earnings forgone		
1. Transfers from migrants	−1.9	−3.1
2. Commodity output	−3.2	−7.2
Savings made		
3. Amortization of capital	0.7	1.1
4. Purchased inputs	4.4	9.2
Total	0.0	0.0

and earnings from seasonal migrations decline (row 1 of Table 17.4). Most of the earnings forgone results, however, from the reduction in the level of commodity output (row 2). Receipts thus forgone (rows 1 and 2) are exactly offset by savings made on the amortization of capital (row 3) and purchased inputs (row 4).[3] Savings on purchased inputs (row 4) exceed the reduction in commodity output (row 2), because the more labor-intensive technology requires less of intermediate inputs.

The comparison between cases 3 and 4 shows that when the interest rate increases from 10 to 20 percent along the isoquant, the average rate of substitution between capital and labor is equal to CFAF25 thousand (at 1970 prices) per man-month. With an average interest rate of 15 percent, this corresponds to a wage of CFAF3.8 thousand per man-month (at 1970 prices), which is approximately the shadow price of labor in Case 3. As further capital is replaced by labor, the rate of substitution declines. Thus, the comparison between cases 4 and 5 shows that an additional worker can replace only CFAF15.3 thousand worth of capital, which is substantially less than the CFAF25 thousand worth of capital which was replaced by one worker when the interest rate was raised from 10 to 20 percent.

This second series of experiments shows that there is a substantial scope for substitution between labor and capital. Raising the interest

---

3. Capital amortization does not include interest charges on capital which are part of the value added by land, labor, and capital. Purchased inputs cover intermediate products (such as chemicals and fertilizers) used on the farm as well as products and services required for the transportation and processing of farm products.

rate is not enough to increase employment, however. The opposite occurs between cases 3 and 1; because of the fall in production, employment in the north declines. Employment is raised by increasing the interest rate and constraining the value added by land, labor, and capital to remain constant but this results in a lower return to land (columns 3 and 5 of row 4 in Table 17.3). Landowners would need to be induced to adopt the production pattern found in case 4. Higher prices for their output or subsidies on their inputs would be required to compensate farmers for the higher cost per unit of capital.

The Development of the Southwest

One of the government's objectives is to reduce migrations from rural areas to urban by providing additional agricultural employment in the north. Another is to develop the southwest. Approximately the size of Switzerland, the southwest has 11 percent of the area of the Ivory Coast and less than 4 percent of its population. It is covered by forests which contain most of the timber resources remaining in the country. After the timber has been cut in a given area, the land can be cleared and replanted with pulp-producing species or used for growing tree crops, such as cocoa, coffee, or rubber.

Real export earnings from timber increased rapidly during the 1960s and the early 1970s. Such a rapid growth cannot, however, continue much longer; export earnings may start declining within a decade or so, once the most valuable species have been exploited. Before that occurs, it would be desirable to initiate a replanting program so that earnings from timber export could be progressively replaced by earnings from tree crop exports. Such a program should identify the most profitable tree crops; it should also indicate the desirable size of the plantations and the time schedule of the investments required.

The most serious constraints to the expansion of tree crops are the availability of labor, the infrastructure required for receiving additional migrants, and the equipment for clearing land. Because requirements of labor and equipment for setting up a plantation are spread unevenly over time, costs can be reduced by appropriate scheduling of the exploitation of forest tracks, the clearing of land, and the planting of different types of tree crops. Interactions among these various activities have been analyzed in the context of a dynamic programming model of the southwest.

For each representative year (1972, 1975, 1980, 1985, and 1990), approximately 100 activities are available. Their nature is summarized in Table 17.5. To avoid wastage of valuable species, exploitation of timber for export or domestic utilization should always precede cultivation. The establishment of a plantation is represented in the model by an activity which describes the entire life of the plantation. In the year when the investment is initiated, the land is cleared and the trees are planted. During the following representative year, the plantation which is not yet in production must nevertheless be maintained. During the latter representative years, in addition to normal maintenance, the crop is harvested and the commodity is conditioned for the export market and transported to the port. In each representative year, there is a choice between investing in seven different types of tree crops. Each tree crop can be grown in small holdings or large estates by applying alternative production technologies.

Table 17.5. Principal Activities of the Southwest Model

Commodity or service supplied	Special feature
Forestries	
Timber for export	7 cubic meters per hectare
Timber for domestic utilization	13 cubic meters per hectare
Full clearing and replanting for paper pulp	180 cubic meters per hectare
Tree crops	
Coffee	
Cocoa	
Coconut	Choice between small holdings and large
Palm oil	estates. Within each category, choice
Rubber	between alternative technologies
Pineapple	
Citrus	
Annual food crops	
Rice	
Others	Choice between alternative technologies
Fisheries	
Nonprimary production	
Transportation of timber	
Transportation of other products	
Construction	Including public works
Administration	Recurring expenditures only
Other services	Produced in the southwest
Purchases of domestic goods and services	Imported from the rest of the Ivory Coast
Imports	Imported from abroad

In the case of annual food crops, production must satisfy the needs of the rural population, while the food required by the urban population can be either produced locally or imported. Finally, nonprimary production and trade are summarized in the form of seven activities.[4]

For all crops except those grown on large estates, labor requirements are specified quarterly, and the supply of labor consists of settlers and seasonal migrants from neighboring countries. In the case of large estates, forestries and administrative services, labor balances are specified yearly instead of quarterly. Apart from an overall land constraint for the southwest, there are specific constraints regarding the total area which can be planted in some types of tree crops and the acreage which can be cleared each year. The objective function is the discounted sum of the excess of the value of commodity output over the costs of factors and products bought from outside the area. During the terminal year, not only the current output but also the capital accumulated during the planning period (the new plantations in particular) are valued in the objective function.

The model, which contains approximately 350 rows and 550 columns, was used in the preparation of the first development plan of the southwest. The model has been solved nine times to test the sensitivity of the results to variations in the premium on foreign exchange, the f.o.b. prices of export crops, the cost of labor, and the upper limit on migrations.

Although the relative profitability of tree crops was not identical in all solutions, tree crops could generally be ranked according to decreasing profitability in the following order: cocoa, rubber, palm oil, coffee, and coconut. In the case of rubber and palm oil, large estates were always more profitable than small holdings. Export crops also were always more profitable than annual food crops; it was therefore always optimal to import from other regions the food needed for the urban population of the southwest.

In the solution of the model which was considered as fitting most closely national objectives, the size of the permanent agricultural labor force was six times higher in 1990 than in 1970, while the average number of working days a year increased from 160 in 1972 to 200 in 1990. Although the targets included in the official plan were somewhat higher than the results of the model (Table 17.6), the model had an impact on the formulation of the plan and on the recommendations made.

The model provided a systematic framework for collecting statistics

---

4. ªThe model excludes the iron mine and the pulp and paper factory, which may or may not be constructed.

*Table 17.6. Comparison between the Plan of the Southwest
and the Solution of the Model*
(Billions of CFAF)

Item	1975	1980	1985
Government receipts			
Plan	8.6	17.3	26.3
Model	7.2	16.5	20.1
Wage bill			
Plan	13.9	23.2	29.5
Model	8.7	21.1	26.5

Source: Working paper by P. Baron, "Schema-Directeur du Sud-Ouest," *Aménagement de la Région du Sud-Ouest*, 1973.

and for checking their consistency. It highlighted the role of constraints which would have otherwise been overlooked. It was also useful to assess tradeoffs and to test the robustness of the solutions to changes in exogenous variables. Perhaps the most critical tradeoff was the one related to the timing of public expenditures. Between the time disbursements are made and the time tax proceeds from exports and other activities are received, a period of six to ten years generally elapses. A problem of liquidity may therefore arise, and the timing of the investments may have to be revised with changes in the scarcity of foreign exchange.

The Problem of Linkages

Whether the development plan for the southwest is too ambitious or not cannot be judged by considering that region in isolation. The tree crops which can be produced in the southwest are already grown in the rest of the south, and a choice has to be made between expanding the frontier to the west or consolidating existing plantations. The plan for the southwest had to be integrated within an overall development plan for the forest area. The model of the southwest was therefore revised and expanded to cover the entire south of the Ivory Coast.

The model of the south had to be dynamic because of the importance of tree crops in that region. The static model of the north was transformed into a dynamic one in order to facilitate analysis of interdependencies between north and south. In the absence of any aggregation, going from a one-period model to a four-period model could be very costly.⁵ For this reason, the monthly constraints on labor and tractors were replaced by quarterly constraints in the dynamic model of the north.⁶

A third model, dealing with livestock, was constructed because the Ivorian authorities expressed interest in setting up a livestock industry. Since cattle can be raised essentially only in the savanna area, it would have been preferable to integrate livestock activities into the model of the north. This was not done, however, because the size of the model would have become too large. Relatively little was known about the possibilities of developing a livestock industry in the Ivory Coast, and the livestock model remained essentially experimental.

The three rural models were constructed at about the same time. The resources shared among the three subsectors were treated in a consistent manner, and the three models could have been solved at once as a single model of the rural sector. This would clearly have been the best way of taking linkages into account. It was not done because the size of the full sectoral model would have become exceedingly large and its solution too costly.⁷ Clearly, some type of aggregation was needed. The procedure followed has already been described in Chapters 12 and 15. Each of the three rural models was solved separately, and from the solutions thus obtained the columns of the matrix representing the rural sector in the central model were derived. Through this procedure, linkages among the three rural models and between the rural sector and the rest of the economy were taken into account simultaneously by solving the central model.

In the linkage experiments described in Table 15.4, a distinction has been made between low and high production vectors. The difference between the growth patterns associated with these two vectors is illustrated in Table 17.7. When the annual growth rate of production is raised from 3.6 percent to 5.8 percent, the growth rate in the use of purchased inputs more than doubles (from 3.3 percent to 7.1 percent) and the growth rate of capital formation increases by more than half (from 7.9 percent to 12.1 percent). The most rapid increase occurs in the case of fertilizers (from 2.3 percent to 13.6 percent) and oxen (from 1.9 percent to 14.3 percent). Accelerating the growth of production leads, however, to some decline in the return imputed to land; the

5. Taking into account postterminal constraints, the number of rows would have been multiplied by 4.3 and the cost of computation by about 20.

6. As shown in Table 17.1, the monthly constraints account for approximately 80 percent of the total number of rows of the one-period model.

7. The full rural model, which contained more than 2,000 rows, was solved only once.

Table 17.7 Two Alternative Growth Patterns
of the Rural Sector[a]
(Average yearly percentage, 1970–80)

Item	Low	High
Commodity production	3.6	5.8
Purchased inputs	3.3	7.1
Fertilizers	2.3	13.6
Chemicals	5.0	11.8
Capital formation	7.9	12.1
Building	7.3	10.0
Machinery	14.2	16.1
Tractors	4.0	13.1
Other vehicles	4.9	9.3
Oxen	1.9	14.3
Unskilled labor	1.4	3.2
Return imputed to land[b]	6.6	5.8

a. The sector defined is the sum of the three subsectors.
b. Returns calculated from the solutions of the rural models.

latter rises 5.8 percent a year instead of 6.6 percent. It is therefore not obvious that producing more would be profitable. As a matter of fact, when the rural sector was linked with the rest of the economy through the central model, it was generally optimal to use a mix between the high and the low production vectors for the south, and to use the low production vector only for the north (Table 15.4).

When the rural models are solved with the shadow prices of the central model, they should indicate the production patterns which are socially optimal under the national policy option retained in solving the central model. In practice, this may not be the case because of the many imperfections of the models. Even when these imperfections are ignored, the production pattern found to be socially optimal could be infeasible if the agents responsible for the production and investment decisions did not receive appropriate incentives.

Because of the existence of taxes and subsidies, the profits accruing to farmers and corporations do not coincide with the value of the maximand. In some cases, these profits were measured in nonbinding rows which did not affect the solution. In other cases, the model was solved by imposing minimum profits for farmers and corporations, or by constraining public expenditures not to exceed a given amount. Such constraints had, unfortunately, to be expressed at constant prices in the same way as the constraint on savings described in Chapter 10; they did not take into account changes in prices that could be derived only from the dual solution. In calculating the high production vectors referred to in Table 17.7, the model was solved by imposing minimum production constraints for key commodities.

There is clearly a limit to the number of factors which can be taken into account, and the optimal design of a model is a function of the use which is to be made of that model. Although the static model of the north was not formally linked with the rest of the economy, that model was useful for assessing the relative advantages of mechanical and animal tractions.[8] In transforming the one-period model of the north into a four-period model, something was gained by taking into account the effects of a progressive transformation in cultural practices, but something was lost by replacing monthly requirements for labor and tractors by quarterly requirements. More would have been lost by further aggregating the dynamic models of the north and the south.[9] This would, however, have made it possible to solve the rural models under a greater variety of conditions. As a result, the number of rural vectors incorporated into the central model could have been increased and the quality of the linkage between the agricultural sector and the rest of the economy improved.

Allocating research funds optimally is perhaps more difficult than allocating resources optimally among economic sectors or projects. In this study, the rural models should have been revised after experimentation with the central model, and a greater number of rural solutions should have been incorporated into the central model. The shortcomings as well as the achievements may nevertheless be useful to those who conduct further research in the field of multilevel programming.

8. The two models can be solved with the shadow prices from the central model, which establishes a downward linkage. There was an informal upward linkage between the static and dynamic models of the north as well as between the models of the southwest and the south. A formal upward linkage with the central model exists, however, in relation to the dynamic models of the north and south.

9. As noted in Chapter 12, another solution would have been to optimize the model of the north sequentially from one representative year to the next instead of simultaneously for all years.

Bibliography

Adelman, Irma. 1966. "A Linear Programming Model for Educational Planning: A Case Study of Argentina." In *The Theory and Design of Economic Development*, edited by Irma Adelman and Erik Thorbecke. Baltimore: Johns Hopkins University Press.

Arrow, Kenneth J., Hollis B. Chenery, B. S. Minhas, and Robert M. Solow. 1961. "Capital Labor Substitution and Economic Efficiency." *Review of Economics and Statistics*, vol. 43 (August), pp. 225–50.

Balassa, Bela A. 1965. "Tariff Protection in Industrial Countries: An Evaluation." *Journal of Political Economy*, vol. 73, no. 6 (November–December), pp. 573–94.

———, and Daniel M. Schydlowsky. 1968. "Effective Tariffs, Domestic Cost of Foreign Exchange, and the Equilibrium Exchange Rate." *Journal of Political Economy*, vol. 76, no. 3 (May/June), pp. 348–60.

———, and Associates. 1971. *The Structure of Protection in Developing Countries*. Baltimore: Published for the World Bank and Inter-American Development Bank by the Johns Hopkins University Press.

Blitzer, Charles R. 1975. "Employment and Human Capital Formation." In *Economy-Wide Models and Development Planning*, edited by Charles R. Blitzer, Peter B. Clark, and Lance Taylor. London: Published for the World Bank by Oxford University Press.

Bowles, Samuel. 1969. *Planning Educational Systems for Economic Growth*. Harvard Economic Studies, vol. 133. Cambridge, Massachusetts: Harvard University Press.

Bruno, Michael. 1967. "Optimal Patterns of Trade and Development." *Review of Economics and Statistics*, vol. 49, no. 4 (November), pp. 545–54.

———. 1972. "Domestic Resource Costs and Effective Protection: Clarification and Synthesis." *Journal of Political Economy*, vol. 80, no. 1, pp. 16–33.

Burk, Abram. 1936–37. "Real Income, Expenditure Proportionality, and Frisch's New Methods of Measuring Marginal Utility." *Review of Economic Studies*, vol. 4, pp. 33–52.

Chakravarty, Sukhamoy. 1969. *Capital and Development Planning*. Cambridge: MIT Press.

[**403**]

Corden, Warner Max. 1966. "The Structure of the Tariff System and the Effective Protective Rate." *Journal of Political Economy*, vol. 74, no. 3 (June), pp. 221–37.

———. 1974. *Trade Policy and Economic Welfare*. Oxford: The Clarendon Press.

Dantzig, George B., and Philip Wolfe. 1961. "The Decomposition Algorithm for Linear Programs." *Econometrica*, vol. 29, no. 4 (October), pp. 767–78.

Das Gupta, Partha, Amartya Sen, and Stephen Marglin. 1972. *Guidelines for Project Evaluation*. Project Formulation and Evaluation Series, vol. 2 ([Document] ID/SER 4/2).

Debreu, Gerard. 1960. "Topological Methods in Cardinal Utility Theory." In *Mathematical Methods in the Social Sciences*. Proceedings, 1959, edited by Kenneth J. Arrow, Samuel Karlin, and Patrick Suppes. Stanford, California: Stanford University Press.

Diamond, Peter A., and J. A. Mirrlees. 1971. "Optimal Taxation and Public Production." *American Economic Review*, vol. 61, nos. 1 and 2 (March), pp. 8–28.

Domar, Evsey D. 1957. Essays in the Theory of Economic Growth. New York: Oxford University Press. (Chapter 5, "The Problem of Capital Accumulation," and Chapter 7, "Depreciation, Replacement, and Growth.")

Duloy, John H., and Roger D. Norton. 1973a. "CHAC, a Programming Model of Mexican Agriculture." In *Multi-level Planning: Case Studies in Mexico*, edited by Louis M. Goreux and Alan S. Manne. Amsterdam and London: North-Holland Publishing Company; New York: American Elsevier Publishing Company.

———. 1973b. "Linking the Agricultural Model and the Economy-Wide Model." In *Multi-Level Planning: Case Studies in Mexico*, edited by Louis M. Goreux and Alan S. Manne. Amsterdam and London: North-Holland Publishing Company; New York: American Elsevier Publishing Company.

Evans, Henry David. 1972. *A General Equilibrium Analysis of Protection: The Effects of Protection in Australia*. Amsterdam: North-Holland Publishing Company.

Food and Agriculture Organization of the United Nations. 1972. *Income Elasticities of Demand for Agricultural Products*. (Projections Research Working Paper No. 1.) Committee on Commodity Problems, Forty-seventh Session, October 30–November 10, 1972. (CCP/WP 1.)

Frisch, Ragnar. 1959. "A Complete Scheme for Computing All Direct and Cross Demand Elasticities in a Model with Many Sectors." *Econometrica*, vol. 27, no. 2 (April), pp. 177–96.

Goreux, Louis M. 1960. "Income and Food Consumption." Food and Agriculture Organization, *Monthly Bulletin of Agricultural Economics and Statistics*, vol. 9, no. 10 (October), pp. 1–12.

———. 1969. "Impact of Urbanization on the Accuracy of Demand Projections Based on National Averages." Annex 1 to "Prospects for Agricultural Trade of Developing Countries." In *The Role of Agriculture in Economic*

Development, edited by Erik Thorbecke. New York: National Bureau of Economic Research.

———. 1972. "Private, National, and International Returns: An Application of Commodity Lending." *European Economic Review*, vol. 3, no. 2, pp. 131–80.

———. 1973. "Comparative Analysis of the Programming Models." In *Multi-Level Planning: Case Studies in Mexico*, edited by Louis M. Goreux and Alan S. Manne. Amsterdam and London: North-Holland Publishing Company; New York: American Elsevier Publishing Company.

———, and Alan S. Manne. 1973. *Multi-Level Planning: Case Studies in Mexico*. Amsterdam: North-Holland Publishing Company; New York: American Elsevier Publishing Company. (Introduction, pp. 1–14.)

Hadley, George F., and Murray C. Kemp. 1971. *Variational Methods in Economics*. Amsterdam: North-Holland Publishing Company; New York: American Elsevier Publishing Company.

Houthakker, H. S. 1960. "Additive Preferences." *Econometrica*, vol. 28, no. 2 (April), pp. 244–57.

Ivory Coast, Minister of Planning. 1971. *Deuxième Esquisse du plan quinquennal de développement*. Abidjan.

Jorgenson, Dale W. 1971. "The Economic Theory of Replacement and Depreciation." Mimeographed. Cambridge, Massachusetts: Harvard Institute of Economic Research, September.

Keesing, Donald B., and Alan S. Manne. 1973. "Manpower Projections." In *Multi-Level Planning: Case Studies in Mexico*, edited by Louis M. Goreux and Alan S. Manne. Amsterdam and London: North-Holland Publishing Company; New York: American Elsevier Publishing Company.

Kendrick, David A., and Lance J. Taylor. 1969. "A Dynamic Non-linear Planning Model for Korea." In *Practical Approaches to Development Planning: Korea's Second Five-Year Plan*, edited by Irma Adelman. Baltimore: Johns Hopkins University Press.

Kornai, János. 1969. "Man-Machine Planning." *Economics of Planning*, vol. 9, no. 3.

———. 1969. "Multi-level Programming—a First Report on the Model and on the Experimental Computation." *European Economic Review*, vol. 1, no. 1 (Fall), pp. 134–91.

———. 1973. "Thoughts on Multi-level Planning Systems." In *Multi-Level Planning: Case Studies in Mexico*, edited by Louis M. Goreux and Alan S. Manne. Amsterdam and London: North-Holland Publishing Company; New York: American Elsevier Publishing Company.

———, and Thomas Liptak. 1962. *Ketszintu tervezes* [Two-Level Planning]. Budapest: Computing Center of the Hungarian Academy of Sciences. Eng. tr., "Two-Level Planning." *Econometrica*, vol. 33, no. 1 (January 1965), pp. 141–69.

Koopmans, Tjalling C. 1960. "Stationary Ordinal Utility and Impatience." *Econometrica*, vol. 28 (April), pp. 287–309.

Langoni, Carlos Geraldo. 1973. "Income Distribution and Economic Development in Brazil" (in Portuguese). *Conjunctura Economica*, vol. 27, no. 9 (September).

Lluch, Constantino, and Ross Williams. 1973. Cross Country Demand and Savings Patterns: An Application of the Extended Linear Expenditure System. Washington, D.C.: World Bank Discussion Paper No. 6. Circulation restricted—for World Bank internal use only.

Manne, Alan S. 1970. "Sufficient Conditions for Optimality in an Infinite Horizon Development Plan." *Econometrica*, vol. 38, no. 1 (January), pp. 18–38.

———. 1973. "On Linking Energeticos to Dinamico." In *Multi-Level Planning: Case Studies in Mexico*, edited by Louis M. Goreux and Alan S. Manne. Amsterdam and London: North-Holland Publishing Company; New York: American Elsevier Publishing Company.

———. 1974. "On the Efficiency Price of Capital in the Dual Economy." *Quarterly Journal of Economics*, vol. 88, no. 4 (November), pp. 574–95.

Mirrlees, J. A. 1967. "Optimum Growth When Technology is Changing." *Review of Economic Studies*, vol. 34 (January), pp. 95–124.

OECD. 1968. *Manual of Industrial Project Analysis*, vol. 1; *Methodology and Case Studies*, prepared by the Societé d'économie et de mathématiques appliquées, Ian M. D. Little, and the Centre. Paris: Organisation for Economic Co-operation and Development, Development Center.

Phelps, Edmund S. 1966. *Golden Rules of Economic Growth: Studies of Efficient and Optimal Investment*. New York: W. W. Norton and Company.

Psacharopoulos, George. 1973. *Returns to Education: An International Comparison*. Amsterdam, London, and New York: Elsevier Scientific Publishing Company.

Pursell, Garry, Dirck Stryker, and Terry Monson. 1975. "Incentives and Resource Costs in the Ivory Coast." Mimeographed. May 23.

Ramsey, F. P. 1928. "A Mathematical Theory of Saving." *Economic Journal*, vol. 38 (December), pp. 543–59.

Samuelson, Paul A. 1965. "A Catenary Turnpike Theorem Involving Consumption and the Golden Rule." *American Economic Review*, vol. 55, no. 3 (June), pp. 486–96.

———, and Robert M. Solow. 1956. "A Complete Capital Model Involving Heterogeneous Capital Goods." *Quarterly Journal of Economics*, vol. 70, no. 4 (November), pp. 537–62.

Sato, Kazuo. 1972. "Additive Utility Functions with Double-Log Consumer Demand Functions." *Journal of Political Economy*, vol. 80, no. 1 (January–February), pp. 102–24.

Sen, Amartya K. 1972. "Control Areas and Accounting Prices: An Approach to Economic Evaluation." *Economic Journal*, vol. 82, no. 3255 (March), pp. 486–501.

Srinivasan, T. N. 1975. "The Foreign Trade Sector in Planning Models." In *Economy-Wide Models and Development Planning*, edited by Charles R.

Blitzer, Peter B. Clark, and Lance Taylor. London: Published for the World Bank by Oxford University Press.

Takayama, Takashi, and George G. Judge. 1971. *Spatial and Temporal Price and Allocation Models*. Amsterdam: North-Holland Publishing Company.

Taylor, Lance. 1975. "Theoretical Foundations and Technical Implications." In *Economy-Wide Models and Development Planning*, edited by Charles R. Blitzer, Peter B. Clark, and Lance Taylor. London: Published for the World Bank by Oxford University Press.

Tendulkar, Suresh D. 1971. "Interaction between Domestic and Foreign Resources in Economic Growth: Some Experiments in India." In *Studies in Development Planning*, edited by Hollis B. Chenery, with Samuel Bowles and others. Harvard Economic Studies, vol. 136. Cambridge: Harvard University Press.

Thenevin, P. 1973. *Utilisation d'un modèle pour la planification régionale*. Paris: Ministère de le Coopération.

Unesco. 1973. Côte d'Ivoire: Education et développement. (Rapport confidential, EFM/57.) Vol. 1, Problèmes et recommandations. Paris.

Vaurs, René, Louis M. Goreux, and Apostolos Condos. 1972. "An Agricultural Model from the Ivory Coast Programming Study." Economic Staff Working Paper No. 125. Washington, D.C.: The World Bank.

Weizsäcker, Carl Christian. 1965. "Existence of Optimal Programs for Accumulation for an Infinite Time Horizon." *Review of Economic Studies*, vol. 32, no. 2 (April), pp. 85–104.

World Bank, Development Research Center. 1975. Working Papers on Rural Sector Model in the Ivory Coast. Washington, D.C.: The World Bank.
1. René Vaurs, *General Description of the Model System*;
2. Henri Quaix and René Vaurs, *Exports, Food Demand and Population*;
3. René Vaurs, *North Region Model*;
4. L. Guinard, *Techniques for the South Region Model*;
5. René Vaurs, *South Region Model*;
6. Jacques Loup, *Livestock Model*.

World Bank. 1974. *Current Economic Situation and Prospects of the Ivory Coast*. Washington, D.C.: World Bank Report No. 296-IVC, April 11. Circulation restricted—for World Bank internal use only.

Index

199, 200, 201, 204–05; and interpolation periods, 239–40

Trade: free, 76–80; government policies on, 316; and production, 142–43; terms of, 115–17

Traditional approaches: versus optimization, 4–7

Tree crops, 395–96, 397

Two-level decomposition, 143–47

Turnpike theorem, 204

Underemployment, 322–31

Unemployment, 93; agricultural, 322–23; disguised urban, 323–37; seasonal, 26

Urban sector, 371–86; and capital goods and stocks, 229; competing imports in, 278–84; deliveries, 283–84; model of, 28–30, 371–84; model solved, 381–86; reduced model of, 270–74; versus rural sector, 142–43

Utility functions, 136–37, 175–80, 207–08; additive, 173; disaggregated, 209–13; marginal, 136–37, 138, 188, 189

Wage bill, 69–75

Wages: -employment interactions, 331; equilibrium, 263–69; migrant, 319–22; urban versus rural, 36, 54. *See also* Incomes